# The Japanese Marketing System:
## ADAPTATIONS AND INNOVATIONS

**THE MIT PRESS**
Cambridge, Massachusetts, and London, England

# The Japanese Marketing System:

## ADAPTATIONS AND INNOVATIONS

M. Y. Yoshino

*To my mother*

# Contents

**8**

# Acknowledgments

This book represents my continuing interest in the dynamic economic and social development in contemporary Japan. As is typical of a major undertaking of this type, I owe so much to so many people that it defies extending individual acknowledgment to everyone who has contributed to it. Certainly, this study would have been impossible without the cooperation of numerous Japanese executives, government officials, trade association officials, and professors, who generously contributed their time and expertise. They provided the basic data, helped refine my hypotheses, challenged my assumptions, and guided my interpretation of the data. I sincerely regret that our original agreement that they would remain anonymous prevents individual mention from being made, but I do wish to acknowledge their assistance. Through this study, I have indeed gained a profound respect for the dynamic innovations in the Japanese marketing scene and for those who have made them possible.

After having analyzed the data and prepared a draft, I had opportunity to discuss my findings and analysis with a group of well-informed individuals in Japan. Particularly helpful was counsel extended by the Consumer Research Group at Nomura Research Institute, which included some of my former students at the University of California, Los Angeles. I am especially grateful to Mr. Mikio Abe, a good personal friend and the very able director of this group.

A number of individuals graciously have read the manuscript and provided constructive criticism and new insights. In this regard I am grateful to Professors Richard D. Robinson of Massachusetts Institute of Technology and Professor John Fayerweather of New York University, who provided very thoughtful and penetrating comments. I would like to take this opportunity to thank them for their continuing interest in my research on Japanese development. Comments provided by Professors Raymond Vernon and Ezra Vogel, both of Harvard University, have also contributed to the improvement of this book.

I would like to acknowledge the generous financial support provided by a Ford Foundation grant administered through the UCLA Chancellor's Committee on International and Comparative Studies. The study was also supported in part by a grant from the Research Committee of the Academic Senate of UCLA.

Throughout this study I was indeed fortunate to have the competent and conscientious assistance of a number of individuals. Miss Ann Dunn most willingly typed several drafts of the manuscript. Miss Kay Fujimoto performed yeoman service in typing the final draft and assisted in preparation of the manuscript for publication. I am also deeply indebted to Mrs. Grace Marshall. In the final stage of this research, I assumed a major administrative responsibility in the Business School, which meant that many of the important yet detailed tasks associated with the preparation of the manuscript for publication fell on her shoulders. She discharged these responsibilities with a competence that would be the envy of any author.

Finally, I would like to acknowledge my gratitude to my wife and two small children, who bore the major burden of this research so willingly, patiently, and understandingly. Only they know what it means to have a husband and father who is absorbed in an exciting but long-term research effort. While many people contributed to this book, the responsibility for the final product rests solely with the author.

Spring 1971                                              M.Y.Y.
Pacific Palisades, California

# Introduction

## The Conceptual Framework and Significance of This Study

It was not so long ago that marketing was viewed simply as a mechanistic process, performing rather specific and limited functions in the distribution of goods and services. This traditional and limited view is well reflected in the more or less official definition of marketing adopted by the American Marketing Association, as articulated slightly over two decades ago. It states: "Marketing is the performance of business activities directed toward and incident to the flow of goods and services from producer to consumer or user."[1]

With the fuller understanding of the nature of marketing attained during the last decade or so, we have come to recognize that marketing is far more than a simple mechanistic process involved in the distribution of goods and services. It is, in fact, an important socioeconomic process, as well as a collection of varied physical tasks designed to help in satisfying certain human needs. Indeed, marketing is a basic component of the social structure in all but the most primitive societies. Cyril Belshaw, an economic anthropologist, goes so far as to note: "As a specific institution, exchange penetrates through the social fabric and may be thought of as a network holding societies together."[2] To view marketing in this broader context is useful in enhancing our understanding of its role and functions in a society. A number of significant implica-

[1] "Report of the Definition Committee," *Journal of Marketing*, 13 (October 1948), 209.
[2] Cyril S. Belshaw, *Traditional Exchange and Modern Markets* (Englewood Cliffs, N.J.: Prentice-Hall, Inc., 1965), p. 6.

tions emerge from this broad conceptualization. The most important implication is the growing interest in the whole issue of the marketing-environment relationship. While the marketing system seeks to satisfy basically the same human needs, the manner in which it performs its function varies widely among different societies; furthermore, these variations are related to the differences in the environment. In fact, this approach represents a major thrust of the growing interest in investigation of comparative marketing systems. In recent years a number of empirical studies have been undertaken in the attempt to understand the influence of the environment on the marketing system, particularly to identify the variables that have a direct bearing on shaping the marketing system in different societies. Although specific relationships between environmental variables and the marketing system have yet to be established, this approach has provided a useful avenue of exploration.

Closely related to the preceding issue is an effort to develop meaningful classifications or taxonomies to categorize marketing systems of different societies according to environmental variables. Here again, a number of different schemes have been offered, and, indeed, the number of taxonomic categories is limited only by the classifier's imagination.

The broad conceptualization of marketing raises another important consideration — that is, that the marketing system, being a key socioeconomic institution operating in the broader environmental milieu, is affected by certain changes in the environment. If it is to maintain its functional viability as a key socioeconomic institution, it cannot remain oblivious to relevant environmental changes. In other words, it must adapt to new needs created by environmental changes. Thus, in a dynamic economy the marketing system must reassess its basic mission, evolve new patterns, design new structures and institutions, and assume new functions.

Finally, while the marketing system is shaped by its environment, the causality is by no means one-sided. As a dynamic and basic social institution, the marketing system is capable of generating changes with far-reaching implications. The potential power of marketing as a change agent is succinctly described by Nicosia and Glock in the following manner:

> Tensions and harmony are the salient features of a viable society. Tensions, of course, imply change, and a society, to be viable, must find organizational designs which provide the means for harmonious change

through time. These means consist of a variety of structures and mechanisms: political, religious, economic, and so forth. Marketing is a socioeconomic mechanism that contributes to the society's search for harmonious patterns of tension. Marketing both reflects and contributes to social change.[3]

Marketing fills as well as creates needs in a society. Marketing is indeed a potent mechanism for social change in an adaptive way.

It is encouraging to note that a growing body of empirical studies is now being undertaken to examine critically the concepts just discussed; though still limited, the research to date has produced some significant results. Of course, it marks only a beginning, leaving a number of unexplored issues.

A major limitation of past research in this area is the fact that it has focused almost exclusively on marketing systems in developing economies. As a result, we know very little concerning marketing systems in developed or highly industrialized economies other than the United States. Understanding the interacting relationship between marketing and its environment is just as important in advanced nations as it is in developing ones. In fact, the marketing system becomes more complex and its functions become even more critical to the welfare of the entire society as the society reaches an advanced stage of economic development. No doubt, the detailed investigation of the marketing system in highly industrialized societies deserves a high priority.

There is a widely held view among certain social scientists interested in economic development that societies will become increasingly similar, not only in economic but in social and cultural characteristics, as they reach a high level of industrialization. It would be of considerable interest to see if this convergence will also take place in the area of marketing. Moreover, greater understanding of the marketing systems of highly developed societies may be of considerable value as a guideline for developing nations as they aspire to achieve a higher level of economic development. These factors also point to the need for greater emphasis on the investigation of marketing systems in highly developed societies.

There is yet another area that past research has scarcely touched. Little attention has been given to the dynamic process of change

3 Francesco M. Nicosia and Charles Y. Glock, "Marketing and Affluence: A Research Prospectus," in Robert L. King (ed.), *Marketing and the New Science of Planning* (Chicago: American Marketing Association, 1968), p. 561.

in the marketing system. Past studies have focused almost exclusively on the description and analysis of the marketing system in a given society at a particular moment in time and have largely neglected to examine the evolutionary pattern of the marketing system in response to environmental changes in a given society. Without discounting the value of the static type of research, there is no doubt that examination of the change process would be indeed significant. We are almost totally ignorant on such key questions as: How is change in the marketing system initiated? Does the marketing sector lead development or lag behind it? What changes do or must occur in the marketing system as the nation achieves economic growth? What is the process of this change? Do these changes occur automatically? In other words, is marketing really a self-adjusting mechanism that readily adapts in response to environmental changes? Examination of these questions is meaningful at every level of economic development, but it would be particularly significant as a society reaches the level of a mass consumption economy in which the role of marketing becomes extremely important.

The research upon which this book is based has been designed to examine these issues in one environmental setting. The setting for this study is Japan, a society that has been experiencing almost unprecedented economic growth and rather remarkable social change during the last two and a half decades, where we are witnessing the rapid emergence of a mass consumption economy.

To investigate the dynamic adaptive behavior of a marketing system in response to rather dramatic environmental changes, Japan provides an excellent setting on several bases. First, the traditional development of Japan's marketing system has lagged behind her economic development. The rapid economic development prior to World War II exerted virtually no impact on the traditional marketing system. This was largely due to the conscious government policy to emphasize the development of strategic industries at the expense of consumer industries. Thus, Kindleberger was indeed correct when he observed: "Industrialization [in Japan] moved very rapidly and capacity at marketing increased pari passu rather than in advance. Government preserved order, provided the necessary expansion of money, but marketing grew up along with capacity at administering production without the necessity for prior condition."[4] Thus, the level of economic development of the

4 Charles P. Kindleberger, *Economic Development* (New York: McGraw-Hill Book Company, 1965), p. 164. Kindleberger goes on to note that the

marketing system that existed prior to World War II was very underdeveloped, retaining many of the features carried over from the marketing system in the preindustrial era.

The postwar pattern of economic growth marked a basic departure from the prewar model described earlier, and it has been instrumental in creating a truly viable mass-consumption-based economy. Moreover, the economic growth in postwar Japan has been dynamic. An affluent mass consumer market has emerged from the ruins of the war in a very short period of time. Given the backward state of the Japanese marketing system and the speed with which a mass consumption economy was created in Japan, the traditional marketing system has come under serious strains and tensions, having to adapt to meet the demands of the new environment. Almost every conceivable strain that might accompany such changes has been present in the Japanese context in an exaggerated form, since not only has the magnitude of the changes been great but they have taken place in a brief period of time.

In addition, Japan is so far the only non-Western nation that has succeeded in creating a highly developed mass consumption society. This makes the Japanese model unique. Comparative analysis of the Japanese pattern with Western models would be highly useful to students of marketing as well as of economic development. Moreover, there is considerable interest among a number of developing nations today in emulating the Japanese strategy of economic development. While the Japanese model of economic growth has received considerable attention in recent years, from both theoretical and practical points of view, the marketing aspect has almost invariably been all but excluded from these examinations. Moreover, in terms of the Gross National Product (GNP), Japan now is second in the free world, surpassed only by the United States. Thus, aside from the comparative point of view, understanding of the workings of the marketing system in such a vital economy would of itself be of considerable importance.

### The Design and Organization of This Study

This study will examine in some depth the following major issues:

1. What impact has Japan's recent entry into a highly indus-

---

Japanese situation is rather a remarkable case, but it is in his judgment the exception rather than the pattern.

trialized and mass-consumption-oriented society had on her marketing system? How is the marketing system seeking to adapt to these developments? What strains have been experienced in the process? What institutional and structural changes have been occurring?

2. What does the emerging pattern look like? Is the emerging system taking on those characteristics commonly associated with marketing systems in other mass-consumption-oriented societies? Can one detect a trend for convergence to a common pattern, or is the Japanese marketing system following a unique pattern of development?

3. What impact, if any, have changes in the marketing system had on the rest of the society? Has the marketing system in fact served as an agent of change? Has the dynamic two-way interaction really occurred in Japan?

Data for this research have been drawn from both primary and secondary sources. Very few secondary data on the Japanese marketing system are available in the English language, and many of those data are of limited value, since most are outdated or based on casual impressionistic observations by individuals with a limited background on Japan. Because of its obvious importance to the Japanese economy, much has been written in Japanese on recent developments in the nation's marketing system. Here, selectivity has been the major problem, inasmuch as the quality of the secondary data available in Japanese varies widely. Primary data were obtained through personal interviews with marketing executives of large manufacturing firms and owners and managers of various types of marketing intermediaries. Also interviewed were a score of experts on the Japanese marketing system, including professors of marketing at Japanese universities, consultants, officials of relevant trade associations, journalists, and government officials.

The organization of this book is as follows: Chapter 1 is designed to give the reader essential background. Included in the chapter is a brief examination of the historical evolution of the nation's distribution sector as well as salient features of the contemporary marketing system. Also discussed in this chapter are the major forces that have caused serious strains in the nation's marketing system. Chapter 2 examines the emergence of a mass consumer market in postwar Japan. The chapter analyzes in some depth salient aspects of the character and magnitude of the burgeoning consumer market in contemporary Japan. Chapter 3 examines changes in the marketing orientation of Japan's large manufacturers of consumer goods. These firms now are attempting to adapt their policies, programs, and organizations to seize upon the emerging mass consumer market. The change in this area has been indeed remarkable.

Chapters 4 and 5 examine the changing pattern of Japan's distribution structure. In Chapter 4, we shall examine first the basic structural changes that are currently taking place in the distribution sector, and then the emergence of new marketing institutions. Chapter 5 seeks to examine how the traditional marketing institutions are attempting to cope with the very rapid environmental changes to assure their continued viability.

One of the most significant marketing developments in postwar Japan is the tremendous growth of consumer financing, particularly in the form of installment credit. Installment credit, though not entirely unknown in prewar Japan, has taken on added significance in postwar Japan, contributing importantly to the growth of a mass consumption market. Consequently, Chapter 6 examines the evolution and present status of installment credit in Japan. In this chapter we shall also treat briefly the recent surge in the use of credit cards.

Chapter 7 examines the role of government in the modernization of Japan's marketing system. Throughout the last century the government has been involved actively in guiding the nation's economic activities, and it is often contended that this unique but highly effective blend of public and private efforts has been a key to Japan's economic success. Until recently, however, the government was preoccupied with the promotion of large-scale strategic industries, and showed virtually no concern for the distribution sector. In recent years, for a variety of reasons, the government has begun to show increasing interest in problems related to the nation's marketing system and its modernization. In Chapter 7, the government's role in modernization of the distribution sector will be examined critically.

The concluding chapter summarizes recent developments in the Japanese marketing system and problems encountered in the process of its adaptive behavior. Also discussed in this chapter are the theoretical relevance and implications of the Japanese case to interactions between marketing and its environment.

It is appropriate here to recognize explicitly the major limitations of this study. First, the study basically takes a macro approach. Although throughout this book micro issues, such as managerial problems of specific marketing institutions, are by no means ignored, the research was designed to examine significant developments in the nation's marketing system as a whole. Reference to management practices of a specific institution is made only to illustrate major trends in the overall system.

Second, of necessity, the coverage of this study has been selective. The marketing system in a complex society such as Japan's is, needless to say, highly complicated. Given the scope of this study, comprehensive treatment of every aspect of the nation's marketing system is impossible. Rather, the treatment has been selective, and the emphasis has been placed on significant trends and developments in the field of consumer marketing. Moreover, marketing of fresh food products has been deliberately excluded from this study, inasmuch as this whole area possesses a set of unique and complex issues that deserve much more penetrating analysis than would have been possible in this limited effort.

Third, changes in the marketing system are by no means completed. In some respects they are just beginning. It is expected that the Japanese marketing system will continue to undergo very dynamic changes, and the rate of change is likely to accelerate. Thus, any research with such a dynamic topic cannot help but become a historical analysis by the time the study is published, despite the author's effort to keep it current throughout the period of data analysis and writing. The reader is urged, therefore, to look for major patterns and dominant trends in a changing process rather than for specific developments.

# The Japanese Marketing System:

## ADAPTATIONS AND INNOVATIONS

# 1

# The Setting

As we have noted in the Introduction, the Japanese marketing system has traditionally lagged behind Japan's economic development. As a result, despite the nation's entry into a highly advanced stage of industrial development, the marketing structure has retained many of the features that are associated with the premodern period. In recent years, however, the tradition-bound marketing system has come under considerable strain as a result of rather dynamic environmental changes, and in order for the system to regain its functional viability, it must adapt to the new conditions. Herein lies the basic challenge confronting the Japanese marketing system. In this chapter we shall first review the evolution of Japan's traditional marketing structure and its salient characteristics. We shall then attempt to examine a series of environmental changes that are making the traditional system obsolete and inefficient.

## The Historical Perspective

### The Tokugawa Era

In examining the historical evolution of the Japanese marketing system, we shall begin with the Tokugawa period, the last of the premodern eras during which the development of commercial institutions received much impetus. Of particular interest to this study is the sociopolitical milieu of this period in which the marketing system evolved.[1]

[1] The ensuing discussion of the commercial system during the Tokugawa era draws heavily from the following sources: Charles D. Sheldon, *The Rise of the Merchant Class in Tokugawa Japan, 1600-1868* (Locust Valley, N.Y.:

1

When the Tokugawa family came to power at the beginning of the seventeenth century, its overriding concern was the perpetuation of the family hegemony. Toward this end the regime sought to create a stable society hospitable to it by introducing a series of rigid, detailed, and elaborate devices for social control. One such attempt was to freeze the society into a legally immutable class structure by classifying the entire populace into the rigid hereditary hierarchy of statuses, consisting of four classes: warriors, farmers, artisans, and merchants. Very precise and rigid rules of conduct were prescribed to control the thought patterns and behavior of each class in minute detail. Heavy penalties were imposed on those who were not willing to conform. A wide gulf separated the warrior class from the other three classes, who were considered to be commoners. The commoners were ranked, in turn, according to the Confucian view of productivity. Significantly, merchants were ranked at the very bottom, because they were considered to be socially unproductive, and they became subject to social contempt and humiliation.

Despite the low status of the merchant class, during the early Tokugawa era commercial activities began to flourish, as the Tokugawa regime achieved a degree of political stability and national integration that had not been known until that time. The regime also took steps toward standardization of the currency and weights and measures, contributing further to the expansion of economic activities. Improvements in transportation, though still inhibited by limited technology and the particular political structure of the time, did help the development of a nationwide economy.

During the first century of the Tokugawa era, in the wake of the expanding economy, the merchant class quietly ingratiated itself with the feudal authorities and sought self-protection in the hostile world by gradually and skillfully evolving a complex commercial system. Despite its low social status, the merchant class enjoyed considerable freedom in evolving its own commercial system. Indeed, to assure continued survival and to maintain autonomy, the merchant class demonstrated considerable ingenuity by developing

J. J. Augustin, Inc., 1958); Mataji Miyamoto, *Kinsei Shonin Ishiki no Kenkyu* [*Studies in the Merchant Mentality of the Early Modern Period*] (Tokyo: Yuhikaku, 1941); Mataji Miyamoto, *Nihon Shōgyō Shi* [*Commercial History of Japan*] (Tokyo: Ryuginsha, 1943).

extremely complex institutional arrangements bound by a very strict code of commercial ethics, which could be ignored only at great peril. In the best Japanese tradition the merchant class developed a strong group solidarity with well-defined particularistic ties.

Also to protect their self-interest, merchants developed ingenious means for collusive actions to prevent competition. Thus, price fixing and other restrictive monopolistic business practices became quite common. During the early Tokugawa period commercial centers began to emerge, which later blossomed into prosperous and busy urban enclaves. Particularly prominent among them was Osaka, where, at its height, some 70 percent of the nation's monetary wealth was believed to be concentrated.[2]

The marketing system thus evolved came to possess a number of characteristics that are typically associated with marketing systems in developing nations today. Among them two were particularly noteworthy. The first was that the system was dominated by wholesalers. Large wholesalers came to occupy the pivotal position in the distribution system and were at the hub of commercial activities. These wholesalers tended to be specialized both in functions and in products handled.

The second notable characteristic was the fact that the distribution system that had thus evolved was highly complex and fragmented, merchandise having to pass through multiple levels of highly specialized intermediaries. Describing the complexity of the Tokugawa distribution system, Sheldon states:

A typical pattern of the flow of commercial goods from individual producers was: (1) fisherman or farmer to (2) middlemen to (3) loading tonya (wholesalers); when the goods reached the market such as Osaka, goods would ordinarily be taken over by (4) unloading tonya. If they were sold without delay, they went through a (5) middleman again, then to the (6) retailers and to the (7) consumer. (If not sold immediately, goods went first to a storage tonya, involving an additional step.) If the goods were reshipped to another market to (3) loading tonya to (4) unloading tonya to (5) middleman to (6) storage tonya to (7) tonya for the other market to (8) middleman to (9) retailers to (10) consumers.[3]

---

[2] Yasuzo Horie, "Entrepreneurs in Meiji Japan," in William W. Lockwood (ed.), *The State and Economic Enterprise in Japan* (Princeton, N.J.: Princeton University Press, 1965), p. 194.

[3] Sheldon, *The Rise of the Merchant Class*, p. 47.

This pattern was attributable to such factors as the prevalence of small production units with unsophisticated technology and limited financial resources, the dominance of small retail units, inadequate flow of information, and poor transportation methods.

With the increasing level of commercial activities, a number of prominent merchants emerged in key commercial centers; they came to be known as city merchants in contrast to those who were in the outlying areas. In fact, for that period some of these city merchants developed extremely large commercial organizations. For example, Mitsui's stores in Edo (Tokyo) reportedly grew to the point of employing more than 1,000 men and women by the mid-eighteenth century.[4] It is interesting to note that these commercial houses were organized along the lines of the traditional Confucian-based family system, with strong paternalistic and particularistic ties. It was among these prominent commercial houses that the tradition concept of *ie,* or "house," was first applied to the organization of economic activities, providing the basic framework for unrelated persons to function together in an artificial or simulated kinship relationship.[5] It is noteworthy that some of these great commercial houses developed into prominent Zaibatsu in the early Meiji era and dominated Japan's industrial and financial scene until 1945. Most notable among them were Mitsui and Sumitomo. Also, some of the large contemporary department stores have their historical roots in these prominent commercial houses.

Along with the emergence of large city merchants, the Tokugawa era also witnessed the growth of provincial merchants, many of whom were of peasant origin and often remained peasant landholders. The development of the money and credit economy resulted in the growth of itinerant trade. Thus, commercial activities began to spread throughout the country. With growing financial power, an increasing number of prominent merchants began to engage in usury or money-lending activities, which proved to be a highly lucrative source of income as well as a relatively painless method of capital accumulation.

One noteworthy development was that, with the rapid growth

---

[4] *Ibid.,* p. 65.

[5] For an illuminating discussion of the organization of commercial houses during the Tokugawa era, see Robert N. Bellah, *Tokugawa Religion: The Values of Pre-Industrial Japan* (Glencoe, Ill.: The Free Press, 1957), pp. 48-51.

of commercial activities, these influential merchants with considerable financial resources began to extend control over the production of goods. They did this through a variety of means: by extending loans, by advancing raw materials and equipment to producers, or even by acquiring outright ownership of productive facilities. This practice, particularly prevalent among large wholesalers, had far-reaching implications for future development of the nation's marketing system.

With growing commercial activities, a subtle but rather basic change began to occur in the social status and political power of the prominent merchants. As noted earlier, during the first century of the Tokugawa era the merchant class tried to seek security in a hostile environment through the development of highly monopolistic and complex trade practices and institutional arrangements. During the period the feudal authorities paid virtually no attention to the growth of the commercial sector. The ruling elite was never able to understand the real implications of the rising commercialism (which eventually undermined the very foundation of the feudal power structure). This was partly because of their long-held disdain for commercial activities and partly because of the very complexity of the distribution and financial systems that the merchant class had so ingeniously evolved. The Confucian ideology, which was espoused officially by the Tokugawa regime, was essentially agrarian in its orientation and lacked an ideological basis for dealing with the rising tide of commercial development.

Without realizing its long-term implications, both the warrior class and the farmers became gradually dependent on the merchant class for their material welfare. Peace and prosperity fostered the ruling classes' growing taste for luxuries. When combined with the inept financial management in many of the semiautonomous fiefs, this forced the ruling class to become financially indebted to prominent merchants. Also, to increase their badly needed revenue, a number of progressive fiefs began to sell their surplus agricultural commodities in the commercial centers. At the same time they encouraged manufacturing activities in their domains. To distribute the output of the growing manufacturing sector outside their own territories, the fief governments had to enlist the services of influential city and provincial merchants. In this process it was not uncommon for the fief authorities to give monopoly rights to certain favored influential merchants. Thus developed a powerful alliance, albeit informal, based on practical necessity between the feudal authority and the influential merchants, that is, between the highest and the lowest class in the social hierarchy. In return for providing commercial services that were rapidly becoming essential to the very survival of the fief government, the influential merchants obtained official protection and reaped huge monopolistic profits.

It is important to note that the Tokugawa era, particularly in the earlier period, produced a number of outstanding merchants and innovative business practices. Resourcefulness, careful calculation, and control were emphasized, and it is observed by a prominent Japanese business historian that the introduction of a one-price policy at retail level in Japan preceded a similar practice in England by nearly half a century.[6] A number of thoughtful and articulate merchants emerged and contributed significantly to the evolution of a viable merchant ideology. Toward the end of the Tokugawa era, however, the monopoly status and alliance with the political elite began to dull the initiative and ingenuity of the merchant class. Their mentality became characterized by a strong conservative orientation and well-entrenched tradition. This result had far-reaching implications in shaping the pattern of Japan's subsequent industrialization. For one thing, as Professor Horie notes, these practices and this mentality failed to breed the spirit of progressive industrial entrepreneurship among prominent merchants.[7]

For these reasons, it is generally believed that the merchant class did not play a very significant role, at least in the initial phase of Japan's industrialization and modernization. The leadership of the Meiji Restoration movement was primarily in the hands of a small number of young men of the impoverished lower warriors' class. Given their rather conservative orientation, a number of prominent commercial houses were unable to survive the great upheavals and traumas immediately preceding and subsequent to the Meiji Restoration. Sir George Sansom, a noted Japanese historian, succinctly summarized this condition in the following manner: "Their

---

[6] A number of outstanding books are written in Japanese on this subject. For example: Takao Tsuchiya, *Nihon Keei Rinenshi [A History of Japanese Managerial Ideology]* (Tokyo: Nihon Keizai Shinbunsha, 1964), pp. 99-255; and Miyamoto, *Kinsei Shōnin Ishiki no Kenkyu,* pp. 3-290. Two of the best sources in English on this topic are Sheldon, *The Rise of the Merchant Class,* pp. 131-164; and Bellah, *Tokugawa Religion,* pp. 107-177.

[7] Horie, "Entrepreneurship," p. 194.

outlook was too narrow, they had thrived on protection, and with a few key exceptions, they fell back to huckstering, while ambitious samurai of low and middle rank became bankers, merchants, and manufacturers."[8]

## The Modern Era

The Meiji leadership introduced sweeping reforms, including abolishing the status hierarchy, and establishing freedom in the choice of occupation. Also abolished were the monopolistic privileges enjoyed by prominent merchants during the Tokugawa era. While the new government actively encouraged industrialization, the development of strategic industries received primary emphasis during the initial stage because of external and internal threats. This trend was given further impetus as the Japanese leadership began to espouse the mercantile ideology toward the end of the nineteenth century. As a result, government policy gave the development of consumer industries and a consumer market a low priority. However, political reforms and subsequent economic growth, coupled with rapid improvement in transportation and communication, contributed to the development of a national market and to a growing surge of commercial activities.

During the early Meiji era the distribution system was virtually unaffected. Prominent wholesalers still maintained a strong control over a myriad of small manufacturers and retailers. As Japan's industrialization progressed and as the Zaibatsu system became well established around the turn of the century, the industrial sector began to gain prominence over the commercial sector. Throughout the period prior to World War II, however, despite the rapid growth of large-scale enterprises, small establishments continued to be an important part of the Japanese economic system. For example, as late as in 1934 plants with fewer than 100 workers accounted for over 96 percent of the total number of establishments, nearly half the total number of employees, and about a third of the total factory production.[9] Particularly in the production of consumer products, small factories remained dominant.[10]

The prevalence of small manufacturing establishments required

[8] G. B. Sansom, *Japan: A Short Cultural History* (New York: D. Appleton-Century, Inc., 1943), p. 509.

[9] William W. Lockwood, *The Economic Development of Japan: Growth and Structural Change, 1868-1938* (Princeton, N.J.: Princeton University Press, 1958), p. 202.

[10] *Ibid.*

a large number of marketing intermediaries. Moreover, marketing intermediaries, particularly wholesalers, provided an important link between large-scale Zaibatsu manufacturing establishments with advanced technology and a myriad of small independent ones with primitive, labor-intensive production methods. True, the relative importance of the commercial sector declined. Nevertheless, in many product lines, particularly in traditional ones, wholesalers retained their importance and maintained their control over small and poorly capitalized manufacturers as well as smaller retail outlets through a variety of intricate means. Indeed, wholesalers in this era provided a number of very vital functions for both manufacturers and retailers, most important of which was the extension of trade credit.

In the retailing sector during this period several innovations were notable, such as widespread acceptance of the one-price policy, improvement of displays, and introduction of rudimentary sales promotion. Perhaps the most significant institutional innovation in retailing was the development of department stores around the turn of the century. Most of the original department stores grew out of prominent dry goods stores, and within a short period of time they experienced significant growth. For example, the sales of Mitsukoshi, the leading department store, grew almost fivefold between 1903 and 1911.[11] It is interesting to note that the rapid growth of department stores brought about familiar organized resistance from small independent retail stores.

Unfortunately, statistics dealing with the distribution sector are almost totally lacking throughout the period prior to World War II. Although systematic collection of statistics, particularly those relating to production, goes back to the early Meiji era, it was not until 1952 that a commercial census was first taken in Japan. Given the paucity of reliable statistics in this sector, one meaningful indicator of its growth during the prewar era is the employment figures by industry. Between 1920 and 1930 the number of persons employed in the distribution sector recorded more than a 50 percent gain, while the total labor force increased only by 9 percent, and the number of persons employed in the manufacturing sector showed a mere 5 percent increase.[12]

[11] Shotaro Takebayashi, *Shōgyō Keei no Kenkyu [Research on Management of Commercial Enterprises]* (Tokyo: Yuhikaku, 1955), p. 217.

[12] *Hundred-Year Statistics of the Japanese Economy* (Tokyo: The Bank of Japan, 1966) p. 58.

When Japan entered into World War II, the distribution sector became highly regulated. A strict rationing system and price controls were enforced. The government also sought to mobilize the labor force in the distribution sector for the war effort. As a means of attaining greater efficiency and labor saving, the government also directed, though in a haphazard manner, mergers of small wholesalers and retailers. Thus, toward the end of the war, given the serious shortage of merchandise, the strict ration system, and tight regulation, distribution activities had all but stopped functioning.

The severe destruction during the war and dislocations in its immediate aftermath dealt the Japanese economy a very serious blow, so serious that many questioned whether Japan could ever recover completely. Economic confusion, rampant inflation, and a high rate of unemployment plagued the immediate postwar Japanese economy. Black markets for all types of goods thrived. Some merchants made huge windfall gains from black market operations, but to the great majority this was indeed a very traumatic era.

In the late 1940s, because of the changes in the international political situation, the American Occupation policy underwent a radical change from demilitarization and democratization of the defeated nation to industrial recovery. The Japanese government, with active encouragement from the Occupation Forces, began to pursue positive steps for the economic recovery of Japan. In this process the government gave strong support and assistance in a variety of forms to a few basic industries deemed essential for general economic recovery. This government support provided the much-needed impetus to recovery of large-scale manufacturing firms, and, of course, the Korean War gave these industries further momentum for their subsequent growth.

In the meantime, the distribution sector received no such assistance from the government. Wholesalers and retailers were left entirely to their own devices to struggle through their postwar chaos. The government, which traditionally had been production-oriented, was almost totally oblivious to the needs of the commercial sector. Without government assistance and encouragement, the Japanese distribution sector did achieve recovery, albeit at a slower rate. It is indeed remarkable that the commercial sector was able to recover from wartime damages on its own in a relatively short period of time.

## An Overview of the Distribution System in Contemporary Japan

Having looked briefly at the historical development of the Japanese marketing system, we shall now examine salient features of the distribution system in present-day Japan to provide a necessary background for further discussion. We shall begin by examining the relative importance of the distribution sector in the Japanese economy. In the fiscal year 1968 the distribution sector contributed to the net domestic product the sum of ¥7,419 billion, or roughly 17.3 percent of the total.[13] Also in the same year approximately 9,260,000 people, representing roughly 18.2 percent of the total labor force, were engaged in distribution and related activities. There were some two million establishments engaged primarily in distribution activities, accounting for nearly half the total number of business establishments.

Throughout the postwar decades, the distribution sector has kept up with the rapid general economic growth. The sector's contribution to the net national product increased from ¥919 billion in 1953 to ¥7,419 billion in 1968, recording an eightfold increase, slightly exceeding the comparable growth rate of the net national product during the same period.[14] Between 1954 and 1969 the number of establishments in the distribution sector increased by 30 percent, which was slightly higher than the growth rate of all business establishments during this period. Particularly noteworthy is the increase in the number of people gainfully occupied in the distribution sector. The number nearly doubled, which was considerably greater than the 21 percent increase in the overall labor force recorded during this period. Also, between 1960 and 1969 the combined sales of the wholesale and retail sectors increased by almost five times. The details are presented in Table 1.1.

Having briefly examined the overall picture of the distribution sector in the Japanese economy, let us now analyze its salient features. In doing so, we shall draw heavily from the *Census of Commercial Statistics* published biennially by the Ministry of International Trade and Industry. The latest Census data now available are those collected in 1968 and published in 1970.

One striking feature of the Japanese distribution sector is that

---

[13] *Economic Statistics Annual, 1969* (Tokyo: The Bank of Japan, 1970), p. 286.
[14] *Ibid.*

TABLE 1.1

INDEXES OF WHOLESALE AND RETAIL SALES, 1960–1969

(1965 = 100)

| Year | Total | Wholesale | Retail |
|------|-------|-----------|--------|
| 1960 | 44.2 | 43.5 | 47.0 |
| 1961 | 54.3 | 53.8 | 56.2 |
| 1962 | 61.4 | 60.2 | 66.3 |
| 1963 | 72.3 | 71.7 | 79.9 |
| 1964 | 89.4 | 88.8 | 91.1 |
| 1965 | 100.0 | 100.0 | 100.0 |
| 1966 | 117.0 | 117.6 | 113.1 |
| 1967 | 129.8 | 129.4 | 130.3 |
| 1968 | 152.0 | 152.3 | 149.3 |
| 1969 | 195.2 | 201.7 | 166.7 |

Source: *Economic Statistics Annual, 1969* (Tokyo: The Bank of Japan, 1970), p. 208.

it is highly fragmented, consisting of a large number of small establishments. According to the Commercial Census, there were more than 281,000 wholesale establishments in Japan in 1968. They averaged less than ¥238 million or roughly $640,000 in annual sales and had an average of about eleven employees. As might be expected, the retailing sector is even more fragmented. In 1968 the Census reported that there were more than 1,389,000 retail establishments. They averaged no more than ¥9.6 million, or approximately $27,000 in annual sales, with an average of three employees. Since the population of Japan was slightly over 100 million in 1968, there was one wholesale store for every 356 persons and one retail store for every 72 persons. A statistical over-

TABLE 1.2

COMMERCIAL ESTABLISHMENTS IN JAPAN, 1968

| Type of Firm | No. of Stores | No. of Employees | Annual Sales (¥ million) | Average No. of Employees per Store | Annual Sales per Store (¥ million) |
|------|------|------|------|------|------|
| Wholesalers | 281,081 | 3,035,648 | 65,711,472 | 10.8 | 237.6 |
| Retailers | 1,389,222 | 4,241,825 | 13,615,365 | 3.1 | 9.6 |
| Total | 1,670,303 | 7,277,473 | 79,326,837 | 4.4 | 45.1 |

Source: Adapted from *Wagakuni no Shōgyō, 1969 [Commerce in Japan, 1969]* (Tokyo: The Ministry of International Trade and Industry, 1970), pp. 1–11.

view of Japanese wholesaling and retailing sectors is presented in Table 1.2.

TABLE 1.3

DISTRIBUTION OF WHOLESALE AND RETAIL ESTABLISHMENTS BY SIZE
AS MEASURED BY NUMBER OF EMPLOYEES, 1968

| Size | Wholesale Trade | | Retail Trade | |
|---|---|---|---|---|
| No. of Employees | No. of Establishments | Percent of Establishments with No. of Employees | No. of Establishments | Percent of Establishments with No. of Employees |
| 1–2 | 63,571 | 22.6 | 932,951 | 67.1 |
| 3–4 | 62,076 | 22.1 | 295,481 | 21.3 |
| 5–9 | 80,453 | 28.5 | 116,148 | 8.4 |
| 10–19 | 43,733 | 15.6 | 30,829 | 2.2 |
| 20–29 | 13,430 | 4.8 | 7,080 | 0.5 |
| 30–49 | 9,483 | 3.4 | 4,163 | 0.3 |
| 50–99 | 5,609 | 2.0 | 1,801 | 0.1 |
| 100 and over | 2,730 | 1.0 | 769 | 0.1 |

Source: *Wagakuni no Shōgyō, 1969 [Commerce in Japan, 1969]* (Tokyo: The Ministry of International Trade and Industry, 1970), pp. 120-123

Table 1.3 provides further evidence of the fragmentation of the distribution sector. Even in wholesale trade nearly half of all establishments had four employees or less. Almost three-quarters of the total had nine employees or less. In 1968 only 8,339 wholesale establishments, or 3 percent of the total, had fifty employees or more. In the retailing sector the situation is far more striking. Stores with four employees or less accounted for nearly 90 percent of some 1.4 million retail establishments.

TABLE 1.4

PERCENTAGE DISTRIBUTION OF RETAIL STORES ACCORDING TO SALES
FLOOR SPACE, 1968

| Sales Floor Space (square meters)* | 1-9 | 10-19 | 20-29 | 30-49 | 50-99 | 100-199 | 200-499 | 500-999 | 1,000 & Over |
|---|---|---|---|---|---|---|---|---|---|
| Percent of All Retail Establishments | 11.8 | 36.2 | 22.3 | 18.4 | 8.1 | 1.7 | 0.8 | 0.2 | 0.1 |

*1 square meter = 10.8 square feet.
Source: *Wagakuni no Shōgyō, 1969 [Commerce in Japan, 1969]* (Tokyo: The Ministry of International Trade and Industry, 1970), p. 84.

Furthermore, as indicated in Table 1.4, nearly half of all retail establishments had sales floor space of less than 19 square meters, or roughly 200 square feet, and nearly three-quarters consisted of establishments with floor space of less than 30 square meters, or roughly 320 square feet. The preponderance of small establishments still prevails, despite the fact that there has been a trend for increase of the average size of establishments, as indicated in Table 1.5. Between 1952 and 1968 the average wholesale sales

TABLE 1.5

GROWTH OF WHOLESALE AND RETAIL SECTORS, 1952–1968

| Year | No. of Establishments | Adjusted* Sales per Store (¥ million) | Average Employees per Store | Sales per Employee. (¥10,000) |
|---|---|---|---|---|
| | | WHOLESALE SECTOR | | |
| 1952 | 131.2 | 50.53 | 6.27 | 807 |
| 1954 | 155.3 | 56.78 | 6.70 | 848 |
| 1956 | 171.4 | 69.23 | 7.33 | 944 |
| 1958 | 185.7 | 78.51 | 8.15 | 963 |
| 1960 | 215.9 | 87.05 | 8.70 | 1,001 |
| 1962 | 218.1 | 129.46 | 9.69 | 1,336 |
| 1964 | 223.8 | 174.86 | 11.20 | 1,562 |
| 1966 | 279.7 | 181.84 | 10.80 | 1,666 |
| 1968 | 276.6 | 226.03 | 10.93 | 2,069 |
| | | RETAIL SECTOR | | |
| 1952 | 1,079.7 | 2.56 | 2.13 | 120 |
| 1954 | 1,189.1 | 3.03 | 2.26 | 134 |
| 1956 | 1,201.3 | 3.58 | 2.56 | 143 |
| 1958 | 1,244.6 | 4.02 | 2.63 | 153 |
| 1960 | 1,288.3 | 4.51 | 2.71 | 167 |
| 1962 | 1,272.0 | 5.96 | 2.79 | 206 |
| 1964 | 1,304.5 | 6.82 | 2.92 | 233 |
| 1966 | 1,375.4 | 7.41 | 3.05 | 243 |
| 1968 | 1,389.2 | 8.51 | 3.05 | 279 |

*The wholesale and retail sales reported here have been adjusted by the wholesale price index and consumer price index, respectively, to remove the effects of inflation.

Source: *Wagakuni no Shōgyō, 1969 [Commerce in Japan, 1969]* (Tokyo: The Ministry of International Trade and Industry, 1970), p. 12.

per establishment more than quadrupled (in real terms) and that of retail stores increased nearly 3.4 times.

Many retailers depend exclusively on family members as the source of labor. In 1966, 29 percent of wholesale establishments and as high as 77 percent of all retail stores belonged to this category.[15] Typically, in these establishments only a very loose accounting record is kept and no clear distinction is drawn between the store's operations and the household budget. Furthermore, in many instances the physical facilities of the store and the family living quarters are separated in a very informal manner.

Indeed, typically, the owners of these very small stores have been barely eking out their daily existence, and some, in fact, have found it necessary to seek other employment to supplement the meager income derived from the operations of their stores. Of course, in some cases, retail operations are considered a supplement to the main source of family income. It is not uncommon to find a situation in which wives operate small stores while their husbands have full-time employment elsewhere. In 1967 a survey by the Small-Medium-Size Enterprise Agency revealed that over 15 percent of the owners of the stores with four employees or less had other sources of income. In small cities, one out of every four owners of these rather marginal retail establishments reported another source of income.

Closely related to the foregoing conditions are the striking dif-

TABLE 1.6

ANNUAL SALES OF WHOLESALE AND RETAIL
ESTABLISHMENTS OF THE UNITED STATES AND JAPAN ACCORDING
TO SIZE OF ESTABLISHMENT, 1966
(Sales of Establishments with 0–2 Employees = 1.0)

| No. of Employees | Wholesale Establishments | | Retail Establishments | |
|---|---|---|---|---|
| | USA | Japan | USA | Japan |
| 0–2 | 1.0 | 1.0 | 1.0 | 1.0 |
| 3–4 | 2.0 | 3.3 | 2.8 | 3.5 |
| 5–9 | 3.4 | 7.7 | 4.9 | 8.7 |
| 10–19 | 5.7 | 19.6 | 10.2 | 18.4 |
| 20–29 | ⎱ | 39.9 | | 30.2 |
| | 12.6 | | 24.2 | |
| 30–49 | ⎰ | 72.4 | | 47.4 |
| 50–99 | 31.9 | 145.8 | 54.0 | 94.6 |
| 100 or more | 86.3 | 999.0 | 183.3 | 818.9 |

Source: *Wagakuni no Shōgyō, 1967 [Commerce in Japan, 1967]* (Tokyo: The Ministry of International Trade and Industry, 1968), p. 6.

15 *Chūshō Kigyō Hakusho: Showa 43 nen ban [White Paper on Small- to Medium-Size Enterprises, 1968 Edition]* (Tokyo: Small-Medium-Size Enterprise Agency, 1969), p. 113.

ferences existing in annual sales volume according to the size of establishments, another indication of the marginal nature of very small marketing intermediaries in Japan. As revealed in Table 1.6, comparison with the United States highlights this disparity. For example, the average sales of wholesale establishments with 100 employees or more in Japan were nearly 1,000 times greater than those of the establishments with two employees or less. In contrast, the disparity between the similar sizes of establishments in the United States is 86 times.

Equally revealing is the international comparison of sales per person according to size of enterprise. In Japan, according to the 1968 data, the sales per person become progressively larger with the increase in size of the establishment. The sales per person of retail establishments with two employees or less were about one-fourth those of establishments with 100 or more employees.[16] Significantly, per-employee sales of stores with two employees or less were half of those of the stores with five to nine employees. In contrast, in Great Britain, virtually no variation was found in sales per employee according to different sized firms. In the United States the sales per person were reported to be highest among stores with 50 to 99 employees, but even here they are only about 50 percent greater than those of stores with two employees or less, in contrast to more than a threefold difference in Japan. These figures reveal the relative inefficiency of very small establishments in the Japanese distribution sector.

Virtually everywhere the distribution sector is known for its high turnover, characterized on one hand by ease of entry, on the other by a high rate of attrition. This characteristic is certainly applicable to the Japanese situation. Respectively, 82 percent and 72 percent of wholesale and retail establishments operating in 1968 were established after 1945. Moreover, in both cases nearly half were established after 1955. For example, as can be seen from Table 1.7, between 1964 and 1966 63,000 retail establishments went out of business, while during the same period, 133,000 new entrants were reported.

As might be expected, the great majority of new establishments are small in size with only limited capital. The average initial capital reported by small retail stores (with four employees or less)

---

[16] *Wagakuni no Shōgyō, 1967 [Commerce in Japan, 1967]* (Tokyo: Ministry of International Trade and Industry, 1968, p. 81.

TABLE 1.7

CHANGES IN THE NUMBER OF RETAIL ESTABLISHMENTS, 1958–1966

| Year | No. of Estab. at the End of the Period (1,000) | No. of New Establishments (1,000) | No. of. Estab. Gone Out of Business (1,000) | Net Increase or Decrease (1,000) |
|---|---|---|---|---|
| 1958–60 | 1,290 | 154 | 111 | 43 |
| 1960–62 | 1,272 | 118 | 136 | −18 |
| 1962–64 | 1,305 | 114 | 81 | 33 |
| 1964–66 | 1,375 | 133 | 63 | 70 |

Source: *Chūshō Kigyō Hakusho, Showa 43 nen [White Paper on Small- to Medium-Size Enterprises, 1968]* (Tokyo: Small–Medium-Size Enterprise Agency, 1969), p. 116.

established in 1966 was only ¥780,000, or slightly over $2,000. Even for stores with 10 to 19 employees, the average initial capital was no more than ¥2.7 million, or less than $8,000.[17]

The existence of a large number of small stores is well illustrated in food retailing. In 1968 there were more than 711,000 retail establishments handling foodstuffs (in contrast to 320,000 in the United States), accounting for more than half of the total number of retail establishments in Japan and approximately 40 percent of the total retail sales. The average annual sales of these stores in 1966 was only ¥7.5 million, or about $20,000. On a daily basis this was only ¥20,000, or less than $60.

Because of their limited financial resources and their limited physical size, there is a tendency for retail stores to be highly specialized in the types of products they handle. This characteristic is also illustrated by conditions prevailing in food retailing. In 1968 there were more than 100,000 stores specializing in liquor and seasonings, 20,000 meat shops, some 49,000 stores handling fish and related products, more than 60,000 fruit and vegetable stands, more than 238,000 confectionery and candy shops.

Although the Japanese distribution system is dominated by small-size establishments, a limited number of large establishments is responsible for a disproportionate share of the total sales. In 1966, the last year for which data are available at the time of this writing, in wholesaling, some 2,600 establishments with 100 employees or

[17] *Chūshō Kigyō Hakusho: Showa 42 nen ban [White Paper on Small- to Medium-Size Enterprises, 1967]* (Tokyo: Small-Medium-Size Enterprise Agency, 1968), p. 116.

more, or 1.3 percent of all stores, were responsible for over 21 percent of the total sales volume. Likewise in 1966, 769 retail establishments, or less than 0.1 percent of all retail establishments, accounted for over 15 percent of the total retail sales. As we shall see in detail in a subsequent chapter, the trend toward concentration of sales among a small number of large stores is very evident in both the wholesaling and the retailing sectors.

Another notable feature of the Japanense distribution system is that it is highly complex and circuitous. Merchandise, particularly consumer goods, must pass through multiple levels of marketing intermediaries, each performing narrow and highly specialized functions. Particularly complex is the wholesaling structure. It is not uncommon for merchandise to pass through several different types of wholesalers — primary, secondary, regional, or local wholesalers. This is evident when one notes that the volume of transactions among wholesalers far exceeds total retail sales. In 1968 total wholesale sales in Japan were about 4.8 times greater than total retail sales. The Japanese case becomes particularly striking when compared with the situation in the United States, where the total wholesale sales are only 1.3 times the total retail sales. The breakdown of wholesale sales according to major customer groups further substantiates this point. In Japan in 1966 over 37 percent of wholesale sales were made to other wholesalers, 24 percent to institutional and industrial customers, and only 24 percent directly to retailers.[18] The comparable figures for the United States are roughly 15 percent, 44 percent, and 41 percent, respectively.

It is estimated that less than 20 percent of wholesalers in Japan buy directly from manufacturers and sell to retailers. These wholesalers are responsible for some 15 percent of total wholesale sales. Slightly over 12 percent of wholesalers buy from producers and sell to other wholesalers. This group of wholesalers accounts for 27.5 percent of total wholesale sales. Nearly half of the wholesalers in Japan are so-called secondary wholesalers (accounting for 22.7 percent of wholesale sales). As high as 8.5 percent of wholesale establishments not only buy from wholesalers but sell to other wholesalers. Details are presented in Table 1.8.

The patterns of distribution and the degree of complexity of the distribution structure vary widely among product lines. For illustrative purposes, channels of distribution for selected consumer products are presented in Figures 1.1, 1.2, and 1.3.

---

[18] *Wagakuni no Shōgyō, 1967 [Commerce in Japan, 1967]*, p. 54.

## TABLE 1.8

NUMBER OF WHOLESALE ESTABLISHMENTS AND THE PERCENTAGE OF
WHOLESALE SALES ACCORDING TO TYPES OF ACTIVITIES, 1968

| Sales | No. of Establishments | Total Sales |
|---|---|---|
| Total wholesalers | 100.0 | 100.0 |
| Primary wholesalers | 45.9 | 64.3 |
| From producers to institutional users | 12.1 | 17.9 |
| From producers to overseas market | 1.1 | 1.8 |
| From overseas sources to institutional users | 0.2 | 1.2 |
| From overseas sources to overseas market | 0.2 | 0.2 |
| From producers to retailers | 19.8 | 14.7 |
| From overseas sources to retailers | 0.1 | 0.2 |
| From producers to wholesalers | 12.1 | 27.5 |
| From overseas sources to wholesalers | 0.3 | 0.8 |
| Secondary wholesalers | 48.0 | 22.7 |
| From wholesalers to wholesalers | 8.5 | 6.9 |
| From wholesalers to institutional users | 16.0 | 6.4 |
| From wholesalers to overseas market | 2.6 | 0.8 |
| From wholesalers to retailers | 20.9 | 8.5 |
| Others | 6.1 | 13.0 |

Source: *Wagakuni no Shōgyō, 1969 [Commerce in Japan, 1969]* (Tokyo: The Ministry of International Trade and Industry, 1970), p. 57.

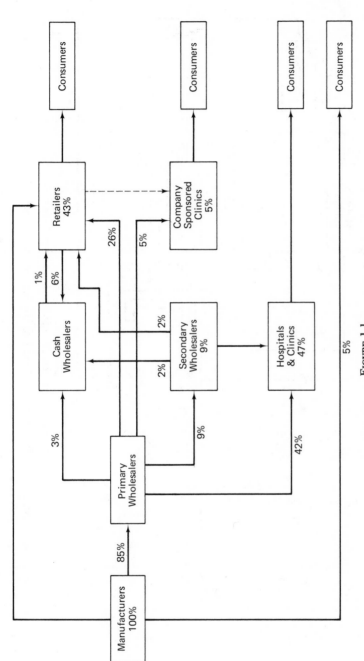

FIGURE 1.1
*The Distribution Channel for Pharmaceutical Products*

Source: *Nihon Keizai Shinbun [The Japan Economic Journal]*, October 11, 1968, p. 27.

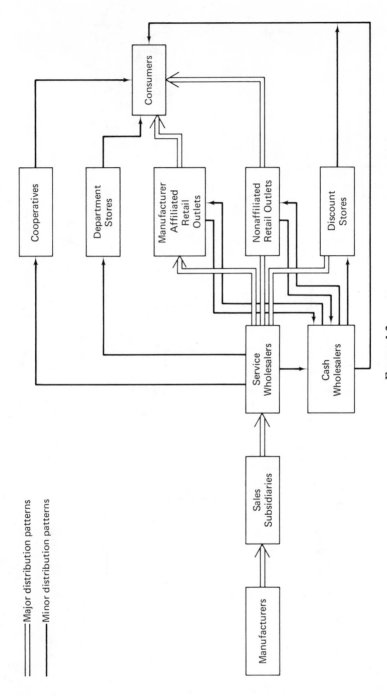

FIGURE 1.2

*The Distribution Channels for Electric Home Appliances*

Source: *Bushibetsu Ryutsu Jittai Chosa Hokokusho [A Report on Distribution by Product]* Tokyo: The Ministry of International Trade and Industry, 1968), p. 206.

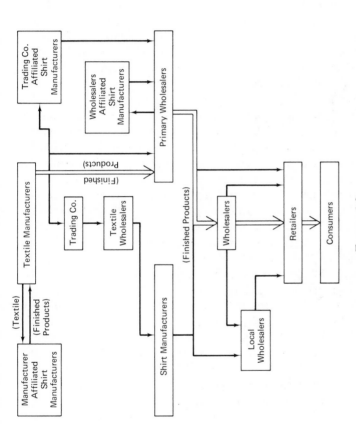

FIGURE 1.3
*The Distribution Channels for Dress Shirts*

Source: *Bushibetsu Ryutsu Jittai Chosa Hokokusho [A Report on Distribution by Product]* (Tokyo: The Ministry of International Trade and Industry, 1968), p. 291.

In addition to circuitous channels of distribution consisting of multiple levels, trade customs that have evolved over the years have become rather complicated. The small size of most retailers, and their limited financial resources, coupled with strong competitive pressure in many industries force wholesalers to sell to retailers in small quantities at frequent intervals, and return privileges are indeed liberal. In highly competitive industries such as drugs, processed food, or home appliances, and certain lines of soft goods, daily shipment of merchandise from wholesalers to retailers is not unusual. In a number of industries, rather elaborate and complicated discount and rebate structures have evolved out of traditional commercial custom and competitive pressures. These discount and rebate practices are often manipulated according to the prevailing competitive conditions and rather particularistic relationships between the seller and the buyer. The very liberal extension of trade credit is also commonplace at every stage of the distribution process. Customarily, notes with the payment period extending as long as 60 or even 90 days are accepted by the seller. Given the extreme scarcity of capital at the retail level, financing has been a very important aspect of wholesalers' functions. In addition to the presence of multiple levels and circuitous channels, these practices tend to make the Japanese distribution system highly complicated.

We have briefly examined salient features of the distribution system in Japan. We have noted that it is dominated by a large number of small establishments, and typically, the distribution channels are long and circuitous. Also noteworthy are the complicated trade customs that have evolved over many years. In fact, in a number of aspects the contemporary Japanese distribution system has undergone little basic change in the last century and still retains many features of the premodern system. This is rather remarkable, considering the very basic and dynamic changes that have taken place in almost every other aspect of the Japanese economy in the last century. Indeed, one cannot help wondering why the distribution sector has been virtually unaffected by the rather sweeping changes that have taken place elsewhere in the economy.

Among several reasons accounting for this situation, the most important was the absence of a broad consumer market. The particular pattern of Japan's industrial development throughout the prewar era did not give rise to a large consumer market. Given the rather limited size of his discretionary income, the average consumer was severely constrained in his consumption. Not only was the average consumer's expenditure limited, but small income forced him to purchase goods in small quantities at frequent intervals. This was particularly true for daily necessities, including food. Limited income, lack of storage facilities, and the strong preference for freshness led housewives to make frequent shopping trips, sometimes several daily. And of necessity, they had to confine themselves to neighborhood shops. Women had ample time on their hands and lacked opportunities to utilize their spare time for economically productive activities. Besides, shopping constituted to many housewives the only opportunity for social interactions.

Even as late as in the mid-1960s, according to a survey sponsored by a commercial research organization, an average housewife in Tokyo did her shopping for convenience goods within a 300-meter radius, or considerably less than a quarter of a mile from home. The same survey revealed that about 72 percent of 889 respondents said that they bought fresh vegetables, meat, and fish daily. Thus, the lack of consumer mobility and the need to shop frequently have provided a powerful rationale for the existence of a large number of small stores.

The second reason is the continued importance of small manufacturing establishments in Japan. As indicated in Table 1.9, small

TABLE 1.9

Size of Establishments in the Manufacturing Industry of Japan, 1967

| No. of Employees | Percent of Establishments | Percent of Employees | Value of Shipment (%) | Value Added (%) |
|---|---|---|---|---|
| 1–9 | 74.0 | 16 | 6 | 7 |
| 10–29 | 16.6 | 17 | 11 | 12 |
| 30–99 | 7.0 | 20 | 16 | 16 |
| 100–299 | 1.7 | 16 | 17 | 16 |
| 300–999 | 0.5 | 14 | 22 | 20 |
| 1,000 and over | 0.1 | 16 | 28 | 29 |

Source: Adapted from *Chushō Kigyō Hakusho: Showa 42 nendo [White Paper on Small–Medium-Size Enterprises, 1967]* (Tokyo: The Ministry of International Trade and Industry, 1968), pp. 437–441.

manufacturing establishments have long occupied an extremely important place in the Japanese economy, particularly in the production of consumer goods. The multiplicity of small manufacturers, with each providing only a limited output, requires a large number of middlemen to supply their needs as well as to distribute their products. Less than reliable production schedules and the absence of uniform quality standards require a large number of middlemen to assemble and distribute these products. Thus, the continued presence of a large number of highly fragmented small production units requires the services of equally many marketing intermediaries.

Despite the small size of the country, Japan developed rather extensive geographic specialization for a variety of products, particularly in handicraft industries. This was due, in part, to the fact that Japan was divided into some 300 semiautonomous fiefs during the Tokugawa era. In order to improve their own economic conditions, these fiefs encouraged the development of certain handicraft industries and agricultural products that were deemed particularly appropriate for their resource endowments. Thus, one certain area became well known for a type of silk product, while another became noted for a particular type of chinaware. Each producing area took pride in its specialized products and guarded its monopoly position with great care. In many cases, these products gained nationwide distribution and recognition. This tradition of geographic specialization of production remains important for a number of specialty products even now. Since the great majority of these producing units typically have been small, the marketing of their output also requires complex arrangements and multiple levels of marketing intermediaries.

The third reason for the continued presence of a highly fragmented and complex marketing system is that the distribution sector in Japan, as in a number of other countries, has absorbed a large share of the surplus labor force. Throughout the prewar decades, as well as during the early postwar years, unemployment was a most serious and nagging problem in Japan. Entry into commercial activities, particularly small-scale retailing, has been relatively easy, thus attracting a large number of the unskilled who would otherwise have been unemployed. This greatly increased the number of small stores, resulting in the proliferation of marketing establishments. Competition among a myriad of small wholesale and retail establishments has been extremely keen. Many are eking out a meager existence and are unable to grow to the minimum size for economic operation.

Finally, inadequate infrastructure has contributed to producing a complex distribution system. Poor road conditions, storage facilities, communication, and transportation have constituted major deterrents to the smooth flow of information and materials, which, of course, is essential for the efficient and effective performance of distributive functions. Road conditions, though gradually improving, are just about the worst in any industrialized country in the world. Roads are not only narrow but poorly surfaced and maintained. Even in the late 1960s less than half the 18,000 miles of national highways were paved. Only 12 percent of the prefectural roads and only 3 percent of municipal roads were paved.[19] Telephone services are still inadequate in comparison with other advanced nations. These inadequacies in infrastructure have been an important factor contributing to the development of highly fragmented and specialized marketing intermediaries.

### Forces of Change

We have described briefly the salient characteristics of the Japanese distribution system and examined the basic reasons that have led to these conditions. Until recent years the Japanese system was adequate to serve the needs it had to fill. However, significant environmental changes that have been taking place during the past decade are now making new demands on the system, calling for its basic reassessment and restructuring.

The strains that are now being experienced by the Japanese marketing system can be traced back to two basic and closely related factors—the rapid postwar economic growth and the significant social changes that the nation has been undergoing concurrently. Japan's phenomenal postwar economic growth is a familiar story and needs no detailed elaboration here. We shall attempt only to indicate its magnitude. After the shattering defeat and destruction of World War II, Japan's industrial output reached its prewar level by 1952. Subsequently, the GNP grew at the rate of 10 percent or more annually, recording a more than threefold increase in real terms between 1955 and 1968. Between 1960 and 1968 it more than doubled. In 1968 the GNP reached $142 billion, demonstrating a 14 percent real growth over the preceding year. In the free world Japan's GNP is now second only to that of the United States.

---

[19] *Hundred-Year Statistics of the Japanese Economy*, p. 126.

A very important consequence of this rapid growth in national product is the emergence of a mass consumption market. Between 1953 and 1968 private consumption expenditure grew by more than five times, reaching over ¥26.6 trillion in 1968[20] and accounting for slightly more than 50 percent of the GNP. In 1968 alone the growth in personal consumption expenditure accounted for nearly half of the 14 percent real growth of GNP over the preceding year.

Extensive social reforms introduced in the immediate aftermath of the war made it possible for the fruits of the economic growth to be diffused widely among the masses. Of course, once this widespread diffusion of economic benefits began to take place, it stimulated further social change, making the postwar Japanese society considerably different from that of the prewar era. Japan has begun to take on those characteristics and orientations that are commonly associated with mass consumption societies elsewhere in the world. Because of the extreme importance of this phenomenon, we shall devote the next chapter to examination of the characteristics of the emerging consumer market in postwar Japan. Let it suffice to point

TABLE 1.10

DISTRIBUTION OF NATIONAL INCOME AND LABOR FORCE BY INDUSTRIAL SECTORS FOR SELECTED PREWAR AND POSTWAR YEARS

| Sector of Industry | 1934–1936 Average | | 1925 | |
| | Percent of National Income | Percent of Labor Force | Percent of National Income | Percent of Labor Force |
| --- | --- | --- | --- | --- |
| Primary Sector | 19.8 | 49.4 | 24.7 | 45.3 |
| Secondary Sector | 30.8 | 20.4 | 31.1 | 23.6 |
| Tertiary Sector | 49.4 | 30.2 | 44.2 | 31.1 |
| | 100% | 100% | 100% | 100% |
| | 1960 | | 1967* | |
| Primary Sector | 14.8 | 32.6 | 12.5 | 23.7 |
| Secondary Sector | 36.4 | 29.2 | 36.1 | 32.3 |
| Tertiary Sector | 48.8 | 38.2 | 51.4 | 44.0 |
| | 100% | 100% | 100% | 100% |

*Adapted from *Keizai Yoran, 1969 [A Summary of Economic Statistics, 1969]* (Tokyo: The Economic Planning Agency, 1969), pp. 68 and 282.

Source: *Hundred-Year Statistics of the Japanese Economy* (Tokyo: The Bank of Japan, 1967), p. 53.

[20] *Economic Statistics Annual, 1968* (Tokyo: The Bank of Japan, 1969), p. 287.

out now that herein lies the single most fundamental and immediate source of the strains now being experienced by the traditional marketing system in Japan.

Rapid economic growth has brought about a basic structural change in the Japanese economy. Indeed, the contemporary Japanese economy is substantially different, in terms of both scale and level of development, from that of prewar times or even that of a decade ago. This is well reflected in changes in the sectoral composition of national income and the labor force.

As can be seen from Table 1.10, the primary sector has steadily declined in relative importance and the secondary and tertiary sectors have made substantial gains. Even the casual comparison between the sectoral distribution of income and labor force between the prewar and postwar years reveals striking differences. Particularly significant, of course, has been the growth of manufacturing industries.

In the early 1950s Japanese manufacturing industries began a most intense round of capital investment. These investments initially were designed to rebuild war-torn facilities and to replace obsolete equipment, but once the economic recovery gained its momentum, they were made to capitalize on the rapidly growing domestic mar-

TABLE 1.11

GROWTH OF CAPITAL INVESTMENT IN THE PRIVATE SECTOR, 1954–1968

| Year | Index 1960=100 | Percentage Change over Preceding Year |
|------|------|------|
| 1954 | 29.8 | — |
| 1955 | 34.9 | 17.1 |
| 1956 | 48.3 | 38.4 |
| 1957 | 59.4 | 23.0 |
| 1958 | 54.8 | -7.7 |
| 1959 | 70.6 | 28.8 |
| 1960 | 100.0 | 41.6 |
| 1961 | 126.1 | 26.1 |
| 1962 | 122.6 | -2.8 |
| 1963 | 130.5 | 6.4 |
| 1964 | 150.4 | 15.4 |
| 1965 | 141.0 | 6.3 |
| 1966 | 160.7 | 14.0 |
| 1967 | 210.9 | 31.2 |
| 1968 | 261.3 | 24.3 |

Source: *Keizai Yoran, 1970 [A Summary of Economic Statistics]* (Tokyo: The Economic Planning Agency, 1970), pp. 18–19.

ket. Indeed, as can be seen from Table 1.11, the aggressiveness and vigor with which Japanese manufacturing industries undertook new capital investments have no close parallel elsewhere.[21] Between 1952 and 1957 the annual capital investment in the private sector doubled in real terms, increasing from ¥903 billion to over ¥1.8 trillion; between 1957 and 1961 the amount again more than doubled, reaching the staggering sum of nearly ¥4 trillion. Since 1961 it has continued to increase, and by 1969 the figure reached over ¥8 trillion.

Naturally, such dynamic capital investment behavior in the private sector has provided a further impetus for economic growth. Furthermore, it has resulted, of course, in the very rapid growth of output. Between 1955 and 1969 the total manufacturing output increased more than sevenfold. During this period the output of capital goods gained more than twelve times; that of consumer nondurables more than tripled. The output of consumer durables showed an amazing twenty-six-fold growth. The details are presented in Table 1.12.

TABLE 1.12

INDEX OF INDUSTRIAL PRODUCTION FOR SELECTED PREWAR AND POSTWAR YEARS

(1960 = 100)

| Yea | Total Manu- facturing | Capital Goods | Construc- tion Materials | Durable Consumer Goods | Nondurable Consumer Goods | Pro- ducers Goods |
|-----|-----------------------|---------------|--------------------------|------------------------|---------------------------|-------------------|
| 1935 | 27.9 | 12.7 | 27.4 | 7.7 | 29.3 | 29.0 |
| 1940 | 44.3 | 36.7 | 30.0 | 10.8 | 54.0 | 42.1 |
| 1950 | 20.4 | 15.4 | 28.6 | 6.2 | 30.2 | 25.1 |
| 1955 | 45.7 | 34.3 | 52.6 | 18.9 | 69.0 | 48.2 |
| 1958 | 65.7 | 72.3 | 81.1 | 75.2 | 91.8 | 80.0 |
| 1960 | 100.0 | 100.0 | 100.0 | 100.0 | 100.0 | 100.0 |
| 1961 | 119.9 | 130.0 | 115.0 | 125.8 | 109.0 | 118.5 |
| 1963 | 143.7 | 157.3 | 132.8 | 160.1 | 129.1 | 139.7 |
| 1967 | 240.7 | 303.8 | 210.1 | 246.5 | 190.1 | 203.4 |
| 1968 | 280.2 | 366.9 | 246.7 | 388.9 | 204.0 | 266.7 |
| 1969 | 328.7 | 437.7 | 304.5 | 475.5 | 221.0 | 311.0 |

Source: Adapted from *Hundred-Year Statistics of the Japanese Economy* (Tokyo: The Bank of Japan, 1967), pp. 92–93, except for 1967 and 1968 figures, which were taken from *Economic Statistics Annual, 1969* (Tokyo: The Bank of Japan, 1970), pp. 187–189.

[21] For details see M. Y. Yoshino, *Japan's Managerial System: Tradition and Innovation* (Cambridge: The M.I.T. Press, 1968), pp. 162–178.

TABLE 1.13

GROWTH OF OUTPUT OF SELECTED PRODUCTS FOR PREWAR AND POSTWAR
YEARS

| Year | Synthetic Fibers (millions of tons) | Sewing Machines (1,000 units) | Electric Refrig- erators (1,000 units) | Radio Receivers (1,000 units) | TV Sets (1,000 units) | Passenger Cars (units) |
|---|---|---|---|---|---|---|
| 1936 | — | 12 | — | 427 | — | 100 |
| 1953 | 6,485 | 1,318 | 7 | 1,391 | 14 | 8,489 |
| 1955 | 15,755 | 1,696 | 31 | 1,789 | 137 | 20,261 |
| 1958 | 46,396 | 2,216 | 415 | 4,897 | 1,205 | 50,642 |
| 1960 | 118,274 | 2,749 | 908 | 12,851 | 3,578 | 165,094 |
| 1963 | 239,193 | 3,353 | 3,421 | 17,062 | 4,916 | 407,830 |
| 1966 | 460,481 | 3,820 | 2,565 | 25,297 | 5,652 | 877,656 |
| 1967 | 577,979 | 3,853 | 3,181 | 28,180 | 7,039 | 1,375,735 |
| 1968 | 685,398 | 4,203 | 3,471 | 30,811 | 9,139 | 2,055,821 |
| 1969 | 806,311 | 4,342 | 3,140 | 34,090 | 12,683 | 2,611,499 |

Source: Adapted from *Economic Statistics Annual, 1969* (Tokyo: The Bank
of Japan, 1970), pp. 199–202.

Table 1.13 presents the growth of output for a few key products
for selected prewar and postwar years. Japan is now first in the
production of such consumer goods as color television sets, cameras,
watches, and motorcycles. Also, it is second only to the United
States in production of a number of other consumer products,
including automobiles, pharmaceuticals, synthetic fibers, and
cosmetics.

Within a very short period of time, Japanese industries have
rapidly reequipped themselves with most up-to-date facilities and
machinery in order to increase their productive capacity and efficiency. For example, according to a survey conducted in 1964, 73
percent of all equipment and machinery used in all incorporated
business establishments in Japan at the time of the survey were less
than six years old.[22] In this process, a modern mass production system has been installed for the first time in many of Japan's key
industries, particularly in the consumer field.

A particularly noteworthy aspect of the postwar economic growth
in Japan is the development of consumer industries. For the reasons

[22] Masao Sakisaka (ed.), *Nihon Sangyo Zue [An Overview of Japanese In-
dustries]* (Tokyo: Toyo Keizai Shinpo Sha, 1968) p. 13.

noted earlier, the consumer industries in prewar Japan were very underdeveloped. During much of the prewar era most of Japan's consumer industry was no more than cottage industries, employing labor-intensive primitive techniques with poor quality standards. In less than two decades, however, the condition has changed radically. Not only does contemporary Japan boast fully developed consumer industries, but they have come to occupy an important position in the nation's economy.

A significant factor in the rapid postwar development of the consumer industry is the entry of large-scale firms into this field. Until the end of World War II large-scale firms had been almost exclusively engaged in the production of strategic industrial goods, but with the total loss of the military market, after the defeat in World War II, large firms were compelled to shift to peacetime industries, and many for the first time entered the consumer market. Now these large firms dominate many of the key consumer industries. For example, among the ten largest manufacturing firms ranked in terms of sales volume are two leading automobile manufacturers and three manufacturers of diversified electrical products in which home appliances comprise an important share. What is more significant is the fact that ranked according to profitability, three leading firms in consumer industries—Matsushita Electric, Toyota Motors, and Nissan Motors—occupy the first three positions among the ten largest manufacturing firms. In fact, in 1968, for the first time in the nation's history, the income of a private corporation exceeded that of the Bank of Japan; significantly, this feat was achieved by Matsushita Electric, a leading manufacturer of electric home appliances.

Another noteworthy aspect in connection with rapid growth of consumer industries is the remarkable rate with which new consumer products have been introduced during the last decade and a half. In consumer durables, for example, virtually every product except such rudimentary ones as electric irons or fans was new. Among products newly introduced are television sets, washing machines, refrigerators, air conditioning units, transistor radios, and vacuum cleaners. In the food industry, new products range from instant coffee, breakfast cereals, and frozen food to ready-to-eat packaged food. Similar patterns are found in automobiles, apparel, cosmetics, pharmaceuticals, and a number of other consumer products. Here again large manufacturing firms took the initiative, since advanced foreign technology has played a very vital role in the rapid introduction of new products. Between 1950 and 1968 Japanese firms, mostly large ones, signed more than 9,800 licensing contracts with foreign firms, for which they paid a staggering sum of nearly $1.5 billion in royalties.

In summary, during the postwar decades we have witnessed major changes in the production sector that have had far-reaching impact on the marketing system. These changes include (1) the extensive development of consumer industries, (2) active entry of large firms into consumer fields, (3) the widespread adoption of the mass production system in consumer industries, (4) the rapid growth of output, and (5) the introduction of numerous new products. Understandably, these changes have placed entirely new demands on the marketing system. One can easily imagine the strains that very rapid growth in output in less than a decade alone would create in the traditional marketing system, not to mention the appearance of a large number of new products and the active entry of large oligopolistic firms into consumer fields.

The traditional marketing system in Japan has been rather slow, at least until recently, in responding to these changes. Reasons are not difficult to find. As we have seen, the distribution sector has been highly fragmented, consisting of a large number of small establishments, and characteristically, they lack financial and managerial resources to generate meaningful change. World War II dealt many of the small establishments a severe blow, which they could ill afford. Moreover, unlike more fortunate large manufacturing firms with close ties to the government, marketing intermediaries were not favored by extensive government assistance in their postwar recovery efforts. They had to carry the entire burden themselves.

The traditional conservatism that characterized Japanese merchants also inhibited rapid response to the environmental changes. Some failed to recognize the implications of the changes discussed earlier. Some simply were oblivious to them. For the majority, however, eking out their daily existence in a highly competitive environment absorbed all their energies. Thus, with the passage of time, the gaps between the new demands and the ability of the distribution sector to perform the newly required functions have widened steadily.

In addition to the two fundamental forces—the emergence of a mass consumer market and fundamental changes in the production sector—there are yet two other forces that are now impinging on the Japanese marketing system. One is the increasingly serious labor shortage, which is another important by-product of the rapid postwar economic growth. The distribution sector in Japan, as in many other countries, has traditionally served, along with the agricultural sector, as a haven for those who would have been otherwise unemployed. This is no longer true, however. The rapid postwar economic growth has created a serious labor shortage, particularly among younger workers, whose wage level has been especially low, given the seniority-based wage system. The labor shortage has resulted, of course, in a steady increase in the wage level, as indicated in Table 1.14.

TABLE 1.14

CASH EARNINGS INDEXES OF REGULAR WORKERS FOR SELECTED POSTWAR
YEARS

(1965 average = 100)

| Year | All Industries | | Manufacturing | | Wholesale and Retail Trade | |
|------|---------|------|---------|------|---------|------|
| | Nominal | Real | Nominal | Real | Nominal | Real |
| 1957 | 52.3 | 73.8 | 52.0 | 73.3 | 53.4 | 75.3 |
| 1963 | 83.0 | 92.7 | 83.2 | 93.0 | 86.3 | 96.4 |
| 1965 | 100.0 | 100.0 | 100.0 | 100.0 | 100.0 | 100.0 |
| 1966 | 110.8 | 105.4 | 111.6 | 106.2 | 110.5 | 105.1 |
| 1967 | 124.2 | 113.6 | 126.7 | 115.9 | 124.1 | 113.4 |
| 1968 | 141.8 | 123.2 | 146.6 | 127.4 | 141.8 | 123.1 |
| 1969 | 164.7 | 136.0 | 171.8 | 141.3 | 167.1 | 137.4 |

Source: Adapted from *Economic Statistics Annual, 1969* (Tokyo: The Bank of Japan, 1970), pp. 271–272.

Furthermore, the number of family workers, who traditionally had constituted an important source of labor in the nation's distribution sector, has been declining rapidly because of increasing availability of more lucrative employment opportunities elsewhere. The percentage of family workers in the total labor force declined from 34 percent in 1953 to less than 17 percent in 1967.[23]

It is fully expected that the labor shortage will intensify in the future. According to a recent forecast prepared by the Ministry of International Trade and Industry, the distribution sector can expect, on the average, only a 2.6 percent annual increase in the labor force between 1967 and 1972, in contrast to a 4.7 percent

[23] *Rodo Hakusho: Showa 43 nen ban [White Paper on Labor, 1968]* (Tokyo: Ministry of Labor, 1968), p. 220.

average annual increase between 1960 and 1966, despite the fact that during this period the total wholesale and retail sales volumes are expected to double.[24] The labor shortage and the rapidly rising wage level are now forcing the distribution sector to reassess its traditional *modus operandi*.

In slightly over a decade the wage level has almost tripled, and between 1965 and 1969 it has grown by nearly 65 percent. The rate of increase has been accelerating rapidly. The manufacturing sector has been able by and large to absorb the rising wage cost by an increase in productivity, as evidenced by the fact that between 1963 and 1969 the increase in the wholesale price index was kept down to 7.4 percent.[25] In contrast, however, the consumer price index showed a 21 percent gain during the same period.[26] The disparity is accounted for at least in part by growing inefficiency in the distribution sector.

The other important source of pressures impinging on the Japanese marketing system is the potential foreign competition. The very impressive record of Japan's postwar economic growth invited increasing pressure for liberalization of its stringent restrictions on direct foreign investment. In response to this pressure, the government committed itself to a step-by-step liberalization of restrictions on direct foreign investment to be completed by 1972. It took the first step in 1967 and implemented the second phase in March 1969. At the time of this writing, the distribution sector has been virtually unaffected, but it is anticipated that by 1972 substantial liberalization will be undertaken in this field, making it possible for large-scale foreign, particularly American, retailing firms to enter the Japanese market. In fact, some of the well-known American retail chains, supermarkets, and franchise operations already have expressed their keen interest in entering Japan. In addition, of course, a number of multinational corporations are already manufacturing and marketing their products in Japan, and with increasing liberalization of foreign investment restrictions the trend is likely to accelerate. The Japanese business community and government officials are fearful of the advanced marketing skills, resources, and experience that these firms can bring to bear in their

---

[24] *Ryutsu Kindaika no Tenbo to Kadai [A Perspective and the Challenge of Modernization of the Distribution Sector]* (Tokyo: Ministry of International Trade and Industry, 1968), p. 8.

[25] *Economic Statistics Annual, 1969*, p. 251.

[26] *Ibid.*, p. 249.

Japanese operations. Indeed, the growing threat of foreign competition is a powerful stimulus for the modernization of Japan's traditional marketing system.

The forces that we have examined have one thing in common; that is, they are exogenous to the marketing system. We should not ignore, however, the innovative forces that are surging within the system itself. As we shall see in the chapters to follow, there are elements within the Japanese marketing system that are able to see tremendous opportunities in the changing environment and are anxious to capitalize on them. Thus, both external and internal pressures are interacting vigorously to create powerful forces for change.

# 2

# Emergence of a
# Mass Consumption Society

The single most important and immediate force prompting changes
in Japan's marketing system is the rapid emergence of a mass consumer market in postwar Japan. In the first chapter we reviewed
briefly the spectacular postwar growth of the Japanese economy
and noted that a most significant asepect of this economic growth
is that its benefits have become diffused widely. For the first time
in the nation's history, a truly viable middle class has emerged, and
with it a mass-consumption-oriented society. Not only has economic growth greatly improved the material welfare of the masses,
it is bringing about important changes in their attitudes and value
systems. Indeed, there is convincing evidence that the emerging
middle class is quickly taking on attributes that are commonly associated with the middle class in other highly industrialized and
urbanized societies.[1] In this chapter we shall examine in detail this
emerging mass consumption economy and accompanying social
changes in postwar Japan.

As a point of departure, we shall note briefly the conditions prevailing in the prewar period. Throughout much of this era, Japan
maintained a high rate of economic growth resulting in consider-

---

[1] George Katona, in his thought-provoking book, *The Mass Consumption
Society*, identifies three features of this society: the general affluence, per-
mitting discretionary purchasing; consumer power to influence the economy;
and the importance of consumer psychology. For further details, see George
Katona, *The Mass Consumption Society* (New York: McGraw-Hill Book
Company, 1964), p. 3.

able improvement in living standards, as evidenced from the fact that per capita consumption in real terms doubled between 1875 and 1920. For a number of reasons, however, only a fraction of the aggregate growth of output went directly into improvement of the standard of living.[2]

Moreover, the macrostatistical data indicating the improvement in the standard of living fail to take into account the great disparity that had existed in income distribution in prewar Japan. As late as 1930 nearly 90 percent of Japan's 12.6 million families earned less than ¥300 annually, and this group received only half of the total national income. At the other extreme, some 24,000 families representing only 0.2 percent of the total number of families received over 10 percent of the total income.[3] The following statements made by two leading authorities on Japan aptly summarize the prewar conditions. Describing the poverty of the masses, Reischauer states:

> While Japan as a whole became a modernized and industrialized nation, her peasant masses were left behind, living not far above the miserable economic levels of feudal days. Moreover, by threatening to glut the labor market, they kept urban labor down to these same pitiful levels. The result has been something new and as yet unique in the world—an industrialized nation supported by the toil of people living not far above the subsistence level.[4]

Having noted a gradual improvement in the consumption level in prewar Japan, Lockwood states:

> For most of the Japanese people, nevertheless, the prewar plane of living remained far below the minimum requirements of health, comforts and security, even by Japanese standards. On an income of 3 yen a day—the average earning of an urban worker family in 1935–36—over a third of family expenditures still went for a simple diet of boiled rice, soybean soup, pickled radishes, and a few vegetables, and now and then some fish. The mass of small farmers managed to eke

2 For detailed analysis see William W. Lockwood, *The Economic Development of Japan: Growth and Structural Change, 1868–1938* (Princeton, N.J.: Princeton University Press, 1954), pp. 140–142: and Alan H. Gleason, "Economic Growth and Consumption in Japan" in William W. Lockwood (ed.), *The State and Economic Enterprise in Japan* (Princeton, N.J.: Princeton University Press, 1965), pp. 291–346.

3 Lockwood, *Economic Development of Japan*, p. 141.

4 Edwin O. Reischauer, *The United States and Japan* (Cambridge, Mass.: Harvard University Press, 1965), p. 66.

out an even more meager existence only by unremitting seasonal toil on the part of the whole family. The bare necessities of existence were leavened by only a few comforts, mostly of traditional variety.[5]

Indeed, the conditions prevailing prior to World War II present a striking contrast to the contemporary situation, which we shall now examine. Since the early 1950s, when the Japanese economy again reached the prewar level, the country's GNP has been increasing rapidly. The annual real growth rate has averaged around 10 percent, and at its peak it even exceeded 15 percent. Between 1953 and 1968 the country's GNP quadrupled in real terms (see Table 2.1). Significantly, Japan has been able to sustain a rather brisk pace of economic growth, as evidenced by the fact that in 1968 the GNP showed more than 14 percent real growth over 1967.

Comparison between the prewar and postwar consumption levels further reveals the magnitude of the improvement of the standard of living. After having sunk to about half the prewar amount in the immediate postwar years, the consumption level has steadily improved, and in the early 1950s it again reached the prewar level. Between 1952 and 1968 private consumption expenditure more than tripled in real terms. In the later years it reached ¥26.7 trillion, accounting for slightly more than 50 percent of the GNP for that year. The growth of personal consumption expenditure was responsible for 8.1 percent of the 18.7 percent nominal growth in GNP in 1968 over the preceding year. The details of economic progress made during the postwar decades are presented in Table 2.1.

Though frequently hidden under the phenomenal economic growth, a series of rather basic social changes that have taken place in the postwar era are equally significant. Indeed, Japanese society has been undergoing most remarkable social changes since the end of World War II. For one thing, the humiliation of the defeat—an unprecedented event in Japanese history—repudiated the traditional value system. More direct effects of the change came in the form of the Occupation-sponsored reforms. To make Japan into a democratic nation, the Allied Occupation, dominated by the United States, instigated most extensive and vigorous social reforms that touched almost every aspect of Japanese life.

On the economic scene, the all-important Zaibatsu were dissolved, followed by passage of the Anti-Monopoly Act, designed

5 Lockwood, *Economic Development of Japan*, p. 148.

TABLE 2.1

SELECTED INDICES OF ECONOMIC PROGRESS MADE IN POSTWAR JAPAN,
1953–1968

| Year | Real Growth of GNP (1960=100) | Real Growth in Personal Consumption (1960=100) | Per Household Consumption Expenditure (1965=100) Urban Areas | Per Household Consumption Expenditure (1965=100) Rural Areas |
|---|---|---|---|---|
| 1953 | 54.0 | 60.4 | 58.8 | 59.0 |
| 1954 | 55.5 | 63.2 | 58.7 | 61.1 |
| 1955 | 62.2 | 68.9 | 61.1 | 61.3 |
| 1956 | 67.5 | 73.6 | 64.4 | 63.1 |
| 1957 | 74.0 | 78.5 | 67.1 | 63.8 |
| 1958 | 76.7 | 84.2 | 71.5 | 65.4 |
| 1959 | 86.8 | 91.6 | 75.4 | 67.9 |
| 1960 | 100.0 | 100.0 | 78.9 | 72.7 |
| 1962 | 120.0 | 121.2 | 88.9 | 83.4 |
| 1963 | 134.4 | 132.7 | 93.4 | 88.4 |
| 1964 | 149.5 | 144.6 | 98.7 | 95.1 |
| 1965 | 155.5 | 154.1 | 100.0 | 100.0 |
| 1966 | 174.8 | 166.9 | 103.9 | 107.1 |
| 1961 | 113.9 | 110.2 | 84.1 | 78.4 |
| 1967 | 197.9 | 184.0 | 109.4 | 119.1 |
| 1968 | 227.6 | 229.3 | 113.8 | 125.7 |

Adapted from: *Keizai Yoran, 1970 [A Summary of Economic Statistics 1970]*
(Tokyo: The Economic Planning Agency, 1970), pp. 13, 281.

to preserve a competitive economic structure. The Occupation implemented a wholesale purge of wartime leaders, including a large number of senior executives of major corporations. The Occupation also undertook reforms in labor-management relations. Under its open encouragement and guidance, and reinforced by serious economic distress, spectacular progress was achieved in the labor union movement. More than half of the nonagricultural labor force was unionized by 1949.[6] The Occupation also sought to broaden the democratic base of postwar Japan by undertaking an extensive land reform program. The reforms resulted in a wide distribution of land ownership, which heretofore had been concentrated in a small number of landlords. It is estimated that in a period of

[6] For details, see Solomon B. Levine, *Industrial Relations in Postwar Japan* (Urbana, Ill.; University of Illinois Press, 1958), p. 200; Alice Cook, *Japanese Trade Unionism* (New York: New York State School of Industrial Relations, Cornell University, 1965), p. 216; and Iwao F. Ayukawa, *A History of Labor in Modern Japan* (Honolulu: East-West Center Press, 1966), pp. 232-301.

four years nearly two million farmers came to own the land they cultivated.[7]

Other major reforms took place in the area of education. Here, two significant changes were introduced. The period of compulsory education was lengthened from six to nine years. Moreover, education was no longer to serve as an instrument of the state, promoting traditional moral values and political ideology; it was now designed to stress democratic values, including the duties and rights of citizens in a democratic society. The Occupation directed the Japanese government to draft a new constitution, which was enacted in 1947. Of all the sweeping changes introduced in the Constitution of 1947, the concept of the sovereignty of the people is undoubtedly the most important. For the first time in the history of Japan, sovereignty now rested with the people.

In spite of the often-mentioned reactionary or "reverse" course notion, retreat from the reforms of the Occupation has been very slight. This has prompted some observers to claim that many of the more basic and sustained changes were not actually instituted by the Occupation but could be attributed to trends that had already been taking place in Japanese society for a number of years. Reischauer, for example, is of the opinion that most of the truly significant and sustained postwar changes seem to be the acceleration of changes that had already been taking place earlier. The Occupation removed barriers to the forward movement of these forces and stimulated their growth and rapid dissemination.[8]

Nonetheless, these extensive Occupation-sponsored reforms are considered major factors contributing to rapid growth of the postwar Japanese economy, particularly to the emergence of a mass consumption society, which, in turn, promoted further social changes. Thus, rapid economic growth and socioeconomic reforms vigorously interacted to create a society that is significantly different from its prewar counterpart.

## Emergence of a Viable Middle Class—Economic Aspects

### Widespread Diffusion of Economic Benefits

Before undertaking a detailed examination of this topic, it would be appropriate to present a few geographic facts about Japan.

[7] John M. Maki, *Government and Politics in Japan: The Road to Democracy* (New York: Frederick A. Praeger, 1961) p. 134.

[8] Reischauer, *The United States and Japan*, p. 292.

Japan, which consists of four major islands and several groups of smaller islands extending in an arc, lies off the eastern coast of Asia. The total area is approximately 142,700 square miles, larger than Great Britain but smaller than the state of California. Japan's population has grown steadily during the modern period, from about 30 million in 1868 to 102.6 million in 1969. Japan is the seventh-largest nation in population in the world, behind China, India, the USSR, the United States, Pakistan, and Indonesia. In terms of population density per square mile, however, Japan is higher than any of these other nations. The population density of Japan in 1969 was slightly over 700 persons per square mile. She ranks fourth in world population density, exceeded only by Belgium, the Netherlands, and Great Britain. In terms of density of population per square mile of arable land, Japan leads all other nations.

There are two notable features about the Japanese population that are pertinent to this study. One is a steady trend toward urbanization. In 1930 roughly 25 percent of Japan's entire population lived within incorporated city limits. Today over 68 percent live in some 560 cities. Roughly 20 percent of the population now live in cities of one million or more. Tokyo alone claims 10 percent of the nation's entire population. Indeed, Japan has become one of the world's most urbanized societies, with the attendant problems. Coupled with this trend is a rapid decrease in the agricultural population. By 1968 the agricultural population declined to 27 million from the postwar height of nearly 38 million in 1953.[9] Even more remarkable is the decline of so-called pure agricultural households—those relying exclusively on income derived from agriculture. By 1968 the number of pure agricultural households declined to one-third of the 1953 level. In 1968 less than 20 percent of all agricultural households derived their income solely from agriculture.

The second notable feature is the age composition of the population. Over 53 percent of the population consists of persons younger than thirty years old. Those between fifteen and twenty-nine years of age account for roughly 29 percent of the population. Nearly 43 percent of the entire population was born after

[9] *Keizai Yoran, 1969 [Summary of Economic Statistics, 1969]* (Tokyo: The Economic Planning Agency, 1970), p. 41.

World War II, a fact that obviously has far-reaching economic as well as social implications.

We have noted earlier that a most remarkable aspect of Japanese postwar economic growth is the wide diffusion of its benefits among the masses. In this section we shall examine this phenomenon in detail. All classes have gained from this rapid economic advance, but differently, of course.

The achievement of an advanced stage of industrialization in the postwar years has significantly altered the structure of employment. The number of wage earners has steadily increased, and by the late 1960s it came to account for nearly 63 percent of the total labor force. This increase has been offset by a significant decline in the labor force in the primary sector as well as in the number of family workers. The decline of the latter has been particularly significant, since Japan had traditionally had a large segment of family workers, a substantial portion of which represented disguised unemployment. Between 1955 and 1968 the percentage of family workers in the total labor force declined from a third to about 17 percent.[10]

Particularly striking have been the gains made by wage earners. Postwar industrial growth has all but wiped out unemployment, a problem that had long plagued Japan. In fact, Japan is now experiencing a serious labor shortage for the first time in her history. The wage level has been steadily going up, even at an increasing rate, as revealed in Table 2.2.

This shift is reflected in the national income distribution, as presented in Table 2.3. The wage earners now claim more than half of the national income, in contrast to 39 percent in the prewar years. A striking development in this regard is a significant relative decline in the income from rent, interest, and dividends. Property income now accounts for less than 11 percent of the national income, as contrasted to 22 percent in the prewar years. The combination of wartime destruction and dislocation, postwar inflation, and Occupation reforms has all but wiped out the traditional rentier class in Japan.

The total income of wage earners' households has been sizably increasing, as indicated in Table 2.4. For the past several years,

10 *Rodo Hakusho, Showa 44 nen ban [White Paper on Labor, 1969]* (Tokyo: The Ministry of Labor, 1969) p. 38.

TABLE 2.2

INCREASE IN THE NUMBER OF WAGE EARNERS AND
GROWTH IN THE REAL WAGE LEVEL, 1959–1968

| Year | Index of Growth No. of Wage Earners (1965=100) | Real Monthly Wage Level per Worker (¥, 1965 price level) |
|---|---|---|
| 1959 | 62.5 | 31,664 |
| 1960 | 71.1 | 32,939 |
| 1961 | 76.3 | 34,180 |
| 1962 | 86.3 | 35,406 |
| 1963 | 91.4 | 36,566 |
| 1964 | 96.9 | 38,508 |
| 1965 | 100.0 | 39,360 |
| 1966 | 102.5 | 41,794 |
| 1967 | 105.6 | 47,341 |
| 1968 | 108.9 | 48,178 |

Source: *Kokumin Seikatsu Tokei Nenpo: Showa 44 nen ban [Annual Statistics on National Life, 1969]* (Tokyo: Kokumin Seikatsu Kenkyujo, 1969), p. 1.

the total average household income has shown a steady and substantial increase each year over the preceding year. The annual rate of growth over the preceding year for the years 1964, 1965, 1966, 1967, and 1968 was 12.0 percent, 9.1 percent, 9.5 percent, 10.3 percent and 11.3 percent.[11] In 1968, for the first time, the average

TABLE 2.3

DISTRIBUTION OF NATIONAL INCOME BY TYPES

| Type of Income | 1934–1936 Average (%) | 1953 (%) | 1960 (%) | 1968 (%) |
|---|---|---|---|---|
| Employee's Wages | 38.8 | 49.7 | 49.8 | 54.2 |
| Unincorporated Proprietor's Income | 31.2 | 37.2 | 26.7 | 21.7 |
| Property Income | 22.2 | 5.3 | 9.3 | 10.7 |
| Other | 7.8 | 8.2 | 14.2 | 13.3 |

Source: Data for 1934–1936 and 1953 were obtained from *Hundred-Year Statistics of the Japanese Economy* (Tokyo: The Bank of Japan, 1967) pp. 46–47. The data for 1960 and 1968 were obtained from *Keizai Yoran, 1970 [A Summary of Economic Statistics]* (Tokyo: Economic Planning Agency, 1970), pp. 52–53.

11 *Annual Report on the Family Income and Expenditure Survey, 1968* (Tokyo: The Office of the Prime Minister, 1969), p. 1.

annual income of wage earner households exceeded ¥1 million, with an average disposable income of ¥960,000.

Not only has the wage level been steadily rising, but the growing labor shortage is also reducing long-standing inequalities in wages among various types of wage earners. For one thing, the wage disparity between large and small enterprises, a well-known feature of the Japanese economy, has narrowed substantially. As late as in 1959 the average cash wage level of small- to medium-size enterprises was considerably lower than that of large enterprises. For example, the average cash wage of enterprises with 100 to 422 employees was roughly 70 percent of the average wage level of large enterprises (500 employees or more). The wage level of enterprises with 30 to 99 and 5 to 29 employees were 56 percent and 44 percent, respectively, of that of large enterprises. Although these inequalities have not disappeared totally, they have been narrowed considerably. By 1968, the disparity was reduced to 80 percent, 69 percent, and 63 percent, respectively.[12]

Another equalizing development is the reduction of inequality in the wage levels between age groups. Because of the traditional seniority-related wage payment system commonly practiced in Japan, a substantial disparity was found in the wage level among workers of different ages. Because of this age-related wage system, the greatest demand is for younger workers. As a result, the wage level for these workers has increased at a much faster rate than for older workers. For example, between 1958 and 1968 the wage level for eighteen- to twenty-year-old blue-collar workers in large

TABLE 2.4

MONTHLY INCOME OF WAGE EARNERS' HOUSEHOLDS, 1963, 1965, 1968

|  | 1963 | 1965 | 1968 |
|---|---|---|---|
| Number in Household | 4.19 | 4.07 | 3.96 |
| Number in Household with Income | 1.54 | 1.54 | 1.54 |
| Total Monthly Income (¥) | 53,298 | 71,347 | 87,599 |

Source: *Kokumin Seikatsu Hakusho, Showa 44 nen ban [White Paper on National Life, 1969]* (Tokyo: The Economic Planning Agency, 1969), p. 31.

12 *Ibid.*, p. 353.

enterprises (1,000 employees or more) tripled, whereas the wage level for older workers (forty to forty-nine) only doubled.[13] This has resulted in a general compression of the wage scale according to age categories.

It is also significant that the wage level of blue-collar workers has improved relatively more than that of the white-collar workers. For example, in 1958 the average cash wage of a blue-collar worker with a secondary education was about 64 percent of that of a white-collar worker with a college education. By 1968 the difference was narrowed to 74 percent.[14]

Along with wage earners, farmers have made substantial relative gains. In the immediate aftermath of the war, the serious food shortage gave farmers a relative advantage. In 1946, for example, the agricultural sector accounted for nearly a third of the GNP. Not only did the agricultural sector experience this significant windfall gain, but the Occupation-sponsored land-reform program greatly contributed to the equalization of income distribution in this sector.

Whereas in 1941 only slightly over 30 percent of the farmers owned the land they cultivated, by the late 1960s over 80 percent were in this category; another 18 percent owned some land, and only 2 percent could be considered as purely tenant farmers.[15] The land cultivated by tenant farmers declined to 5 percent of the total by the mid-1960s. Moreover, the rent paid for the use of land has been reduced substantially (the land rent is controlled by government). Until 1967 it had remained unchanged for 12 years.

Although the relative advantage initially enjoyed by the agricultural sector was wiped out by the phenomenal industrial growth during the late 1950s and early 1960s, the agricultural sector has made substantial strides during the last several years. By 1968 the average per-household income reached ¥1 million, recording nearly a 10 percent increase over the preceding year.[16]

A recent gain made by the agricultural sector has all but wiped

13 Kokumin Seikatsu Hakusho, Showa 44 nen ban [White Paper on National Life, 1969] (Tokyo: The Economic Planning Agency, 1969), p. 69.
14 Ibid., p. 66.
15 Yano Kotaro Kinen Kai (ed.), Nihon Kokusei Zue, 1968 [National Profiles of Japan, 1968] (Tokyo: Kokusei Sha, 1968), p. 201.
16 Kokumin Seikatsu Hakusho, Showa 44 nen ban, [White Paper on National Life, 1969], p. 30.

out the income disparity between wage earners' households and agricultural households. In fact, as evidenced by Table 2.5, farmers' income has surpassed that of wage earners on a per-household basis, and even on a per capita basis farmers' income is rapidly approaching that of the wage earners.

Contributing significantly to the recent prosperity in the agricultural sector are the increasing level of price support for rice, quite significant gains in agricultural productivity, and the rapid growth in income derived from nonagricultural sources. According to the latest agricultural census, only 22 percent of the farmers' households derive their income exclusively from agriculture. Among 40 percent of farmers' households, the income from nonagricultural sources exceeded that from agricultural sources. For an average agricultural household, the income from nonagricultural sources exceeded that obtained from agricultural sources at least during the past several years.

We have now seen that the benefits of Japan's phenomenal postwar economic growth have been diffused widely. Two deprived segments of prewar Japan—farmers and wage earners—have gained most from the postwar economic growth, which has contributed to the reduction of inequality in income distribution that characterized prewar Japan. Since this trend is extremely significant, it deserves further examination. In Figure 2.1 the Lorenz diagram compares the income distribution between 1930 and 1965. As clearly shown in this diagram, income was more equally distributed in 1965 than it was in 1930. Another meaningful measure of the trend of income distribution toward equality shows how various income classes have changed during the postwar years. As shown in Table 2.6 in 1956 nearly three-fourths of the households earned less than ¥300,000. Substantial relative gains are shown in the four higher income classes in 1965.

Between 1965 and 1968 the number of households whose annual income exceeded ¥1 million tripled, reaching 7.7 million households, accounting for 27 percent of the total in 1968. Even more significant is the fact that during this period the number of households earning ¥2 million or more a year almost tripled, reaching the 1.3 million mark.[17] (See Table 2.6.)

---

[17] *Keizai Yoran, 1970 [Summary of Economic Statistics, 1970]* (Tokyo: The Economic Planning Agency, 1970), p. 294.

## TABLE 2.5

### COMPARISON OF THE TOTAL ANNUAL INCOME AND DISCRETIONARY INCOME OF WAGE EARNERS AND FARMERS, 1968

(wage earners = 100%)

| | No. of Members of Household | Per Household | | Per Capita | |
| --- | --- | --- | --- | --- | --- |
| | | Real Income (¥) | Disposable Income (¥) | Real Income (¥) | Disposable Income (¥) |
| Wage Earners' Households (Nationwide) | 3.96 | 1,051,188 (100.0) | 964,992 (100.0) | 265,452 (100.0) | 243,685 (100.0) |
| Agricultural Households | 5.06 | 1,138,491 (108.3) | 1,045,338 (108.3) | 224,998 ( 84.8) | 206,589 ( 84.8) |

Source: *Kokumin Seikatsu Hakusho, 1969 [White Paper on National Life, 1969]* (Tokyo: The Economic Planning Agency, 1969), p. 35.

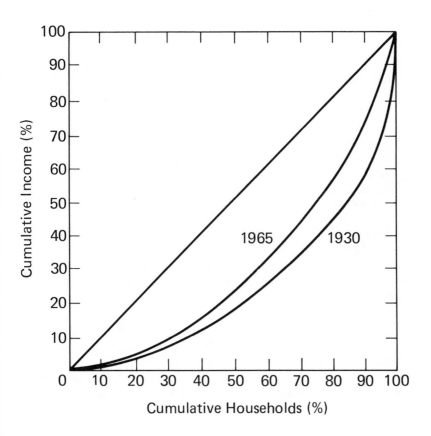

FIGURE 2.1

*Income Distribution in Japan, 1930 and 1965*
*(Lorenz curve)*

Source: For 1930 data, Alan H. Gleason, "Economic Growth and Consumption in Japan" in W. W. Lockwood (ed.), *The State and Economic Enterprise in Japan* (Princeton, N.J.: Princeton University Press, 1965), p. 404. For 1935 data, *Kokumin Seikatsu Hakusho: Showa 44 nen ben [White Paper on National Life, 1969]* (Tokyo: Economic Planning Agency, 1969), p. 185.

TABLE 2.6

NUMBER OF JAPANESE HOUSEHOLDS ACCORDING TO
MAJOR INCOME CATEGORIES, 1956, 1965, 1968

| Income | *Households, 1956* | | *Households, 1965* | | *Households, 1968* | |
|---|---|---|---|---|---|---|
| | *Number (thousands)* | *%* | *Number (thousands)* | *%* | *Number (thousands)* | *%* |
| Less than ¥300,000 | 15,288 | 73.8 | 6,640 | 27.8 | | |
| | | | | | 12,127 | 42.5 |
| ¥600,000–599,999 | 3,952 | 19.1 | 9,676 | 32.2 | | |
| ¥300,000–799,999 | 1,183 | 5.7 | 4,115 | 17.3 | | |
| | | | | | 8,684 | 30.5 |
| ¥800,000–999,999 | 154 | 0.7 | 2,219 | 9.3 | | |
| Over ¥1,000,000 | 145 | 0.7 | 3,209 | 13.4 | 7,708 | 27.0 |
| Total | 20,722 | 100.0 | 25,859 | 100.0 | 28,519 | 100.0 |

Source: Adapted from *Keizai Yoran 1968 [A Summary of Economic Statistics, 1968]* (Tokyo: The Economic Planning Agency, 1969), pp. 298–299.

How does the income distribution in postwar Japan compare with that of other advanced nations? One useful measure for international comparison is the magnitude of dispersion from the median income. Particularly useful is the degree of the dispersion between the median income of all households and that of the lowest and the highest income groups. In 1968 the median income of the lowest and the highest quintile in Japan was 48.6 percent and 173.6 percent, respectively, of the median income of all households.[18] Great Britain has the least dispersion (55.5 percent and 151.8 percent) among the countries compared. In the United States, the median income of the lowest quintile was 39.6 percent of the median income of all households and that of the highest income group was 162.4 percent. In West Germany the dispersion was 61.1 percent and 151.2 percent. In France, where the data were expressed in terms of quartiles, the median income of the lowest and the highest quartiles was 46.9 percent and 171.3 percent, respectively. Thus, Japan now compares favorably with these three other advanced nations.

*Changes in Consumption Patterns*

Let us now examine changes in the consumption pattern of Japanese consumers. In this connection we shall draw heavily on

[18] *Kokumin Seikatsu Hakusho, Showa 44 nen ban [White Paper on National Life, 1969]*, p. 186.

TABLE 2.7

HOUSEHOLD EXPENDITURE PATTERNS OF NONAGRICULTURAL HOUSEHOLDS
IN CITIES WITH POPULATION OF 50,000 OR MORE, 1956–1968

| Year | Persons per Household | Total Living Expenditures | Food | Housing | Fuel and Light | Clothing | Miscellaneous | Engel Coefficient | Living Expenditure Level* (1965=100) |
|---|---|---|---|---|---|---|---|---|---|
| | | | (monthly expenditures in yen) | | | | | | |
| 1956 | 4.61 | 23,958 | 10,786 | 1,625 | 1,225 | 2,920 | 7,402 | 45.0 | 64.4 |
| 1957 | 4.56 | 25,608 | 11,368 | 1,819 | 1,331 | 3,096 | 7,994 | 44.4 | 67.1 |
| 1958 | 4.57 | 27,171 | 11,898 | 2,239 | 1,353 | 3,135 | 8,546 | 43.8 | 71.5 |
| 1959 | 4.56 | 28,902 | 12,260 | 2,600 | 1,396 | 3,376 | 9,270 | 42.4 | 75.4 |
| 1960 | 4.51 | 31,276 | 13,000 | 2,790 | 1,597 | 3,755 | 10,134 | 41.6 | 78.9 |
| 1961 | 4.34 | 34,329 | 13,842 | 3,399 | 1,731 | 4,326 | 11,031 | 40.3 | 84.1 |
| 1962 | 4.29 | 38,587 | 15,063 | 3,951 | 1,906 | 4,933 | 12,734 | 39.0 | 88.9 |
| 1963 | 4.30 | 43,616 | 16,793 | 4,394 | 2,021 | 5,432 | 14,985 | 38.5 | 93.4 |
| 1964 | 4.28 | 47,834 | 18,139 | 4,703 | 2,171 | 5,683 | 17,138 | 37.9 | 98.7 |
| 1965 | 4.24 | 51,832 | 19,738 | 5,157 | 2,389 | 5,916 | 18,632 | 38.1 | 100.0 |
| 1966 | 4.17 | 56,097 | 20,836 | 5,686 | 2,554 | 6,206 | 20,815 | 37.1 | 103.9 |
| 1967 | 4.13 | 61,091 | 22,355 | 6,424 | 2,730 | 6,725 | 22,858 | 36.6 | 109.4 |
| 1968 | 4.06 | 66,440 | 23,665 | 7,665 | 2,867 | 7,338 | 24,906 | 35.6 | 121.5 |

*Indices of living expenditure are adjusted for the average number of persons per household and deflated by the consumer price index.

Source: *The Annual Report on the Family Income and Expenditure Survey, 1968* (Tokyo: The Office of the Prime Minister, 1969), p. 32.

## TABLE 2.8

### Household Expenditure Patterns of Agriculture Households in Cities with Population of 50,000 or More, 1956–1967

| Year | Persons per Household | Total Living Expenditures | Food | Housing | Fuel and Light | Clothing | Miscellaneous | Engel Coefficient | Living Expenditure Level* (1960=100) |
|------|------|------|------|------|------|------|------|------|------|
| | | | (monthly expenditures in yen) | | | | | | |
| 1956 | 6.23 | 25,475 | 12,483 | 1,917 | 1,250 | 2,883 | 6,942 | 49.0 | 86.8 |
| 1957 | 5.93 | 25,425 | 12,175 | 1,825 | 1,292 | 2,933 | 7,200 | 47.9 | 87.7 |
| 1958 | 5.86 | 25,817 | 12,225 | 1,950 | 1,233 | 2,925 | 7,483 | 47.4 | 89.9 |
| 1959 | 5.80 | 27,342 | 12,400 | 2,550 | 1,283 | 3,117 | 7,992 | 45.4 | 93.4 |
| 1960 | 5.70 | 29,542 | 12,717 | 3,100 | 1,433 | 3,467 | 8,825 | 43.0 | 100.0 |
| 1961 | 5.64 | 33,192 | 13,592 | 4,000 | 1,600 | 3,908 | 10,092 | 40.9 | 107.8 |
| 1962 | 5.52 | 36,733 | 14,492 | 4,392 | 1,842 | 4,325 | 11,682 | 39.5 | 114.7 |
| 1963 | 5.42 | 41,075 | 15,842 | 4,908 | 2,008 | 4,742 | 13,575 | 38.6 | 121.5 |
| 1964 | 5.31 | 46,258 | 17,608 | 5,717 | 2,200 | 5,117 | 15,616 | 38.1 | 130.8 |
| 1965 | 5.29 | 52,067 | 19,350 | 6,392 | 2,475 | 5,767 | 18,083 | 37.2 | 137.5 |
| 1966 | 5.18 | 57,471 | 20,828 | 7,117 | 2,655 | 6,055 | 20,816 | 36.2 | 143.8 |
| 1967 | 4.97 | 72,625 | 23,517 | 13,650 | 3,058 | 7,250 | 25,150 | 32.4 | 163.7 |

*Indices of living expenditure are adjusted for the average number of persons per household and deflated by the consumer price index.

Source: *The Annual Report on the Family Income and Expenditure Survey, 1968* (Tokyo: The Office of the Prime Minister, 1969), p. 33.

data provided by the annual household expenditure surveys conducted by the Japanese government. The Office of Prime Minister conducts a Family Income and Expenditure Survey annually among a nationwide sample of nonagricultural families. The Ministry of Agriculture undertakes a similar study among agricultural households. These studies follow well-accepted research methodology and provide comprehensive and reliable data.

Tables 2.7 and 2.8 present summary data of household expenditures in absolute amounts for each of the major categories over a decade for both urban, nonagricultural households and rural agricultural households. Tables 2.9 and 2.10 present the changes in

TABLE 2.9

INDICES OF EXPENDITURE LEVELS BY MAJOR CATEGORIES FOR
URBAN NONAGRICULTURAL HOUSEHOLDS, 1956–1968

(1965 = 100)

| Year | Total Living Expenditures | Food | Housing | Fuel and Light | Clothing | Miscellaneous |
|------|------|------|---------|------|----------|--------|
| 1956 | 46.2 | 54.6 | 31.5 | 51.3 | 49.4 | 39.7 |
| 1957 | 49.4 | 57.6 | 35.3 | 55.7 | 52.3 | 42.9 |
| 1958 | 52.4 | 60.3 | 43.4 | 56.6 | 53.0 | 45.9 |
| 1959 | 55.8 | 62.1 | 50.4 | 58.4 | 57.1 | 49.8 |
| 1960 | 60.3 | 65.9 | 54.1 | 66.8 | 63.5 | 54.4 |
| 1961 | 66.2 | 70.1 | 65.9 | 72.5 | 73.1 | 59.2 |
| 1962 | 74.4 | 76.3 | 76.6 | 79.8 | 83.4 | 68.3 |
| 1963 | 84.1 | 85.1 | 85.2 | 84.6 | 91.7 | 80.4 |
| 1964 | 92.3 | 91.9 | 91.2 | 90.9 | 96.1 | 92.0 |
| 1965 | 100.0 | 100.0 | 100.0 | 100.0 | 100.0 | 100.0 |
| 1966 | 108.2 | 105.6 | 110.3 | 106.9 | 104.9 | 111.7 |
| 1967 | 117.9 | 113.3 | 124.6 | 114.3 | 113.7 | 122.7 |
| 1968 | 128.2 | 119.9 | 148.6 | 120.1 | 124.1 | 133.7 |

Source: The Annual Report on the Family Income and Expenditure Survey, 1968 (Tokyo: The Office of the Prime Minister, 1969), p. 32.

each of the categories during the period under examination in index form.

Several significant observations can be made about the data presented here. First, the consumption level has increased steadily throughout the years indicated for urban and rural housholds, both absolutely and relatively. Second, the Engel's coefficient, an im-

TABLE 2.10

INDICES OF EXPENDITURE LEVELS BY MAJOR CATEGORIES FOR
AGRICULTURAL HOUSEHOLDS, 1956–1967

(1965 = 100)

| Year | Total Living Expenditures | Food | Housing | Fuel and Light | Clothing | Miscellaneous |
|------|------|------|------|------|------|------|
| 1956 | 48.9 | 64.5 | 30.0 | 50.5 | 50.0 | 38.4 |
| 1957 | 48.8 | 62.9 | 28.6 | 52.2 | 50.9 | 39.8 |
| 1958 | 49.6 | 63.2 | 30.5 | 49.8 | 50.7 | 41.4 |
| 1959 | 52.5 | 64.1 | 39.9 | 51.8 | 51.0 | 44.2 |
| 1960 | 56.7 | 65.7 | 48.5 | 57.9 | 60.1 | 48.8 |
| 1961 | 63.7 | 70.2 | 62.6 | 64.6 | 67.8 | 55.8 |
| 1962 | 70.5 | 74.9 | 68.7 | 74.4 | 75.0 | 64.6 |
| 1963 | 78.9 | 81.9 | 76.8 | 81.1 | 82.2 | 75.1 |
| 1964 | 88.8 | 91.0 | 89.4 | 88.9 | 88.7 | 86.4 |
| 1965 | 100.0 | 100.0 | 100.0 | 100.0 | 100.0 | 100.0 |
| 1966 | 110.4 | 107.6 | 111.3 | 107.3 | 105.0 | 115.1 |
| 1967 | 139.5 | 121.5 | 213.5 | 123.6 | 125.7 | 139.1 |

Source: *The Annual Report on the Family Income and Expenditure Survey, 1968* (Tokyo: The Office of the Prime Minister, 1969), p. 33.

portant measure of the standard of living, steadily declined from 45 to 35.6 for urban households and from 49 to 32.4 for rural households during the years examined. Since the lowest Engel's coefficient in the prewar era was around 50, this is a rather significant achievement. Third, for both urban and rural households the most significant relative gains were made in the areas of housing and miscellaneous expenditure. The miscellaneous category includes expenditures for cultural, social, recreational, and educational activities. In both urban and rural households real expenditures for these categories about tripled during the period.

Finally, the data reveal very little difference in consumption levels between the urban nonagricultural and rural agricultural households. We should also note that despite the rapid rate of increase in consumption levels, the average propensity to save has been increasing. In 1968, the personal savings rate (the amount of savings as a percentage of total disposable income) reached 19.7 percent, and the average household had savings of ¥970,000. We mention parenthetically that nearly 93 percent of Japanese households have some form of savings: 85 percent have savings accounts,

TABLE 2.11

YEARLY AVERAGE OF MONTHLY DISBURSEMENTS FOR LIVING EXPENDITURES PER HOUSEHOLD
BY MONTHLY INCOME QUINTILE GROUPS, 1968

(figures in parentheses indicate percent of total)

| Annual Income Quintile Group | Total Living Expenditures | Expenditures in Yen | | | | |
| --- | --- | --- | --- | --- | --- | --- |
| | | Food | Housing | Fuel and Light | Clothing | Miscellaneous |
| I. Less than ¥575,000 | 37,878(100) | 15,797(41.7) | 4,626(12.2) | 2,170(5.7) | 3,557(9.4) | 11,722(31.0) |
| II. ¥575,000–764,000 | 50,108(100) | 19,546(39.0) | 6,236(12.5) | 2,471(4.9) | 5,039(10.1) | 16,800(33.5) |
| III. ¥764,000–968,000 | 59,962(100) | 22,179(37.0) | 7,183(12.0) | 2,647(4.4) | 6,393(10.7) | 21,589(36.0) |
| IV. ¥968,000–1,291,000 | 71,017(100) | 24,422(34.4) | 8,346(11.8) | 2,902(4.1) | 8,091(11.4) | 27,177(38.3) |
| V. Over ¥1,291,000 | 93,550(100) | 29,489(31.5) | 9,427(10.1) | 3,686(3.9) | 11,501(12.3) | 39,394(42.1) |
| Average | 62,503(100) | 22,286(35.7) | 7,163(11.5) | 2,795(4.5) | 6,928(11.1) | 23,330(37.3) |

Source: *The Annual Report on the Family Income and Expenditure Survey, 1968* (Tokyo: The Office of the Prime Minister, 1969), pp. 194–196.

74 percent have life insurance, and over 13 percent own stock.[19]
Let us now examine how the expenditure patterns vary according to income class. Table 2.11 presents the expenditure pattern by
income quintile groups for the nationwide sample of nonagricultural households. As might be expected, the expenditure for food
declines with the increase in the income level, and just the reverse
trend is apparent for expenditure in the miscellaneous category.
The highest income bracket allocated nearly 42 percent of the total
expenditure in this latter category. In this group, the expenditure
for cultural and recreational activities alone accounted for slightly
over 8 percent of the total expenditure.

One segment we cannot ignore in discussing consumption patterns is the growing importance of youth. As we noted earlier,
contemporary Japan is a youth-oriented society in which 43 percent
of the entire population is 25 years of age or younger. In the face
of serious labor shortages and rapidly rising wages, the youth
market is becoming increasingly important. The total annual expenditure by persons in the 15 to 24 age bracket is estimated to be
over ¥2,900 billion. A recent survey of the income and expenditure
of single male and female wage earners up to the age of 25 reveals
the consumption patterns of this group. The results are summarized in Table 2.12. We note here parenthetically that for manu-

TABLE 2.12

AVERAGE MONTHLY EXPENDITURE PATTERNS
OF SINGLE WAGE EARNERS, 1968

| Kind of Expenditure | Monthly Total (¥) | Percentage Increase over Preceding Year | Percentage Distribution |
|---|---|---|---|
| Basic Essentials | 12,424 | 10.3 | 45.4 |
| Cultural and Recreational Activities | 4,828 | 11.5 | 17.6 |
| Clothing | 3,981 | 16.3 | 14.6 |
| Transportation | 1,522 | 31.8 | 5.6 |
| Consumer Durables | 1,191 | 54.9 | 4.4 |
| Health | 641 | 17.0 | 2.3 |
| Others | 2,773 | 40.0 | 10.1 |
| Total Consumption | 27,360 | 16.6 | 100.0 |

Source: *Kokumin Seikatsu Hakusho, Showa 44 nen ban [White Paper on
National Life, 1969]* (Tokyo: The Economic Planning Agency, 1969), p. 19.

[19] *Shohi to Chochiku no Doko: Showa 43 nen ban [A Survey of Consumption and Savings, 1968].* (Tokyo: The Economic Planning Agency, 1968),
pp. 153–159.

facturers of certain products the youth market has become extremely important. For example, 79 percent of the total sales of small portable television sets is derived from this segment. Likewise, this market accounts for 65 percent of the total sales of guitars, stereo sets, and skiing equipment, 60 percent of the total sales of tape recorders, and nearly 50 percent of men's toiletries.[20]

*The "Consumption Revolution"*

The very rapid economic growth has substantially improved the standard of living of the masses and has altered their mode of living in important ways. The Japanese themselves are very aware of these developments, and such terms as *Shohi Kakumei,* or "consumption revolution," have been popularized to describe these changes. Indeed, in many aspects the changes have been revolutionary. Moreover, postwar changes mean to an average Japanese much more than material improvements. They mean a new way of life with a greater amount of leisure time, emancipation from time-consuming daily household chores, greater individual freedom, and Westernization of tastes. Also, there is widespread expectation among the masses that the amenities of middle-class life are finally within their reach.

Almost every aspect of daily life has been affected. For one thing, the diet has improved markedly in recent years. Per capita daily calorie intake has been increasing steadily from 2,097 in 1949 to 2,456 in 1967. Qualitative changes are even more impressive. An average Japanese now can afford to buy a much wider range of food than was possible a generation ago. Also significant is the extent to which the Japanese have been departing from their traditional diet pattern. For instance, in 1938 nearly 72 percent of the calorie intake of an average Japanese was derived from various types of cereal products, but by the mid-1960s, as can be seen from Table 2.13, the consumption of rice has been steadily declining, whereas the consumption of meat, eggs, and dairy products has grown substantially.

In the area of clothing some significant improvements are notable. Per capita consumption of clothing has steadily increased, and synthetic fibers now account for nearly 50 percent of the total clothing purchased. Ownership of various clothing items has also increased rather rapidly. By the mid-1960s a Japanese woman on

[20] "Wakamono no Hijuwa masu" ["A Growing Importance of the Youth"], *Nihon Keizai Shinbun,* August 19, 1969, p. 22.

TABLE 2.13

PER CAPITA DAILY CONSUMPTION OF SELECTED FOOD ITEMS, 1946–1967

| | | | | *Items in Grams* | | | | |
|---|---|---|---|---|---|---|---|---|
| *Year* | *Rice* | *Fish* | *Meat* | *Eggs* | *Dairy Products* | *Sugar* | *Vege-tables* | *Fruits* |
| 1946 | 254.0 | 25.0 | 2.6 | 1.0 | 4.3 | 2.0 | 151.0 | 19.0 |
| 1950 | 302.0 | 40.0 | 6.3 | 2.3 | 14.6 | 8.0 | 174.0 | 42.0 |
| 1955 | 302.2 | 71.8 | 8.8 | 9.3 | 33.0 | 33.7 | 225.0 | 33.6 |
| 1960 | 313.3 | 76.1 | 13.8 | 13.3 | 61.0 | 41.2 | 273.1 | 61.2 |
| 1961 | 319.1 | 81.6 | 17.4 | 17.8 | 68.4 | 43.6 | 256.7 | 63.8 |
| 1962 | 321.2 | 81.8 | 21.5 | 18.9 | 77.7 | 46.5 | 281.0 | 64.0 |
| 1963 | 317.7 | 81.8 | 21.6 | 20.4 | 89.8 | 45.7 | 304.8 | 70.3 |
| 1964 | 314.3 | 79.3 | 23.5 | 23.7 | 97.1 | 48.3 | 285.9 | 77.8 |
| 1965 | 302.6 | 80.3 | 25.0 | 24.2 | 102.8 | 51.5 | 300.5 | 77.9 |
| 1966 | 286.2 | 80.0 | 28.4 | 25.3 | 114.2 | 54.9 | 317.0 | 88.0 |
| 1967 | 278.5 | 84.4 | 30.2 | 27.5 | 118.2 | 57.3 | 317.9 | 90.1 |

Source: *Kokumin Seikatsu Hakusho: Showa 44 nen ban [White Paper on National Life, 1969]* (Tokyo: The Economic Planning Agency, 1969), p. 434.

the average owned 6.5 dresses and suits, 1.6 coats, and 15.6 kimonos, while men on the average owned 5.5 suits, 1.9 overcoats, and 4.5 kimonos.[21] These statistics unfortunately do not convey adequately the qualitative improvements that have taken place. Fashion has become very important, particularly in women's apparel. The latest Paris or New York fashions are quickly adopted by the Japanese. Even men's clothing has now become quite susceptible to Western fashion. Ready-to-wear has made great strides in both men's and women's clothing.

Perhaps the most striking measure of the material progress achieved by an average Japanese consumer in the past decade or so is the wide diffusion of consumer durable goods. As presented in Table 2.14, in 1969 over 94 percent of Japanese households owned at least one television set, nearly 88 percent owned washing machines, and 85 percent owned refrigerators. One out of every seven families now owns an automobile. Equally significant is the speed with which consumer durables have been diffused. In 1958, for example, less than 30 percent of urban families had washing machines, only 16 percent owned television sets, and only 5.5 percent had refrigerators. As evidenced in Table 2.15, there is little difference in ownership of the more popular consumer durables

[21] *Zude Miru Kokumin Seikatsu [Pictorial Analysis of National Life]* (Tokyo: The Japan Productivity Center, 1967), p. 80.

TABLE 2.14

OWNERSHIP OF SELECTED CONSUMER DURABLES AMONG URBAN
HOUSEHOLDS FOR SELECTED YEARS, 1958–1969

(percent of households owning item)

| Items | 1958 | 1961 | 1967 | 1969 |
|---|---|---|---|---|
| Television Sets | | | | |
| (black and white) | 15.9 | 62.5 | 96.4 | 94.7 |
| Television Sets (color) | — | — | 1.6 | 13.9 |
| Electric Refrigerators | 5.5 | 17.2 | 77.6 | 84.6 |
| Washing Machines | 29.3 | 50.2 | 84.8 | 88.3 |
| Vacuum Cleaners | — | 15.4 | 53.8 | 62.6 |
| Room Air Conditioners | — | 0.4 | 3.9 | 4.7 |
| Passenger Cars | — | 2.8 | 13.1 | 17.3 |
| Sewing Machines | 66.3 | 74.1 | 82.6 | 84.6 |

Source: Adapted from *Kokumin Seikatsu Hakusho, Showa 44 nen [White Paper on National Life, 1969]* (Tokyo: The Economic Planning Agency, 1969), p. 322.

between urban and rural households. Moreover, consumer durables are well diffused even among the low-income brackets. Table 2.16 presents ownership data of consumer durables according to income levels. It is significant to note that as high as 82 percent of households whose annual income is less than ¥300,000 ($830) own television sets, and 45 percent of these households own sewing machines, 45 percent own washing machines, and 34 percent have refrigerators.

Another sign of improvement is an increasing expenditure for leisure activities. Growing discretionary income and increasing leisure time, through gradual reduction of work hours, are contributing to an increase in the expenditure for cultural and recreational activities. The expenditure for these activities among urban households nearly quadrupled between 1956 and 1968 (during this time total expenditures grew by slightly over two and a half times).[22] Between 1965 and 1968 leisure-related expenditures grew by 42.5 percent, while total household expenditures increased by 28 percent.

Particularly significant is the rapid rise in both domestic and foreign travel for pleasure. A recent nationwide survey conducted by the Ministry of Health and Welfare estimates that some 35 mil-

[22] *Annual Report on the Family Income and Expenditure Survey, 1968,* pp. 184–186.

TABLE 2.15

OWNERSHIP OF SELECTED CONSUMER DURABLE GOODS BY MAJOR OCCUPATIONAL CATEGORY OF HOUSEHOLD, 1967

| Type of Household | | Percentage of Households Owning Item | | | | | | |
|---|---|---|---|---|---|---|---|---|
| | Sewing Machines | Television Sets | Passenger Cars | Washing Machines | Refrig-erators | Vacuum Cleaners | Living Room Sets | Room Coolers |
| All Households | 81.7 | 96.2 | 9.5 | 79.8 | 69.7 | 47.2 | 16.3 | 2.8 |
| Farmers | 80.8 | 94.7 | 6.6 | 75.7 | 49.3 | 21.9 | 7.2 | 0.3 |
| Nonfarmers | 82.1 | 96.7 | 10.6 | 81.3 | 76.3 | 56.1 | 19.6 | 3.7 |
| Wage Earners | 83.7 | 97.4 | 7.5 | 81.0 | 76.8 | 55.8 | 18.6 | 1.4 |
| Proprietors and Others | 78.9 | 95.2 | 16.5 | 81.9 | 77.0 | 56.7 | 21.9 | 8.1 |

Source: *Shōhi to Chochiku no Dōkō: Shōwa 42 nen ban [A Survey of Consumption and Savings, 1967]* (Tokyo: The Economic Planning Agency, 1967), pp. 80–81.

TABLE 2.16

OWNERSHIP OF CONSUMER DURABLE GOODS BY INCOME CATEGORY OF HOUSEHOLD, 1967

(percentage of all households owning item)

| Annual Income | Sewing Machines | Television Sets | Passenger Cars | Refrigerators | Vacuum Cleaners | Air Conditioners | Living Room Sets | Dining Room Sets | Washing Machines | Color TV |
|---|---|---|---|---|---|---|---|---|---|---|
| Less than ¥300,000 | 44.6 | 82.1 | 0.7 | 33.8 | 16.4 | 1.1 | 3.9 | 3.3 | 44.4 | 2.2 |
| ¥300,000- 599,999 | 74.9 | 97.2 | 4.5 | 65.3 | 33.7 | 1.2 | 6.8 | 9.6 | 75.0 | 1.3 |
| ¥600,000- 899,999 | 86.4 | 98.3 | 10.0 | 80.6 | 54.1 | 2.5 | 13.1 | 19.1 | 88.8 | 3.7 |
| ¥900,000- 1,299,999 | 87.4 | 95.0 | 18.5 | 87.3 | 67.8 | 3.8 | 21.4 | 27.0 | 94.0 | 6.2 |
| ¥1,300,000- 1,499,999 | 92.8 | 98.5 | 22.9 | 93.2 | 75.3 | 5.9 | 33.2 | 32.7 | 94.1 | 7.1 |
| ¥1,500,000- 1,799,999 | 94.0 | 98.4 | 28.4 | 93.6 | 79.4 | 7.9 | 41.7 | 41.3 | 94.6 | 15.5 |
| Over ¥1,800,000 | 95.7 | 96.6 | 40.9 | 95.1 | 88.4 | 23.6 | 60.7 | 53.3 | 97.5 | 26.6 |

Source: *Shohi to Chochiku no Dōkō: Showa 43 nen ban [A Survey of Consumption and Savings, 1968]* (Tokyo: The Economic Planning Agency, 1968), pp. 108–109.

lion, adults, or over 47 percent of the entire adult population, took sight-seeing trips lasting more than overnight during the one-year period ending in October 1966.[23]. According to another survey, one of every three families surveyed took at least one pleasure trip lasting more than overnight during the year.[24] This survey also estimates that a total of 815 million people visited resorts during 1966. Also during the same year the total number of people visiting Japan's 23 national parks exceeded 220 million (more than twice the country's population). The number doubled between 1960 and 1966. During 1968 some 321,674 people have made trips overseas, recording nearly two-and-a-half-fold growth since 1964.[25] About half of these trips were intended for pleasure. Indeed, the Japanese have become an extremely mobile people. These figures provide convincing evidence of the significant improvement in the standard of living of the middle class.

Western sports such as bowling, skiing, golfing, and swimming are now widely enjoyed. It is estimated that there are as many as one million golfers. Spectator recreational activities such as baseball and cycle racing are also very popular. Closely related to the expenditure for cultural and recreational activities is the almost fivefold increase in expenditure for professionally prepared food. The volume of sales of eating and drinking establishments was nearly five times as large in 1968 as it had been in 1958.

### Emergence of a Mass Consumption Market and Its Effects

We have just examined the rather striking material improvements achieved by the Japanese in the last decade or so. What is most remarkable is that these benefits have been diffused widely among all segments of the population, and there is every indication that Japan is on the verge of developing a mass consumer market. Such a basic and sweeping change cannot help but have a major impact on the value system. We alluded earlier to the fact that the consumption revolution the Japanese so frequently and enthusiastically talk about involves much more than material improvements, however significant they may be, but it also is producing basic changes in their attitudes.

[23] *Kanko Hakusho: Showa 43 nen ban* [White Paper on Sight-Seeing, 1968] (Tokyo: The Office of the Prime Minister, 1968), p. 67.
[24] *Kokumin Seikatsu Hakusho, Showa 44 nen ban* [White Paper on National Life, 1969], p. 32.
[25] *Ibid.*

In view of the rather dynamic social changes that have been taking place, it is essential to examine them further. Among many interesting implications a most intriguing one is the direction of the change, more specifically, whether or not these changes are bringing contemporary society closer to the Western pattern. In the remainder of this chapter we shall explore a number of significant attitude changes, particularly as they relate to the consumption behavior and life style of the contemporary Japanese. While this is a widely debated topic, little systematic analysis has been undertaken, and the ensuing discussion has been drawn from a number of different empirical studies; as a result, many of the observations made here are still very tentative.

*The Acceptance of Material Values and Consumption Orientation*

Traditionally, the Japanese culture emphasized aesthetic values and a nonmaterial orientation. Social position and prestige in Japan were not dependent on possession of material wealth. While conspicuous consumption was not entirely unknown in Japanese history, it was not pervasive nor well accepted. In fact, the Confucian morality that was dominant in the Tokugawa period emphasized the importance of thrift and saving. It held that production was socially useful but that consumption was not. According to its teachings, curbing one's desire for worldly possessions was a virtue, and the code of ethics of the ruling elite in the premodern era laid strong emphasis on frugality and nonmaterial values.

The elite that led Japan to industrialization in the Meiji era essentially subscribed to the same philosophy. They found the traditional ideology consistent not only with their own background and upbringing but with the practical necessity of curbing consumption and encouraging saving in order to attain the overriding goal of rapid industrialization. Of course, for the masses, frugality was not a matter of choice, simply because they could not afford much more than the bare necessities of life. Throughout the prewar era, austerity, cultivation of aesthetic or nonmaterial values, and frugality received much emphasis. In fact, the Imperial Edict on Education that set the framework for prewar education clearly emphasized, among other things, the importance of frugality. As Japan entered the quasi-war period in the late 1930s and more directly as she started all-out war efforts in the early 1940s, consumption was further discouraged. The mood of the era was well represented by one of the prevailing slogans: "Luxury is Enemy." In postwar years, the traditional emphasis on Puritanlike asceticism and the denial of materialism have undergone significant change. A number of forces are responsible for this rather revolutionary development. For one thing, World War II, as far as the Japanese were concerned, was a direct confrontation of materialism on one hand and nonmaterialistic or even antimaterialistic values on the other. In the face of overwhelming American material superiority, the Japanese experienced on the battlefronts as well as at home the very hollowness of fanatic spiritualism not supported by material strength. The strict rationing brought about by the acute shortage of essential materials, and the inevitable widespread black market that the Japanese experienced during the war and its immediate aftermath, made them very conscious of the importance of material wealth. The presence of affluent American Occupation Forces in the poverty-stricken nation also was telling evidence of the comforts of material superiority. The desire for consumption and material welfare had been checked for so long that when the restrictions were taken off it burst with a strong thrust.

There are yet two other considerations that are more basic than those already mentioned. One is that in the darkest days of the immediate postwar era, the Japanese went through a most thoroughgoing self-criticism and repudiated many of their traditional values. The other is the tremendous material improvements that the masses have experienced during the past decade and a half. For the first time the average Japanese has been able to raise himself above the level of the bare subsistence. He has been emancipated from perpetual poverty, and the amenities of life have finally come within his reach. This burgeoning material expectation has been further heightened by the steadily increasing bombardment of advertising and the ever-increasing flood of new products.

No longer is the desire for consumption held as evil and something to be repressed. The cry for frugality is seldom heard. On the contrary, an average consumer is constantly exposed to mass media advertising and to propaganda that the nation's prosperity is based on mass consumption and that people have a "duty" to consume to sustain this prosperity. Implicit in this change is the widespread recognition of the legitimacy of financial and material aspirations and of a desire to make one's life more comfortable and pleasant. This is very evident in a study conducted in 1962 by Kokumin

Seikatsu Kenkyujo, a leading research institute in Japan. This study sought to obtain data on consumption patterns and the behavior of consumers in Tokyo and Osaka, the two major urban centers in Japan. The data for this study were gathered from carefully chosen samples of 691 and 680 respondents, respectively, in each city. To measure respondents' attitudes toward consumption, the study asked the following question: "There is a view that consumption is a virtue. What do you think about it?" The results are summarized in Table 2.17.

TABLE 2.17

JAPANESE ATTITUDES TOWARD CONSUMPTION, 1962*

|  | Very Much Agree with the Statement | Agree with the Statement | Disagree with the Statement | Very Much Disagree with the Statement | Don't Know | Total |
|---|---|---|---|---|---|---|
| Tokyo | 1.9 | 32.3 | 46.5 | 3.9 | 15.4 | 100 |
| Osaka | 1.5 | 27.8 | 46.8 | 4.1 | 19.8 | 100 |

*"There is a view that consumption is a virtue. What do you think about it?"
Source: *Toshi ni Okeru Shohisha no Ishiki to Kōdō [Consumers' Orientation and Behavior in Large Cities]* (Tokyo: Kokumin Seikatsu Kenkyujo, 1965), p. 39.

Surprisingly, despite the strong positive connotation of the term "virtue," about 34 percent and 29 percent, respectively, of the respondents in Tokyo and Osaka said that they were basically in agreement with the statement. Also significant is the relatively large percentage of "don't knows," which can be interpreted as a manifestation of ambivalence.

Further analysis of the data is revealing. As indicated in Table 2.18, a considerable variation in the response pattern is notable among various age categories. For example, in Tokyo 40 percent of the respondents in the age bracket twenty to twenty-nine agreed with the statement, while only 23 percent of the respondents in the age bracket fifty to fifty-nine shared this view. While it is reasonable to assume that the older generation is apt to be more conservative than the young, nevertheless, this does represent a considerable generation gap.

It is also interesting to note, as is evident from Table 2.19, that the highest percentage of those agreeing with the statement is found among the white-collar workers. Housewives, laborers, and

TABLE 2.18

ATTITUDE TOWARD CONSUMPTION BY AGE CATEGORY, 1962

| | Tokyo Respondents | | | Osaka Respondents | | |
|---|---|---|---|---|---|---|
| Age | Agree with the State- ment | Disagree with the State- ment | Don't Know | Agree with the State- ment | Disagree with the State- ment | Don't Know |
| 20–29 | 40.1 | 43.5 | 16.4 | 35.8 | 39.6 | 24.5 |
| 30–39 | 36.2 | 46.7 | 17.0 | 26.7 | 52.9 | 20.4 |
| 40–49 | 28.2 | 61.9 | 10.0 | 28.9 | 60.0 | 11.1 |
| 50–59 | 22.9 | 57.5 | 19.5 | 23.7 | 55.6 | 20.5 |
| Total | 34.2 | 50.4 | 15.5 | 29.3 | 50.9 | 19.8 |

Source: *Toshi ni Okeru Shohisha no Ishiki to Kōdō [Consumers' Orientation tion and Behavior in Large Cities]* (Tokyo: Kokumin Seikatsu Kenkyujo, 1965), p. 68.

TABLE 2.19

ATTITUDE TOWARD CONSUMPTION BY MAJOR OCCUPATIONAL CATEGORIES, 1962

| | Tokyo | | | Osaka | | |
|---|---|---|---|---|---|---|
| Occupation | Agree with State- ment | Dis- agree with State- ment | Don't Know | Agree with State- ment | Dis- agree with State- ment | Don't Know |
| Individual Proprietors | 30.4 | 56.9 | 12.7 | 32.1 | 51.8 | 16.0 |
| Self-Employed Professionals | 44.4 | 48.1 | 7.4 | 28.6 | 52.4 | 19.0 |
| Managerial Personnel | 50.0 | 50.0 | – | 33.3 | 55.6 | 11.1 |
| Skilled Professionals | 49.2 | 40.9 | 9.8 | 21.8 | 58.7 | 19.6 |
| Clerical Workers | 35.6 | 56.8 | 7.7 | 28.6 | 51.7 | 19.8 |
| Laborers | 27.5 | 48.4 | 24.2 | 30.5 | 48.9 | 20.6 |
| Housewives | 26.8 | 54.4 | 18.9 | 27.8 | 53.9 | 18.3 |
| Others | 45.5 | 34.2 | 20.3 | 34.5 | 32.8 | 32.8 |
| Total | 34.2 | 50.4 | 15.5 | 29.3 | 50.9 | 19.8 |

Source: *Toshi ni Okeru Shohisha no Ishiki to Kōdō [Consumers' Orientation and Behavior in Large Cities]* (Tokyo: Kokumin Seikatsu Kenkyujo, 1965), p. 68.

individual proprietors appear to be more conservative. Interestingly, however, as indicated in Table 2.20, the response patterns to this question are little related to income.

TABLE 2.20

ATTITUDE TOWARD CONSUMPTION ACCORDING TO INCOME CLASS, 1962

| Income | Tokyo | | | Osaka | | |
|---|---|---|---|---|---|---|
| | Agree | Dis-agree | Don't Know | Agree | Dis-agree | Don't Know |
| Less than ¥20,000 | 33.8 | 50.1 | 16.1 | 21.6 | 43.2 | 35.3 |
| ¥20,000–29,999 | 28.7 | 58.3 | 13.0 | 30.2 | 50.8 | 19.1 |
| ¥30,000–39,999 | 37.5 | 47.9 | 14.6 | 32.4 | 51.6 | 15.9 |
| ¥40,000–59,999 | 36.4 | 51.5 | 12.1 | 27.9 | 55.9 | 16.2 |
| ¥60,000–99,999 | 35.8 | 52.9 | 11.3 | 30.3 | 56.2 | 13.5 |
| Over ¥100,000 | 33.3 | 48.9 | 17.8 | 31.3 | 54.2 | 14.6 |
| Don't Know | 26.1 | 30.5 | 43.5 | 26.0 | 36.2 | 37.7 |
| Total | 34.2 | 50.4 | 15.4 | 29.3 | 50.9 | 19.8 |

Source: *Toshi ni Okeru Shohisha no Ishiki to Kōdō [Consumers' Orientation and Behavior in Large Cities]* (Tokyo: Kokumin Seikatsu Kenkyujo, 1965), p. 50.

Another trend toward consumption orientation can be seen from consumers' attitudes toward advertising. One of the surveys conducted by Kokumin Seikatsu Kenkyujo included the following question:

What impact do you feel advertising has on your life? Out of the following views, please check the one that most closely represents your view.
  1. Advertising is designed to entice customers to buy things that they do not need.
  2. Advertising informs consumers on new product features and designs.
  3. Advertising is designed to entice consumers to keep up with the latest fashion.
  4. Advertising aids consumers in their buying decisions.
  5. Advertising is designed to increasing earnings of large firms.
  6. Advertising increases the price of products advertised.
  7. Advertising enriches our life.

The responses are presented in Table 2.21. Significantly, over 70 percent of the respondents expressed positive views about advertising.

Japanese consumers are now caught up in an incessant search

TABLE 2.21

CONSUMERS' ATTITUDES TOWARD ADVERTISING, 1968

$(N = 1,098)$

| Statement | Percentage of Respondents Choosing Each of the Statements |
|---|---|
| 1 | 7.3 |
| 2 | 35.4 |
| 3 | 8.2 |
| 4 | 22.6 |
| 5 | 4.4 |
| 6 | 10.0 |
| 7 | 11.4 |
| Don't Know | 0.7 |

Source: *Seikatsu Ishiki ni Kansuru Kenkyu [A Study of Views on Life]* (Tokyo: Kokumin Seikatsu Kenkyujo, 1969), p. 41.

for a "bright new life," to borrow Vogel's apt expression.[26] With characteristic zeal the Japanese have turned to improving their living conditions. An important means to this end is their acquisition of consumer durables. The Japanese consumers talk of wanting "three Imperial treasures." By this they do not mean the three national treasures (mirror, jewel, and sword), traditionally handed down in the Imperial Household, but three consumer durable goods that are highly desired to make everyday life pleasant and comfortable. The identity of the "three treasures" has changed with the improvement in the standard of living, as former "treasures" become commonplace. Initially, the most common "three treasures" were television sets, refrigerators, and washing machines; but now the treasures that many aspire to are a car, a central heating system, and a cottage at a resort.

The search for a better and more comfortable life has become a legitimate and acceptable goal for the masses. Significantly, the aspiration level continues to elevate as former goals are achieved. This is evidenced very eloquently by the results of the annual government survey on national living standards, based on a nationwide sample of 20,000. Comparison of the results obtained between 1962 and 1967 illustrates the very rapid upgrading of the aspiration level. Each year respondents were asked to define the aspired

[26] Ezra F. Vogel, *Japan's New Middle Class: The Salary Man and His Family in a Tokyo Suburb* (Berkeley and Los Angeles: University of California Press, 1963), p. 25.

standard of living in terms of ownership of certain consumer durable goods.
As evident from Table 2.22, not only has the aspiration level

TABLE 2.22

CHANGES IN THE ASPIRATION LEVEL FOR MATERIAL GOODS, 1962–1967

| Item Desired | 1962 | 1964 | 1965 | 1966 | 1967 |
|---|---|---|---|---|---|
| Radio and Sewing Machine | 2% | 1% | 0% | 0% | 0% |
| The Above plus Television Set and Washing Machine | 23 | 13 | 9 | 5 | 3 |
| The Above plus Refrigerator and Vacuum Cleaner | 43 | 51 | 43 | 37 | 29 |
| The Above plus Automobile and Piano | 15 | 29 | 39 | 46 | 53 |
| Don't Know | 17 | 6 | 9 | 12 | 15 |

Source: *Kokumin Seikatsu ni Kansuru Seron Chōsa, Showa 42 nen [A Public Opinion Survey on National Life, 1967]* (Tokyo: The Office of the Prime Minister, 1967), p. 13.

been improving continuously but there is considerable optimism concerning the future outlook. For example, 44 percent of the respondents surveyed in 1967 felt that their living standard would continue to improve in the future, and only 7 percent anticipated a decline.[27]

In the foregoing brief analysis we have seen that with the development of a mass consumer market there is a clear trend toward consumption orientation. The traditional nonmaterial, ascetic value orientation has rapidly declined, and in its place a strong material value system and consumption orientation has emerged. The search for material welfare has now become a legitimate and widely shared goal.

### The Wane of Traditional Collectivity Orientation

Along with rapidly emerging consumption orientation, another noteworthy development taking place in postwar Japan is a trend toward greater individual freedom. This is a rather significant development in view of the strong collectivity orientation that characterized traditional Japanese culture. The collectivity orien-

[27] *Kokumin Seikatsu ni Kansuru Seron Chōsa, Showa 42 nen [A Public Opinion Survey on National Life, 1967]* (Tokyo: The Office of the Prime Minister, 1968), p. 13.

tation of the Japanese is said to go back almost to the dawn of Japan's history. The Japanese gave up their nomadic life early in their history and settled down to cultivate rice fields, thus establishing permanent settlements. In such settlements families tended to stay together and perpetuate themselves for generations, even to the stage where the entire settlement took on the characteristics of one large family.[28] Moreover, this specific form of economic life required cooperative relationships, and the family in fact constituted the very basic economic unit. In such a society individuals either were, or soon came to be, closely interrelated with one another, forming an "exclusive social nexus."[29] Out of this relationship developed a considerable degree of interdependence not only among individuals within a family but also among families within a given settlement. One's welfare and prosperity were most closely tied to the life of the group. The individual was identified with a collectivity to such an extent that whatever he did almost immediately and totally reflected on the entire collectivity.

In such a society the individual hardly existed as a distinct entity. In almost every aspect of life he was tightly bound to a group and was allowed few private emotions and virtually no freedom for individual action. The group imposed the norms of conduct on the individual, whose lot was to conform. Much emphasis was given to group loyalty, and the group's disapproval was very much feared, since one could hardly survive without group membership.

The importance placed on the collectivity meant that the interest of the totality was the dominant concern of individuals. Certainly, one was expected to subordinate his own interests and welfare to those of the group. In return he was given protection and security. The ruling elite that guided Japan's industrialization made deliberate use of this collectivity orientation to its own purposes. The collectivity orientation was generalized into the nation-state in an attempt to achieve national integration and to mobilize resources to attain its goals. In fact, the Japanese people were taught that the entire nation was one vast family, and loyalty to the nation-state and to the Emperor were to receive the utmost priority. The prewar educational system greatly emphasized the importance of loyalty to the family system, the community, and above all to the

[28] For details, see Hajime Nakamura, *Ways of Thinking of Eastern Peoples: India, China, Tibet and Japan* (Honolulu: East-West Center Press, 1964) p. 413.
[29] *Ibid.*

nation-state. No amount of individual sacrifice was too great for the sake of the family as an institution, and for the nation-state. A crying slogan of the time, "Meshi Hokō," literally meaning "sacrificing oneself for the good of the whole," well represented the accepted mood of the era. Individualism was traditionally equated with selfishness, and a very negative connotation was attributed to the term *kojin shugi*—individualism.[30]

In traditional Japan one belonged to a number of different collectivities, such as one's family, neighborhood groups, occupational groups, the village. The extent and the nature of collectivity naturally varied considerably, depending upon one's status. Among the various types of collectivities the family was most important. In the idealized model of the traditional Japanese family system each member of the family was prescribed a status in the familial hierarchy and was related to the other members through a code of specific moral obligations and acceptable conduct.

The traditional family system became the very foundation of Japan's prewar civil code. Dore characterizes the prewar family system as "a system of legal and political organizations whereby the family is the major unit of social organization, is a legal personality in which property rights and duties are vested, and is represented externally by a family head who exercises wide power of control over family members."[31] While industrialization and urbanization did contribute to some decline of collectivity orientation in the prewar period, the ruling elite was, on the whole, successful in arresting the tide for change and in maintaining the traditional anti-individualistic ethic in a position of unassailable supremacy.

A host of developments in the postwar years have contributed to the gradual decline in collectivity orientation. The notion that the nation-state constituted the supreme collectivity, and that national loyalty had a prior claim over anything else, was totally repudiated in the immediate aftermath of the war. The concept of family as a legal instrument was abolished. Unlike the prewar version, a most fundamental premise of the postwar Constitution is recognition of the rights of the individual citizen. The postwar educational system is designed to train a citizen for a democratic society rather than to develop a docile subject. The land reforms greatly weak-

---

[30] R. P. Dore, *City Life in Japan: A Study of a Tokyo Ward* (Berkeley and Los Angeles: University of California Press, 1958), p. 338.
[31] *Ibid.*, pp. 93–94.

ened the highly collectivity-oriented traditional village structure.
The postwar prosperity, with its benefits widely diffused, has
given the average Japanese a greater degree of economic independence than ever before, thus reducing his dependence for material
welfare from the collectivities. It must be remembered that economic deprivation was a powerful force that had supported the
traditional collectivity orientation. The rapid urbanization trend, a
product of the phenomenal economic growth, further weakened
traditional family and village ties.

Industrialization, urbanization, and economic prosperity, coupled
with the legal change, brought about a basic alteration in the
character of Japan's family system. The traditional idealized family
institution as a legal and political system virtually has been
destroyed, and a typical family in contemporary Japan, particularly
in urban areas, is hardly distinguishable in its size, composition,
and orientation from that of other highly industrialized nations.

Average family size has been steadily declining: in 1965 the
nationwide average had declined to 4.08.[32] In metropolitan areas,
the average was as low as 3.91, only slightly larger than the overall
United States average. It is anticipated that the average family
size will continue to decline, and by 1975 it is projected to drop to
3.5.[33] The number of households nearly doubled between 1930 and
1965, while the population increased by one and a half times.

Closely related to the declining family size is the increasing
importance of the conjugal or nuclear family (composed of a
married couple, with or without children). By 1960 over 55.6
percent of Japan's households consisted of these basic family units,
and the ratio was as high as 60 percent among nonagricultural
households.[34] Young couples are increasingly living in their own
homes and not with parents or grandparents, as was so commonly
done in the past. Households in which three generations were
living together accounted for only 19 percent of the total, and
among nonfarm households the percentage was as low as 11
percent. The strong hierarchical orientation and dominance-obe-
dience relationships among family members that characterized the
traditional family system have all but disappeared. The relationship

---

[32] Keizai Yoran, 1968 [A Summary of Ecnomic Statistics, 1968] (Tokyo:
The Economic Planning Agency, 1968), p. 62.
[33] Kokumin Seikatsu Tokei Nenpō, Showa 44 nen ban [Annual Statistics on
National Life, 1969] (Tokyo: Kokumin Seikatsu Kenkyūjo, 1969), p. 8.
[34] Ibid.

between family members in a typical nuclear family is democratic and egalitarian.

Thus, postwar Japan has witnessed a clearly discernible trend toward the weakening of collectivity orientation. This has resulted in two closely related changes: one is an increase in the range of individual decision making; the other is a change in the criteria by which decisions are made.[35] In traditional Japan, the dominant decision criterion was the good of the collectivity, although the specific collectivity depended on the nature of decisions to be made. In other words, whatever the range of freedom one enjoyed, he was to be guided, above anything else, by the welfare of the relevant collectivity.

In contemporary Japan, however, an average citizen is likely to be guided in his decision making more by his own welfare or by that of certain other individuals than by the collectivities of which he is a member. For example, an individual no longer makes a critical decision on the basis of what is good for the family collectivity as an institution, but he is more likely to be guided by what is good for him and the specific members of his immediate family. The concern here is for *individual* members of the family as parents, husband, wife, or children rather than for the impersonal family collectivity.[36]

It is highly significant to note that much of the stigma once attached to the search for an individual's own welfare and happiness (and those of his immediate family) is almost completely gone. In fact, the search for private joy and comfort has now become an accepted goal. Findings of a number of opinion surveys conducted in recent years tend to confirm this trend. Let us examine the results of a recent study conducted by Kokumin Seikatsu Kenkyujo.[37] Included in this survey was the following question:

> We all have certain aspirations for our life. Among the following, please choose the statement that most closely approximates your aspirations. You may choose only one.
>
> 1. To have a rich, abundant, and comfortable life.
> 2. To enjoy everyday life.

[35] R. P. Dore, "Mobility, Equality, and Individuation in Modern Japan," in R. P. Dore (ed.), *Aspects of Social Change in Modern Japan* (Princeton, N.J.: Princeton University Press, 1967), p. 149.

[36] *Ibid.*

[37] *Seikatsu Ishiki ni Kansuru Kenkyu [A Study of Views on Life]* (Tokyo: Kokumin Seikatsu Kenkyūjo, 1969), pp. 41–50.

3. To be absorbed in challenging work.
4. To be able to make useful social contributions.
5. To have a peaceful and happy family life.
6. Don't know.[38]

The results are presented in Table 2.23.

TABLE 2.23

ASPIRATIONS OF LIFE, TOKYO, 1968

$(N = 1,098)$

| Statement | Percentage of Respondents Choosing Each of the Statements |
|---|---|
| 1 | 7.0 |
| 2 | 13.0 |
| 3 | 23.3 |
| 4 | 3.6 |
| 5 | 51.4 |
| 6 | 1.6 |
| Total | 100.0 |

Source: *Seikatsu Ishiki ni Kansuru Kenkyu* [*A Study of Views on Life*] (Tokyo: Kokumin Seikatsu Kenkyujo, 1969), p. 34.

Granted that the respondents were limited to the urban adult population, where traditional collectivity orientation is expected to be weak, it is extremely significant to note that over half of the respondents chose the statement "to have a peaceful and happy family life." Needless to say, the "family" they had in mind was certainly not the traditional family collectivity but a nuclear family, or the modern type. Only slightly less than 4 percent of the respondents chose the "community-oriented" statement as the overriding goal of life.

In this survey, as in others, it is interesting to note that only a small percentage of respondents cited accumulation of wealth as their primary goal. At first glance this may appear contradictory to the trend toward materialism discussed earlier. Further analysis would indicate however, that these replies are not inconsistent. After all, opportunities for amassing a large fortune are extremely limited in contemporary Japan. This is particularly true for salary and wage earners. Moreover, even if it were possible, realization of such a goal would require a high risk and enormous effort. The basic aspiration of an average citizen is a comfortable middle-class

[38] *Ibid.*, p. 41.

life. Surely, an average citizen is becoming increasingly materialistic in his basic orientation, but all he could reasonably aspire to
are sufficient material comforts to enable him to maintain a re-
spectable middle-class life.

Table 2.24 sheds further light by presenting the same data

TABLE 2.24

LIFE ASPIRATIONS OF TOKYO RESPONDENTS
CLASSIFIED ACCORDING TO OCCUPATION AND AGE, 1968

(N = 1,098)

| Occupation | Total | Statement 3 | Statement 5 | Others |
|---|---|---|---|---|
| | | Percent of Total | | |
| Proprietors | 100%<br>(206) | 30.6 | 47.1 | 22.3 |
| White-Collar<br>Workers | 100%<br>(238) | 31.1 | 44.1 | 24.8 |
| Blue-Collar<br>Workers | 100%<br>(237) | 24.5 | 44.7 | 30.8 |
| Housewives | 100%<br>(338) | 10.7 | 67.8 | 21.6 |
| Others | 100%<br>( 79) | 31.6 | 34.2 | 34.2 |
| *Age* | | | | |
| 20–29 | 100%<br>(374) | 27.8 | 41.7 | 30.5 |
| 30–39 | 100%<br>(326) | 25.5 | 56.6 | 17.8 |
| 40–49 | 100%<br>(198) | 20.7 | 56.1 | 23.2 |
| 50–59 | 100%<br>(200) | 13.5 | 56.5 | 30.0 |

Source: *Seikatsu Ishiki ni Kansuru Kenkyu [A Study of Views on Life]*
(Tokyo: Kokumin Seikatsu Kenkyujo, 1969), p. 45.

classified according to major occupation groups and age categories.
As might be expected, those choosing statement 5 were most
numerous among housewives, but it is interesting to note that 47
percent, 44 percent, and 45 percent of individual proprietors, white-
collar workers, and blue-collar workers, respectively, have also
chosen this statement. As for breakdowns according to age groups,
over 56 percent of all but those in their twenties chose the family-
oriented goal.

Closely related to this is the changing attitude toward work and leisure. The aforementioned study of behavior of consumers in Tokyo and Osaka conducted by Kokumin Seikatsu Kenkyujo included a question designed to probe the respondent's attitude toward work and leisure. It asked each respondent to identify one among the following six statements that came closest to his view:

1. Work is duty; therefore, I must work to the limit of my time.
2. One should work diligently during his working hours, but one should forget his work, and play during off-duty hours.
3. Work is only a means to livelihood. I do an adequate amount of work, then enjoy myself as much as possible.
4. Work is a form of enjoyment. I have not particularly felt like taking time off from work to enjoy myself.
5. I like to work, but I devote adequate time for rest and recreation to store up enough energy for work.
6. One cannot determine the course of one's life, so he should simply do what he wants at a given moment. (Includes "don't know.")

The study revealed some very interesting results. As can be seen in Table 2.25, only a small minority of respondents accepted

TABLE 2.25

ATTITUDES TOWARD WORK AND LEISURE, 1965

| City | Total % (no. of respon- dents) | Percentage of Respondents Choosing Each Statement | | | | | |
|------|------|------|------|------|------|------|------|
| | | State- ment 1 | State- ment 2 | State- ment 3 | State- ment 4 | State- ment 5 | State- ment 6 |
| Tokyo | 100 (691) | 16.2 | 41.2 | 6.7 | 9.6 | 21.6 | 4.8 |
| Osaka | 100 (686) | 19.2 | 37.3 | 7.0 | 9.0 | 20.6 | 6.9 |

Source: *Toshi ni Okeru Shohisha no Ishiki to Kōdō [Consumers' Orientation and Behavior in Large Cities]* (Tokyo: Kokumin Seikatsu Kenkyujo, 1965), p. 32.

the traditional, almost Puritanlike commitment to work as one's duty to the society. Significantly, over 40 percent of the respondents took a balanced view between work and relaxation. They tended to compartmentalize work, on one hand, and rest, recreation, and relaxation, on the other.

There is a rather clear-cut difference in the response patterns between age groups. For example, as evident in Table 2.26, among the Tokyo respondents less than 4 percent of those in their twenties considered work as their duty to the society, whereas over a third of those in their fifties agreed with the statement. Occupational breakdowns also reveal some interesting insights, as indicated by Table 2.27. As might be expected, the highest percentage of the respondents who chose the second statement are found among white-collar workers. While a similar trend is found for both Tokyo and Osaka respondents, it is interesting that the Osaka respondents tend to be more conservative. This is likely to stem from long-standing differences in cultural heritage between the two urban centers.

The average person's attitude toward life has undergone a considerable change between the prewar and postwar years. This is evident in the comparison of nationwide surveys among a sample of the male population who came of age in 1931, 1941, and 1964. The three surveys, though administered in different settings, contained a number of common questions. The data collection method differed somewhat among the three surveys, which unfortunately makes strict comparison of the results impossible. The surveys are still useful, however, in indicating the trend. Particularly significant from our point of view are the differences in the responses to the following question common to the three surveys:

Please choose one statement among the following which most closely approximates your goal in life:

1. To become extremely wealthy.
2. To become famous.
3. Do not aspire to become wealthy or famous, but to live according to the dictates of one's desire and taste.
4. Live day by day without becoming overconcerned about the future.
5. To lead a clean life.
6. To forget about oneself, and to devote oneself to the good of the society.

The responses to the question are presented in Table 2.28.

The data reveal a very clear-cut trend toward individualism and privatization among the postwar youth. As high as 67 percent of the postwar youth chose either statement 3 or 4, as contrasted to 16 percent and 6 percent of the prewar generations. Only 2 percent of the postwar generation as contrasted to 24 percent and 30 per-

## TABLE 2.26

### ATTITUDE TOWARD WORK ACCORDING TO AGE, 1965

(percent of respondents agreeing with each statement)

| Age | Statement 1 | | Statement 2 | | Statement 3 | | Statement 4 | | Statement 5 | | Statement 6 | |
|---|---|---|---|---|---|---|---|---|---|---|---|---|
| | Tokyo | Osaka | Tokyo | Osaka | Tokyo | Osaka | Tokyo | Osaka | Tokyo | Osaka | Tokyo | Osaka |
| 20–29 | 3.8 | 13.2 | 52.3 | 43.6 | 5.7 | 5.9 | 6.9 | 5.9 | 26.0 | 25.5 | 5.3 | 5.9 |
| 30–39 | 17.0 | 21.2 | 36.2 | 38.9 | 7.1 | 7.5 | 13.2 | 8.4 | 22.5 | 19.5 | 3.8 | 4.0 |
| 40–49 | 25.0 | 21.5 | 35.6 | 35.5 | 7.5 | 8.2 | 8.8 | 12.6 | 17.5 | 17.0 | – | 5.1 |
| 50–59 | 34.5 | 22.9 | 28.7 | 25.4 | 6.9 | 6.6 | 11.5 | 11.5 | 13.8 | 18.0 | 4.5 | 12.3 |
| Total | 16.2 | 19.2 | 41.2 | 37.3 | 6.7 | 7.0 | 9.6 | 9.0 | 21.6 | 20.6 | 4.8 | 6.9 |

Source: *Toshi ni Okeru Shohisha no Ishiki to Kōdō [Consumers' Orientation and Behavior in Large Cities]* (Tokyo: Kokumin Seikatsu Kenkyujo, 1965), p. 71.

## TABLE 2.27

### ATTITUDE TOWARD WORK ACCORDING TO MAJOR OCCUPATIONAL CATEGORY, 1965

(percent of respondents agreeing with each statement)

| Occupation | Statement 1 | | Statement 2 | | Statement 3 | | Statement 4 | | Statement 5 | | Statement 6 | |
|---|---|---|---|---|---|---|---|---|---|---|---|---|
| | Tokyo | Osaka | Tokyo | Osaka | Tokyo | Osaka | Tokyo | Osaka | Tokyo | Osaka | Tokyo | Osaka |
| Individual Proprietors | 17.7 | 37.0 | 32.9 | 21.0 | 8.9 | 8.6 | 25.3 | 12.7 | 19.7 | 8.6 | 2.5 | 4.4 |
| Self-Employed | 18.5 | 32.8 | 44.4 | 28.6 | 11.1 | 4.8 | 7.4 | 14.8 | 33.3 | 4.8 | 3.7 | 4.8 |
| Managerial Employees | 31.5 | 11.1 | 59.0 | 44.4 | — | — | 9.1 | — | 33.3 | 11.1 | — | — |
| Skilled Employees | 11.5 | 15.2 | 52.5 | 39.1 | 8.2 | 4.3 | 21.3 | 3.3 | 34.8 | 6.5 | 3.2 | — |
| Clerical Employees | 13.5 | 17.6 | 44.2 | 44.0 | 2.9 | 3.3 | 29.8 | 23.1 | 8.7 | 7.7 | 1.0 | 4.4 |
| Laborers | 23.1 | 20.6 | 41.7 | 38.3 | 8.8 | 7.1 | 19.8 | 5.5 | 19.8 | 6.4 | 1.1 | 7.8 |
| Housewives | 16.2 | 14.8 | 35.5 | 38.3 | 7.0 | 8.3 | 21.1 | 12.7 | 17.4 | 13.9 | 7.5 | 7.4 |
| Others | 8.9 | 15.5 | 46.8 | 43.1 | 5.1 | 10.3 | 19.0 | 8.9 | 12.1 | 1.7 | 13.4 | 17.2 |
| Total | 16.2 | 19.2 | 41.2 | 37.3 | 6.7 | 7.0 | 21.6 | 9.6 | 20.6 | 9.0 | 21.6 | 6.9 |

Source: *Toshi ni Okeru Shohisha no Ishiki to Kōdō [Consumers' Orientation and Behavior in Large Cities]* (Tokyo: Kokumin Seikatsu Kenkyujo, 1965), p. 71.

TABLE 2.28

PREWAR AND POSTWAR COMPARISON OF ATTITUDE TOWARD LIFE

| Year | Percentage Choosing Statement | | | | | | | |
|------|----|----|----|----|----|----|----------------------|-----|
|      | 1  | 2  | 3  | 4  | 5  | 6  | Others and Don't Know | All |
| 1931 | 19 | 9  | 12 | 4  | 32 | 24 | 0 | 100 |
| 1941 | 9  | 5  | 5  | 1  | 41 | 30 | 9 | 100 |
| 1964 | 10 | 2  | 50 | 17 | 16 | 2  | 3 | 100 |

Source: *A Study of Japanese National Character* (Tokyo: The Research Committee of Japanese National Character, 1966), p. 22.

cent, for answers in 1931 and 1941, respectively, chose statement 6, self-sacrifice for the sake of the society, as their goal in life. There is a clear indication that high achievement orientation, which traditionally characterized the prewar generation, now tends to be replaced by greater emphasis on the search for private comforts and enjoyment. Many Japanese youths have learned to tailor their ambitions to their realistic prospects and have begun to attach greater importance to family life and middle-class amenities than to career or professional success. These trends are indeed disturbing to older generations, who are still vocal in Japan. They deplore what Dore calls "the privatized pettiness of the young men who have lowered their sights to a cosy little home in the suburbs, a pretty wife, a couple of kids and the occasional game of golf." They also object to "the meanness of these aims, but also to the consumption orientation revealed in the openness with which so many young men nowadays acknowledge them."[39] These trends, however, appear to be too strong to be checked merely by the cries and deplorations of the traditionalists.

As we have seen in this section, the trend toward greater emphasis on individualism and the search for private comforts and enjoyment is very much approved. These developments have far-reaching marketing implications. For one thing, an individual can now exercise more freedom in his purchasing decisions. He or she is less constrained financially as well as culturally by the will of the collectivity. Also, these developments encourage consumption orientation designed to enrich a person's daily life and that of his immediate family. The trend toward individualism and privatiza-

[39] Dore, "Mobility, Equality and Individuation," p. 141.

tion, working hand in hand with materialistic consumption orientation, has reinforced the demand for consumer goods, particularly consumer durables.

One point worth noting in this connection is that there are indications of a more generalized type of group pressure emerging to replace the specific and rather narrow collectivity orientation. This is a growing trend toward social class consciousness. Social class, as viewed in the Western context, had been less important in Japan, since in traditional Japan one was forced to accept a specific set of collectivities whose norms he was compelled to respect. Moreover, one's status and position within this narrow and rather specific collectivity were prescribed for him. With weakening of the traditional collectivity orientation, the Japanese may well now turn to the social class as their reference group. This trend is further reinforced by the development of the very extensive mass communication system in Japan. One's reference group is no longer imposed by a specific collectivity. One now enjoys a considerable amount of discretion in selecting his own reference group and the degree to which he wishes to be identified with this group. Admittedly, this observation is still in the realm of hypothesis, but it would be very interesting to investigate the implication of this apparent change in the realm of consumer behavior.

## The Emergence of Egalitarian Values

Premodern Japanese society was highly structured and rigidly hierarchical. Hierarchy, ascription of status at birth, and status by group affiliation were extremely important to an individual. Everyone was prescribed a station in life and a very specific code of conduct, and he was expected to behave in a way appropriate to that status. The formal hierarchical class structure was abolished at the time of the Meiji Restoration (1868); the attainment of higher status through ability and achievement then became possible. In fact, upward mobility has become an openly emphasized aspect of modern Japanese society.[40] Industrialization and urbanization also helped loosen the very rigid social structure. Despite these developments in prewar Japan, hierarchical orientation remained strong. Since the end of World War II, however, the combined forces of the democratic reforms and great economic growth have significantly weakened the traditional pattern, giving

[40] *Ibid.*, pp. 113–150.

rise to egalitarian value orientation. For example, hereditary factors have all but disappeared as a basis for status determination. Indeed, the allocation of income, prestige, and power now depends, to a much greater degree, on demonstrated ability than on prescribed status. Several factors have contributed to this development. Postwar economic growth, with its benefits widely diffused, has given the masses a degree of economic independence beyond the fondest dreams of a generation ago. Land reforms have contributed greatly to the democratization of a very conservative and hierarchically based rural social structure. Unionization of the labor force and the dominance of salaried professional managers closed the status gap between management and labor.

The status gap between male and female, which had been quite striking up through World War II, has been closed considerably. Under the new Constitution women have been given equal rights and status. Women are now active in a number of professional and occupational activities that previously had been closed to them. The number of women seeking higher education has increased significantly in postwar years. In 1967 over 70 percent of some 269,000 students attending two-year colleges were women. In the same year women accounted for 17 percent of the 1.1 million students attending four-year colleges and universities.[41]

Another interesting development is the trend toward rapidly increasing opportunities for part-time employment for housewives, whose ability to earn extra income had been limited traditionally to extremely menial piecework that could be performed at home. It is estimated that there are now more than one million working wives in Japan. In 1968, for example, the income reported by employed housewives in wage earners' households showed a 21 percent increase over 1967.[42]

Along with the factors already observed, we should note two additional forces that have significantly strengthened egalitarian value orientation. One is popularization of higher education beyond the compulsory level and the other is the phenomenal development of mass communication. Compulsory education has been lengthened to nine years. More important, by 1967 over 76 percent of those completing the compulsory education are going on for another three years of schooling, in contrast to 52 percent in

41 *Keizai Yoran, 1969 [A Summary of Economic Statistics, 1969]*, p. 287.
42 *Kokumin Seikatsu Hakusho, Showa 44 nen ban [White Paper on National Life, 1969]*, pp. 22–23.

1956. Nearly a fourth of those completing twelve years of education are going on to college, in contrast to 16 percent in 1956.[43]

The rapid development of mass communication in recent years has also had great impact on the diffusion of egalitarian values. In 1968 there were 118 daily newspapers with a combined circulation of over 33.7 million,[44] or one daily for slightly over three persons, or 1.25 newspapers per household. The circulation of the morning edition of the *Asahi*, the leading daily, alone exceeded five million copies in 1968. In 1968 there were 1,398 different types of monthly magazines which in aggregate published some 724 million copies. Also during the same year there were 42 weekly magazines, with 943 million copies per year.[45] It is estimated that some 32 million radios are in use in Japan.[46] Over 96 percent of the householders own a television set, and over 10 percent of the families own multiple sets.

*Masu Komi*, a newly coined Japanese term for mass communication, has indeed had a tremendous impact on postwar Japanese society. While some say that the Japanese now suffer from mass media hypnosis, widespread diffusion of information has indeed contributed to strengthening egalitarian values by bridging regional, status, and class gaps in contemporary Japanese society. These developments have made the already homogeneous Japanese even more so. Indeed, homogeneity is one of the most basic and important characteristics of Japanese society.

The emergence of egalitarian value orientation is affecting almost every aspect of life in Japan. This is nowhere more evident than in relationships among family members in modern Japan. Hierarchical orientation, clear-cut division of responsibilities among family members occupying different prescribed roles, and the highly authoritarian family head are things of the past. Rather, cooperative and democratic patterns dominate most Japanese families.

This trend is well depicted in the decision-making patterns of urban households as reported in the study of Tokyo housewives cited earlier. Respondents were asked to indicate who in their

---

[43] *Monbu Tokei Yoran, Showa 42 nen ban [A Summary of Educational Statistics, 1967]* (Tokyo: The Ministry of Education, 1968), p. 8.

[44] *Dentsu Kōkoku Nenkan, 1969 [The Dentsu Advertising Annual, 1969] 1969]* (Tokyo: Dentsu Advertising Agency, 1969), p. 111.

[45] *Ibid.*, p. 115.

[46] *Ibid.*, p. 120.

family made the following types of decisions: savings, daily shopping, the purchase of consumer durables, the selection of gifts, and children's education. The results are presented in Table 2.29.

TABLE 2.29

FAMILY DECISION-MAKING PATTERNS, 1966:
Family Member Primarily Responsible for Selected Types of Decisions

(percent of total sample of 1,808)

| Type of Decision | Parents or Parents-in-Law | Hus-band | Wife | Chil-dren | Others | Consul-tation | Don't Know |
|---|---|---|---|---|---|---|---|
| Savings | 0.9 | 30.1 | 40.4 | 1.4 | 1.7 | 24.3 | 1.2 |
| Daily Shopping | 1.9 | 0.9 | 92.3 | 1.3 | 0.7 | 2.4 | 0.5 |
| Purchase of Consumer Durables | 0.4 | 20.8 | 25.8 | 1.9 | 0.7 | 48.9 | 1.4 |
| Selection of Gifts | 1.8 | 8.2 | 45.6 | 0.8 | 1.4 | 41.2 | 1.1 |
| Education of Children | 0.2 | 11.3 | 28.8 | 2.4 | 2.9 | 48.9 | 5.5 |

Source: *Shohisha no Seikatsu Ishiki to Shohi Chochiku Kōdō ni Kansuru Kenkyu [A Study of Consumers' Attitudes Toward Consumption and Savings]* (Tokyo: Kokumin Seikatsu Kenkyūjo, 1967), p. 50.

In daily shopping, as might be expected, housewives hold the undisputedly dominant voice. It is interesting to note, however, that in the purchase of consumer durables and matters relating to children's education, nearly half of the respondents reported that decisions were made on the basis of consultation among family members. In the selection of gifts 41 percent of respondents also reported consultation.

The emerging egalitarian value system is not confined solely to family relationships but applies even to the society as a whole. A striking indication of the emergence of the egalitarian values in contemporary Japan is revealed in a nationwide government-sponsored opinion survey conducted every year.[47] One of the questions asked respondents to indicate what social class they identified themselves with. In the 1967 survey as high as 88 percent (6 percent upper middle, 53 percent mid-middle and 29 percent lower middle) of 16,358 respondents perceived themselves as be-

[47] *Kokumin Seikatsu ni Kansuru Seron Chōsa, Showa 43 nen [A Public Opinion Survey on National Life, 1968]*, p. 7.

longing to the middle class. Only 1 percent said they belonged to the upper class and 7 percent to the lower class. The others (4 percent) said they did not know. More than half of the respondents viewed themselves as belonging to the middle of the middle class. Also significant is the fact that those who identified with the middle class have increased from 72 percent to 88 percent in the past decade.

Precise definition of social class is obviously difficult, but it is interesting to note that 88 percent of the nationwide sample viewed themselves as belonging to the middle class. As indicated in Table 2.30, the respondents who identified themselves as belonging to the middle class cut across various occupational categories.

TABLE 2.30

RESPONDENTS CLAIMING TO BELONG TO SOCIAL CLASS,
BY MAJOR OCCUPATIONAL CATEGORY, 1968

| | *Percent in Social Class* | | | | | |
|---|---|---|---|---|---|---|
| *Major Occupational Categories* | *Upper and Upper Middle Class* | *Middle Middle Class* | *Lower Middle Class* | *Lower Class* | *Don't Know* | *Total* |
| Farming and Fishery | 6 | 52 | 29 | 8 | 5 | 100 |
| Proprietors | 11 | 57 | 24 | 5 | 3 | 100 |
| White-Collar Employees | 9 | 64 | 22 | 2 | 3 | 100 |
| Blue-Collar Employees | 2 | 44 | 38 | 11 | 5 | 100 |
| All | 7 | 52 | 31 | 7 | 3 | 100 |

Source: *Kokumin Seikatsu ni Kansuru Seron Chosa [A Public Opinion Survey on National Life, 1968]* (Tokyo: The Office of the Prime Minister, 1969), p. 8.

What impact has the shift toward egalitarian values had on the behavior of contemporary Japanese as consumers? While still in the realm of hypothesis, it may be noted that the average Japanese is now less constrained in his consumption pattern by a web of prescribed hierarchical relationships in his narrow social nexus. Previously, a consumer might have been reluctant to purchase a particular product, even if he had been financially capable of doing so, for fear of social disapproval for possessing goods deemed incompatible with his station in life. Now, however, he is less concerned with keeping his consumption pattern and behavior in line with any prescribed status. Opportunities for upward social mobility are now widely diffused, and it is legitimate for *everyone* to aspire for a higher social and economic status and to improve his material welfare. This change in attitude is very apparent in the rapidly increasing aspiration level of an average Japanese consumer.

### Westernization

Another noteworthy development in contemporary Japan is a trend toward Westernization. Throughout her history Japan has borrowed heavily, though selectively, from foreign cultures. Chinese influence was especially profound throughout the premodern era; throughout the modern period, Western culture, particularly its technological component, has played a key role. Despite extensive cultural borrowing throughout the nation's history, Japan has retained much of its own tradition and has adapted what it did borrow from other cultures to fit its own traditions and needs. The Japanese have shown an amazing degree of flexibility and have felt nothing incongruent with selective acceptance of foreign cultures.

Although Western, particularly American, influence has been very pervasive in almost every aspect of life since the end of World War II, it has been especially evident in the daily living pattern. Let us examine a few examples to identify the extent to which Westernization has progressed in postwar Japan.

TABLE 2.31

GROWTH OF PER HOUSEHOLD CONSUMPTION OF
SELECTED WESTERN-TYPE FOOD PRODUCTS, 1963–1968

(100g except when otherwise indicated)

| Items | 1963 | 1964 | 1965 | 1966 | 1967 | 1968 |
|---|---|---|---|---|---|---|
| Fresh Milk | | | | | | |
| (bottles 180 cc) | 322.20 | 375.10 | 389.20 | 432.90 | 458.70 | 483.80 |
| Cheese | 3.59 | 4.07 | 5.16 | 7.02 | 8.08 | 9.89 |
| Mayonnaise | 13.42 | 15.58 | 17.50 | 19.62 | 20.82 | 23.87 |
| Catsup | 7.48 | 8.96 | 9.35 | 10.75 | 11.18 | 11.35 |
| Coffee | 1.84 | 2.07 | 2.44 | 2.62 | 3.03 | 3.32 |
| Lettuce | – | – | 12.93 | 16.52 | 20.65 | 26.70 |
| Whiskey (100 ml) | 7.32 | 8.18 | 8.77 | 11.72 | 13.21 | 15.63 |

Source: Adapted from *Annual Report on the Family Income and Expenditure Survey, 1968* (Tokyo: The Office of the Prime Minister, 1969), pp. 206–243.

We have previously noted changes in the dietary habits of the Japanese in recent years. Western types of foods have become commonplace in the daily diet of an average Japanese. As can be seen in Table 2.31, the use of some Western-type food products experienced a significant increase between 1963 and 1968. At the same time, it is noteworthy that the consumption of rice, soy sauce, and miso (bean paste), considered essential to traditional Japanese diets, is steadily declining.

Equally significant is a trend toward Western-style living patterns. This trend is partially evidenced by the diffusion of Western-style furniture as indicated in Table 2.32, and occurs in all

TABLE 2.32

OWNERSHIP OF SELECTED WESTERN-STYLE FURNITURE AMONG HOUSEHOLDS ACCORDING TO MAJOR OCCUPATIONAL CATEGORIES, 1966 and 1968

| Occupational Categories | Western-Style Items (percent of households) | | | | | |
| | Living Room Sets | | Dining Room Sets | | Beds | |
| | 1966 | 1968 | 1966 | 1968 | 1966 | 1968 |
|---|---|---|---|---|---|---|
| All Households | 14.1 | 17.8 | 18.9 | 21.0 | 14.6 | 18.7 |
| Farmers | 3.9 | 9.1 | 3.7 | 9.5 | 5.1 | 8.0 |
| Wage Earners | 16.4 | 20.1 | 18.0 | 24.3 | 17.1 | 21.3 |
| Individual Proprietors and Others | 19.2 | 21.7 | 15.3 | 25.6 | 18.5 | 23.7 |

Source: For 1966 data, Economic Planning Agency, *Shohi to Chochiku no Dōkō: Showa 41 nen* [*A Survey of Consumption and Savings, 1966*] (Tokyo: Economic Planning Agency, 1966), p. 77. For 1968 data, the 1968 version of the same publication.

occupational groups. Table 2.33 shows a very definite relationship between income level and ownership of Western-style furniture.

In many of the new homes constructed in recent years, Western architectural features are incorporated extensively. Clothing style has also undergone a significant change; Western-style clothing now dominates the Japanese scene.

The previously cited survey of Tokyo housewives included a series of questions to measure the degree of Westernization in several aspects of their daily life. The study attempted to find out from each respondent her present practice and future plans in each of these areas. Key findings are summarized in Table 2.34. The data

86    CHAPTER TWO

TABLE 2.33

Ownership of Selected Western-Style Furniture Among
Households According to Income Groups, 1968

| Monthly Income Categories | Western-Style Items (percent of households) | | |
|---|---|---|---|
| | Living Room Furniture | Dining Room Sets | Beds |
| Less than ¥30,000 | 3.9 | 3.3 | 1.5 |
| ¥30,000–59,999 | 6.8 | 9.6 | 9.2 |
| ¥60,000–89,999 | 13.1 | 19.1 | 17.9 |
| ¥90,000–119,999 | 21.4 | 27.0 | 28.7 |
| ¥120,000–149,999 | 33.2 | 32.7 | 28.7 |
| ¥150,000–179,999 | 41.7 | 41.3 | 32.7 |
| More than ¥180,000 | 60.3 | 53.3 | 46.6 |
| All Households | 17.8 | 21.0 | 18.7 |

Source: *Shohi to Chochiku no Dōkō: Showa 43 nen [A Survey of Consumption and Savings, 1968]* (Tokyo: The Economic Planning Agency, 1968), p. 109.

TABLE 2.34

The Westernization Trend in Selected Items Among Tokyo Households, 1966

| Style | Percent of Sample of 1,808 Households | | | | |
|---|---|---|---|---|---|
| | Type of Breakfast | Clothing Worn at Home | Dining Room Sets | Sleeping Equipment | Attire for Wedding |
| Western Style | 17.8 | 66.1 | 22.2 | 6.5 | 12.2 |
| Japanese Style | 68.3 | 21.6 | 71.2 | 86.6 | 83.5 |
| Mixture of the Two | 13.3 | 9.1 | 6.1 | 7.4 | 3.5 |
| Don't Know | 0.6 | 3.2 | 0.5 | 0.6 | 0.8 |
| Total | 100.0 | 100.0 | 100.0 | 100.0 | 100.0 |

Source: Adapted from *Shohisha no Seikatsu Ishiki to Shohi Chochiku Kodo ni Kansuru Kenkyu [A Study of Consumers' Attitudes Toward Consumption and Savings]* (Tokyo: Kokumin Seikatsu Kenkyujo, 1967), pp. 45–46.

must be interpreted with some caution, since the survey was confined to Tokyo housewives. Nevertheless, it reveals some interesting results concerning the trend toward Westernization. For example, nearly 18 percent of the respondents said that they ate Western-style breakfasts regularly, 66 percent wore Western-type clothing regularly at home, 22 percent had Western-style dining rooms sets, and 6.5 percent slept on beds.[48] The study was undertaken in 1966; therefore, it is reasonable to believe that the Westernization trend has now progressed even further. It is interesting to note that there is considerable variation among the items listed. The Westernization trend is most apparent in clothing and least in the use of beds. Noteworthy is the overwhelming majority of respondents (83.5 percent) who said that they prefer to wear the traditional kimono for weddings and other ceremonies and would continue to do so in the future.

Thus, amidst a strong Westernization trend there appears to be a significant exception. This is a desire to retain selectively certain aspects of the Japanese tradition for special or ceremonial occasions. The Westernization trend has not replaced, and is not likely to replace completely, the traditional mode of living. Rather, with growing discretionary income, the Japanese have begun to develop dual patterns. They selectively have adopted Western styles of living, but at the same time have retained their traditions for certain occasions to enrich their lives. This stems from a view that although the Western mode of living is highly functional and well suited for daily living, at least in the Japanese view it lacks the beauty and charm associated with things that are traditionally Japanese. This is nowhere more apparent than in the area of clothing. For work the Japanese have almost totally adopted more functional Western types of clothing, but for ceremonial occasions they still prefer the traditional kimono. This is very evident in the increase in household expenditures for kimonos. In 1968, for example, there was a 15.5 percent increase in spending for kimonos over 1967, while the increase in the total expenditure for clothing was around 10 percent.[49]

### Problems Facing Japanese Consumers

Despite a tremendous improvement in the standard of living of an average citizen, there are many problems that remain unsolved. An examination of the emerging mass consumption market in Japan is incomplete without at least a look at some of the major problems that still plague an average consumer. While the material

[48] Shohisha no Seikatsu Ishiki to Shohi Chochiku Kodo ni Kansuru Kenkyu [A Study of Consumers' Attitudes Toward Consumption and Savings] (Tokyo: Kokumin Seikatsu Kenkyujo, 1967) pp. 45–47.
[49] Annual Report on the Family Income and Expenditure Survey, 1968, p. 15.

progress made by an average Japanese consumer during the last decade has been remarkable by any standard, the rapid economic growth and the accelerating trend of urbanization have resulted in some imbalances, creating new problems. Despite continued prosperity, there are still some 660,000 families, or over a million and a half people, dependent on government welfare of some sort.[50]

Although economic progress has been very rapid in recent years, per capita annual income in Japan is only slightly over $1,100, considerably lower than that of other highly industrialized societies. For the fiscal year 1969, Japan ranked second in the Free World in terms of the GNP, but in terms of per capita income it was still fifteenth, falling behind such countries as Denmark, New Zealand, and Australia.

Perhaps the utmost concern to an average Japanese, particularly in urban areas, has been housing. Wartime destruction of homes (some 2.7 million homes were destroyed), population increase, and a trend toward urbanization and toward nuclear families have combined to create a tremendous demand for housing. The great majority of those who live in urban areas are crowded into small quarters. The living space of an average residence in Tokyo is less than 500 square feet.

Despite government efforts to build low-rent apartment complexes, the problem is far from solved. Soaring real estate prices in cities forced the urban population to the suburbs, and many must commute great distances to work every day. A recent survey reveals that over 50 percent of those living in publicly financed housing developments must spend at least an hour each way commuting to work.[51] A survey conducted in 1967 by the Toyko city government revealed that 41 percent of the respondents were dissatisfied with the housing conditions in Toyko.[52]

In addition to the housing shortage, public facilities such as roads and sewers are glaringly inadequate, and Japanese urban centers, like those of other nations, suffer from traffic congestion, air and water pollution, a high noise level, and other urban ills. Road conditions, for example, are just about the worst in any

[50] *Kokumin Seikatsu Hakusho, Showa 44 nen ban [White Paper on National Life, 1969]*, p. 31.

[51] *Kokumin Seikatsu Hakusho, Showa 41 nen ban [White Paper on National Life, 1966]* (Tokyo: The Economic Planning Agency, 1966), p. 54.

[52] *Kokumin Seikatsu Hakusho, Showa 42 nen ban [White Paper on National Life, 1967]* (Tokyo: The Economic Planning Agency, 1967), p. 14.

industrialized country. Despite the presence of superhighways in some areas, only about a fourth of the national and prefectural highways are paved, and in all areas less than 11 percent of the roads are paved.[53] In the Toyko metropolitan area, only 11 percent of the total area is devoted to roads, as compared to 43 percent in Washington, D. C., and 35 percent in New York City.[54] Construction of new roads and improvement of the existing ones have fallen behind the very rapid rate of increase in automobile ownership, and traffic congestion in large urban centers has become very serious. The number of traffic accidents has been steadily increasing. For example, in 1968, there were some 635,000 traffic accidents, in which more than 14,000 people were killed and nearly 830,000 were injured.[55]

Public expenditure for infrastructure sadly has lagged behind the need. Furthermore, Japan's welfare and social security measures are still very inadequate. Per capita annual expenditure for social welfare is by far the lowest among industrialized nations. Thus the very rapid postwar economic growth has created some serious imbalances. In some aspects the Japanese enjoy a very high standard of living, while in others it is considerably lower than the level enjoyed by citizens of other advanced nations. In terms of ownership of consumer durables, the diffusion of mass communication, and educational standards, Japan ranks among the world leaders; but in terms of such things as roads, social welfare, and housing, it still has a long way to go.

Another serious problem confronting Japanese consumers is a mild inflationary pressure, resulting in part from the aggressive growth policy followed by the government. During the last several years the consumer price index has been increasing continuously. Between 1965 and 1969 it increased as much as 23 percent. Understandably, checking this inflationary trend is a concern of the utmost importance to many consumers. In the government survey quoted earlier, 56 percent of the respondents indicated that this problem deserved the first priority in government policies.[56]

In this chapter we have reviewed in some detail the emergence

[53] *Kokumin Seikatsu Hakusho, Showa 44 nen ban [White Paper on National Life, 1969]*, p. 399.
[54] *Ibid.*, p. 396.
[55] *Ibid.*, p. 66.
[56] *Kokumin Seikatsu ni Kansuru Seron Chōsa, Showa 42 nen [A Public Opinion Survey on National Life, 1967]*, p. 18.

of a mass consumer market in postwar Japan. We have noted that rapid economic growth and social reforms have interacted in a most powerful way to create a mass consumption society. Once created, of course, this burgeoning development has become a powerful instrument for further social and economic changes. Its impact has been most keenly felt by Japan's traditional marketing system.

# 3

# Marketing Behavior
# of Large Manufacturing Firms

Having analyzed the emergence of the mass consumption market in Japan, we shall now examine how various elements in the marketing system responded to this all-important phenomenon. In this chapter we shall analyze the adaptive behavior of large manufacturing firms. It is highly significant that these firms were the first to recognize and seize upon opportunities in the rising mass consumer market. Marking a rather basic departure from their prewar pattern, they have now become actively involved in marketing. In the process they have made significant changes in their organizational structure, policies, and management outlook in their efforts to transform themselves into marketing-oriented firms. In fact, their very aggressive marketing actions have further encouraged the growth of the mass consumer market in Japan. Let us now consider in detail the specific ways in which large consumer goods manufacturers have responded to the rapidly expanding mass consumer market, and the problems that they have encountered in this process.

## Forces for Change

Until the end of World War II, large manufacturing firms, the great majority of which belonged to a handful of Zaibatsu (family-owned and controlled diversified financial and industrial combines), confined their activities primarily to heavy industries of a strategic nature. This pattern was determined initially by the circumstances under which Japan's industrialization began, and later was perpetuated by the mercantilistic ideology espoused by the political elite as well. The limited consumer market was served by a myriad of highly fragmented small manufacturers and merchants. There existed a rather clear-cut line of demarcation between large-scale strategic industries controlled by a handful of Zaibatsu, on the one hand, and numerous small firms serving the highly fragmented consumer market on the other. In the latter, large wholesalers dominated the scene, occupying a pivotal position in both the production and distribution of consumer goods.

The success of the firms in strategic industries depended largely on their ability to satisfy the needs of a limited number of customers, the most important of which was the military establishment. True, certain types of sales functions were necessary even under these circumstances, particularly since each of the leading Zaibatsu was highly diversified and competed against the others in a number of industries and products. Given the conditions prevailing in prewar Japan, however, technical capacities of the firm, political connections, and personal ties were often the overriding factors in making sales. In addition, the fact that the major Zaibatsu were highly integrated, with strong interdependence among member firms, and with each of the subsidiary firms typically deriving a substantial portion of its sales from intragroup transactions, further minimized the need for active marketing efforts. The very organization of the Zaibatsu made it unnecessary for its manufacturing component to perform active marketing functions. A major Zaibatsu typically consisted of the holding company at its helm and a number of manufacturing subsidiaries, financial institutions, and a trading company, with clear-cut functional specialization of these units. Manufacturing subsidiaries confined their activities solely to production of goods, while the trading company, supported by powerful financial institutions, not only served as the sales and procurement agent for the manufacturing arm but often played a critical organizational and coordinating role within the group.

The situation in which large manufacturing firms found themselves in the aftermath of World War II was radically different from that of the prewar period. The Zaibatsu were dissolved by the Occupation, and each of the former subsidiaries now became an independent concern. Once-strong intercorporate ties were severed, at least formally. Moreover, the two prominent Zaibatsu trading firms, Mitsui Bussan and Mitsubishi Shoji, were dissolved into hundreds of fragmented independent corporations, forcing former manufacturing subsidiaries of these two prominent Zaibatsu to assume many of the marketing functions previously performed by their respective trading companies. In addition, the total loss of the military market meant that these large manufacturing firms now had to shift completely to peacetime industries. Most of the former Zaibatsu manufacturing firms have achieved this difficult transition with considerable effectiveness. It should also be noted that the dissolution of the well-entrenched Zaibatsu system encouraged rapid growth of non-Zaibatsu firms in postwar Japan. In a number of industries, particularly in consumer-related fields, these firms without traditional ties have been most innovative, particularly in their approaches to marketing, and have attained a commanding position in their respective industries.

We noted in Chapter 1 that the development of full-scale consumer industries has been a very recent phenomenon. Within a rather short period of time—less than a decade and a half in most cases—Japanese consumer industries have gained maturity with the aggressive entry of large-scale manufacturing firms. To illustrate the very rapid growth of consumer industries in postwar Japan, let us consider two prime examples: electric home appliances and automobiles.

The electric home appliance industry in prewar Japan was still in its infancy, manufacturing only a small number of very rudimentary products such as radios, electric irons, and electric fans. The diffusion of electric home appliances was very limited, as can be seen from the following statistics. As late as in 1938 only 12,215 refrigerators, 6,610 vacuum cleaners, and 3,199 electric washing machines were in use in Japan. The only popular electric home appliance was the electric iron, with some three million units in use in 1938. In fact, it was only in the 1930s that small-scale domestic production of these appliances began, and this was soon suspended because of the war.

The industry began its postwar growth in the mid-1950s. In 1955 the value of total output of all electrical home appliances was slightly over ¥40 billion, but two years later it had nearly tripled. By 1968 the industry reached the ¥1 trillion output level, recording a staggering twenty-five-fold growth in value of output in a mere 13 years. The home appliance industry now accounts for over a third of the total annual value of all electrical machinery and equipment produced. During the past decade and a half the industry introduced a number of new products, including refrigerators, washing machines, television sets, vacuum cleaners, and room air conditioning units. The output of these new products has made remarkable gains. The annual production of black-and-white television sets increased from 60,000 units in 1957 to over 6 million units in 1968, that of washing machines increased from 1 million units to 3.5 million units, and the output of refrigerators grew from 20,000 to 4 million units during these years, The production of color television sets increased from 10,000 units in 1965 to nearly 1.5 million units in 1968.

Unlike in the prewar era when the industry was largely controlled by influential wholesalers with small manufacturing firms serving as their subcontractors, it is now dominated by a handful of giant manufacturing firms bearing such names as Matsushita, Hitachi, Toshiba, and Mitsubishi Electric. Matsushita Electric, the leader in the home appliance industry in Japan, is the sixth largest corporation in Japan. It ranks twenty-fourth in *Fortune's* listing of the 200 largest non-U.S. firms.

Another consumer product that has shown tremendous growth is the automobile. It was in the mid-1930s that Japan began to have a semblance of a domestic automobile industry, but it served almost exclusively the military need. In 1949 the industry began the small-scale production of passenger cars for the first time in the postwar era. In less than two decades the Japanese automobile industry has become second largest in the world in volume of output, next to the United States. In 1969 Japan produced a total of 4,046,000 cars (2,055,000 passenger cars), recording a nearly 38 percent growth in output over the preceding year. The total output grew twenty-two-fold in the last ten years and tripled during the last five years. Toyota Motors is now the sixth-largest automobile manufacturer in the world, and Nissan Motors ranks eighth. Within two or three years it is quite likely that the annual output of Toyota and Nissan combined will reach 1.5 million units, the present production level of the Chrysler Corporation. Remarkable as they are, the foregoing are but two examples of Japan's rapidly growing consumer industries. Similar feats have been achieved in a number of other industries, including pharmaceuticals, cosmetics, synthetic fibers, and processed foods.

As large manufacturing firms aggressively sought to capitalize on the growing consumer market, they soon discovered that they had to become actively involved in marketing for a variety of reasons. First, many of these large firms, attracted by opportunities in the rapidly growing consumer market, undertook a series of vigorous expansion programs. For a number of reasons examined in detail elsewhere,[1] the postwar generation of professional managers of large Japanese manufacturing firms has been highly growth-oriented. The very structure of these industries and the mass production system they began to employ also put strong pressure on them to expand to take advantage of the economies of scale. This pressure for capacity expansion and the desire to obtain a greater share of the growing market have created the need for active marketing efforts by large manufacturing firms.

The second compelling reason for the involvement of large manufacturing firms in marketing activities is the need for market information. Timely and accurate market information is essential for capacity planning, new product introduction, and production planning. This need was particularly pronounced in capital-intensive large-scale industries. The third reason for these firms to become deeply involved with marketing is the inability and unwillingness of the traditional distribution sector to meet the new conditions created by the rapid rise in output level and the high rate of new product introduction. Up until the end of World War II it was quite common for manufacturing firms to delegate or relegate the entire distribution function to distributors and dealers. The manufacturing firms considered their mission completed when the merchandise was shipped out of their warehouse. Frequently they did not know nor care how their products were distributed. However, the highly fragmented and typically small-scale marketing intermediaries proved to be wholly inadequate to distribute the ever-increasing flow of output as well as to develop actively the market for new products.

To illustrate this problem, we can cite the example of Toyo Rayon, a leading synthetic fiber manufacturer in Japan. In 1950 Shigeki Tashiro, then president of the company, successfully negotiated a technical licensing agreement with du Pont to acquire the know-how for production of nylon for the sum of $3 million. This was indeed an unprecedented feat for the company and represented a major risk. The license fee alone exceeded the total paid-in capital of the firm at that time. As it was an entirely new inven-

---

[1] M. Y. Yoshino, *Japan's Managerial System: Tradition and Innovation* (Cambridge, Mass.: The M.I.T. Press, 1968), pp. 163–177.

tion, much uncertainty surrounded the product itself. Tashiro, exercising his excellent entrepreneurial leadership, took this calculated risk.

While production of nylon products was no easy task, marketing them posed even more difficult problems. Both industrial and consumer demand for nylon had to be created. The right use of the products had to be shown. Moreover, processors and intermediary users of nylon products had to be convinced of the merits of the product and had to be shown its appropriate uses. Understandably, textile mills, apparel manufacturers, and other potential users and marketing intermediaries were less than enthusiastic about this new man-made fiber. The company had to prod these reluctant users, to share in the risks, and to provide them with appropriate incentives. In effect, the company had to create new channels of distribution for the products, had to become heavily involved in demand creation, and had to assume considerable marketing risks. Under Tashiro's leadership, by trial and error to be sure, the company was able to devise effective marketing programs. Indeed, the very successful introduction of nylon, which laid the foundation for the phenomenal postwar growth of the company, owes much to the development of imaginative marketing programs.

Another example can be seen in the electric home appliance industry, where the great majority of wholesale and retail distributors were and still are very small, with extremely limited financial and managerial capacities. In fact, until very recently many of the outlets were no more than one-man repair shops, carrying a small inventory on the side. The reader will recall from our earlier discussion that between 1955 and 1968 the value of output of electrical home appliances experienced a twenty-five-fold growth. In addition, a number of new products were introduced, most of which were items of high unit price, such as refrigerators and television sets. Obviously, without extensive assistance from large manufacturers it would have been an insurmountable task for small wholesalers and retailers to distribute this rapidly increasing flow of output. We should also note here that at least in the initial stage large consumer goods manufacturers assumed an active role in marketing only very reluctantly, perceiving no other alternative; but many of these firms soon realized that such involvement would bring substantial benefits to the firm. As a result they began to intensify their marketing efforts.

Finally, we should not ignore American influence in making large Japanese consumer goods manufacturers recognize the importance of marketing activities. American influence has been very pervasive in shaping almost every aspect of life in postwar Japan, and the field of marketing was no exception. The term *marketing* itself was imported and so were many concepts and techniques of marketing. A large volume of American marketing literature, though not always well selected, was devoured by academicians and businessmen. Here, too, large firms had decided advantages. Well-educated professional executives who manage Japan's leading corporations were already equipped to read and digest American literature on marketing. Also, training teams sent overseas were selected, at least initially, from managers of large firms. Not to be ignored is that, through licensing and joint venture agreements entered with American firms, managers of large firms were given firsthand opportunity to observe new concepts and techniques of marketing.

### Analysis of Specific Adaptive Behavior

Having examined forces that have prompted large Japanese manufacturing firms to become more marketing-oriented, we shall now examine specific changes that have taken place during the last decade or so.

Professor Laurence Dowd, in describing the lack of marketing orientation in Japanese manufacturing firms, made the following statement as late as 1959: "Even large manufacturers seldom undertake marketing of their products intensively. Most firms have no marketing or sales department as such; and even those firms having such a department usually relegate it to a completely subordinate position."[2]

This description, which may have been relevant in 1959, certainly does not apply to the present-day situation, at least among large consumer goods manufacturers. During the past decade or so most large Japanese manufacturing firms have gone through a series of organizational changes to accommodate rapid growth and to cope with challenges arising from the new operating environment.[3] It is worth noting that in many instances the primary

[2] Laurence P. Dowd, "Wholesale Marketing in Japan," *The Journal of Marketing*, 23 (October 1959), 257.
[3] For details see Yoshino, *Japan's Managerial System*, pp. 196–224.

objective in corporate reorganization was to sharpen the firm's marketing capabilities. In fact, this very objective has become increasingly important in recent years, as evidenced by a recent survey of corporate practices. According to this survey conducted among Japan's leading corporations in March 1967, 41 percent of 317 responding firms indicated that they underwent major organizational change during the preceding year. Significantly, 61 firms, or over 40 percent of those that had undergone major organizational realignments, stated that the chief objective for their reorganization was to improve their marketing capacities.[4] It is now well accepted among Japan's leading corporations that marketing is a key and essential business function. In fact, marketing has become an important route for promotion to top management positions.

Two major patterns are notable in the manner in which marketing activities are now organized among large consumer goods manufacturers in Japan. The first is the functional pattern, in which the corporation is organized on the basis of various functions, such as production, finance, engineering, and marketing. This pattern, as may be expected, is most commonly found among firms with a limited range of highly specialized product lines.

The second type of corporate organization takes the form of product divisions. The product division concept has been widely adopted in the last decade or so by a number of Japan's leading corporations, particularly those with highly diversified product lines. One of the main reasons for adopting this form of organization is management's recognition that the marketing task and approaches differ significantly for different types of products. The divisional form of organization makes it possible to exploit specialized marketing skills and to bring about closer coordination between production and marketing. While the divisional management concept in Japan differs somewhat from the common pattern found in the United States, it was generally observed that in highly diversified firms this form of organization has resulted in more effective marketing management.

In addition, there are two patterns that are much less prevalent than either of the two already discussed. One is the incorporation

4 Tsuneo Suzuki, "1966 Nendo Keiei no Ugoki—Wagakuni Shuyo 317 Sha no Anketo Bunseki Kara" ["Major Managerial Developments in 317 Major Japanese Corporations in Fiscal Year 1966], in Fujiyoshi Sakamoto, Keiei Nenpo, 1967 [Management Annual, 1967] (Tokyo: The Diamond Publishing Co., 1967), p. 14.

of a separate subsidiary to undertake marketing activities. The other is a geographically based organization. Given the limited physical size of the domestic market, geographical division as the principal criterion of marketing organization is seldom used.

The formation of a separate marketing subsidiary is observed in some of the companies with diversified product lines. For example, Hitachi and Toshiba, two leading diversified manufacturers of electrical machinery and equipment, chose to establish wholly owned subsidiaries to market their home appliances and related products. Both companies entered the consumer product field only since the end of World War II, and their establishment of a separate marketing subsidiary stems, at least in part, from their recognition that the marketing task for consumer products is different enough from their previous operations to warrant formation of a separate corporate entity to devote undivided attention to marketing.

Regardless of the particular manner in which marketing functions are organized, the marketing unit has a complement of both line and staff personnel. Line units in a large manufacturing firm are organized on the basis of products, geographic areas, or customer groups, or any combinations of these factors. Typically, large firms have a network of branch offices throughout the nation whose primary task is to perform sales and service functions. Most large manufacturing firms have a full marketing staff, including marketing planning, advertising, sales promotion, customer relations, marketing research, product development, and so on. Many of these staff functions are duplicated at the divisional and branch level.

A recent study conducted by the Research Department of the Japan Chamber of Commerce provides evidence for the growing emphasis given to marketing activities by Japan's leading corporations as reflected in their organizational structure. The study was based on mail questionnaires sent out to 952 major manufacturing firms in a variety of industries; 412 usable returns were received. Among the responding corporations, 76 percent were organized on a functional basis, 16 percent were organized along major product lines, 3 percent were organized on a geographic basis, and 5 percent were organized in some combination of the other three.[5]

---

[5] *Wagakuni ni Okeru Meika no Hanbai Katsudo [Marketing Activities by Manufacturers in Japan]* (Tokyo: The Japan Chamber of Commerce, 1966), p. 14.

Branch sales offices were reported by 374 firms. There were a total of 3,087 sales offices, averaging about 8 offices per company. The survey also revealed that approximately 10 percent of the total company personnel were engaged in some form of marketing activity.[6] Details according to major industry group are presented in Table 3.1.

TABLE 3.1

PERSONNEL ENGAGED IN MARKETING AS A PERCENTAGE
OF TOTAL EMPLOYEES, 1965

| Industry | Average Number of Total Employees per Company (A) | Average Number of Marketing Employees per Company (B) | (B)/(A) (%) | Number of Responding Firms |
|---|---|---|---|---|
| Food | 1,740 | 265 | 15.2 | 21 |
| Textile | 5,267 | 315 | 5.9 | 30 |
| Pulp and Paper | 3,526 | 80 | 2.3 | 8 |
| Chemical | 1,946 | 321 | 16.5 | 55 |
| Petroleum and Coal | 2,467 | 511 | 20.7 | 5 |
| Rubber Products | 2,148 | 212 | 9.9 | 7 |
| Glass | 2,195 | 175 | 8.0 | 21 |
| Steel | 5,837 | 209 | 3.6 | 27 |
| Nonferrous Metals | 2,635 | 107 | 4.1 | 16 |
| Metal Products | 1,418 | 92 | 6.0 | 24 |
| Machinery | 1,845 | 488 | 26.8 | 56 |
| Electric Machinery | 2,810 | 369 | 13.1 | 50 |
| Transportation Equipment | 4.396 | 215 | 4.9 | 33 |
| Precision Instruments | 2,289 | 324 | 14.4 | 11 |
| Others | 1,975 | 321 | 16.3 | 10 |
| Average | 2,822 | 294 | 10.4 | 374 |

Source: *Wagakuni ni Okeru Meika no Hanbai Katsudo* [*Marketing Activities by Manufacturers in Japan*] (Tokyo: The Japan Chamber of Commerce, 1966), p. 16.

This survey showed the further breakdown of those engaged in marketing by specific functions. Among the 374 firms responding to this question, 63 percent of those engaged in marketing were in line activities, while 25 percent were occupying staff positions of various types, and 12 percent were performing functions that are

6 *Ibid.*, p. 16.

related to physical distribution, such as storage and transportation. Details are presented in Table 3.2.

TABLE 3.2

PERCENTAGE DISTRIBUTION OF MARKETING PERSONNEL
IN MAJOR JAPANESE MANUFACTURING FIRMS ACCORDING TO MAJOR TYPES
OF ACTIVITIES AND THEIR ORGANIZATIONAL LOCATIONS, 1965

| Location | Line Marketing Personnel | Market- ing Staff | Staff Engaged Primarily in Physical Distribution | Total | Number of Responding Firms |
|---|---|---|---|---|---|
| Corporate Headquarters | 46.4 | 37.8 | 15.8 | 100 | 355 |
| Branch Office I* | 71.5 | 19.5 | 9.0 | 100 | 325 |
| Branch Office II† | 54.0 | 22.5 | 23.5 | 100 | 90 |
| Overseas Offices | 69.7 | 28.1 | 2.2 | 100 | 67 |
| Total | 62.8 | 25.3 | 11.9 | 100 | 374 |

* Branch Office I denotes those branches whose primary activities are in marketing.
† Branch Office II denotes those whose primary functions are not in marketing.
Source: *Wagakuni ni Okeru Meika no Hanbai Katsudo* [*Marketing Activities by Manufacturers in Japan*] (Tokyo: The Japan Chamber of Commerce, 1966), p. 16.

We have seen indications of how large Japanese manufacturing firms, particularly those in consumer industries, have adjusted their organizational structures to cope with challenges of the rapidly growing consumer market. This trend, which began in the late 1950s, has continued and is likely to intensify, as evidenced by the aforementioned survey conducted by Suzuki in 1967. The survey revealed that 142, or 45 percent of the 317 responding firms, indicated that they had increased their marketing personnel during the preceding year. Eighty-three firms, or 26 percent of the responding firms, stated that they had strengthened their marketing research functions. Sixty-three firms, or 20 percent, expanded staff functions relating to marketing. Significantly, 44, or 14 percent of the responding firms, revealed that during the preceding year they had either established or expanded their sales engineering or service department.[7]

[7] Suzuki, "1966 Nendo Keiei no Ugoki," pp. 20–21.

Closely related to the growing emphasis given to marketing in corporate organization is the increasing importance attached to the use of scientific decision-making tools in marketing. Marketing research data are becoming increasingly important in key marketing decisions. In addition to the creation of a marketing research staff within the corporate organization, growing interest in marketing research in recent years has led to the emergence of a number of independent organizations that specialize in marketing research. A recent directory of marketing research firms compiled by the Japan Marketing Association lists 56 firms that provide a variety of marketing research services. Since the directory lists only major firms, the total number is believed to be considerably greater than those named. Also noteworthy is the fact that quite sophisticated research concepts and techniques are being employed by these organizations. In fact, large Japanese corporations are frequently the first foreign firms to import or adopt advanced marketing research techniques developed in the United States. Marketing research activities have also been facilitated by the rather rapid diffusion of computers in Japan.

Finally, large Japanese manufacturing firms have made some progress in the area of marketing planning. The concept of formal planning is a rather recent innovation in Japanese corporations. As discussed elsewhere,[8] traditional Japanese management practices are not generally suitable for the introduction of the concept of formal planning, but in recent years considerable progress has been made in this regard. Most of Japan's leading corporations now have a planning department or section, whose chief responsibility is to develop strategic plans. In addition, the marketing departments of most leading firms have a group charged with development of the marketing aspects of strategic planning as well as with formulation of tactical marketing plans.

Among various phases of marketing planning, the area of product planning has received most attention. This is consistent with the fact that the Japanese industries have vigorously pursued new product introduction and diversification strategies mainly through the importation of foreign technology. Ready access to foreign technology made it possible for Japanese firms in many cases to introduce new products without having to undertake their own research and development. Still, the successful commercialization

8 Yoshino, *Japan's Managerial System*, pp. 262–272 .

of new technical know-how was no easy task but required careful planning and coordination. This need led to the introduction of the product planning concept in a number of Japan's leading consumer goods manufacturing firms, and in many of them a formal organizational unit was established to coordinate such activities. This group took on added significance as Japan's leading manufacturing firms began to strengthen their own research and development efforts in recent years. In the face of growing domestic as well as international competition, marketing planning is expected to take on even greater significance in the years to come.

### Manufacturers' Efforts toward Demand Creation and Stimulation

Another significant evidence of an increasing trend toward marketing orientation among the nation's large consumer goods manufacturers is their intense interest in activities related to the creation and stimulation of demand. Throughout the prewar era, the management of even those few large manufacturing firms that produced consumer goods had operated under the assumption that the demand was relatively fixed and that, therefore, advertising and sales promotion efforts would not significantly expand it. Also, as was typical of production-oriented firms elsewhere, the management of most large manufacturing firms in the prewar era had the notion that good products would sell themselves and that active promotion was not necessary.

In recent years, however, there has been a clear shift in their outlook. Large manufacturers of consumer goods are now making intense efforts to create and stimulate both primary and selective demand for their products through direct appeals to consumers, using a variety of means. First, as we noted earlier, large manufacturers of consumer goods now manufacture and distribute their products under their own brand names, and they are making substantial financial commitments to establish and promote their brands. While manufacturers' brands were not totally unknown in prewar Japan, their use was rather limited. But now virtually every type of mass-produced consumer goods—home appliances, cosmetics, drugs, processed food, and soft drinks, just to mention a few—is marketed under manufacturers' brand names, and in almost every product line national brands enjoy undisputed leadership in the marketplace. For example, in the home appliance field such names as Hitachi, Toshiba, Mitsubishi, Matsushita, and Sanyo literally have taken on the same degree of familiarity among Japanese consumers as General Electric, Westinghouse, and RCA have among their American counterparts.

Obviously, the single most important means for demand creation and stimulation is mass media advertising. Such advertising was not totally unknown in prewar Japan, but it was done only on a small scale and was limited to the printed media. The phenomenal growth of mass communication, coupled with the postwar institutional reforms that placed broadcasting media in the private sector, and the addition of television as an advertising medium, laid ground for the rapid development of mass media advertising in postwar Japan. Japan represents an ideal setting for mass media advertising, given the fact that the population density is extremely high, with more than 100 million people concentrated in a land area smaller than the state of California, coupled with the extremely high literacy rate and the characteristically intense curiosity of the Japanese.

The postwar growth of mass·media advertising can be seen from Table 3.3. In 1969 the total advertising expenditure reached nearly ¥629 billion, or just over $1,750 million, recording greater than an 18 percent increase over the preceding year and accounting for roughly 1 percent of the nation's Gross National Product. Looking

TABLE 3.3

GROWTH OF TOTAL ADVERTISING EXPENDITURE IN JAPAN, 1955–1969

| Year | Total Amount (¥ billion) |
|------|--------------------------|
| 1955 | 60.9 |
| 1956 | 74.5 |
| 1957 | 94.0 |
| 1958 | 106.5 |
| 1959 | 145.6 |
| 1960 | 174.0 |
| 1961 | 211.0 |
| 1962 | 243.5 |
| 1963 | 298.2 |
| 1964 | 349.1 |
| 1966 | 383.1 |
| 1967 | 459.4 |
| 1968 | 532.0 |
| 1969 | 628.7 |

Source: *Dentsu Advertising Annual, 1969* (Tokyo: Dentsu Advertising Agency, 1969), p. 223.

at the breakdown of the total expenditure by major medium for the year 1968, we find that newspapers account for approximately 35 percent of the total expenditure, television 33 percent, and magazines and radio are responsible for 5.6 percent and 4.4 percent, respectively. Altogether, the four major media account for 78 percent of the total advertising expenditure. Particularly remarkable is the very rapid growth of television as an advertising medium.

As can be seen in Table 3.4, the growing importance of tele-

TABLE 3.4

DISTRIBUTION OF ADVERTISING EXPENDITURE BY MAJOR MEDIA, 1968

| Medium | Amount (¥ billion) | Percentage |
|---|---|---|
| Newspaper | 188.4 | 35.4 |
| Television | 174.5 | 32.8 |
| Magazines | 29.7 | 5.6 |
| Radio | 23.3 | 4.4 |
| Direct Mail | 21.3 | 4.0 |
| Outdoor | 79.9 | 15.0 |
| Export | 14.9 | 2.8 |
| Total | 532.1 | 100.0 |

Source: *Dentsu Advertising Annual, 1969* (Tokyo: Dentsu Advertising Agency, 1969), p. 223.

vision as an advertising medium has radically changed the relative importance of other media. Television has become particularly important in consumer-oriented industries. For example, in 1968 the food industry spent nearly 68 percent of its total advertising budget on this single medium. Likewise, the cosmetics industry spent 70 percent, the sundry goods industry 60 percent, and the pharmaceutical industry 54 percent of their total advertising budgets on television.[9]

Looking further at the advertising expenditure patterns, let us examine breakdowns by major industries. The machinery industry was responsible for over 21 percent of the total expenditure for the four major media: newspaper, television, magazine, and radio. Included in this category are such important consumer products as

[9] *Dentsu Kōkoku Nenkan, 1969 [The Dentsu Advertising Annual, 1969]* (Tokyo: Dentsu Advertising Agency, 1969), p. 227.

home appliances, sewing machines, watches, cameras, and automobiles. Next comes the processed food industry, accounting for
nearly 18 percent. The pharmaceutical industry was responsible
for over 8 percent of the total, followed by the cosmetic industry,
which accounted for 7 percent of the total spent for the four major
media.[10]

Significantly, the four consumer-oriented industries just mentioned were responsible for 53 percent of the total spent for the
four media, or over 40 percent of the total advertising expenditure.
It is important to note that each of these industries is dominated
by a small number of large firms. For example, Matsushita Electric
led all firms in terms of the total size of its advertising budget.
During 1969 the company spent ¥11.4 billion (approximately $31
million). The second was Toshiba, a diversified manufacturer of
electrical products (¥8.7 billion). Closely trailing Toshiba were
Nissan Motors (¥7.89 billion), Takeda Pharmaceuticals (¥7.7
billion), and Toyota Motors (¥6.6 billion). This is indeed convincing evidence of the extent of commitment made by large manufacturers of mass-produced consumer goods to the creation of
demand.

To describe the sheer growth of advertising expenditure tells
only part of the story. Equally impressive is the marked improvement in the quality of advertising. The Japanese have applied their
recognized artistic ability to creating most attractive advertise-
ments. With the rapid growth of advertising, a number of advertising agencies have emerged; there are some 80 agencies now
aggressively vying for the growing advertising business in Japan,
including a number of affiliates of American agencies. Dentsu, the
largest agency in Japan, ranks fourth in the world in terms of total
billings. Indeed, both qualitative improvement and quantitative
growth of advertising in postwar Japan have been remarkable, and
it is important to note that a relatively small number of large
marketing-oriented firms has been primarily responsible for its
growth.

Another important means that large manufacturers of consumer
goods are now employing rather extensively to stimulate demand
is packaging. Prior to World War II it was customary for manufacturers in a number of consumer industries such as food, drugs,
and even cosmetics to sell their products in bulk, leaving the func-

10 *Ibid.*, p. 226.

tions of sorting and packaging to marketing intermediaries. In fact, this was one of the major functions performed by marketing intermediaries. In contrast, however, large manufacturers of these product lines are now engaged extensively in prepackaging as a tool for sales promotion. With the remarkable growth of national brands and development of self-service retail operations, the role of packaging as a marketing tool is becoming all the more important. The growth of packaging in postwar Japan is summarized in Table 3.5. Unfortunately, the information contained in this table is not

TABLE 3.5

OUTPUT OF PACKAGING MATERIALS, 1962–1968
(in billions of yen; numbers in parentheses
are index numbers, 1962 = 100)

|  | 1962 | 1963 | 1964 | 1965 | 1966 | 1967 | 1968 |
|---|---|---|---|---|---|---|---|
| Plastic |  |  |  |  |  |  |  |
| Containers | 208.9 | 248.9 | 307.1 | 330.0 | 375.2 | 429.6 | 509.7 |
|  | (100) | (124) | (147) | (158) | (180) | (206) | (244) |
| Cellophane | 26.2 | 31.9 | 53.4 | 62.8 | 93.6 | 108.6 | 124.7 |
|  | (100) | (122) | (204) | (240) | (358) | (415) | (476) |
| Metal Packag- |  |  |  |  |  |  |  |
| ing Materials | 93.9 | 104.9 | 113.1 | 129.9 | 133.4 | 144.3 | 156.6 |
|  | (100) | (111) | (120) | (138) | (142) | (154) | (166) |
| Glass Containers | 34.2 | 39.0 | 39.3 | 39.1 | 43.8 | 49.7 | 56.5 |
|  | (100) | (114) | (115) | (115) | (128) | (145) | (165) |
| Total | 464.3 | 560.6 | 646.9 | 707.9 | 815.9 | 925.5 | 1068.7 |
|  | (100) | (121) | (139) | (152) | (176) | (199) | (230) |

Source: "Statistics of Production of Packaging Materials and Packaging Machinery in Japan," *JPI Journal*, March 1969, pp. 42–43.

broken down by user's categories such as manufacturers, wholesalers, and retailers; however, with the exception of paper, which is extensively used at the retail level, the greater portion of the materials used is consumed at the manufacturing level. The table also indicates the rapid growth of new types of packaging materials such as plastics.

Again, as in the case of advertising, the statistics indicating quantitative growth tell only a part of the story. Though difficult to measure precisely, qualitative improvements in packaging have been equally impressive. Here again, large manufacturers of consumer goods have taken the initiative in improving design and quality. In addition to its potent role as a means for sales promotion, extensive prepackaging now undertaken by large manufacturers has given them more flexibility and freedom in distribution of their products by reducing their dependence on marketing intermediaries. Moreover, by assuming this function, large manufacturers now have greater control over pricing as well as over quantity of purchase through all the distributive channels.

Another means that manufacturers of consumer durables have found particularly effective for demand creation and stimulation is their direct involvement in consumer financing. Since this topic is taken up in detail in Chapter 6, let it suffice here to note that virtually all major manufacturers of consumer durables such as automobiles, home appliances, and pianos are now actively engaged in consumer financing, and their efforts have contributed to a substantial expansion of the effective demand for these products.

Finally, large manufacturers of consumer goods have been actively engaged in sales promotion. Here again, most of the really imaginative programs have been developed by large manufacturers, often in cooperation with major advertising agencies. These promotional efforts are geared both to the ultimate consumer and to the marketing intermediaries. A number of large consumer goods manufacturers now regularly sponsor a wide variety of contests for consumers. In fact, as these contests became popular, prizes have become increasingly expensive, even to a point where the Fair Trade Commission was recently compelled to direct some manufacturers to curtail such sales promotion activities.

A few of the more aggressive and innovative firms are now attempting to organize consumers to increase their patronage. This trend is particularly notable in such industries as cosmetics, cameras, home appliances, and automobiles. To illustrate, let us examine a nationwide network of consumer clubs organized by Shiseido, the leading manufacturer of cosmetics. Customers who buy Shiseido cosmetics are automatically enrolled in Shiseido Camellia Club, which boasts 10 million members, representing nearly 20 percent of the entire female population in Japan. Individual records are carefully kept on all members, and they receive an attractive monthly magazine, direct mail advertising, and promotional pieces as well as a variety of gifts annually depending upon their total annual purchase of the company's products. Other benefits include invitations to free lectures on makeup and personal grooming. Not only does the club serve to strengthen Shiseido's consumer franchise but it provides the company with a wealth of valuable market and consumer data.

In the home appliance field both Matsushita and Toshiba have organized similar consumer clubs. Matsushita's Izumi-Kai is estimated to have 1.8 million members who also receive a monthly magazine and annual gifts. Moreover, members are invited to free cultural events, cooking classes, and new product exhibits. In addition to these consumer-oriented programs, large consumer goods manufacturers are also actively engaged in sales promotion activities geared to marketing intermediaries. These programs range from providing point-of-sale displays, sales materials, and sales instructions to sponsoring sales contests and providing a wide variety of recreational activities, including foreign tours.

These firms now devote rather intensive efforts to demand creation and stimulation by appealing directly to their marketing intermediaries as well as to ultimate consumers. They now rely on extensive use of various elements of marketing mix—branding, packaging, advertising, and sales promotion—to establish and strengthen consumer franchise and dealer support for their products. Large manufacturing firms are taking the initiative in these efforts.

### Manufacturers' Control over Channels of Distribution

One of the most significant developments in Japan's postwar marketing scene is the very extensive control attained by large manufacturers of selected consumer goods over their channels of distribution. In a number of consumer goods industries we have witnessed the emergence of centrally coordinated distribution systems under the initiative of large manufacturers. Indeed, this has resulted in a rather basic alteration of the power relationship between manufacturers and marketing intermediaries. We have repeatedly noted that in most consumer industries large wholesalers and trading firms occupied a pivotal position in the marketing system prior to World War II. Indeed, as the captain of the channel, they exercised almost uncontested leadership. A typical pattern was for large wholesalers to dictate to small manufacturers under their control what and how much to produce; at the same time they enjoyed considerable influence over the actions of retail outlets.

*Vertically Integrated Distribution Systems*

In the postwar decades, however, this situation has undergone a radical change in a number of industries in which large manufacturers have completely replaced traditional wholesalers in the leadership role. Large manufacturing firms have all but taken over distribution functions through outright ownership of outlets or by bringing independent wholesalers and retailers under their control. As a result, in a number of consumer industries we have witnessed the emergence of a manufacturer-dominated vertically integrated distribution system. This pattern is most commonly found in those consumer industries dominated by oligopolistic firms and those that have experienced extraordinarily rapid growth, including the automobile, electric home appliance, pharmaceutical, and cosmetics industries.

Several factors are responsible for the development of this pattern. First, we must cite intense efforts now being made by major manufacturers toward building a consumer franchise for their national brands through advertising, sales promotion, and packaging. Certainly, to the extent that manufauturers are successful in achieving the consumer franchise through direct appeals it will weaken the relative power of marketing intermediaries. When manufacturers can successfully establish a consumer "pull" for their products, wholesalers and retailers have little choice but to bow to the manufacturers' leadership.

Another important reason lies in the inability of old-style marketing intermediaries to cope with the new demands placed on them by the emergence of the mass consumer market and entry of large manufacturing firms into consumer industries. Marketing intermediaries for the most part were not able to distribute adequately the rapidly increasing output now being produced by the streamlined mass production system. It is not difficult to imagine the kinds of strains traditional marketing intermediaries were subject to when the output of the products they were handling increased manyfold within a very short period of time. Neither were they always able or willing to carry new products. As we have seen, marketing intermediaries were small, highly fragmented, seriously undercapitalized, and had only limited space. Moreover, unlike many of the large manufacturers, they had to struggle on their own to recover from wartime losses and postwar dislocations. This further handicapped their ability to keep up with the growth rate achieved by major manufacturers. The traditional conservative mentality was, of course, another factor inhibiting their adaptation to the new condition. Thus, it became increasingly evident to large manufacturers in a number of fast-expanding consumer industries that, if they were to market a rapidly growing output successfully and to create sufficient demand for their new products, they had to become actively involved with the distribution process.

As a result, some innovative large manufacturers in certain industries began to make concerted efforts to establish a vertically controlled distribution system. Indeed, this is a major departure from the traditional orientation of a manufacturing firm of the prewar era which had so typically viewed its sole mission as that of producing goods. Now a number of major manufacturing firms have established a vertically controlled and coordinated distribution system all the way down to the consumer. Such an arrangement gives manufacturers considerable competitive advantage.

*Patterns of Manufacturer-Controlled Distribution Systems*

Basically, there are three patterns in the manufacturer-controlled distribution system. The first pattern is most complete in terms of degree of control. This is where manufacturers distribute their products through their own outlets. Under this arrangement the channel of distribution becomes highly compressed, and it gives the manufacturer complete control over how the products are to be sold and serviced. This practice is not widely practiced. For example, this pattern is adopted most extensively in the sewing machine industry: roughly 60 percent of the total sales in the domestic market are distributed through manufacturers' own outlets. A similar practice is also followed in the distribution of beds.

The second pattern is the manufacturer-controlled franchise system. This is common in the distribution of gasoline and automobiles. Recently, some confectionery manufacturers have attempted to use this approach to increase their number of outlets.

The third pattern is for large manufacturers to bring existing independent marketing intermediaries under their control by organizing them into a group of affiliated wholesalers and retailers. Since this pattern is by far the most common, we shall examine it in some detail. Within this approach several different variations are found, with a varying degree of control exercised by manufacturers. In some cases the control is rather tight and the relationship is permanent, while in others it is loose and constantly shifting. To illustrate the different approaches, let us consider the patterns developed in three key consumer industries.

### Examples of Manufacturer Control by Use of Affiliates

THE COSMETIC INDUSTRY. One of the most tightly controlled and smoothly functioning systems has been developed by a leading manufacturing firm in the cosmetic industry. The cosmetic industry in Japan has been growing at a very rapid rate, and the total output in 1967 reached nearly ¥134 billion. In terms of output Japan is now second only to the United States. The industry is made up of some 150 manufacturers, the great majority of whom are small, and as a result a wide variety of distribution methods are employed. Most successful, however, is the pattern developed by Shiseido, which enjoys more than a third of the domestic cosmetic market. The company derives roughly 80 percent of its sales from cosmetics and the remaining 20 percent from various types of toiletries. To distribute its cosmetic products, the company divided the entire nation into 73 territories. In each territory it established a wholesaling subsidiary in which Shiseido owns controlling, if not the majority, interest. These sales subsidiaries, in turn, sell to some 13,000 controlled or affiliated retail outlets, including virtually all of Japan's outstanding cosmetic retail concerns. They are independent stores, but they are known as Shiseido Chain Stores. Many of the large retail outlets generally set aside a certain portion of store space for Shiseido products that is known as "Shiseido Corner," and the company provides attractive display cases as well as point-of-sale promotional devices. These chain outlets are organized into six classes according to their sales volume, and the company has a separate discount policy for each category of store. As one of the conditions for chain membership, retail firms are required to agree to resale price maintenance at the retail level. The company has several thousand beauty consultants who visit these retail outlets at regular intervals to perform demonstration services for customers.

The company distributes its toiletries through the Shiseido Trading Co., a wholly owned subsidiary, which in turn sells to some 400 wholesalers and eventually to 100,000 retail outlets. In both cosmetics and toiletries the company controls the price structure of its products at every stage of distribution. Shiseido maintains its control over the distribution channels through the effective combination of ownership, administrative relationship, and contractual ties. The company places a great deal of emphasis on trade relations and has a large complement of staff personnel assigned to this function.

The company's outstanding success owes much to its imaginative distribution policy. This policy has enabled the company to establish an orderly distribution pattern, to avoid price cutting in a highly competitive industry in which such a practice is extremely common, and to encourage active sales efforts by retailers. As we noted earlier, the company's organization efforts have gone even beyond retail outlets by establishing a direct link with consumers through consumer clubs. Thus, the company has skillfully organized its entire marketing channel up to and including consumers.

THE HOME APPLIANCE INDUSTRY. Major manufacturers of home appliances also have been making concerted efforts to develop a vertically controlled distribution system. Prior to World War II, when the country's home appliance industry was still in its infancy, wholesalers occupied a dominant position. To a large degree, these wholesalers controlled both production and distribution of these products. A rather limited line of home appliances was available at that time; in fact, most were manufactured by small subcontractors for large distributors. With the very rapid growth of output in this industry and the introduction of high-unit-price items such as refrigerators, television sets, and washing machines, it became apparent that traditional marketing intermediaries could no longer perform distribution functions adequately. To distribute an increasing volume of output, especially of high-unit-price items, manufacturers were compelled to become actively involved in distribution functions. Also, new entrants in the home appliance field, such as Hitachi and Toshiba, were confronted first with the task of having to develop a national distribution network. Since the difference in technical capabilities of these large firms in production of such products was minimal, the success of a particular firm depended largely on its marketing ability. One of the first essential steps was to build a strong dealer organization.

Manufacturers initially sought to strengthen their ties with existing wholesalers through offering a generous discount, rebates, and credit, as well as providing them with substantial promotional, managerial, and even financial assistance. Financial assistance, largely in the form of a liberal credit policy, was particularly important in view of the fact that, as is typical of Japanese marketing intermediaries, appliance wholesalers suffered from chronic capital shortage.

Some manufacturers have gone a step further and have established their own sales subsidiaries throughout Japan. A typical pattern is for the manufacturers to encourage their wholesalers in a given area to pool their resources to form a company with equity participation by the manufacturing firm. Generally, the manufacturer has a controlling interest, and the company thus formed becomes the exclusive distributor for the manufacturer. Matsushita Electric has been most aggressive in this regard, having created some 165 such controlled wholesale outlets throughout the country.

It is indeed remarkable that within a very short period of time, large manufacturers have attained such power vis-à-vis wholesalers that they literally could insist on mergers among these typically independent-minded wholesalers. In fact, in this industry truly independent wholesalers have all but disappeared. The manufacturers' efforts to organize a controlled distribution system did not stop at the wholesale level. Obviously, if manufacturers were to develop a vertically integrated network of distribution, they had to reach the retail level. Ultimately, it is at this level that the real battles are fought. This was particularly true in the home appliance industry, in which retailers' capacity was desperately inadequate for the task that they now had to perform.

Manufacturers competed vigorously to develop their own network of retail outlets, each seeking to bring retailers under their exclusive control. Each manufacturer gave cooperating retail outlets various kinds of assistance, including promotional aids, generous rebates, liberal credit terms, and managerial assistance. These outlets have become known as *keiretsu*, or affiliated stores. These stores, though independent, became clearly indentified as to their affiliation with a particular manufacturer. The manufacturers, who were anxious to expand retail coverage, also encouraged the establishment of new retail outlets. Between 1956 and 1966 the number of retail outlets handling home appliances nearly doubled, reaching more than 40,000 in the latter year. There is little doubt that the aggressive and liberal assistance provided by manufacturers was a major impetus to this growth.

In most cases, however, it has been impractical for manufacturers, as powerful as they are, to insist that these retail outlets become their exclusive agents. Retailers generally carry products of at least one other manufacturer. This is due in part to retailers' fear of totally losing their independence and also to their desire to broaden their appeal to consumers by offering competing brands. Typically, however, the affiliated outlets derive 70 percent to 80 percent of their sales from products of the company with which they have an affiliated relationship. Judging from the results, the manufacturers' efforts to establish vertical control over retail outlets have been quite successful. They had achieved it between the mid-1950s and early 1960s. By the early 1960s, it was estimated that about two-thirds of the 40,000-odd retail outlets handling home appliances were affiliated with a particular manufacturer.

In the early 1960s the home appliance industry, along with a number of other growth industries, reached a turning point. The rapid expansion of productive capacity finally caught up with what once appeared to be an insatiable demand, and the industry entered the era of intense competition. For the reasons noted earlier, manufacturers, who were anxious to expand their market share, refused to make quick downward adjustment of their level of production. Instead, they intensified their promotional efforts and accelerated the tempo of model changes. Anxious to sell an ever-increasing level of output, the manufacturers stepped up their pressure on their affiliated wholesale and retail outlets. In many cases they literally attempted to dump their products onto their affiliated wholesalers and retailers by offering all sorts of incentives such as liberal rebates, special discounts, and attractive credit. Lured by these incentives, many wholesalers and retailers took on extra inventories. Manufacturers also intensified their efforts to increase their wholesale and retail coverage. They encouraged large retail outlets to engage in wholesaling. They also competed vigorously and even indiscriminately at times to bring even the smallest and weakest retail outlets under their control.

The consequence of such an ill-conceived and short-sighted sales approach was obvious. Price cutting became commonplace. Wholesalers who presumably were affiliated with a given manufacturer competed against each other in the same territory, encouraging retail outlets to pit one wholesaler against another. There was excess inventory at every stage of the channel. This, of course, slowed down their stock turnover, tying up their already tight working capital. Since wholesalers and retailers typically rely heavily on borrowing as a source of funds, they became burdened with increasingly high financial charges to service their debts. They were compelled to cut prices to dispose of their excess inventory, and because of high rebates provided by manufacturers they were often able to make some profit, even if they resold at their purchase price. In fact, because of the liberal credit terms offered by manufacturers (90 to 120 days), many wholesalers engaged in a practice of reselling their inventory at cost for payment in cash, in order to have "free use" of the capital for three to four months.

The situation deteriorated quickly, and weaker wholesalers and retailers were on the verge of bankruptcy. Considerable hostility developed among wholesalers and retailers, particularly smaller ones, against the high-pressure tactics employed by the manufacturers to move their inventory. By 1964 the situation deteriorated to a point at which manufacturers were compelled to take some action.

Matsushita Electric, the leading manufacturer, took the initiative in overcoming this grave problem. Konosuke Matsushita, the charismatic founder of the company, came out of retirement to take charge of the company's marketing operations. The company made a number of drastic changes in both production and marketing policies. The remedies in the area of production included production cutbacks and the realignment of product lines. In the area of distribution the company streamlined the wholesaling structure by strengthening its sales subsidiaries. Each of the 200 sales subsidiaries was given a strict territorial assignment, which was to be tightly enforced. These subsidiaries are supported by 22 sales branches, 72 installment credit companies, and 18 subsidiaries specializing in postsale servicing. Operations of these subsidiaries are tightly controlled by the parent company. The company now controls resale price and discount structure throughout the channel. The steps are designed both to reduce severe price cutting and to prevent Matsushita products from flowing to discount stores.

Other manufacturers followed suit. They, too, have established sales subsidiaries on a territorial basis and have tightened their control over them. For example, Sony divided the country into 72 territories and designated one distributor for each territory. In most cases, as with Matsushita, a number of wholesalers handling Sony products in a given area were encouraged to merge to form one company, with Sony's equity participation. Sony ships its merchandise to these outlets on a consignment basis to be sold at a specified price to retail outlets, thus taking pricing out of the hands of the distributors. Wholesalers or the sales company receive commissions on the sales made to retailers. Along with streamlining the wholesaling structure, large manufacturers are now trying to strengthen their affiliated retail outlets. In the process they gradually have become more selective in their choice of affiliated outlets. Matsushita reportedly has some 10,000 retail outlets under its affiliation. Likewise, it is estimated that Toshiba and Hitachi have about 5,000 retail outlets under their control.

THE PHARMACEUTICAL INDUSTRY. Pharmaceuticals provide another example of the attempt by large manufacturers to develop a vertically integrated distribution system. The Japanese pharmaceutical industry also has achieved very rapid growth in the postwar period. During the decade ending in 1968 the value of output of this industry grew fivefold, reaching the ¥700 billion level in 1968. The Japanese pharmaceutical industry is second only to that of the United States. Unlike the home appliance industry, it is made up of some 2,000 to 3,000 manufacturers of varying sizes and descriptions. These manufacturers range from small shops of no more than three or four employees to a firm with more than 10,000 employees whose annual sales exceed ¥127 billion (350 million). A dozen or so leading manufacturers are responsible for over 50 percent of the total pharmaceutical sales. Another characteristic of this industry is its sheer number of products. According to one estimate there are some 20,000 different items currently available on the market, and new products constantly are being introduced.

This industry, too, traditionally had been dominated by large wholesalers; in fact, some of the prominent manufacturers began as wholesalers. The distribution channel has been circuitous and complicated, with the presence of a myriad of primary and secondary wholesalers and small retail outlets. The reader may recall the diagram depicting the distribution channels of pharmaceutical products presented in Chapter 1. According to the latest Commercial Census, there are some 39,000 retail outlets and 3,500 wholesalers handling pharmaceutical products.

The pharmaceutical industry responded to the rapidly growing demand in a manner typical of other growth industries in postwar Japan. Large manufacturers, having reequipped themselves with the most up-to-date production facilities, increased their capacity rapidly and introduced a large number of new products by taking advantage of licensed foreign technology. Medium-size and small manufacturing establishments tried hard to keep up with their larger competitors. Characteristically, they competed vigorously to seek a greater share of the growing market. Here again a familiar situation of oversupply and extensive price cutting developed. In fact, by the early 1960s the pharmaceutical industry had become one of the most competitive industries in Japan, characterized by frequent discounting practices. The characteristics of this industry described earlier made the situation even worse.

To combat this situation, major manufacturers began to seek greater control over certain wholesale, and particularly retail, outlets. The aforementioned characteristics of the industry made it difficult to achieve this objective. Because of the large number of products, obviously no single manufacturer, regardless of size, can possibly supply the entire range of products to wholesale and retail outlets. As a result, in seeking to establish a network of affiliated outlets, large manufacturers in this industry are in a weaker position than those in less diversified industries such as home appliances. Aware of their limited power, they tend to emphasize cooperation rather than control in forging a network of affiliated outlets. In fact, it is not uncommon for a retail firm to belong to several different manufacturers' groups. To offset this disadvantage, however, pharmaceutical manufacturers do enjoy one important advantage not commonly shared by other manufacturers. Pharmaceuticals are one of the few industries in which resale price maintenance is permitted legally. In attempting to develop a network of affiliated outlets, large pharmaceutical manufacturers have made good use of this legal provision.

Let us examine patterns developed by several leading firms. Tanabe Seiyaku was the first among the major firms to attempt to organize marketing intermediaries. This network includes about 100 wholesalers and nearly 13,000 retail drug outlets, covering some 60 items. The company divided the country into 172 market areas, and affiliated wholesalers and retailers in each area were organized into an association that, in turn, is a member of the nationwide federation. The officers of this federation consist primarily of representatives of retail outlets, supplemented by persons representing the wholesalers and the manufacturing company. The representatives of this federation are consulted regularly on important matters affecting them, such as new product introduction and credit terms. Requirements for membership are also determined by each association. Tanabe gives special promotional and managerial assistance to these stores. Other major pharmaceutical manufacturers have followed suit. Takeda Seiyaku, the largest pharmaceutical manufacturer, though the last one to adopt this approach, is estimated to have more than 23,000 retail outlets as its affiliated stores.

In discussion of both pharmaceutical and cosmetic industries, references have been made to resale price maintenance by manufacturers. The resale price maintenance agreement is, indeed, a potent weapon for large manufacturers, allowing them legally to bind actions of their wholesale and retail outlets. Because of extensive reliance made on this practice by manufacturers in some industries, we shall discuss it in greater detail.

Retail price maintenance is legally prohibited under Japan's Anti-Monopoly Act, which was enacted immediately after World War II; but certain products are exempted from this Act. Initially, nine product categories were exempted, but four subsequently have been taken off the list. In 1969, resale price maintenance was legally allowed for the following product groups: cosmetics, dyes, toothpaste, soap for home use, and drugs. There are some 4,000 specific items within these broad product categories.

TABLE 3.6

NUMBER OF JAPANESE MANUFACTURERS REQUIRING RESALE PRICE MAINTENANCE FOR SELECTED PRODUCTS, 1954–1968

| Year | Cosmetics | Hair Dyes | Toothpaste | Soap | Drugs |
|------|-----------|-----------|------------|------|-------|
| 1954 | 10 | 13 | — | 1 | — |
| 1955 | 23 | 15 | — | 1 | 1 |
| 1956 | 23 | 2 | — | 1 | 1 |
| 1957 | 24 | — | — | 1 | 1 |
| 1958 | 33 | — | — | 1 | 1 |
| 1959 | 34 | — | — | 3 | 1 |
| 1960 | 24 | — | — | 3 | 1 |
| 1961 | 25 | — | — | 1 | 1 |
| 1962 | 30 | — | 2 | 4 | 1 |
| 1963 | 30 | — | 2 | 4 | 5 |
| 1964 | 33 | 1 | 2 | 4 | 14 |
| 1965 | 34 | 1 | 4 | 6 | 29 |
| 1966 | 35 | 1 | 4 | 7 | 36 |
| 1967 | 34 | 1 | 2 | 9 | 39 |
| 1968 | 34 | — | 2 | 9 | 44 |

Source: *Kokumin Seikatsu Hakusho: Showa 44 nen [White Paper on National Life]* (Tokyo: The Economic Planning Agency, 1969), pp. 282–283.

As indicated in Table 3.6, the number of manufacturing firms that engage in resale price maintenance has been increasing steadily during the past 13 years. Growing competitive pressure and a rising trend toward price cutting in those industries in which the practice is allowed are considered to be the major reasons for this increase. While the total annual sales of the products covered by resale price maintenance agreements are estimated to account for only about 2 percent of total retail sales, in some industries they are extremely important. For example, in cosmetics sales virtually all the major firms insist on resale price maintenance for certain products. It is estimated that the products covered by this practice account for as high as 85 percent of total cosmetic sales. It is further estimated that altogether as many as 42,000 wholesalers and retailers are bound by resale price agreements of some sort. In those industries in which this practice is allowed, it is a very potent weapon for manufacturers to establish and maintain control over the channels of distribution. In addition, even in those industries in which resale price maintenance is not permitted legally, large manufacturers are engaged in covert or underground attempts to control prices and terms of sale at various levels of the channel. For several reasons the Japanese government was lax, at least until recently, in enforcing the Anti-Monopoly Act, including resale price maintenance; this attitude, of course, encouraged large companies to resort to informal agreements to control the price structure through the various channels.

By the sheer power that these large manufacturing firms enjoy vis-à-vis their distributors, they can bind to an important degree the actions of their marketing intermediaries. They are often in a position to exert strong pressure against recalcitrants, including refusal to sell to distributors who are not responsive to manufacturers' requirements. A recent estimate by the Fair Trade Commission indicates that these "underground" or "informal" arrangements for resale price maintenance affect transactions totaling some ¥2,300 billion, accounting for some 20 percent of total retail sales.

We have seen how large manufacturers in certain industries have taken over leadership in the distribution system. In many cases, as we have seen, these patterns have been developed not by conscious design or strategy but through a series of groping experiments as a by-product of the search for better alternatives to the traditional methods.

It is significant to note, however, that within a very short period of time in a number of industries we have witnessed the emergence of a well-organized and disciplined manufacturer-controlled distribution system. In doing so, manufacturers have devised a variety of ingenious means and by and large have been flexible and pragmatic. The patterns thus emerging range from tightly controlled and autocratic relationships, as in the case of automobiles or even home appliances, to the cooperative and democratic type, as in the case of the pharmaceutical industry. The degree of success, of course, depends on a number of factors, but to an important measure, it is related to large manufacturers' ability:

1. To establish a strong consumer franchise for their products through aggressive promotion.
2. To extend financial and managerial assistance to selected marketing intermediaries.
3. To develop alternate channels, if necessary.
4. To bind marketing intermediaries legally on resale price and terms of sale or to insist on informal "understandings" on resale price maintenance.

The apparent success achieved in a number of industries is largely due, of course, to intense efforts by manufacturers, but it is interesting to speculate on the degree to which such efforts have been facilitated by a strongly entrenched collectivity orientation, particularly of the hierarchical type, in Japanese cultural tradition. At least, manufacturers' appeals for group solidarity and identification, when appropriately supported by practical incentives, are consistent with a dominant aspect of Japanese cultural heritage.

### Problems of Manufacturer Control over Distribution

As we have seen, the attainment of control over vertical distribution channels offers a number of significant advantages to the manufacturer. Of course, establishing and maintaining such a system solves some problems but also creates problems of its own.

First, this practice imposes a serious burden on the manufacturer, making heavy demands on his already strained financial and managerial resources. To remain effective, a manufacturer's control over the distribution system requires his continuing attention. The fact that the majority of marketing intermediaries are small and inadequately financed makes it imperative for the sponsoring manufacturer to make substantial financial advances. In addition, administering a complex system of distribution whose membership consists of a large number of independent units requires a considerable amount of managerial skill. There frequently exists a wide ideological gap between high-level professional managers of large manufacturing firms and typically independent-minded owners of small retail outlets. This further complicates the task of administration. Such a system also imposes on the sponsoring firms a certain degree of operating rigidity. For one thing, in order to assure total cooperation from retailers, the manufacturer must maintain full product lines, making it difficult to discontinue less-profitable products or even certain models of a given product.

Finally, the practice sometimes has resulted in the intensification of competition among retailers. This practice tends to draw a clear line of demarcation among retailers by identifying them with specific manufacturers, in many cases worsening the already intense competition in the retailing sector.

While large manufacturers in selected consumer goods industries have now attained considerable control over the distribution channels, there are two important recent developments that may well impede such a system. Because of the very recent origin of these developments, it is too early to assess their full impact, but they are too important to be ignored.

One development is the increasingly stringent attitude of the Fair Trade Commission (FTC) toward manufacturers' attempts to control price structures throughout their channels, particularly in the form of "underground" price maintenance agreements. The Fair Trade Commission, reflecting a growing national concern for the continuing rise of the consumer price level, has begun to take stricter measures against these informal resale price agreements. Soon after an abortive attempt to pass a separate law to impose tighter restrictions on resale price maintenance in 1967, the Commission began to scrutinize several industries in which informal resale price maintenance agreements were believed to be particularly prevalent.

In the summer of 1967 the FTC accused Matsushita Electric of being engaged in resale price maintenance activities illegally on the grounds that the company (1) specified the wholesale price and rebate structure to be followed by its controlled outlets and (2) refused shipment to violators. The Commission interpreted Matsushita's policy as a violation of Article 19 of the Anti-Monopoly Act and directed the company to cease and desist. Matsushita denied the accusation, and at the time of this writing the dispute had yet to be solved.

Likewise, in November 1967 the FTC accused Sony of being engaged in similar acts. The Commission claimed that the contract among three parties—Sony (specifically Sony Trading Co., a wholly owned marketing subsidiary of Sony), its wholesalers, and its retail outlets—contained clauses that were deemed in violation of the Anti-Monopoly Act. Specifically, the contract contained a clause suggesting that retail outlets conduct their operations in such a way as to yield a satisfactory profit based on the manufacturer's recommended price. The contract also confined the activities of retail outlets to sales to ultimate consumers. After considerable discussion, the FTC and Sony reached an understanding in June 1968 that the Commission would suspend further investigation provided that the company would weaken the terms of the contract.

Another indication of the FTC's growing concern for monopolistic practices, resulting in part from manufacturers' control over distribution channels, is reflected in its recent decisions to expand its research and investigation staff to permit watchful eyes to scrutinize such corporate practices. At the time of this writing, discussions were also under way to reassess the current legal provisions for resale price maintenance. Although it is too early to evaluate fully the impact of these developments, if the FTC persists in applying pressures against informal or underground resale price maintenance activities by manufacturers, it will undoubtedly weaken the power of manufacturers.

The other development is even more basic in challenging manufacturers' newly gained leadership in the distribution system. This is the rapid emergence of countervailing power within the distribution sector itself. A chief reason why large manufacturers have been so successful in achieving their control over marketing intermediaries is the fact that the marketing intermediaries characteristically have been small and highly fragmented, with extremely limited resources. The manufacturers' dominance in the distribution system, however, is now being challenged by the emergence of a countervailing power in the distribution structure. This rather recent development takes two forms. One is the phenomenal growth of innovative large-scale mass merchandising firms. Because of its singular importance, we shall examine this development in detail in a subsequent chapter (Chapter 4); suffice it here to note that rapidly emerging new types of large-scale retail firms present a very potent threat to large manufacturers. We already have begun to see a direct confrontation between large manufacturers and large-scale retail establishments in a number of popular product lines. The retail firms are very anxious to reduce the dominant position of large manufacturers in Japan's distribution system, and there is growing evidence that they gradually are eroding the heretofore uncontested position of the manufacturers.

The other development is a trend for smaller retail and wholesale outlets to form cooperative and voluntary chains. We shall have occasion to examine details of this trend, also, in a subsequent chapter (Chapter 5). We should note here that such organized groups will strengthen the otherwise weak position of small wholesale and retail establishments, making them less responsive to pressures exerted by large manufacturers. Suffice it here to note that these developments seem to indicate that the present power contest between manufacturers and marketing intermediaries is rather fluid and dynamic.

**Evaluation and Conclusion**

In this chapter we have examined how large Japanese manufacturing firms have adapted their organization, policies, and strategies to the needs of the emerging mass consumption market. Until the end of World War II most of the large manufacturing concerns represented those characteristics typically associated with production-oriented firms. They not only showed little concern for the consumer market but in fact considered their sole function to be production. Moreover, the Zaibatsu control had limited competition, and there had existed a rather clear-cut distinction between production and marketing by means of the trading company.

In face of the loss of the military market in the postwar era, however, large manufacturers had no choice but to switch to peacetime industry. In order successfully to penetrate a rapidly emerging mass consumer market, large manufacturers soon found that they had to assume a new posture toward marketing. The need to involve themselves actively with marketing functions initially was forced on them by the inability of the traditional marketing intermediaries to respond adequately to new demands placed on them, and this need was further accelerated by an increasing competitive pressure.

In their effort toward greater involvement in marketing activities, large manufacturing firms have realigned their organizational structure, expanded line and staff marketing personnel, initiated marketing research, and established new product development programs. They have begun to seek consumer franchises for their products through extensive promotional efforts and by building a vertically controlled distribution system under the manufacturer's leadership. Indeed, in many industries large manufacturing firms have taken away the intiative that was once vested with large primary wholesalers. In a number of key consumer industries, manufacturing firms clearly have emerged as captain of the channels. All these changes have been accomplished in a relatively short time—less than a decade and a half in most cases. There is every indication that this trend is likely to continue and probably to be intensified in the future. Without doubt, most large Japanese manufacturing firms in consumer industries are now very involved with marketing activities.

By any standard the transition has been remarkable, but have large Japanese firms transformed themselves into truly marketing-oriented firms? Despte the appearance of characteristics that are generally associated with marketing-oriented firms, closer examination of the past behavior of many large Japanese manufacturing firms in consumer industries indicates that they have a considerable way to go to become truly marketing-oriented. In the past there was a tendency even among Japan's leading firms to pay little attention to the realities of the market in planning capacity or entry into a new business. Rather, these key decisions were made on the basis of intuitive judgment, wishful thinking, or unbounded optimism on the part of key executives.

There is a tendency even among otherwise highly capable executives to refuse to recognize market conditions in undertaking their expansion programs. Such aggressive expansion programs often created a mismatch between supply and demand, thus resulting in excess inventories. Confronted with this situation, some manufacturing firms, overly anxious to improve their current profit picture, were not above loading their affiliated marketing intermediaries with their excess inventories, while paying little attention to the long-term impact of such actions. Nearsighted solutions, such as large rebates and liberal discounts, did not solve the problem but only made it worse. Certainly, the behavior of large manufacturing firms was in a number of cases far from what we would expect from truly marketing-oriented firms.

Ironically, in many cases these manufacturing firms strengthened their marketing organization, improved their distribution structure, and expanded their advertising program in order to solve the problems created in the first place by their ill-conceived and over-optimistic capacity planning. What is more curious is that even when the difficulties became obvious, the managements of many of these firms steadfastly refused to adjust their output. Of course, given the very dynamism of postwar economic growth in Japan, one should not be too harsh in judging the behavior of Japanese executives. After all, the very aggressive expansionary policy followed by Japan's leading manufacturing firms has been a major factor in promoting the nation's rapid economic growth. Surely, the difficulties of checking rapid growth momentum must be appreciated fully; and perhaps these inadequacies should be considered as growing pains as firms underwent a difficult transition from production orientation to marketing orientation. Nevertheless, the relative universality of this situation, which prevailed until very recently, is something that we should not ignore.

Most large Japanese manufacturing firms fall short of the ideal model of marketing-oriented firms in another rather basic way. A hallmark of a marketing-oriented firm is that it has a set of clear-cut corporate marketing goals as well as strategies to attain these goals. Moreover, marketing strategies must be well coordinated and integrated. How do large Japanese manufacturing firms handling key consumer goods measure up against these criteria? Careful examination reveals that most large Japanese firms are wanting in these respects, too. True, many firms have developed sophisticated approaches to specific aspects of marketing management such as advertising, new product development, and dealer organization. In marketing research most up-to-date techniques are now being employed in many firms. At the technical level it is difficult to fault the marketing capacities of Japan's leading manufacturing firms. Despite technical sophistication it is uncommon to find firms even among the leading ones that have clearly defined and well-integrated marketing objectives and strategies.

A particular method of decision making that is commonly employed in large Japanese corporations is cumbersome and encourages a piecemeal approach.[11] This tends to mitigate against efforts toward development of well-conceived corporate marketing goals and strategies. Also, the traditional decision-making process makes it difficult to base decisions on objective information provided by marketing research or other staff groups. Thus, despite the apparent prevalence of organizational units specializing in marketing research in large Japanese corporations, only limited use has been made of the research input in strategic decision making. Various elements of the marketing mix have been employed extensively, and in many cases each aspect is well performed; but the coordination of various individual elements in the marketing mix leaves something to be desired, even in the most progressive Japanese manufacturing firms.

Further evidence of the lack of total marketing orientation among large Japanese firms can be seen in their approaches to diversification. Product diversification has been an important strategy for growth for many Japanese corporations during the postwar decades. In determining the direction of diversification, however, there is a tendency even among the more progressive firms to do so chiefly from their strength in production and manufacturing capabilities. Frequently slighted in this decision is the careful assessment of the unfilled needs that the company is capable of supplying in the marketplace. In a large number of major Japanese corporations the potential strength of the firm in the marketing area does not always receive adequate attention in diversification decisions. This is so despite the fact that underutilization of marketing capabilities or less than optimum use of strength in marketing does exist; if these capabilities were utilized effectively, they would constitute a very powerful asset.

In this chapter we have examined how large Japanese manufacturing firms have evolved from traditional production orientation to marketing orientation. Given the very short period of time and the dynamic nature of the corporate environment, these firms have done well, but most have not yet reached the final stage of genuinely marketing-oriented firms. The best characterization that can be applied to most large consumer goods manufacturers in Japan is that they are now in a transitory stage. Given the well-

11 Yoshino, *Japan's Managerial System*, pp. 254–272.

entrenched organizational structure and traditional decision-making system, the next step in their evolution may be a most difficult one. But in the face of growing international and domestic competition, the future success of Japan's large corporations depends, to an important degree, on how effectively and speedily they can achieve the final stage.

# 4

# Innovations in the
# Distribution Sector

Having examined the adaptive behavior of large manufacturers of
consumer goods to the challenges of the rising mass consumer
market, we shall now turn our attention to salient developments
in the distribution sector in recent years. In this chapter we shall
examine the emergence of new institutions and highly innovative
operating concepts, and in Chapter 5 we shall focus our attention
on the adaptive behavior of traditional marketing institutions to
the rapidly changing environment.

The distribution sector in Japan has been undergoing some significant changes in the last decade, particularly in the last several
years, The very fundamental change in the environment that we
discussed earlier has created new consumers' needs, which have
not been adequately met by traditional marketing institutions. In
response to newly created opportunities, we have witnessed the
emergence of innovative and aggressive entrepreneurs who successfully have introduced within a very short period of time new
concepts and institutional arrangements in the tradition-bound
distribution system. The rapidity with which many of the dramatic
innovations have taken firm hold is rather startling. It is significant
to note that most of the very fundamental innovations in the distribution sector thus far have taken place in the retailing sector.
Furthermore, these innovative changes have been introduced by
a very small number of entrepreneurs, but they already have had a
major impact.

A significant recent development in the retailing sector is the

129

gradual decline in the importance of very small establishments and a trend toward greater concentration among larger operating units. As indicated in Table 4.1, the composition of retail stores by

TABLE 4.1

PERCENTAGE DISTRIBUTION OF RETAIL ESTABLISHMENTS
BY NUMBER OF EMPLOYEES, 1952 AND 1968

| Size of Establishment by No. of Employees | 1952 | 1968 |
|---|---|---|
| 1–2 | 95.4 | 67.1 |
| 3–4 | | 21.3 |
| 5–9 | 3.7 | 8.4 |
| 10–19 | 0.7 | 2.2 |
| 20–29 | 0.1 | 0.5 |
| 30–49 | 0.1 | 0.3 |
| 50–99 | 0.0 | 0.1 |
| 100 and over | 0.0 | 0.1 |

Source: *Shōgyō Tokei Sokuho, Showa 43 nen [Preliminary Report on Commercial Statistics, 1968]* (Tokyo: The Ministry of International Trade and Industry, 1969), p. 43, for 1968; and for 1952, *Wagakuni no Shōgyō, 1967 [Commerce in Japan]* (Tokyo: The Ministry of International Trade and Industry, 1968), p. 105.

size has been undergoing some change during the last decade. The percentage of very small stores (those with four employees or fewer) has been steadily declining since 1952, and establishments with five or more employees have been growing.

Similarly, in terms of size as measured by floor space, the relative importance of very small stores has been shrinking. Even during the six-year period 1960 to 1966, the latest year for which such data are available, the relative importance of stores with 19 square meters (203 square feet) or less declined. Particularly noteworthy was the five percentage point decline of stores with 9 square meters (963 square feet) or less. Details are presented in Table 4.2.

Further evidence for this trend is presented in Table 4.3. A considerable shift took place between 1960 and 1966 in the distribution of total sales by size of establishment. In 1960 establishments with four employees or fewer accounted for 47 percent of the total retail sales, whereas six years hence the percentage declined to less than 41 percent. In contrast, the share held by establishments with 50 or more employees increased from 13 per-

TABLE 4.2

PERCENTAGE DISTRIBUTION OF RETAIL ESTABLISHMENTS
BY SIZE OF SALES FLOOR SPACE, 1960 AND 1966

| Sales Floor Space (square meters)* | 1960 | 1966 |
|---|---|---|
| 1–9 | 18.3 | 11.8 |
| 10–19 | 39.9 | 36.2 |
| 20–29 | 20.7 | 22.3 |
| 30–49 | 14.3 | 18.4 |
| 50–99 | 5.3 | 8.1 |
| 100–199 | 1.0 | 1.7 |
| 200–499 | 0.4 | 0.8 |
| 500–999 | 0.1 | 0.2 |
| 1,000 or more | 0.0 | 0.1 |

*One square meter equals 10.8 square feet.
Source: *Wagakuni no Shōgyō, 1969 [Commerce in Japan]* (Tokyo: The Ministry of International Trade and Industry, 1970), p. 84.

TABLE 4.3

PERCENTAGE DISTRIBUTION OF TOTAL RETAIL SALES
ACCORDING TO THE SIZE OF ESTABLISHMENT, 1960 AND 1966

| Size of Establishment by No. of Employees | Percentage of Total Retail Sales | |
|---|---|---|
| | 1960 | 1966 |
| 1–4 | 47.0 | 40.8 |
| 5–9 | 22.6 | 20.6 |
| 10–19 | 10.6 | 11.7 |
| 20–49 | 6.7 | 9.1 |
| 50 and over | 13.1 | 17.8 |

Source: *Chushō Kigyō Hakusho: Showa 43 nen ban [White Paper on Small–Medium-Size Enterprises, 1968]* (Tokyo: The Small–Medium-Size Enterprise Agency, 1969), p. 120.

cent to nearly 18 percent during this period. Particularly striking is a growing trend for concentration of sales among a small number of very large retail establishments. According to a survey conducted by the *Japan Economic Journal* in 1968, the 104 largest retail firms in aggregate were responsible for 13.8 percent of the total retail sales in the year ending March 31, 1968.[1] A year later a similar study of the 102 largest retail

[1] "Kyodai Jidai ni Totsunyu Suru Kourigyo" ["Entry into an Era of Large Business in Retailing"] *Nihon Keizai Shinbun*, April 30, 1968, p. 7.

firms revealed that their share increased to 14.5 percent of the estimated total retail sales for that year.[2] Moreover, in 1969 the 20 largest retail firms were responsible for 8.2 percent of total retail sales.

A trend for greater concentration among large-scale retail establishments is evident even among specialty stores. For example, in home appliances, it is estimated that the 300 largest stores specializing in the sales of home appliances (out of roughly 36,000 establishments) are now responsible for 19 percent of the total home appliance sales. Similarly, the 100 largest camera stores out of some 10,000 stores account for 40 percent of the total sales of cameras. Likewise, the 100 largest stores in watches (25,000 stores), shoes (20,000 stores), and furniture (10,000 stores) are responsible for roughly 13 percent of the total sales in each of these product categories.

## The Emergence of New Retailing Institutions

An important factor responsible for greater concentration in the retailing field is the emergence of a new type of large-scale retailing institution, employing merchandising concepts and techniques radically different from those established traditionally. Within a very short time they have become a dominant force in the Japanese retailing scene. In fact, it is no exaggeration to state that this is the single most important development in the retailing sector in modern Japan.

These newly emerged institutions share two major characteristics. One is that their operating policy is mass-merchandise-oriented, with their major appeal to the mass consumer market; the other is that they are chain-operated. These institutions are of three types. The most important type is what is commonly referred to as "supermarkets" in Japan, which combine characteristics that are commonly associated with American supermarkets and discount stores. They emphasize a merchandising concept characterized by a high volume, low margin, and high turnover. Although they carry a broad line of merchandise, including food, soft goods, household goods, and kitchen utensils as well as consumer durables, they tend to concentrate on high-volume standard items

---

2 "Teikei Gappei de Kyodaika" ["Growing to Giant Scale Through Cooperative Relationships and Mergers"] *Nihon Keizai Shinbun*, May 3, 1969, p. 3.

within each merchandise category. They offer only a limited range of services and follow a very aggressive promotion policy, with the main emphasis on low price, and most are operated on a self-service basis.

The second type is a unique Japanese retailing institution known as an installment department store. As the name implies, these are department stores that are engaged primarily in installment sales. Typically, these stores derive 80 percent to 90 percent of their total sales from this source. These stores are responsible for 2.5 percent of the total retail sales in Japan. The merchandise carried by this type of store consists primarily of apparel and consumer durables.

The third type is the large-scale chain of specialty stores. These are emerging in such fields as home appliances, cameras, watches, shoes, and books. In home appliances, for example, the largest chain in the field has 50 stores, with an annual sales volume of over ¥8.5 billion in 1969. The largest chain for shoes in 1969 operated 22 stores, with total sales of over ¥6 billion. Although there are these three varieties, since the supermarket is by far the most important, we shall confine the discussion primarily to this particular form of mass merchandising institution.

The rise of these large-scale mass merchandise institutions is indeed phenomenal. As late as in 1960 there were but 31 retailing firms whose annual sales volume exceeded ¥5 billion, or roughly $14 million, and all but one were traditional department stores. The exception, Maruzen, was a large specialty store whose management concept was quite similar to that of the traditional department store. By 1969, however, the number of retail firms in this category reached 112, almost quadrupling in less than a decade. It is also highly significant that in a mere nine years the composition of the retail firms in this category underwent a rather radical change. Of these 112 firms there were 46 department stores, and the rest were made up of newly emerged mass merchandising firms. Among the latter there were 52 supermarkets, 5 installment credit stores, and 9 specialty stores.

The first comprehensive survey of the development of large-scale mass merchandising firms was undertaken in November 1966 by the *Japan Economic Journal*. The study revealed that, excluding traditional department stores, there were then 50 mass merchandising firms (with a total of 793 stores) with at least ¥3 billion sales volume. These stores together accounted for roughly 4 percent of total retail sales in 1966. In the same year the department stores in aggregate were responsible for roughly 11 percent of total retail sales. It should be noted, however, that it took the department stores more than half a century to achieve this share, whereas mass merchandising stores had been able to capture as much as 4 percent of the total retail share in less than 10 years.

Out of this study emerges the following picture of a typical mass merchandising firm. In late 1966 a typical chain consisted of 16 stores, with aggregate sales of ¥8.1 billion and total floor space of 144,000 square feet, or slightly less than 9,000 square feet per store. The number of employees among the firms surveyed ranged from 250 to 5,000, with the average around 1,500. Significantly, in terms of average sales per firm, the mass merchandising firms' sales even in 1966 exceeded those of the department stores by a substantial margin (the average figure reported for the department stores for 1966 was ¥6.1 billion), and the mass merchandising firms had almost the same floor space (144,000 square feet for mass merchandising firms and 150,000 square feet for department stores).

The composition of merchandise differs somewhat among these stores. Fourteen of the 50 mass merchandising firms derived more than 50 percent of their sales from food. In 21 firms apparel and related items were responsible for more than 50 percent of the total sales, and the remaining 15 had a somewhat more balanced merchandise composition. They derived 40 percent of total sales from apparel and related soft goods, 30 percent from food, and the remaining 30 percent from other assorted types of merchandise, including consumer durables, household and kitchen wares, cosmetics, drugs, and notions.

In the follow-up study conducted in 1967, mentioned earlier, it was learned that there were 104 retail firms of all types (including department stores) whose annual sales volume exceeded ¥4 billion for the fiscal year ending in March 1967. Again, the composition of the 104 firms is quite revealing. There were 54 mass-merchandising-oriented firms in contrast to 50 traditional department stores. Among the mass merchandising institutions there were 40 supermarket chains, 9 specialty stores, and 5 installment department stores. In terms of total sales, however, the 50 department stores were responsible for some 66 per cent of the total sales. In individual ranking by annual sales, department stores occupied the first four places, then came Daiei, the largest chain of supermarkets, with total sales of ¥58 billion for the year ending March 31, 1967.

These 104 firms can be broken roughly into three groups in terms of total sales volume. The largest group consists of those firms whose annual sales volume exceeds ¥20 billion. Among the 18 firms in this group there were 12 department stores and 6 mass merchandising chains. The next group is those with sales volume ranging between ¥10 billion and ¥20 billion. Among 26 firms in this category there were 12 department stores and 14 chains. The last category consists of firms with annual sales of less than ¥10 billion. There were 36 chain stores of various types and 24 department stores in this category. It is interesting to note that only in the very first category did the department stores outnumber the mass merchandising chains.

A similar study conducted by the *Japan Economic Journal* in May 1969 reveals further growth of the new types of retail institutions. The largest 102 retail firms studied were divided equally between department stores and mass merchandising firms. Among the latter there were 35 supermarket chains, 11 large specialty stores, and 5 installment department stores. The rapid growth of mass merchandising firms can be seen from the fact that the share of total sales held by department stores declined from the previous year's 66 percent to 60 percent in the 1969 study. Among 102 firms there were 17 firms that reported more than ¥30 billion in sales for fiscal year 1968: of these, 11 were department stores and 6 were mass merchandising firms. In the next category, consisting of firms with annual sales between ¥20 billion and ¥30 billion, there were 13 firms, of which 8 were mass merchandising firms. The list of the 20 largest retailing firms is presented in Table 4.4.

In 1969, according to one estimate, the total sales of the Japanese version of the supermarket are estimated to have reached ¥1.7 trillion ($4.7 billion), accounting for roughly 12 percent of total retail sales, overtaking department stores, which were in aggregate responsible for 10 percent of retail sales. By fiscal 1970 it is projected that the share of sales by supermarkets will reach the ¥2 trillion mark.[3]

The studies just cited provide convincing evidence for the very rapid growth of large-scale supermarket or discount chains in the

3 "Sangyo Tokushu" ["Industry Report"], *Nihon Keizai Shinbun*, March 24, 1970, pp. 21–26.

TABLE 4.4

THE TWENTY LARGEST RETAIL FIRMS IN JAPAN, FISCAL YEAR 1969

| Ranking | Name of Firm | Type of Operation | Estimated Annual Sales (¥ billion) | No. of Stores |
|---------|--------------|-------------------|-----------------|---------------|
| 1 | Mitsukoshi | Dept. Store | 145.0 | 11 |
| 2 | Daimaru | Dept. Store | 140.0 | 4 |
| 3 | Takashimaya | Dept. Store | 128.0 | 4 |
| 4 | Daiei | Supermarket | 120.0 | 47 |
| 5 | Matsuzakaya | Dept. Store | 105.0 | 5 |
| 6 | Seiyu Store | Supermarket | 88.0 | 70 |
| 7 | Seibu | Dept. Store | 85.0 | 8 |
| 8 | Jasco | Supermarket | 70.0 | 78 |
| 9 | Isetan | Dept. Store | 65.0 | 3 |
| 10 | Hankyu | Dept. Store | 60.0 | 5 |
| 11 | Sogo | Dept. Store | 55.0 | 4 |
| 12 | Nichiei | Supermarket | 53.0 | 70 |
| 13 | Tokyu | Dept. Store | 52.0 | 3 |
| 14 | Hoteiya | Supermarket | 48.0 | 71 |
| 15 | Fuchigami-Maruei | Supermarket | 45.0 | 21 |
| 16 | Nagasakiya | Supermarket | 40.0 | 46 |
| 17 | Kintetsu | Dept. Store | 38.7 | 2 |
| 18 | Marui | Installment Dept. Store | 38.0 | 29 |
| 19 | Midoriya | Installment Dept. Store | 37.5 | 43 |
| 20 | Hanshin | Dept. Store | 35.1 | 1 |

Source: "Kouri Kyodaika no Honryu" ["Rapidly Emerging Large-Scale Retailing"], *Nihon Keizai Shinbun*, Jan. 4, 1970, p. 92.

last decade. Even more dramatic is the growth of individual firms. To illustrate the very rapid growth achieved by these firms, let us examine the case of Daiei, the largest supermarket chain in Japan. The fantastic story began in 1951 when Isao Nakauchi opened his first drugstore. It was typical of the very small stores on the Japanese retailing scene, with sales space of less than 60 square feet. In 1957 it opened its first self-service store on a very modest scale, with the main merchandising lines consisting of drugs, cosmetics, and other sundry items. The store was no larger than 1,000 square feet, with three employees and with an annual sales volume of around ¥20 million, roughly $55,000. By 1960 the firm had four stores, with a sales volume approaching ¥3.2 billion. By early 1970, or slightly over a decade from its very modest beginning, Daiei had 47 stores, and its sales volume had grown to nearly ¥120 billion ($333 million). The company has set for itself the very ambitious goal of achieving annual sales of ¥400 billion, or $1.1 billion, by 1973.

Few who are knowledgeable about dynamic developments in Japan's current distribution scene doubt that within the next two or three years Daiei's sales will exceed those of the largest department store and will become the largest retail firm in the nation. Daiei's achievement is particularly remarkable, since in early 1970 there were only three other retail firms, all department stores, that had sales of more than ¥100 billion (it was only in 1967 that the ¥100 billion mark was ever achieved). These department stores—Mitsukoshi, Daimaru, and Takashimaya—have nearly 300 years of history as retail stores, and even as department stores they are more than 50 years old. In a little over a decade Daiei, from a very modest beginning, has grown to take over the hegemony of the nation's retailing sector. Though less spectacular, highly impressive growth records have been achieved by a number of other newly emerged mass merchandising firms.

## Factors Promoting Growth of Mass Merchandising Firms

What factors, then, are responsible for such phenomenal growth of large-scale mass merchandising institutions in postwar Japan? The single most important factor is the environmental change in postwar Japan, discussed earlier. This is not in any way to discount individual enterpreneurial foresight and effort; indeed, the handful of innovators who saw in these changes new opportunities and, more important, were able to translate them into action deserve much credit. However, without the very basic environmental change, no amount of enterpreneurial foresight and effort would have been as successful. It is in this context that environmental change is singled out as the most important factor.

Among the environmental changes the most significant are the emergence of the mass consumer market and the rapidly rising consumer expectations. As we have seen in Chapter 2, a large proportion of consumers were suddenly propelled into a position in which they began to enjoy some discretionary income. Those who had struggled for so long merely to eke out a daily living were confronted with opportunities to improve their lives; the amenities of the middle class had finally come within their reach. New products flooded the market and aggressive advertising messages were constantly beamed to consumers by large manufacturers. Consumers indeed found themselves a large number of alternative ways of spending their growing but still limited discretionary income.

Consumers' wants were stimulated and their consumption horizons pushed beyond their available means. In this context price became an extremely important consideration in buying decisions. The existing retail institutions, particularly prestige-oriented and conservatively managed department stores, were unable to fill the needs of this rising middle class. Indeed, these unfilled new consumer needs were the very opportunities that mass merchandising firms capitalized on. Very aggressive merchandising techniques —strong price appeal, extensive use of loss-leader merchandise, active advertising and promotion efforts, and limited service— were consistent with the equally aggressive desire of the rising middle class to improve its standard of living.

Typically, these stores were considerably larger than traditional neighborhood stores. Not only did they offer a broader range of

TABLE 4.5

PERCENTAGE OF EXPENDITURE MADE AT DEPARTMENT STORES AND
SUPERMARKETS ACCORDING TO INCOME CLASS, 1964

| Cash Income (¥) | Department Stores | | Supermarkets | |
| | Total Consumption Expenditure | Food | Total Consumption Expenditure | Food |
|---|---|---|---|---|
| Less than 9,999 | 1.5 | 2.1 | 3.8 | 6.4 |
| 10,000–19,999 | 3.3 | 1.4 | 5.3 | 7.6 |
| 20,000–29,999 | 3.6 | 1.5 | 5.8 | 9.2 |
| 30,000–39,999 | 4.5 | 1.7 | 6.1 | 10.0 |
| 40,000–49,999 | 5.0 | 2.3 | 5.6 | 10.1 |
| 50,000–59,999 | 5.5 | 2.7 | 5.8 | 10.3 |
| 60,000–69,999 | 5.8 | 2.9 | 5.5 | 10.4 |
| 70,000–79,999 | 6.0 | 3.2 | 5.0 | 10.1 |
| 80,000–89,999 | 5.7 | 3.8 | 4.3 | 9.3 |
| 90,000–99,999 | 7.7 | 3.7 | 4.6 | 10.3 |
| 100,000–119,999 | 9.4 | 5.0 | 4.1 | 9.3 |
| 120,000–139,999 | 8.8 | 5.3 | 3.3 | 7.9 |
| 140,000–159,999 | 11.5 | 7.2 | 3.4 | 7.5 |
| 160,000 and over | 9.4 | 4.9 | 5.8 | 17.7 |

Source: *Zenkoku Shohi Jittai Chōsa Hōkoku* [*Report on Consumption Expenditure in Japan*] (Tokyo: The Office of the Prime Minister, 1964), p. 50.

merchandise, but it was more attractively displayed. Moreover, they successfully projected the image that consumers were getting the best value for their money. At the same time they created a store atmosphere in which the emerging-middle-class customers felt comfortable. The fact that mass merchandising retail firms appeal to a lower income class than do department stores can be partially seen from the information presented in Table 4.5.

We should also note that the development of large-scale mass merchandising firms has been greatly encouraged by extensive development of consumer industries and aggressive marketing strategies followed by large manufacturing firms. Not only can large-scale manufacturing firms of consumer goods supply large quantities of merchandise of consistent quality, but their active promotional efforts have facilitated the growth of mass merchandise firms.

Through large-volume purchase of well-selected mass-produced standardized merchandise, as well as through limited customer services, these stores have been able to achieve substantial cost savings, at least a part of which has been passed on to their customers. National brands are carried extensively by large-scale mass merchandising firms, which has helped strengthen their reputation and credibility in the minds of consumers.

Another factor that cannot be ignored is the geographic shift of population. We noted in Chapter 2 the rising trend toward urbanization and the rapid emergence of so-called satellite or suburban towns, which offer new market opportunities. In fact, this market consists primarily of the rising middle class—described earlier— since they live at a considerable distance from major downtown shopping areas, and trips to downtown are not only expensive but time-consuming. Moreover, as the downtown centers become increasingly beset with typical urban ills, such as traffic congestion and air pollution, shopping in downtown centers has become less attractive. Unlike department stores, mass merchandising firms have capitalized aggressively on the rapid emergence of the suburban population by opening new stores in these areas. This expansion policy of creating stores where the market is, or is likely to develop, was a key factor leading to their success.

Of course, to be fair to the department stores, it should be noted that they have been somewhat constrained by legal restrictions from following a similar strategy. As we shall see in the next chapter, department stores in Japan are regulated by the

Department Store Law, whereas mass merchandising firms are not. Thus the latter have enjoyed considerable advantage over department stores in moving into attractive suburban markets. These forces that we have examined have interacted powerfully to prompt the emergence of large-scale mass merchandising retailing institutions.

### Characteristics of Emerging Mass Merchandising Firms

These mass merchandising retail firms have departed from the traditionally accepted merchandising concepts in a number of significant ways. First, as we have noted, they strictly adhere to the mass merchandising concepts of high volume, low margin, high turnover, and limited service. In fact, most are self-service stores. Second, they are typically operated as chains. Rather than building a single large store, their managements' policy has been to locate stores where the present or potential market is to be found. The chain system not only enables them to spread the risk among various stores but, more important, permits them to reduce total distribution costs through central purchasing. According to the aforementioned survey conducted by the *Japan Economic Journal* in 1966, the 50 leading mass merchandising firms bought on the average 60 percent of their merchandise centrally. Sixteen did as much as 90 percent of total buying in this manner. To obtain further savings in purchasing, these firms, unlike their traditional counterparts, minimize the use of credit. Instead, many now practice cash payment for their purchases. The 50 leading firms included in the *Journal's* survey made on the average 80 percent of their total purchases on a cash basis. Twenty-one of the 50 firms reportedly did 100 percent of their buying for cash.

Mass merchandising firms have incorporated a number of other innovative management practices. These include streamlined organizational structures, effective staff groups (particularly in the areas of long-range planning), market and locational analysis, centralized distribution facilities, and elaborate computerized merchandise control systems. A number of these stores also have established extensive management training programs. Indeed, the newly emerged large-scale mass merchandising firms are radically different from traditional types of small retail firms.

Let us now examine the salient characteristics of these newly emerged mass merchandising firms. In so doing, we shall draw from a comprehensive annual survey of the 100 largest mass merchandising chains conducted by Nihon Sen-I-Keizai Kenkyujo (Japan Textile Economic Research Institute). The latest study available at this writing was conducted in 1969, and the period covered in this study was fiscal year 1968.

Among the chains included in this study there are two types. One group consists of those whose principal source of sales is food and related products, while the other is made up of chains that carry broader lines of merchandise, including soft goods, cosmetics, household items, and home appliances as well as food. In the 1969 survey there were 28 food chains; the remaining 72 belonged to the diversified category. Since there are some significant differences between these two types, the study distinguishes between the two whenever appropriate.

Among these 100 chains there were 17 whose sales for fiscal year 1968 exceeded ¥10 billion. The number of chains in this category has increased steadily from 2 in 1963 to 10 in 1966 to 17 in 1968. For the first time, in 1968 3 food chains entered this group. Significantly, these 17 chains were responsible for over 62 percent of the combined sales of the 100 chains. In fact, the top 30 chains accounted for roughly 75 percent of all sales. Here again we see a relatively small number of large chains responsible for the preponderant share of the total.

Let us look first at the salient characteristics of the food chains. A typical chain has 14 stores, with a total sales volume of roughly ¥4,556 million (or around $12.6 million) and some 430 employees. The average store in a chain has annual sales of roughly ¥318 million (or $880,000) and approximately 30 employees. The size of an average store is slightly over 7,000 square feet. While these chains derive the principal share of their sales from food, they also carry some nonfood merchandise. The composition of the merchandise of these 28 food chains is presented in Table 4.6.

Even among these food chains there are some that are giving increasing attention to soft goods as a means of increasing their profitability as well as broadening their customer appeal. There are, on the other hand, those that are consciously staying only with food products. Compared with chains whose sole product is food, those chains carrying a broader line of merchandise have two notable characteristics. One is that this group as a whole has shown a more rapid growth rate than the straight food chains.

TABLE 4.6

MERCHANDISE COMPOSITION OF MAJOR FOOD CHAINS, 1968

| Merchandise Lines | Percent of Total Sales |
|---|---|
| Food | 62.1 |
| Apparel | 16.4 |
| Housewares | 9.5 |
| Drugs | 2.6 |
| Cosmetics | 4.6 |
| Electric Home Appliances | 1.0 |
| Others | 3.8 |
| Total | 100.0 |

Source: *Super Chain 100 Sha no Jittai Chōsa [A Report on Operating Characteristics of 100 Chains]* (Tokyo: Nihon Sen-I-Kenkyujo, 1969), p. 34.

For example, while the sales of food chains increased 26 percent in 1968 over the preceding year, chains with diversified product lines recorded nearly a 50 percent increase. The other feature is that this type of chain is considerably larger than an average food chain. A typical chain in this group had 13 stores, with total sales of ¥7,876 million (or slightly over $21 million) for fiscal year 1968 (73 percent more than the average sales of food store chains). The average chain had 724 employees. The average store in such a chain had annual sales of about ¥584 million ($1.6 million), with

TABLE 4.7

MERCHANDISE COMPOSITION OF MAJOR CHAINS
WITH DIVERSIFIED PRODUCT LINES

| Merchandise Lines | Percent of Total Sales |
|---|---|
| Food | 26.3 |
| Apparel | 54.9 |
| Housewares | 8.2 |
| Drugs | 1.1 |
| Cosmetics | 1.8 |
| Electric Home Appliances | 2.2 |
| Others | 5.5 |
| Total | 100.0 |

Source: *Super Chain 100 Sha no Jittai Chōsa [A Report on Operating Characteristics of 100 Chains]* (Tokyo: Nihon Sen-I-Kenkyujo, 1969), p. 34.

roughly 54 employees. The average store size was around 12,000 square feet, which is considerably larger than an average store in food chains. In terms of composition of merchandise, we note that the single most important category was apparel, which accounted for nearly 55 percent of total sales. This is largely due to the fact that many of these chains started out as clothing stores. Food accounted for 26 percent, while housewares came in a poor third with 8 percent of the total sales of these chains in 1968. The details are presented in Table 4.7.

Again these averages conceal the differences among individual chains. As might be expected, the merchandise composition of individual chains differs widely. Broadly speaking, there are three types, classified according to their merchandising strategy. First, there are those that sell almost exclusively soft goods and related items. The second type consists of those that are making conscious efforts to diversify from apparel lines to other products. Finally, there is a group that has balanced merchandising lines divided among foods, soft goods, home appliances, household wares, cosmetics, and so on.

Let us now examine the performance of these chains. Table 4.8 presents key operating figures for both types of chains. It is noteworthy that in all but one area, stock turnover, the chains with diversified product lines did considerably better than straight food chains.

### Backgrounds of New Entrepreneurs

One intriguing aspect of the new large-scale mass merchandising firms is the backgrounds of the entrepreneurs who were able to see the great profit potentials in the rapidly changing environment and were willing to take risks in challenging the unknown. Who were this handful of innovators who broke away from the traditional mold and concept of retailing? True, these men had the American example to follow, but major adaptations were indeed necessary to make the American type of merchandising workable in Japan. These entrepreneurs are indeed diverse in their individual backgrounds and orientations, but they do have several characteristics in common.

Significantly, the great majority of them have come from the retailing sector itself. With few exceptions, however, these institutional innovators came from outside the established power structure, and their personal backgrounds vary considerably. In fact, the

TABLE 4.8

KEY OPERATING DATA OF SUPERMARKET CHAINS, 1969

| Operating Data | Food Chains (¥1000) | Diversified Chains with Product Lines | All Chains |
|---|---|---|---|
| Sales per Tsubo* | ¥1,593,000 | ¥1,617,000 | ¥1,613,000 |
| Sales per Employee | ¥105,860,000 | ¥109,410,000 | ¥108,820,000 |
| No. of Customers per Chain per Day | 32,672 | 47,442 | 43,306 |
| Average Amount of Purchase per Customer | ¥454 | ¥622 | ¥577 |
| Annual Turnover of Merchandise (times) | 34.3 | 23.7 | 24.9 |
| Gross Margin as Percent of Net Sales | 16.7 | 18.4 | 18.1 |
| Labor Cost as Percent of Net Sales | 6.0 | 6.3 | 6.2 |
| Total Operating Expense as Percent of Net Sales | 14.6 | 16.0 | 15.7 |
| Net Profit as Percent of Net Sales | 2.1 | 2.4 | 2.4 |

* Approximately 35 square feet.
Source: *Super Chain 100 Sha no Jittai Chōsa* [*A Report on Operating Characteristics of 100 Chains*] (Tokyo: Nihon Sen-I-Kenkyujo, 1969), p. 33.

heterogeneity in their social backgrounds presents an interesting contrast to the homogeneity that characterizes professional managers in large-scale industrial and financial corporations. Some were the owners of small retail stores, while others had been employed by small retail establishments. Some inherited their small family stores, while others entered into retailing—a sector known for ease of entry—simply to eke out a living in the dislocations of the immediate postwar years. As a result, their educational backgrounds differ considerably. Some were born and raised in relatively affluent merchant families and had the benefits of higher education, while others had barely completed an elementary education.

They are relatively young, at least by Japanese standards. Most of these men belong to the generation that was severely affected by World War II and its subsequent dislocations and whose career plans and aspirations were at least temporarily shattered by the war. They were young enough not to be tied to traditional ways, perceptive enough to see new opportunities, and bold enough to challenge the established order. It is also interesting to note that most of these men were able to understand the significance of the development of mass merchandising concepts and their success in the United States. More important, they were able to apply these concepts and techniques in the Japanese context with necessary modifications.

It should also be noted that the concept of mass merchandising to these men is much more than a mere technique of doing business; rather, it is their philosophy. In fact, many of these men are promulgating their newly found merchandise doctrine with an evangelical fervor. Indeed, the rise of prominent entrepreneurs in the mass merchandising field in the last decade is an extremely interesting phenomenon and undoubtedly will be a subject of further inquiry in the future. While postwar Japan did produce some notable entrepreneurs in the manufacturing sector, including Konosuke Matsushita of Matsushita Electric, Masaru Ibuka and Akio Morita of Sony, and Sazo Idemitsu of Idemitsu Oil, the large-scale firms in the manufacturing sector are now dominated and tightly controlled by professional managers. Very limited opportunities are now present in large-scale manufacturing firms and financial institutions for entrepreneurs to rise quickly to prominence. In contrast, the distribution sector is indeed a fertile field and offers an attractive alternative to the industrial and financial sector as an outlet for entrepreneurs' skills. Also noteworthy is the time difference in the rise of entrepreneurs between the manufacturing and distribution sectors. It was primarily in the late 1940s and the 1950s that entrepreneurs in the manufacturing sector enjoyed the greatest opportunity to attain prominence; but it was a decade or even two decades later before similar opportunities began to unfold in the merchandising field.

*Entry of Traditional Marketing Institutions into the Mass Merchandising Field*

Although the mass merchandising field is now largely dominated by aggressive entrepreneurs who rose rapidly from obscurity, it is not their exclusive domain. Other elements actively have been seeking opportunities in this rapidly growing field. Particularly notable are the department stores owned and managed by a number of private railroad companies and located in large cities, particularly in Tokyo. These railroads service Tokyo's rapidly growing suburbs. In recent years, taking advantage of their strategic positions, they have diversified into real estate development, sight-seeing, retailing, bus lines, taxis, and other related transportation and service businesses. In retailing they have built department stores at their major terminals, and more recently they have gone into mass merchandising operations. These urban railroad-based conglomerates enjoy several advantages in entering the large-scale mass merchandising field. First, extensive land ownership along their railroad lines is extremely valuable for store sites. Second, they can locate their stores as a part of planned housing developments, and in this regard they have a clear advantage over competitors in the choice of store locations. Third, they often have greater access to managerial and financial resources, including good banking connections. A most successful example of mass merchandising operations of this type is the Seiyu Chain, part of the Seibu Railroad group that now is the second largest mass merchandising firm in Japan.

In addition, there are three other powerful groups that are eyeing the mass merchandising field with increasing interest. Large trading firms have become increasingly active in this field. They have now become deeply interested in mass merchandising. The traditional department stores that until recently had adhered to their own merchandising philosophy now have become increasingly intrigued by rapidly growing opportunities in the mass merchandising field, and a number of prestigious department stores have diversified into mass merchandising operations. We shall examine, in some detail, these activities of the trading companies and department stores in Chapter 5.

There is yet another element that has considerable interest in entry into the mass merchandising field. These are consumer and agricultural cooperatives. Consumer cooperatives in Japan, despite their long history, have not been fully developed. It is estimated that there are some 1,600 consumer cooperatives with approximately 8 million members, and their total annual sales are around ¥150 billion. Most of these stores are still rather small. There are some exceptions, however. For example, several cooperative-sponsored chains are included among the 100 largest chains. The largest of these is the Nada Kobe supermarket, which boasts annual sales of ¥24 billion (fiscal year ending in March 1969). The chain has 27 stores in eight major cities in the Osaka-Kobe areas, serving some 160,000 member households. Its sales experienced some fifteenfold growth in the decade ending in 1969. Many consumer cooperatives are now making concerted efforts to develop along the line of the Nada Kobe chain.

Much more powerful than consumer cooperatives are agricultural cooperatives. There are roughly 7,000 agricultural cooperatives located throughout Japan, with total membership of some 5 million agricultural households. The annual volume of purchasing done through the central purchasing organization of the Agricultural Cooperative Federation exceeds ¥740 billion, to be distributed through their diverse organizations. One of the important services that the agricultural cooperatives provide is retail outlets for daily necessities. More than 4,200 cooperatives maintain altogether nearly 10,000 outlets of this type for their membership, with total sales of some ¥160 billion. Out of these 10,000 outlets roughly 3,000 are self-service stores. At present over 90 percent of these stores are small, with less than 230 square meters of sales space (roughly 2,500 square feet). But they can be a very potent force to become large-scale retail operations because they enjoy several unique advantages. They already have a powerful central buying organization that can be readily mobilized. They can rely on the active support of their membership and also have relatively abundant financial resources. There is growing evidence that agricultural cooperatives are expanding rapidly and are already posing a serious competitive threat to regular supermarket chains.

*Growth of the Self-Service Concept*

We have noted earlier that the self-service concept is now employed extensively by large-scale mass merchandising firms; but it is not confined to large-scale mass merchandising chains. It is also employed by some single-unit smaller retail establishments in certain merchandise lines, such as food and soft goods. Though this concept is closely related to development of large-scale mass merchandising firms, because of its significance we shall afford it separate treatment.

The self-service concept as applied to retailing, however, is strictly a postwar phenomenon, having been first introduced in Tokyo in 1953. Many at that time questioned the applicability of the self-service concept in Japan, claiming that it was the complete antithesis to traditional retailing practices commonly accepted in Japan. Certainly, few were able to predict the very rapid rate at which this rather radical innovation would be accepted by the average Japanese consumer. Indeed, it has now become widely

TABLE 4.9

GROWTH OF SELF-SERVICE STORES, 1964–1968

|  | Total | Seven Major Metropolitan Areas | Others |
|---|---|---|---|
| No. of Stores |  |  |  |
| 1964 | 3,620 | 534 | 3,086 |
| 1966 | 4,790 | 657 | 4,133 |
| 1968 | 7,062 | 889 | 6,173 |
| Rate of Increase (%) |  |  |  |
| 1964–1966 | 32.3 | 23.0 | 33.9 |
| 1966–1968 | 47.4 | 35.3 | 49.4 |
| No. of Employees (1,000) |  |  |  |
| 1964 | 87 | 17 | 70 |
| 1966 | 105 | 19 | 86 |
| 1968 | 143 | 26 | 117 |
| Rate of Increase (%) |  |  |  |
| 1964–1966 | 20.7 | 11.8 | 22.9 |
| 1966–1968 | 36.0 | 40.0 | 35.1 |
| Annual Sales (¥100 million) |  |  |  |
| 1964 | 3,924 | 1,131 | 2,793 |
| 1966 | 5,811 | 1,399 | 4,412 |
| 1968 | 10,286 | 2,469 | 7,817 |
| Rate of Increase (%) |  |  |  |
| 1964–1966 | 48.1 | 23.7 | 58.0 |
| 1966–1968 | 77.0 | 76.4 | 77.2 |

Source: For 1964 and 1966, *Wagakuni no Shōgyō, 1967 [Commerce in Japan, 1967]* (Tokyo: The Ministry of International Trade and Industry, 1968), p. 52. For 1968, *Shōgyō Tōkei Sokuho, Showa 43 nen [Preliminary Report of Commercial Statistics, 1968]* (Tokyo: The Ministry of International Trade and Industry, 1969), pp. 8–9.

diffused, and consumers have come to expect self-service as a *modus operandi* of supermarket operations. Its rapid growth can be seen partially from the following statistics. From its modest beginning in 1953, the number of stores operating on a self-service basis reached 7,062 by 1968. Moreover, it recorded a 47.4 percent increase in the number of establishments and a 77 percent increase in sales over 1966. This is indeed an amazing rate of growth, considering the fact that between 1966 and 1968 the rate of growth of sales by self-service stores was almost three times the rate of growth of total retail sales (27 percent) and more than double

the rate of growth of department stores (32.4 percent).[4]
These stores in aggregate accounted for roughly 7.6 percent of
the total retail sales in 1968, as contrasted to 5.4 percent in 1966.[5]
Some details of the rapid growth of self-service stores in recent
years are presented in Table 4.9. It is also interesting to note that
self-service stores are not solely confined to urban areas but are
well diffused throughout the nation. In fact, in recent years the
rate of increase in the number of such stores in the areas outside
the seven major metropolitan areas exceeded that of the urban
centers, indicating widespread appeal.

The self-service stores have become increasingly important for
certain types of products. An estimate in 1969 based on the (Tokyo-
Yokohama area) panel maintained by the Hakuhodo, a leading
advertising agency in Japan, reveals the penetration of self-service
stores into the daily life of an average Japanese consumer. According to this survey, 81 percent of instant pudding, 71 percent of
cheese, 70 percent of instant coffee, 69 percent of mayonnaise, 65
percent of butter, 60 percent of canned fruits and margarine, 57
percent of seasonings, 49 percent of toothpaste, and 35 percent of
detergents are sold through self-service supermarkets.[6] In a decade
and a half less than 1 percent of some 700,000 food stores have
come to account for more than 50 percent of the sales of the more
popular packaged food products. Self-service outlets also have
become extremely important in selected apparel items. According
to a study conducted in 1969, self-service stores were responsible
for 35 percent and 45 percent, respectively, of the sales of women's
sweaters and blouses and for 23 percent of the total sales of men's
dress shirts.[7] Even for home appliances, the self-service outlets
were responsible for 1.2 percent of the total sales in 1969, rapidly
approaching the share of department stores (1.8 percent).[8] Nationwide data on where certain food products are being bought are
presented in Table 4.10. These data are drawn from a government

[4] *Shōgyō Tokei Sokuho, Showa 43 nen ban [Preliminary Report on Commercial Statistics, 1968]* (Tokyo: Ministry of International Trade and Industry, 1969), p. 8.
[5] *Ibid.*
[6] "Masu masu Fueru Super no Shuchū Shōhin" ["An Increase in the Number
of Products Sold Predominantly by Supermarkets"] *Nihon Keizai Shinbun*
November 17, 1969, p. 5.
[7] *Ibid.*
[8] *Ibid.*

## TABLE 4.10

### Percentage of Sales and Comparison of Retail Prices of Three Major Retail Outlets for Selected Food Products, 1967

(regular retail store prices = 100)

| Items (nationwide) | Regular Retail Outlets | | Supermarkets (self-service) | | Department Stores | |
|---|---|---|---|---|---|---|
| | % of Total Sold | Retail Price | % of Total Sold | Retail Price | % of Total Sold | Retail Price |
| Bread | 93 | 100 | 4 | 93.0 (87.3)* | 0 | 95.8 |
| Instant Noodles | 64 | 100 | 32 | 93.0 (90.0) | 1 | 92.6 |
| Beef | 85 | 100 | 13 | 96.2 (90.0) | 2 | 116.2 |
| Pork | 88 | 100 | 10 | 93.9 (81.9) | 1 | 107.0 |
| Chicken | 86 | 100 | 12 | 96.4 (78.4) | 1 | 111.4 |
| Cabbage | 86 | 100 | 13 | 88.6 (106.5) | 0 | 129.6 |
| Sugar | 71 | 100 | 20 | 93.4 (88.1) | 1 | 99.9 |
| Canned Salmon | 77 | 100 | 21 | 95.5 (92.7) | 1 | 95.9 |
| Margarine | 64 | 100 | 32 | 96.9 (94.1) | 1 | 100.6 |
| Cooking Oil | 72 | 100 | 25 | 92.4 (90.5) | 6 | 93.4 |
| Apples | 88 | 100 | 15 | 94.4 (101.2) | 1 | 119.9 |

* Numbers in parentheses indicate prices charged by supermarkets with annual sales exceeding ¥3 billion.
Source: Adapted from Rodo Hakusho, Showa 44 nen ban [White Paper on Labor, 1969] (Tokyo: The Ministry of Labor, 1969), p. 28.

survey on consumer prices, and as a result they include compari-
sons of average retail price for these products (comparable quality
and size). These data provide further evidence for the growing
strength of self-service outlets in certain standard food products. It
is also noteworthy that among three major outlets, without exception, self-service supermarket prices are considerably lower than
those charged by food specialty stores and in most cases those of
department stores. As may be expected, even among supermarkets
the average prices charged by large-scale establishments are lower
than those of smaller stores.

Having examined the rapid growth of the self-service concept
in Japan, let us now turn our attention to the operating characteristics of these stores. A typical self-service store is much smaller
than its American counterpart, although it is considerably larger
than a regular retail store in Japan. According to the Commercial
Census of 1968 a typical self-service store had an annual sales
volume of ¥147 million, or roughly $400,000, employed 20 full-
time employees, and had approximately 4,300 square feet of sales
space. A typical store derived 57 percent of its total sales from food,
27 percent from soft goods, and nearly 17 percent from assorted
other merchandise lines.[9]

According to the 1968 Census, of the 7,062 stores, 5,395, or
nearly 77 percent, derived most of their sales from food and some
900 stores, or 13 percent, obtained the major share of their sales
from soft goods.

Looking at the distribution of self-service stores by size, we find
that in 1968 92 percent of all establishments had less than 1,000
square meters, or roughly 10,700 square feet, of sales floor space.[10]
In fact, nearly half of the self-service stores in Japan in 1968 consisted of establishments with floor space of less than 200 square
meters, or 2,140 square feet. The details are presented in Table 4.11.
Similarly, as evident in Table 4.12, in terms of sales, over 60 percent
of the self-service stores consisted of establishments with annual
sales of less than ¥100 million ($280,000). There were only 756
stores that had annual sales of ¥300 million or more.[11] However, as
indicated in Tables 4.11 and 4.12, a trend toward increased physical
size and sales volume was apparent in 1968 as compared to 1966.

[9] *Wagakuni no Shōgyō, 1969 [Commerce in Japan, 1969]* (Tokyo: The
Ministry of International Trade and Industry, 1970), p. 7.
[10] *Ibid.*
[11] *Ibid.,* p. 320.

TABLE 4.11

DISTRIBUTION OF SELF-SERVICE STORES BY SIZE OF STORE
MEASURED BY SALES SPACE, 1966 AND 1968

| Sales Space (square meters)* | 1966 | | 1968 | |
|---|---|---|---|---|
| | No. of Stores | % | No. of Stores | % |
| 100–199 | 2,213 | 46.2 | 3,027 | 42.9 |
| 200–299 | 896 | 18.7 | 1,258 | 17.8 |
| 300–399 | 648 | 13.5 | 906 | 12.8 |
| 400–599 | 459 | 9.6 | 735 | 10.4 |
| 600–999 | 370 | 7.7 | 589 | 8.3 |
| 1,000–1,499 | 152 | 3.2 | 333 | 4.7 |
| 1,500 and over | 52 | 1.1 | 214 | 3.0 |
| Total | 4,790 | 100.0 | 7,062 | 100.0 |

* One square meter is approximately 10.8 square feet.
Source: For 1966, Wagakuni no Shōgyō, 1967 [Commerce in Japan, 1967] (Tokyo: The Ministry of International Trade and Industry, 1968), p. 302. For 1968, Shōgyō Tōkei Sokuho, Showa 43 nen [Preliminary Report of Commercial Statistics, 1968] (Tokyo: The Ministry of International Trade and Industry, 1969), p. 54.

Another valuable datum provided by the Commercial Census is the efficiency of self-service stores. The average annual sales per employee in self-service stores was more than twice the average figure in the retail sector. The figure reported for self-service stores

TABLE 4.12

DISTRIBUTION OF SELF-SERVICE STORES BY
ANNUAL SALES VOLUME, 1966 AND 1968

| Annual Sales (¥ million) | 1966 | | 1968 | |
|---|---|---|---|---|
| | No. of Stores | % | No. of Stores | % |
| Less than 50 | 1,860 | 38.8 | 2,546 | 36.0 |
| 50–99 | 1,211 | 25.3 | 1,840 | 26.1 |
| 100–299 | 1,329 | 27.8 | 1,920 | 27.2 |
| 300 and over | 390 | 8.1 | 756 | 10.7 |
| Total | 4,790 | 100.1 | 7,062 | 100.0 |

Source: For 1966, Wagakuni no Shōgyō, 1967 [Commerce in Japan, 1967] (Tokyo: The Ministry of International Trade and Industry, 1968), p. 302. For 1968, Wagakuni no Shōgyō, 1969 [Commerce in Japan, 1969] (Tokyo: The Ministry of International Trade and Industry, 1970), p. 320.

was nearly 7.2 million, as contrasted to ¥3 million for the overall average. Of particular interest is the apparent economy of scale that exists among self-service stores. The sales per employee ranged from ¥5,870,000 for very small stores (less than 200 square meters, or 2,140 square feet) to ¥8,240,000 for stores with floor space of more than 1,500 square meters, or 16,050 square feet. Likewise, the ratio of operating expenses to sales declined progressively with the increase in store size, except for those with 1,500 employees or more. A similar pattern is observed for the ratio of wages and salary expenses to total sales. The details are presented in Table 4.13.

### Development of Shopping Centers

The most recent innovation in the distribution sector is the emergence of shopping centers to serve the rapidly growing suburban population. For some time, Japan has had a semblance of shopping centers in which a number of specialty stores are housed under one roof. They have taken the form of shopping arcades or have been concentrated in major railroad terminals. Suburban shopping centers as known in the United States are, however, a recent phenomenon, and the trend for their growth is very apparent. At the time of this writing only three or four of this type of shopping center were in operation, although a number were under construction and more were in the planning stage.

Shopping centers are being developed by diverse interests, including large department stores, mass merchandising firms, major city banks, trading companies, leading real estate development firms, and even life insurance companies. In fact, the development of shopping centers has provided the mechanism by which some of the corporate and financial interests that had not been active in distribution activities have entered this field. So far, the patterns of development have taken two forms. One is for a single department store or mass merchandising firm to become the primary development agent; the other takes the form of joint actions or consortium of a number of diverse interests. Several department stores and mass merchandising firms are now constructing shopping centers of their own. Examples of this first type are the two centers that were developed by Daiei in Osaka and the Seibu group in a satellite city near Tokyo. The second type is exemplified by Tamagawa shopping center in the suburbs of Tokyo. It was constructed by a consortium organized by a major city bank, a life insurance

## TABLE 4.13

### KEY OPERATING CHARACTERISTICS OF SELF-SERVICE STORES ACCORDING TO SIZE, 1968

| Size (square meters of floor space) | Annual Sales per Store | | Annual Sales per Employee | | Sales per 1 Square Meter Sales Space | |
|---|---|---|---|---|---|---|
| | Amount (¥10,000) | Size Disparity* | Amount (¥10,000) | Size Disparity* | Amount (¥10,000) | Size Disparity* |
| 100–199 | 5,361 | 1.0 | 587 | 1.0 | 38 | 1.0 |
| 200–299 | 8,621 | 1.6 | 612 | 1.0 | 35 | 0.9 |
| 300–399 | 12,453 | 2.3 | 661 | 1.1 | 36 | 0.9 |
| 400–599 | 17,903 | 3.3 | 738 | 1.1 | 36 | 0.9 |
| 600–999 | 26,749 | 5.0 | 780 | 1.3 | 35 | 0.9 |
| 1,000–1,499 | 50,779 | 9.5 | 857 | 1.5 | 41 | 1.1 |
| 1,500 and over | 87,284 | 16.3 | 824 | 1.4 | 36 | 0.9 |

* 100–199 square meters of floor space = 1.0.

| Size (square meters of floor space) | No. of Employees per 100 Square Meters† | Operating Expenses as Percentage of Sales | Wages as Percentage of Sales | Stock Turnover |
|---|---|---|---|---|
| 100–199 | 6.49 | 12.9 | 6.2 | 12.2 |
| 200–299 | 4.39 | 13.6 | 6.2 | 13.8 |
| 300–399 | 4.35 | 13.4 | 5.8 | 13.7 |
| 400–599 | 5.51 | 12.8 | 5.5 | 14.9 |
| 600–999 | 4.95 | 12.8 | 5.3 | 13.4 |
| 1,000–1,499 | 4.80 | 12.3 | 4.8 | 12.6 |
| 1,500 and over | 4.42 | 13.1 | 4.9 | 12.2 |

† One square meter is approximately 10.8 square feet.

Source: Adapted from *Wagakuni no Shōgyō, 1969* [*Commerce in Japan, 1969*] (Tokyo: The Ministry of International Trade and Industry, 1970), p. 74.

company, a leading real estate development firm, and Takashimaya, a well-known department store. It is extremely significant to note that major city banks, trading firms, and leading real estate development firms are showing increasing interest in the development of shopping centers. For example, Mitsubishi Trading Company entered into an agreement in early 1969 with Jasco, a leading mass merchandising firm, to develop a shopping center. Mitsubishi is also planning to build another center with roughly 230,000 square feet in a Tokyo suburb. The construction cost alone is estimated to run about ¥4 billion. Likewise, Mitsui Trading Company is now taking an active interest in the development of shopping centers and has an immediate plan to develop three centers in the Tokyo area.

There are several noteworthy features of the shopping centers being developed in Japan. First, understandably, in comparison with their American counterparts the Japanese version is considerably smaller. The total ground area of the Tamagawa Center, for example is no larger than 215,000 square feet, with parking space for 1,000 automobiles. Second, because of the scarcity of land and extremely high land cost, the Japanese version invariably consists of multiple levels. (The total purchase cost of the 215,000 square-foot area is estimated to be around ¥3 billion, or $8.3 million. The construction cost is estimated to be ¥6 billion, or roughly $17 million.) Thus, the total floor space is likely to exceed the size of the lot. For example, the total floor space of the Tamagawa Center is nearly 440,000 square feet, and it houses a large department store and some 120 smaller specialty shops. The Center draws on the average 30,000 people on weekdays and as many as 70,000 people a day on weekends.

Third, unlike in the United States, the primary mode of transportation used by customers going to shopping centers is not automobiles but rather various means of public transportation, particularly the nation's well-developed railroad network. For example, in the aforementioned Tamagawa shopping center, it is estimated that 60 percent of its customers will travel to the center by train, 30 percent by automobile, and 10 percent on foot. As a result, the availability of public transportation will be an extremely important factor in location decisions.

As pointed out earlier, the development of shopping centers in Japan is still in the very early stage, and its success in Japan is yet to be tested. But, given the very dynamic conditions prevailing in the nation's distribution sector, it is fully expected that shopping centers will gain considerable popularity in the near future. In fact, those firms that are currently developing such centers are already searching for new sites for additional centers, and there is every indication that others will soon do likewise. Since the development of a center is likely to take the form of cooperative actions among a number of different institutions, including some that had never shown interest in retailing before, the implications of such cooperation may well go beyond merely the introduction of another new marketing institution.

### Implications and Future Prospects

The emergence of large-scale mass merchandising firms in Japan is indeed a very recent phenomenon, but already this development has had far-reaching impact and is altering the basic structure of the Japanese distribution system. In this section we shall examine major implications of this development and discuss the prospects for the future. First, the rapid rise of large-scale innovative mass merchandising firms has resulted in the emergence of an entirely new method of distributing mass-produced standard merchandise, providing a new alternative to both manufacturers and consumers. Second, the rapidly growing new mass merchandising establishments have given rise to what Palamountain calls vertical conflict, that is, struggle between different levels of the distribution channel,[12] particularly between large oligopolistic manufacturers and emerging large-scale mass merchandisers.

We have observed in an earlier chapter that during the last decade or so, in a number of key consumer products, the initiative in and control over distribution has shifted from dominant wholesalers to large manufacturers. Indeed, in mass-produced and nationally advertised products, large oligopolistic manufacturers have now assumed the leadership role in the distribution channels. Traditionally, because of their very small size, the power of retailers has been very limited; but now mass merchandising firms are challenging the existing power structure. We have observed that in certain processed food items, the self-service outlets account for more than 50 percent of total sales. Likewise, in certain standard

---

[12] Joseph C. Palamountain, Jr., *The Politics of Distribution* (Cambridge, Mass.: Harvard University Press, 1955), p. 48.

apparel lines they are responsible for an important share. For example, for fiscal year 1968, the 100 largest chains sold over ¥383.3 billion, or over $1 billion, worth of apparel. Jasco, the largest chain in the soft goods line, is reported to have sold 870,000 dress shirts, 1.7 million women's blouses, 1.8 million women's sweaters, 2.1 million slips, 7.9 million pairs of stockings, and more than 4.5 million pairs of men's socks during fiscal year 1968.[13] In the home appliance field, mass merchandising firms in aggregate account for less than 2 percent of the total sales of these products; however, sales by a few leading firms are of significant size. For example, during fiscal year 1968 Daiei sold some ¥6 billion worth of home appliances, and for the 1969 fiscal year it was expected to increase such sales to ¥10 billion. Seiyu, the largest chain, sold ¥3 billion worth of home appliances in 1968 and planned to increase this to ¥5 billion for fiscal year 1969.

Fully aware of their newly gained power, which is rapidly increasing, mass merchandising firms have now begun to exert their power in several ways. First, these firms have grown to a point at which large manufacturers of many consumer products can now hardly ignore them as an important outlet for their products. Mass merchandising firms had initially experienced considerable difficulty in buying national brands, at least through legitimate sources; but this condition no longer exists generally. These firms have now gained a sufficient degree of consumer franchise to accord them a powerful voice in their dealings with manufacturers.

The reactions of large manufacturers to mass merchandising firms have varied widely. A relatively small number of them steadfastly have refused to sell to these firms for fear of antagonizing their existing customers, and they make serious efforts to prevent their merchandise from flowing to mass merchandising firms. Some manufacturing firms are ambivalent. This is reflected in their policy of not actively soliciting sales to mass merchandising firms but yet being relatively lax in policing if their products find their way onto the counters of these firms. An increasing number of manufacturing firms, however, view the growing power of mass merchandising firms as the wave of the future, and they are now actively seeking business from these establishments. As a result, with a few notable exceptions, the newly emerging mass mer-

13 *Super Chain 100 Sha no Jittai Chōsa [A Report on Operating Characteristics of 100 Chains]* (Tokyo: Nihon Sen-I-Kenkyūjo, 1969), pp. 37–41.

chandising firms can now buy whatever they desire from almost any sources at their own terms. Not only do they now enjoy access to a wide variety of the well-known national brands but they enjoy considerable freedom in determining at what price they can be sold to consumers. Pleas by major manufacturers to adhere to manufacturers' suggested prices have often gone unheeded, and national brands have been widely used as loss leaders by supermarket and discount chains to entice customers to their stores.

A very interesting trend that began to emerge in late 1969 was a perceptible change in the attitude of major manufacturers of home appliances toward mass merchandising firms. Until recently their policy was characterized as that of reluctant acquiescence. The "official" posture of these manufacturers was to refuse to sell to mass merchandising firms, particularly to those that were not willing to conform to manufacturer's suggested retail price. As a result, the mass merchandising firms had to obtain their merchandise from "irregular" sources. They experienced little difficulties in doing so. Recognizing the growing importance of mass merchandising firms, however, several major manufacturers have taken the initiative in setting up special outlets to supply merchandise to these firms. Several firms have established special subsidiaries to sell to these mass merchandising firms. Thus, even hitherto most reluctant home appliance manufacturers began to recognize the inevitability of having to "normalize" their relationship with mass merchandising firms. Of course, the latter also were faced with the need to assure a supply of sufficient quantities of merchandise in order to increase their home appliance sales. To do so, in many cases they had to agree to conform to the minimum price suggested by the manufacturers. In this respect, the current development represents a pragmatic compromise between the two.

Second, in a number of product categories, mass merchandising firms are now attempting to bypass wholesalers and to deal directly with large manufacturers. In some cases mass merchandising firms have been forced to purchase directly from manufacturers from sheer necessity, since wholesalers often are not capable of supplying the large demand of the mass merchandising firms. In certain limited product lines, large-scale mass merchandising firms can now generate a sufficient volume to demand direct purchase from large manufacturers. The most immediate advantage to the chains is, of course, the cost savings that give them a competitive edge over their smaller competitors. It also opens up an entirely new horizon to retailers, such as having large well-known manufacturers produce specially designed merchandise, thus paving the way to the adoption of private brand policy.

Third, some large mass merchandising firms have now gone into private branding. In these instances the large mass merchandising firms work closely with wholesalers or directly with manufacturers. This approach, of course, has several well-known advantages, such as avoiding direct price competition with national brands and increasing store loyalty. The extent to which private brand practices have been adopted, of course, varies among firms and among product lines within a firm. For example, in one leading firm, 75 percent of the total sales in ladies underwear, 65 percent of sales in ladies foundations, and 46 percent of sales in blouses came from private brands. Although private brand merchandise has been most commonly found among high-volume food and apparel items, a few large mass merchandising firms have now begun to extend this practice to selected home appliances. This is particularly significant, inasmuch as the home appliance industry has been known for the dominant role occupied by large manufacturers in the distribution structure.

To develop their unique merchandise lines, some of the large retail chains have now established product-planning groups and have strengthened the functions of merchandising managers. Some have incorporated separate subsidiaries for this purpose. These subsidiaries, or satellite firms as they are often called, are frequently financed jointly by wholesalers and manufacturers who are interested in supplying these chains.

The development of private brands, though still in the formative stage, is significant evidence of the growing power of large-scale mass merchandising firms. A recent survey of supermarkets in Tokyo revealed that 36 percent of 376 participating firms indicated that they were selling some merchandise under their own brands.[14] Products that are sold most frequently under private brands include soup, canned fruits, cooking oil, instant coffee, men's socks, dress shirts, sheets, women's blouses, stockings, and underwear.

Large chains follow two different strategies in this regard. One is to persuade large manufacturers with well-known national brands to manufacture private brand merchandise. This is being

14 *Tokyo ni Okeru Supermarket no Genjo: Showa 42 nen [The Status of Supermarkets in Tokyo, Fiscal Year 1967]* (Tokyo: The Tokyo Chamber of Commerce, 1968), p. 20.

done in some of the processed food items such as mayonnaise. For understandable reasons, large manufacturers are ambivalent about entering into private branding; as a result, though there are a few notable exceptions, this practice has not yet gained wide acceptance. It is true, however, that large manufacturers of selected consumers' goods are coming under growing pressure from large chains, and no doubt this will be one of the most important marketing decisions they must make in the next few years. Indeed, the battle of brands, a struggle so familiar on the American distribution scene, has already begun in Japan.

A rather unique and noteworthy compromise has evolved out of this "battle of the brands" between large manufacturers and large chains. This is the use of "dual brands," as they have become known in Japan; that is, merchandise bearing both the manufacturers' and the retailers' brand name. The practice has proved to be advantageous both to chains and to major manufacturers of national brands. Retailers can benefit from the prestige associated with the manufacturer's brand as well as from their own promotional efforts. For example, the Seiyu chain has recently begun to sell salad oil under the dual brands of Seiyu and Mitsubishi Trading Company. A major theme in their promotion is "Mitsubishi quality and Seiyu price." The dual brand also makes the practice more palatable to large manufacturers, who may otherwise be unwilling to manufacture private brands. It is too early to predict at this time whether or not the practice of dual branding may become a permanent and widespread aspect of the nation's distribution scene.

The second approach followed by mass merchandising firms is to have small manufacturers produce private brand merchandise for them. Given the presence of a large number of small manufacturers and the keen competition that exists among them, they are more than willing to supply private brands for large retail chains. Here, however, continued assurance of supply and quality maintenance often present difficult problems.

Some mass merchandising firms have gone a step further by organizing a separate subsidiary to supply certain high-volume standard merchandise to be sold under their brands. For example, Seiyu now has two separate subsidiaries that supply meat to the Seiyu stores. Some have also organized a network of controlled manufacturers. Seiyu, in cooperation with Mitsubishi Trading Company, organized a number of small manufacturers into a centrally coordinated and controlled team to make certain apparel lines, including fashion items. This merchandise is, of course, being sold under Seiyu's private brand name.

Among a number of volatile and dynamic developments now taking place in Japan's distribution scene, particularly significant is the change in the power relationship in the distribution system. As we noted earlier, it is only in recent years that large manufacturers in certain industries have emerged as the dominant force in the distribution channel. These firms have taken the lead in product design, manufacture, and distribution. They have generally acted as "captain of the channel." This newly gained power of large manufacturers in the area of marketing is now being challenged by emerging large-scale mass merchandising firms. The latter are anxious to assume many, if not all, of the marketing functions once performed by manufacturers and to claim a greater share of the profit accruing to the performance of such functions. Large manufacturers of consumer goods are very aware of these developments and are naturally anxious to retain this power and, of course, the profit associated with such power. It is quite likely, therefore, that the contest between large manufacturers and large-scale mass merchandising firms is likely to intensify in the future.

What does the future hold for large-scale mass merchandising firms? There is a wide consensus that they will continue to grow.

TABLE 4.14

PROJECTED CHANGE IN THE NUMBER OF ESTABLISHMENTS
BY MAJOR TYPES OF STORES BETWEEN 1966 AND 1972

(in thousands)

| Type of Store | 1966 | 1972 |
|---|---|---|
| (1) Department Stores ⎫ | 5 | 10 |
| (2) Chain Stores* ⎭ | | |
| (3) Regular Retail Stores† | 320 | 330 |
| (4) Family-Managed Retail Stores‡ | 105 | 105 |
| Number of Self-Service Stores among | | |
| Categories 2, 3, and 4 | 5 | 10 |

*Firms having 10 stores or more.
†Stores with paid employees.
‡Stores owned and operated by family members without paid employees.

Source: *Ryutsu Kindaika no Tenbo to Kadai [A Perspective and Challenges of Modernization of the Distribution Sector]* (Tokyo: The Ministry of International Trade and Industry, 1968), p. 69.

## TABLE 4.15

PROJECTED CHANGE IN SALES BY MAJOR TYPES OF RETAIL STORES
(¥100 billion)

| Type of Store | 1966 | 1972 |
|---|---|---|
| (1) Department Stores | 10 (9.5)* | 20 (9.8)* |
| (2) Chain Stores | 6 (5.7) | 30 (14.6) |
| (3) Regular Retail Stores | 59 (57.2) | 105 (51.2) |
| (4) Family-Operated Retail Stores | 5 (27.6) | 24 (24.4) |
| Number of Self-Service Stores among Categories 2, 3, and 4 | 6 | 26 |
| Total Retail Sales | 105 (100) | 205 (100) |

* Figures in parentheses indicate percentage distribution.

Source: *Ryutsu Kindaika no Tenbo to Kadai* [*A Perspective and Challenges of Modernization of the Distribution Sector*] (Tokyo: The Ministry of International Trade and Industry, 1968), p. 69.

Forces that gave them an initial impetus for growth are still very much present. A recent report prepared by the Council on Industrial Structure, a blue-chip advisory board to the Ministry of International Trade and Industry, predicts continued growth for large-scale chains.

According to this report, by 1972 total retail sales are expected to reach around ¥20.5 trillion, about twice the level reported in 1966, and the total number of retail establishments will increase from 1,370,000 to around 1,390,000. The total number of large-scale retail firms, including department stores and mass merchandising firms, is expected to grow from 5,000 to roughly 10,000. Details are presented in Tables 4.14 and 4.15. Particularly significant is that the total sales of chain stores are expected to grow from roughly ¥600 billion to ¥3 trillion, representing a fivefold growth. On the other hand, the sales of the department stores are expected only to double, or to grow only at the same rate as the increase in the total retail volume. By 1972 the study predicts that large-scale chain stores will account for nearly 15 percent of total retail sales, exceeding the share of the department stores by a substantial margin.

The present trend toward greater concentration of retail sales in a small number of large retailing firms is likely to continue. By the early 1970s it is projected that there will be some 60 firms with annual sales of at least ¥20 billion. Among these firms there will be as many as 15 firms with annual sales exceeding ¥100 billion. It is also projected that the aggregate sales volume of the 60 or so giant retail firms will reach ¥4.4 trillion, accounting for roughly 20 percent of the total anticipated retail sales.

The management of the mass merchandising firms is extremely optimistic about the future. This is very evident in a survey conducted by the *Japan Economic Journal* in 1969. The survey asked each of the 60 leading large-scale retail firms, including department stores, to indicate their anticipated sales volume to be achieved by 1975. The survey revealed that there would be 9 firms whose expected sales volume per firm would reach the ¥400 billion level, or roughly $1.1 billion.[15] If this goal is realized, these 9 firms will be responsible in aggregate for some 17.6 percent of the total projected retail sales for that year. It is recalled that in 1967 the largest 104 firms held 14 percent of the aggregate retail sales, indicating a rapidly accelerating trend for greater concentration in retailing. These estimates are crude and may appear overly ambitious. It is very unlikely that every firm will be able to realize its projected goal. The survey, however, includes only the 60 largest existing firms. Given the dynamic nature of Japan's distribution scene, it is fully expected that there will be a number of new entrants into this field. Despite these qualifications, the survey is a useful indicator of future trends.

To illustrate the magnitude of growth these firms are seeking to achieve, let us examine the goals set by two leading firms. The Seibu distribution group, with Seibu department store and Seiyu stores as its nucleus, is aiming at becoming the nation's largest retail enterprise by 1975. By 1973, Seiyu, the group's supermarket chain, plans to have some 300 stores, with sales of ¥400 billion and ¥1 trillion by 1975 ($2.8 billion). Daiei, Japan's largest supermarket chain, is planning to increase its sales to ¥420 billion ($1.2 billion) by 1972, and to ¥1.15 trillion ($3 billion) by 1975. Daiei plans to have a network of 200 stores by that time.

These are indeed very optimistic goals. Judged by the past growth record, however, these admittedly very ambitious goals may well be within their reach. In order to realize these goals, however, there are a number of challenges that must be met successfully.

First, these chains will be the subject of greater competitive pressure. This will come from several sources. In the formative stage, mass merchandising firms owed their rapid growth at least

---

[15] "Kouri Kyodaika no Honryū ["Entry of Retailing into Large-Scale Business"] *Nihon Keizai Shinbun*, January 4, 1970, p. 8.

in part to the very ineptness of small traditional retail firms. The former had innovative ideas and were able to capitalize on them. The situation, however, has changed radically. In a number of attractive market areas, large retail chains have begun to come into direct competition with one another. Intense competition among giant mass merchandising firms is bidding up already rapidly rising real estate prices in attractive market areas, making addition of new stores extremely costly. Moreover, competition is being further intensified by increasingly active entry of outside elements into this field. We have already noted the entry of consumer and agricultural cooperatives. In addition, traditional department stores, large trading companies, and real estate development firms are eyeing this field with aggressive interest.

In addition to the external challenges, there are several major problems that are internal to these rapidly growing chains. The most immediate problem is the rapidly increasing capital requirement to finance expansion. Not unlike large manufacturing firms in Japan, to finance their growth large mass merchandising firms have depended heavily on debt sources. As a result, their debt-equity ratio is staggeringly high. Daiei, for example, had been capitalized at only ¥4 million, which was recently raised to ¥32 million. Even now, considering the total annual sales of over ¥100 billion, it is extremely small. The cost of new store sites in attractive market areas, as we have noted, is rapidly increasing. Construction costs are also on the rise. For example it is estimated that in 1969 building and equipping a store with roughly 5,000 square feet of floor space in a major metropolitan market would run at least ¥300 million ($830,000).

In order to realize their planned goals, large-scale retailing firms must undertake large capital investment at a rapid rate. A survey of planned capital investment for fiscal year 1970 among the 20 leading firms revealed that they were planning to increase their capital investment substantially over the preceding year.[16] Capital investment planned by these mass merchandising chains for fiscal year 1970 averages about ¥9.3 billion. Six of these firms are planning to spend at least ¥10 billion. (For fiscal year 1969, only two exceeded ¥10 billion.) Seiyu plans to spend ¥30 billion for expansion, while Daiei is planning a ¥25 billion capital investment to

[16] "Zenko Ku Chain Keisei e Hashiru" ["Toward National Chains"], *Nihon Keizai Shinbun,* January 21, 1970, p. 8.

add 33 stores during fiscal year 1970 alone. New stores being planned are considerably larger and, as a result, more expensive than those built in the past. The average size of a new store being planned by Daiei during 1970 is about 90,000 square feet, roughly 30 percent larger than the average built in 1969. Similarly, Seiyu plans to add half a dozen stores with floor space of roughly 170,000 square feet during fiscal year 1970. Significantly, these firms plan to finance at least 70 percent of this capital investment through debt sources. Daiei, for example, is planning to raise nearly 90 percent of the ¥25 billion through debts.[17]

To obtain additional funds, some firms are now planning to go public. At the same time they are developing close banking connections. Japan's leading city banks, which traditionally had favored large manufacturing firms, have become increasingly interested in developing closer ties with the rapidly growing retail chains. Already some of the major city banks have gone beyond ordinary banking relationships. Several major banks now have their former employees in top management positions in a number of large mass merchandising firms. Some have entered into the store-and-equipment-leasing business through their subsidiaries. Others have collaborated in the development of shopping centers. Growing dependence on the major city banks for funds, however, will likely constrain the freedom of action of these stores. Obtaining necessary funds to finance their ambitious expansion programs undoubtedly will be a major challenge to the management of expansion-oriented large mass merchandising firms.

Even more serious problems lie in the areas of organizational development and management resources. It may be recalled that most of the large-scale mass merchandising firms grew out of small-scale operations in a very short period of time. These firms have grown under the very dynamic and capable leadership of aggressive entrepreneurs, but they have now grown into large enterprises, requiring different types of managerial leadership, styles, and skills.

It is axiomatic that problems associated with managing enterprises with ¥400 billion annual sales are considerably different from those of an enterprise with annual sales of ¥50 billion. Particularly, in order to achieve their ambitious goals these firms must undertake active diversification programs. A number of large mass merchandising firms have already begun their diversification

17 *Ibid.*

programs into such leisure-related service fields as restaurants, hotels, drive-ins, amusement centers, travel services, and sport facilities. A number of mass merchandising firms are now developing into large diversified conglomerates. In this context organizational and managerial development becomes of utmost importance. They must evolve an organizational structure and management system appropriate to a large diversified enterprise. Development of strategic planning, formulation of well-defined corporate goals and strategies, and establishment of management information and control systems will become urgent.

The top management of large-scale firms now faces a dual challenge of achieving significant growth, on one hand, but at the same time shaping internal organization and a management system adequate to meet the increasingly complex demands of growing size and diversity. In meeting these challenges, the most critical factor, of course, is managerial capabilities. The future growth potential of the rapidly emerging chains depends, to a large degree, on whether or not these obviously successful entrepreneurs effectively can transform themselves into capable organizational builders and managers of large-scale and highly complex diversified enterprises.

Another closely related critical issue is whether or not the chief executives of these enterprises can develop successfully an effective and capable top management team. Despite this obvious need, some of the top management positions in these rapidly growing chains are now occupied by men who have been propelled to top positions with the growth of their firms but who lack the capacity and skills to become effective members of the top management team in a large enterprise. They are the ones who shared the difficulty and growing pains in the initial phase of the venture and who were highly effective then, but, unlike some of their better-equipped colleagues, they sadly have outlived their usefulness now that the firm has become extremely large and complex. Ironically, the very success the firm has achieved, to which these men had contributed significantly, has made their skills, temperament, and background obsolete. This is a tragedy that is commonly observed in firms that have experienced very rapid growth. Understandably, these men often feel that they are now rightful partakers of the fruits of success, and the entrepreneur can hardly be blamed for his personal attachment to them. What to do with these men presents a very serious dilemma to the chief executives of many of the rapidly growing chains, inasmuch as the continued growth and success of these firms depends on the capacity of an effective top management team.

Another closely related problem is the recruitment and development of middle management personnel. The absence of a sufficient number of well-trained middle management personnel will be a major deterrent to growth. Both line managers and staff specialists in large-scale retailing must be developed in sufficient quantity. With the rapid expansion of large-scale mass merchandising firms, a shortage of qualified middle management personnel and staff specialists is becoming increasingly keen. A particularly crucial need is the development of highly skilled and capable merchandising managers. Trained individuals who readily can assume managerial responsibilities in newly emerging chains are indeed scarce. As a result, the burden of development of middle management falls squarely on the firms themselves.

Most of the large-scale mass merchandising firms are now actively recruiting college graduates. For example, Daiei recruited some 300 college graduates in the spring of 1969, and Seiyu hired about 100. Retailing had not been a very popular field among college graduates, but with the emergence of large-scale retailing, the traditional view is undergoing a gradual change. Particularly among graduates of less prestigious universities who are at a disadvantage in seeking employment with leading Japanese industrial or financial firms, the mass merchandising field provides an attractive alternative. Also appealing to them is the presence of ample opportunities for rapid advancement. The very nature of chain operations requires a certain degree of decentralization, and as a result it demands managers who are willing to assume responsibility. Despite these favorable trends, firms must find, train, and develop their managers.

Since there are few established patterns to follow, mass merchandising firms are learning on a trial-and-error basis. Of course, the very dynamic nature of this industry is a compensating factor, since it does provide a high degree of motivation and ample opportunity for those willing to assume responsibilities to move up in the organization. Top management of mass merchandising firms is keenly aware of the importance of managerial recruitment and development. To most of these firms this is their greatest concern.

Another critical factor relating to personnel is the growing labor shortage and accompanying rise of the wage level. A number of mass merchandising firms, particularly small- and medium-size ones, are experiencing some difficulties in recruiting first-line personnel. Mass merchandising firms operating on low margins are particularly vulnerable to a profit squeeze through rapidly accelerating wage increases. As a result, they are now compelled to rationalize management practices to increase the productivity of each employee.

Closely related to the foregoing is one disturbing mentality that is widely shared by the top management of a number of these mass merchandising firms. This is their preoccupation with the sales volume. This is evidenced by the fact that most frequently the goals to be achieved are defined in terms of total sales. Seldom is reference made to such critical measures as profit or return on investment. This emphasis on sales volume is common among Japanese executives, regardless of industry. This, of course, is not without reason. First, sales volume is the most direct and immediate measure of the relative standing of an enterprise. It is the single most effective measure of their growing importance, and it can be used with considerable effectiveness to demonstrate their newly gained power to outside elements such as manufacturers and wholesalers. While the continued use of this measure may be desirable for external use or public image, for the purpose of internal management planning and control the overemphasis on sales volume is fraught with potential dangers. It tends to bring about cutthroat competition, making profitability a secondary concern and generating dangerous pressure to undertake reckless expansion programs merely to meet the sales target. Thus, the top management of many of the mass merchandising firms now needs to reorient its thinking in this regard.

We have briefly discussed major challenges that are now facing Japan's large-scale mass merchandising firms if they are to achieve their planned goals. In order to meet these challenges and to capitalize on very dynamic growth opportunities, Japan's large-scale retailing firms are mapping out new strategies. Of these, several noteworthy developments are taking shape. One is the already-noted trend for diversification, with the goal of developing a widely diversified enterprise centering around retailing. A number of large retailing firms are planning horizontal diversification into such fields as shopping center development, real estate, housing, and leisure-related industries, including hotels, restaurants, bowling facilities, sight-seeing, and amusement and recreational centers.

Second, the relationship among large-scale firms is becoming increasingly fluid. As noted earlier, truly intense competition among them has just begun, as each of the large chains pushes its own expansion programs, thus bringing them into direct confrontation with one another. It is extremely interesting that, for mutual advantage, many of these firms are willing to enter into cooperative arrangements of various types, ranging from exchange of information to cooperative buying and even to collaboration in opening new stores.

Particularly significant are several cases of joint action taken by competitors in entering into new areas to avoid competition. This trend may well accelerate as the competition becomes more intense and as the attractive new markets become saturated. This approach also enables them to combine their resources and distinctive competence. To cope with the aggressive efforts toward national chains, somewhat smaller regional chains are taking similar actions. For example, in early 1970 seven regional chains formed a joint purchasing subsidiary, which some suspect eventually may lead to mergers among these firms.

What is most significant in interfirm cooperation of various types among large mass merchandising firms is the flexibility and dynamism they demonstrate in entering into these arrangements. They have little tradition to uphold: If they see mutual advantages in these arrangements, they implement them with little hesitation. It is not difficult to conceive that these cooperative arrangements may well eventually lead to mergers among these firms. As growing competition among mass merchandising firms escalates, and especially with the possibility of entry of large-scale American retailing firms, mergers will undoubtedly occur, particularly among medium-size firms, as their very survival may well become endangered.

The most significant merger up to now is the formation of Jasco in 1969 through mergers of three large regional chains. The combined firm now is the third largest mass merchandising chain in Japan. The trend toward greater concentration became even more evident in late 1969 as large chains intensified their efforts to become truly national in scope. Daiei, for example, entered into cooperative arrangements with several local chains in 1969 and also began to resort to franchising operations.

We should also note here that the process of elimination already has begun among some of these firms. This is particularly true among small- to medium-size companies that find it increasingly difficult to withstand aggressive competition from large-scale chains. Many of these small- to medium-size mass merchandising firms had entered this field without adequate planning and re- sources. It is not unlikely that these floundering small- to medium- size establishments will be acquired by large chains as the latter press for expansion.

Last, but not the least important, is the increasingly closer rela- tionship between large-scale mass merchandising firms and large trading firms. This move, which began in early 1969, was surprising to many since it was often thought that, to the innovative mass merchandising firms, the trading companies represented the "es- tablishment" that epitomized the ills and irrationality of the tradi- tional distribution system. For a variety of reasons, however, highly pragmatic managers of mass merchandising firms found it advan- tageous to establish closer ties with large trading firms. One such benefit is the enormous ability of trading companies to supply the large volume of merchandise demanded by large retailing firms. This is particularly true in regard to products such as apparel and certain household items that traditionally have been manufactured and distributed by small firms, many of which have been closely tied to and controlled by large trading firms. The managements of mass merchandising firms found it advantageous to capitalize on the traditional leadership and expertise of trading companies in this field. Another important line of products in which close ties with trading companies will undoubtedly prove beneficial to mass merchandising firms is fresh food: fish, meat, and vegetables. Fresh food traditionally has been marketed through the central wholesale markets, and this manner of distribution is not suitable to supermarket operations. To obtain fresh food in large volume, it is necessary to create new channels. To develop and manage such a system, the expertise of trading companies will be invaluable. Another potentially attractive feature is the extensive network of procurement sources that large trading companies have overseas. The mass merchandising firms have just begun to look toward foreign sources, particularly to Southeast Asia, for certain types of products in order to obtain cost advantages.

The second major advantage to large-scale retail firms is the access to huge financial resources that these large trading firms command. Trading companies not only are willing to extend liberal credit to rapidly growing mass merchandising firms but are pre- pared to purchase store sites and to build and equip new stores and lease them to the chains. To trading companies, this alliance is extremely attractive, inasmuch as it gives them a foothold in this rapidly growing industry in which they hitherto had had only limited participation. It is extremely significant to note that alliance between these two forms typically goes far beyond commercial transactions. The potential ability of large trading companies to develop and supply original merchandise lines is also attractive to mass merchandising firms. For example, in early 1969 Seiyu entered into a four-year agreement with Mitsubishi Shoji, the world-famous trading company, a prominent member of the Mitsubishi group. Among other things, this agreement stipulated that Mitsubishi would extend ¥20 billion credit to Seiyu for the purpose of capital investment, and in return Seiyu has committed itself to make up to 20 percent of its total purchases from Mitsubishi by 1972. Similarly, in early 1969 Daiei and a number of other large supermarket chains entered into similar agreements with large trading companies. Jasco entered into a cooperative arrangement with Mitsubishi Trading Company. Their collaboration will span a wide range of activities, including the development of shopping centers.

The third major advantage is the organization and management capability of major trading companies. We have noted earlier that one of the major problems facing large mass merchandising chains is the relative lack of managerial talent. Large trading companies, on the other hand, have abundant managerial resources. The ability of trading companies to mobilize and organize resources is particularly important, if not essential, to diversification efforts by mass merchandising firms. Especially attractive is the fact that, not infrequently, large trading companies can mobilize resources from other related firms belonging to the same group.

Indeed, this has marked the beginning of a new era in the development of Japan's mass merchandising firms. We shall examine this development in greater detail in the next chapter, but it is highly relevant to speculate about the possible impact of this development on mass merchandising firms. For example, one pertinent question that deserves careful scrutiny is the degree to which they can continue to pursue an independent course. Given their characteristic pragmatism, mass merchandising firms view their alliance with trading companies simply as a marriage of convenience and merely as the means to achieve their highly ambitious growth objectives. Managers of large mass merchandising firms are indeed aware of the potential pitfalls, and most have been careful in structuring their ties with trading companies, particularly seeking ties with not one but several different trading companies. Nevertheless, given the enormous power that the trading companies command, and their increasingly aggressive posture toward the mass merchandising field, the emerging relationship deserves continuing scrutiny.

In this chapter we have examined the development of large-scale mass merchandising retail firms in postwar Japan. Without doubt, this development has had far-reaching impact and has been a key revolutionary force in the dynamically changing Japanese distribution sector.

# 5

# Adaptive Behavior
# of the Traditional Elements
# in the Marketing System

In Chapter 4 we examined a number of significant innovations now taking place in the Japanese distribution system in response to the emerging mass consumer market. Since these innovations are still in the early stage, their full impact is yet to be felt by the traditional elements in the nation's distribution system. In this chapter we shall examine responses of the traditional elements to the rapidly changing environment, and more specifically the innovative forces that are now taking shape. In this analysis we shall focus our attention on four traditional institutions, namely, small retailers, wholesalers, department stores, and trading companies. Although their functions and relative sizes vary, they do have one thing in common; that is, they are seriously affected by the developments discussed in Chapter 4. Thus, it is indeed relevant to examine how these different traditional elements are now attempting to formulate defensive or even counterstrategies to maintain their functional viability in the changing environment.

### Adaptive Behavior of Small Retail Establishments

We noted earlier that the Japanese distribution system, particularly the retail sector, is dominated by a large number of small establishments. The average annual sales of a retail establishment are less than ¥10 million, or roughly $27,000, and nearly 89 percent of establishments have four employees or fewer. Nearly 60 percent have sales space of less than 200 square feet. We have also observed that as high as 77 percent of retail establishments are operated solely by the owner himself or by members of his immediate family.

Because of the predominance of extremely small establishments in the Japanese retailing sector, it is highly relevant to examine how they perceive the threats of the rapidly changing environment and how they are attempting to cope with them. One would think that, given their extremely limited resources, they would be particularly vulnerable to the onslaught of aggressive large-scale retailing. Before we undertake our analysis of their adaptive behavior, we must acquaint ourselves with their present behavior patterns, attitudes, and ideologies, because only against this background can we fully appreciate the risks and threats of the innovative forces as perceived by small merchants and their efforts (or lack of them) for rationalization.

For this purpose we shall present relevant findings of a recent study sponsored by the Ministry of International Trade and Industry.[1] The study was designed to investigate the attitude and behavior patterns of selected owners of small shops. The study was based on extensive personal interviews of a nationwide sample of 1,426 owners of small retail establishments. For the purpose of this study, a small store was defined as one with one or two individuals fully occupied in its management. This is the most comprehensive study conducted to date of the profile of owners of small retail stores in Japan. Looking first at the general character of these stores, we find that 28 percent had an annual sales volume of less than ¥2 million, or roughly $6,000, and stores with sales volume of less than ¥5 million, or $14,000, accounted for 73 percent of the total. Nearly 80 percent of the stores have been established since 1945, and 57 percent were established between 1955 and 1964. It is interesting to note that in 80 percent of the stores surveyed the store and family living quarters were in the same building, and they were separated only in a very rudimentary way.

---

[1] "Shokibo Kouriten ni Kansuru Chosa" ["A Study of Small-Scale Retail Establishments"], in *Shogyō Ryutsu Kozō Chōsa [An Investigation of the Distribution Structure]* (Tokyo: Ryutsu Mondai Kenkyu Kyokai, 1968), pp. 60–99.

In roughly 93 percent of the stores surveyed, the owners themselves are mainly responsible for operations of the store, and in addition, 60 percent of the respondents stated that their wives were also actively involved in its operations.

Another noteworthy finding is that for a substantial number of respondents the store did not constitute the sole source of income. In fact, about one-third of those interviewed indicated that their revenue from the retailing operation accounted for less than 60 percent of their total income. Nearly 20 percent reported that the income from the store represented less than 40 percent of the total. Roughly one-fourth of these stores are operated as a side business by wives while their husbands are employed elsewhere.

The absence of clear-cut separation between the store and living quarters goes beyond the physical setting and is reflected in similar practices in financial matters as well. Over 45 percent of those surveyed indicated that no formal distinction is made between their household budget and operations of the store. Understandably, only a very loose accounting record is kept of the store's operations.

Another extremely interesting finding of this survey is that nearly two-thirds of the stores surveyed derive at least half of their total sales from a rather small group of regular customers with whom the store owners are personally acquainted and who live in their immediate neighborhood. More than one-third of the stores surveyed obtain as high as 70 percent of their total sales from this group of customers. It is also interesting to note that in 60 percent of the stores these regular customers consist of fewer than 100 households; in more than two-thirds of the stores, they represent fewer than 200 households. Moreover, on the average 30 percent of their total sales are made after 6:00 P.M. These evidences clearly point to the fact that these stores serve a very limited number of customers and trade heavily on personal relationships and convenience.

These are some of the salient characteristics of the very small retail establishments that still dominate the Japanese distribution scene. They represent small stores typically found in almost every part of the world. The survey then inquired into how respondents perceived a series of new developments such as those discussed in Chapter 4.

The majority of the respondents were aware of growing competitive pressure from other retail establishments. As the most serious source of competition, 28 percent of the respondents cited stores of similar size, 23 percent mentioned stores that are considerably larger than their own, and 30 percent singled out supermarkets. Roughly 20 percent of the respondents, however, felt that they were virtually unaffected by competition. Asked what they feared most from their main competitors, respondents most frequently mentioned wide assortment of merchandise, low price, liberal use of loss leaders, and aggressive promotion. Those who felt that they were competitively vulnerable were asked to cite how they most effectively could respond to this threat. As their single most important tool, over 38 percent of the respondents mentioned greater emphasis on personal service and strengthening personal ties with their customers. Given their traditional background and the absence of other effective competitive tools, this reaction is readily understandable. It is extremely interesting to note, however, that nearly 30 percent of respondents felt that there was no effective competitive tool available.

As to the future, those participating in the survey singled out three problem areas as the major sources of their concern: (1) profit squeeze, largely resulting from increasing labor cost; (2) intensified competitive pressure; and (3) changes in store patronage patterns and shopping habits of average consumers, particularly their growing preference for one-stop shopping. Despite these problem areas, the study revealed that the majority of the respondents were somewhat optimistic about their future. When they were asked about their prospects five years hence, only 28 percent of the respondents had a rather dim view of the future; 43 percent foresaw no significant change; and 26 percent felt that the performance of their stores would improve significantly.

Furthermore, it is highly interesting to note that 62 percent of the respondents interviewed indicated that they had no specific plans for the future. Twenty-two percent were planning to expand their operations, while only 7 percent were considering either quitting or reducing the size of their operations. The widespread absence of specific plans for the future may well be due partially to the fact that in 41 percent of the stores surveyed, the owner was fifty years old or older. If owners over forty are included, the proportion goes up to over 70 percent. It is not unreasonable to assume that the age factor is an important variable in determining their attitude toward innovation.

An interesting finding of this survey is that only slightly over half of the respondents have used cash wholesalers, despite the fact that this might be a readily accessible means of obtaining lower cost of goods, thus enhancing their competitive capacity. Telling evidence about their attitudes are the reasons cited for their reluctance to deal with cash wholesalers. Interestingly, 52 percent of those not buying from cash wholesalers (or over 21 percent of the retailers studied) gave as the most important reason their long-standing and well-established personal relationships with their service wholesalers. These retailers felt a strong sense of obligation to their wholesalers whom they had dealt with for many years, despite the loss of immediate advantages. Thus, personal relationships are a key factor in retailers' dealings with both their customers and suppliers.

Two dominant characteristics emerge from this study. One is the owners' complacent attitude in the face of the rapidly changing environment. Underlying their lack of sense of urgency are several major factors. One detects a sense of resignation stemming from their pragmatic experiences—they have such limited resources that they could hardly influence the course of events no matter how hard they tried. There is also a widely shared view that somehow they could continue to survive despite the changing environment. This stems in part from their intuitive feeling that changes will not take place at as drastic a rate as others anticipate, and that there will always be a demand for their services. Surely, they do concede that some very marginal stores will be forced out by competitive pressure, but somehow their particular stores will be spared.

Their complacency at least in part stems from the age factor mentioned earlier, which limits their time horizon and alternative opportunities. They are relatively confident that their stores can continue to survive for another five, ten, or even fifteen years. The potential reward for innovation holds little appeal to these men, considering the effort, cost, and risks involved. Moreover, as we have noted, to a substantial number the revenue derived from their stores represents only a supplementary source of income. This fact, too, discourages risk-taking and serious commitment of their efforts.

There is also a strong preference among the owners of small stores for independence of action. This is revealed from another study undertaken by the MITI, designed to examine characteristics of new entrants into retailing in recent years. The data were obtained from a nationwide sample of 470 stores established since January 1, 1965. Among a number of findings, particularly noteworthy is the fact that the most frequently cited reason for establishing their own store is the desire for independence. Nearly 36 percent of the respondents gave this as the prime reason.[2] Moreover, the previously cited survey revealed that over 87 percent of those planning future expansion indicated that they would do so on their own.[3]

The dominant impression that emerged from this study is that the majority of owners of small retail establishments are vaguely aware of the growing competitive pressure from innovative forces in the distribution system, but despite some exceptions the prevailing mood is that of fatalism. Their defensive actions have been largely limited to improvement of personal services and an attempt to adopt a distinctive merchandising policy.

Past efforts by small retailers to increase their competitive position have been rather limited and primarily have taken the form of individual action. However, in recent years, some efforts have been made to formulate counterstrategies on a cooperative basis.

Among various types of cooperative programs, two are particularly noteworthy. One approach is for small retailers to pool their resources, construct a large store in a strategic location, and physically move into a central location. Under this system each participating store may remain independent as to its ownership and management or the stores may merge into one corporation under a unified management. This cooperative effort to bring a number of small stores of a given geographic area physically into a single large establishment, in the form of either a department store or a supermarket, was first promoted by the Ministry of International Trade and Industry as a part of its program to encourage the modernization of small retail stores.

This program seeks to improve operating efficiency of participating stores through reducing duplication of efforts, to increase their customer appeal, and to attain greater economy of scale while maintaining their local identity and independence.

Between 1963 and 1968 some 103 cooperative department stores and 52 supermarkets either were formed or were being organized under the government assistance program. Details are presented in Table 5.1. The combined sales of both types of cooperative stores were estimated to be around ¥41 billion for 1967.

[2] "Shinki Kigyo ni Kansuru Chosa" ["A Study of New Entrants"], in *Shogyō Ryutsu Kozō Chōsa [An Investigation of the Distribution Structure]* (Tokyo: Ryutsu Mondai Kenkyu Kyokai, 1968), pp. 4–32.

[3] "Shokibo Kouriten ni Kansuru Chosa" ["A Study of Small-Scale Retail Establishments"], p. 93.

TABLE 5.1

COOPERATIVE DEPARTMENT STORES AND SUPERMARKETS
FOUNDED EACH YEAR, 1963–1968

| Year | Type of Store | No. of Establishments | No. of Stores Participating |
|---|---|---|---|
| 1963 | Cooperative Dept. Stores | 9 | 201 |
| | Cooperative Supermarkets | 25 | 551 |
| 1964 | Cooperative Dept. Stores | 30 | 509 |
| | Cooperative Supermarkets | 9 | 99 |
| 1965 | Cooperative Dept. Stores | 12 | 272 |
| | Cooperative Supermarkets | 4 | 29 |
| 1966 | Cooperative Dept. Stores | 13 | 234 |
| | Cooperative Supermarkets | 4 | 41 |
| 1967 | Cooperative Dept. Stores | 16 | 266 |
| | Cooperative Supermarkets | 7 | 61 |
| 1968° | Cooperative Dept. Stores | 23 | — |
| | Cooperative Supermarkets | 3 | — |

°The 1968 figures were obtained from *Ryutsu Kindaika Shisaku no Gaiyō* [*A Summary of Government Policies toward the Distribution Sector*] (Tokyo: The Ministry of International Trade and Industry, 1969), p. 7.

Source: *Ryutsu Kindaika no Tenbo to Kadai* [*A Perspective and the Challenge of Modernization of the Distribution Structure*] (Tokyo: The Ministry of International Trade and Industry, 1968), p. 63.

Although in theory this approach is sound and appealing, it has so far enjoyed only a limited success. In fact, the majority of cooperative stores established thus far have largely failed to achieve the expected results. Some have been almost total failures. According to one estimate, there are only a dozen or so that can be considered successful.

Several factors can be cited to explain this generally disappointing result. First of all, the very success of such a cooperative venture depends, to an important degree, on the willingness of each member to give up a certain degree of independence and autonomy for the common good. Given their traditional orientations, they have not always been willing to make this commitment. Some wanted immediate results; when these were not forthcoming, they began to question the value of such a venture. Another common reason for failure is that competition among participating stores frequently destroyed their unity and cooperation.

The absence of effective leadership and capable management has plagued a large number of such projects. Many persons who were elected from their membership to manage the complex did not possess the skills and capacities required for such a task. Except for a few instances, most such ventures have been reluctant to bring in needed managerial talent from the outside. It has not been uncommon for these cooperative projects to suffer from power struggles and factional strifes within the leadership.

Finally, in a number of cases participating stores found their new financial obligations too burdensome, and anticipated cost reduction and operating efficiency proved illusory. Thus, joint efforts, at least in the form of cooperative department stores and supermarkets, have had small impact.

Another recent cooperative effort among independent retailers has been the formation of retail cooperative buying groups commonly known as cooperative chains. Disillusioned with the lack of success of cooperative department stores and supermarkets, the Ministry of International Trade and Industry shifted its policy emphasis in the mid-1960s to encouraging the formation of voluntary and cooperative chains. The Ministry now provides financial assistance as well as managerial guidance to qualified wholesalers and retailers who are interested in establishing cooperative or voluntary chains. While their growth has been rather gradual, this approach appears to have potential significance and appeal of considerable magnitude. A distinct strength of the cooperative chain is that, unlike the first method, it does not involve drastic actions on the part of the participants, such as physically moving their stores and having to give up their independence. Possibilities of conflict of interest among member stores also appear to be considerably less than among the cooperative department stores and supermarkets.

In 1969 there were altogether 41 cooperative chains, with some 5,700 participating stores, that belonged to the Japan Voluntary Chain Association, the national association of cooperative and voluntary chains. As evident in Table 5.2, food stores account for by far the largest proportion of these, both in the number of chains and in the number of member stores. It is interesting to note that cooperative chains have been organized in a variety of merchandise lines.

A recent study conducted by the Research Department of the Tokyo Chamber of Commerce reveals some interesting character-

TABLE 5.2

COOPERATIVE CHAINS ACCORDING TO MAJOR MERCHANDISE CATEGORIES,
1969

| Merchandise Categories | No. of Chains | No. of Member Stores |
|---|---|---|
| Food | 12 | 1,949 |
| Clothing | 7 | 655 |
| Sleeping Equipment and Bedding | 1 | 1,000 |
| Housewares | 2 | 184 |
| Drugs and Cosmetics | 2 | 196 |
| Furniture | 3 | 173 |
| Home Appliances | 3 | 770 |
| Stationery and Office Machines | 1 | 120 |
| Shoes | 1 | 124 |
| Toys | 2 | 79 |
| Watches | 1 | 140 |
| Others | 6 | 233 |
| Total | 41 | 5,715 |

Source: The Japan Voluntary Chain Association.

istics of the cooperative chains in Japan.[4] The study investigated
the operating characteristics and practices of 29 cooperative chains.
Virtually all of these chains were still quite small, as is evident
from the following data. Twenty-one chains had fewer than 75
member stores; two had between 75 and 100; and five had between
100 and 250 member stores. There was only one chain in the entire
group that claimed to have more than 250 member stores.

Retail stores that were members of these cooperative chains
were primarily medium-size stores with 5 to 30 employees. Among
the member stores, only 17 percent were very small stores with
fewer than 4 employees. Medium-size stores were affected most
severely by the newly emerging chains, and, unlike very small
stores, their owners perceived the threats to be significant enough
to take positive steps to improve their competitive position; also,
they were enlightened enough to understand potential benefits of
such a cooperative program.

The study revealed a wide divergence in the degree of commit-

[4] *Wagakuni no Voluntary Chain no Genkyo [Current Status of Voluntary
Chains in Japan]* (Tokyo: Research Department, The Tokyo Chamber of
Commerce, 1968), pp. 219–243.

ment by member stores to the cooperative program. Roughly 60 percent of the member stores did less than 30 percent of their buying from their chain headquarters, while 32 percent bought at least 50 percent of their merchandise from their chain headquarters. The chains surveyed were engaged in a number of joint activities beyond cooperative buying.[5] Twenty-three of the chains studied were undertaking cooperative advertising and promotional activities. Eleven chains had developed their own private brands. One of the most active cooperative chains is that formed by large home appliance stores. This group was organized in 1963, and at the time of this writing it consisted of some 320 firms with more than 800 stores and total estimated annual sales volume exceeding ¥100 billion. The chain known as All Japan Home Appliance Group has developed its private brand merchandise in such products as electric fans, vacuum cleaners, and refrigerators.

In the formation of cooperative chains, however, a number of serious problems also have been encountered. Most serious are those related to the leadership needed to manage the chains and commitment to the project by member stores. To organize independent-minded retailers, often with a narrow point of view, into cooperative ventures requires strong leadership, and even more critical is the ability to manage and sustain the cooperative activities once they are organized. Moreover, member stores are not always willing to support the chain, particularly in its formative stage. Independent orientation and old rivalry often hinder truly meaningful cooperative efforts. True to Japanese tradition, even within the cooperative buying groups there is a frequent tendency for power struggles to emerge among various factions.

Another practical problem facing cooperative chains is that they, unlike most of the wholesale-sponsored voluntary chains, lack facilities for warehousing and distribution. In 1969 only 6 out of 43 chains that are members of the Japan Voluntary Chain Association had merchandise distribution centers. To construct these facilities themselves would be a costly undertaking, which few of the cooperative chains could afford. One solution would be to establish closer ties with selected wholesalers to utilize their existing facilities. To solve this problem, a few large cooperative chains are now planning to undertake backward integration through acquisition of wholesalers. Without distribution facilities and warehouses, the

[5] *Ibid.*, p. 234.

real benefits of cooperative chains are often difficult to reap.

Still another potential problem facing cooperative chains is the tendency among member stores to develop into a regular chain themselves as they expand their operations. As these member stores develop into regular chains with considerable power of their own, they would have less incentive to support the cooperative chain to which they belong. Given the very dynamic environment in the Japanese retailing sector, such a prospect is very evident.

### Adaptive Behavior of Wholesalers

Without doubt the element most vulnerable to recent developments in the Japanese distribution sector is wholesaling. As we noted earlier, large wholesalers traditionally had enjoyed a strong position in the Japanese distribution structure. They had emerged as the dominant marketing institution during the Tokugawa era and had been able to maintain their uncontested leadership until very recently. But in the past few years their position has become an increasingly precarious one, and even their very *raison d'être* in the modern distribution structure has been questioned.

Wholesalers' preeminence in the traditional distribution structure was derived largely from the following conditions that had long prevailed. First, the manufacturing sector traditionally has consisted of a myriad of small-scale establishments with limited output, financial strength, and, most important, marketing ability. They had to look to wholesalers to distribute their products, to obtain needed capital, and sometimes even to procure raw materials. Second, the presence of a large number of small retailers has been an important factor. They, too, were limited in financial capacity, knowledge of the market, and management know-how. Third, wholesalers traditionally have performed risk-absorption functions in a market characterized by a high degree of uncertainty because of poor communication and transportation systems and inadequate storage facilities. Thus wholesalers performed important functions in linking a myriad of small manufacturers with a large number of equally small retailers. Both looked to wholesalers for knowledge of the market, contacts in the market place, and financial assistance. A particularly critical role of the wholesaler has been that of supplier of credit. Wholesalers also absorbed many of the risks that are inherent under such conditions.

As we have already seen, these conditions have undergone a

rather rapid change in recent years. In a number of key consumer industries we have seen the emergence of large-scale manufacturing firms with rather sophisticated marketing capabilities, and many of them now have established vertically integrated and controlled distribution channels. In some cases they have assumed many of the wholesaling functions themselves, either by bypassing the existing wholesalers or by bringing the once-independent wholesalers under their own control. Certainly, these large manufacturing firms are much less dependent on wholesalers than small manufacturers had been previously. In many cases large manufacturers now insist that their wholesalers be exclusive dealers and often dictate the terms under which merchandise is to be resold. In some cases large manufacturers now own equity interest in some of their wholesalers, and among these wholesalers it is not uncommon for representatives of the manufacturer to occupy top management positions.

At the same time, the emergence of large-scale retailing chains have also contributed to the reduction of the wholesalers' power. These large-scale chains have begun to assert their growing power vis-à-vis their wholesalers, and at the same time they have begun to assume some of the key wholesaling functions themselves.

There is a growing trend among large retail chains, if they do not buy directly from large manufacturers, to concentrate their purchases with a small number of large wholesalers. These developments, coupled with improved communication and transportation methods, have deprived wholesalers of many of their traditional functions. At least some of the traditional wholesaling functions now are being performed with greater effectiveness and efficiency by large manufacturers or retailers (or by both). Of course, this situation is by no means found in every industry, but it is becoming increasingly common, particularly in mass-produced consumer products.

We should note at the outset that wholesalers, unlike large manufacturers, had been left to their own devices to recover from wartime destructions and dislocations; it is readily understandable that this had indeed proved to be a difficult task for many. However, the wholesaling sector has by and large been oblivious to the rather basic changes that have been taking place in its environment during the last decade and a half. Particularly serious has been its inability to respond quickly and effectively to new demands and functions that have been created by these changes.

A good case in point is the failure of the majority of the whole-salers to perform adequately the task of market development for new products that have been introduced continuously by large manufacturers in the postwar years. Many wholesalers apparently felt the performance of such a task was beyond what they per-ceived as proper wholesaling functions. Wholesalers' reluctance or even refusal to perform the task of developing markets for new products invited manufacturers' encroachment into this sector, even leading to eventual control of distribution channels by the manufacturers.

Like small retailers, the average wholesaler has been very com-placent. This point is clearly demonstrated in the retailers' evalua-tion of their wholesalers in the aforementioned MITI-commissioned study of small retail establishments. While the retailers included in the study felt that their wholesalers were performing traditional wholesaling functions, such as delivery services, rather well, in other areas the retailers' evaluation of wholesalers' services was less than enthusiastic. For example, one-third of the 1,426 retailers interviewed felt that wholesalers gave only mediocre or inadequate advice on merchandising, and nearly 23 percent reported that they gave no guidance in this area.

In the area of dissemination of useful market or industry infor-mation, 37 percent of retailers interviewed felt that the wholesalers' services were inadequate, and nearly 25 percent reported that they did not receive any information whatsoever. Likewise, in the area of advertising and promotion only 17 percent were satisfied with the amount and the quality of guidance and assistance given by their wholesalers. Over 50 percent reported that they did not re-ceive any help in this regard. In the area of financial assistance only slightly over 14 percent felt that they received either excel-lent or satisfactory service. Details of retailers' evaluations as to the various services provided by their wholesalers are presented in Table 5.3. It is evident from these data that wholesalers have tended in the past to depend complacently on personal relation-ships with their retailers, as the latter have done with their cus-tomers, and they have largely failed to improve their services and their efficiencies. Seldom has the average wholesaler questioned his continued viability in the rapidly changing environment.

In recent years it has become increasingly clear that the very *raison d'être* of wholesalers began to be threatened by the environ-mental changes discussed earlier. The impact has been particularly

TABLE 5.3

SMALL RETAILERS' EVALUATION OF SERVICES PROVIDED BY
WHOLESALERS IN SELECTED AREAS, 1968

| | Percent of 1,426 Respondents Replying | | | | | |
|---|---|---|---|---|---|---|
| Type of Service | Excellent | Satis-factory | Mediocre | Inade-quate | Not Provided at All | Don't Know |
| Delivery Service | 52.4 | 30.8 | 6.9 | 2.0 | 6.3 | 1.6 |
| Merchandising Advice | 12.0 | 28.2 | 23.6 | 10.2 | 22.8 | 4.1 |
| Advice on Pricing | 11.0 | 21.8 | 28.3 | 9.0 | 25.3 | 4.6 |
| Market and Industry Information | 11.1 | 23.1 | 23.7 | 13.5 | 24.7 | 3.9 |
| Financial Assistance | 3.3 | 11.8 | 7.1 | 11.0 | 61.5 | 5.3 |
| Return Privileges | 20.1 | 30.4 | 16.0 | 11.2 | 19.0 | 3.3 |
| Advertising and Promotional Assistance | 4.3 | 12.9 | 16.6 | 11.2 | 50.5 | 4.5 |

Source: Adapted from *Shogyō Ryutsu Kozo Chōsa* [*A Study of the Distribution Structure*] (Tokyo: Ryutsu Mondai Kenkyu Kyokai, 1968), pp. 84–88.

TABLE 5.4

CHANGES IN THE DISTRIBUTION OF WHOLESALE ESTABLISHMENTS BY
SIZE AS MEASURED BY NUMBER OF EMPLOYEES, 1956 AND 1968

| Number of Employees | Number of Establishments as Percentage of Total | |
|---|---|---|
| | 1956 | 1968 |
| 1–2 | 27.8 | 22.6 |
| 3–4 | 25.3 | 22.1 |
| 5–9 | 28.4 | 28.5 |
| 10–19 | 13.0 | 15.6 |
| 20–29 | 2.9 | 4.8 |
| 30–49 | 1.6 | 3.4 |
| 50–99 | 1.0 | 2.0 |
| 100 or more | | 1.0 |
| Total | 100.0 | 100.0 |

Source: *Wagakuni no Shōgyo, 1969* [*Commerce in Japan, 1969*] (Tokyo: The Ministry of International Trade and Industry, 1970), pp. 120–121.

serious among small secondary wholesalers. Small wholesalers are clearly declining in importance. As presented in Table 5.4, between 1956 and 1968 the relative importance of wholesalers with fewer than 10 employees showed a decline, while those with 30 employees or more have showed a significant relative increase. Likewise, between 1960 and 1966 the proportion of sales accounted for by establishments with fewer than 50 employees declined, and the share of establishments with 50 employees or more increased from 44 percent to 56 percent (see Table 5.5).

TABLE 5.5

CHANGES IN DISTRIBUTION OF WHOLESALE ESTABLISHMENTS BY
SALES VOLUME AND NUMBER OF EMPLOYEES, 1960 AND 1966

| Number of Employees | Percent of Sales | |
|---|---|---|
| | 1960 | 1966 |
| 1–4 | 5.6 | 4.3 |
| 5–9 | 12.2 | 9.2 |
| 10–19 | 17.0 | 12.3 |
| 20–49 | 21.6 | 17.8 |
| 50 or more | 43.6 | 56.4 |
| Total | 100.0 | 100.0 |

Source: Adapted from *Chusho Kigyō Hakusho: Showa 43 nen ban [White Paper on Small–Medium-Size Enterprises, 1968]* (Tokyo: Small–Medium-Size Enterprise Agency, 1969), p. 120.

It must be noted that not all wholesalers have been idle in the face of their eroding power. To meet these rapidly changing conditions, some progressive wholesalers are taking a number of concrete steps, which we shall now examine. A number of wholesalers are reorienting their operations to meet the needs of large-scale retail chains. Although there is a trend for large retail chains to buy directly from manufacturers, they still purchase the bulk of the merchandise from wholesalers. With their very rapid growth, one of the chief problems facing large-scale chains is to find wholesalers capable of adequately supplying needed merchandise. A number of large progressive wholesalers have begun to capitalize on this obviously attractive opportunity. This trend is particularly notable in such products as soft goods, housewares, durables, drugs, and cosmetics.

A number of these wholesalers have established a separate section or department within their organization, specializing in servicing large chain accounts. Likewise, a number of wholesalers have improved their physical distribution systems, including construction of new distribution centers, to service large retail chains. Some wholesalers are now developing into chain operations themselves, establishing branch stores and distribution centers in strategic locations in order to serve better the needs of multistore large-scale retail chains.

Some have gone a step further by developing special merchandise and merchandising plans designed specifically for large retail outlets. A few wholesalers, particularly in fashion-oriented soft goods, are now engaged in joint product development programs with large retail chains. Wholesalers not only are providing their merchandising expertise to large chains but are absorbing a part of the risks typically associated with such activities. These efforts have contributed to cementing their relationship with large chains. At the same time the attitude of large chains toward wholesalers has been undergoing a subtle change.

Initially, the chains sought to buy merchandise from any source as long as they could get a low price. This often meant circumventing regular wholesalers and buying directly from manufacturers, or buying from cash wholesalers or whoever else could supply merchandise at low cost. As these retail chains grew, however, they began to need regular and dependable sources of supply; large wholesalers are now attempting to fill this need. There are, of course, two major risks for wholesalers adopting this approach. One is the possibility of alienating smaller wholesalers and retailers who resent the increasing interest of wholesalers in large retail chains. Of particular concern to small wholesalers and retailers are the discriminatory pricing policies followed by large wholesalers, which put the small firms in an even more disadvantageous position in competing with large chains. The other risk is the ever-present possibility that the alliance between wholesalers and large retailers is a temporary one, and that the retailers may well decide to bypass wholesalers when they feel this to be to their advantage.

Another step toward rationalization taken by a number of wholesalers is the cooperative approach. This assumes several different forms. One popular cooperative effort is for wholesalers located in a given area to establish a new joint wholesale distribution center and physically move their operations there. Traditionally, wholesalers have been located in downtown areas, and typically they are highly concentrated in a relatively small area known as the Wholesale District. One of the serious problems facing wholesalers located in crowded cities today is that their ability to move merchandise to and from their stores and warehouses is rapidly deteriorating in the face of the growing volume of merchandise to be handled and ever-worsening traffic congestion. Moreover, the existing buildings occupied by a great many wholesalers often were built scores of years ago and are not designed to perform modern large-scale distribution functions. Being located in highly congested areas, with prohibitively high land cost, many wholesalers find expansion of existing facilities all but impossible. For these reasons, in a number of cities wholesalers jointly have decided to move out of the downtown area to suburbs where they can build a planned wholesale center, or to move into a high-rise building constructed to their specifications. These newly created wholesale centers have a number of common facilities that serve the entire group, including warehouses, distribution terminals, and even a common computer center. Particularly notable is the construction of major wholesale merchandising marts in Tokyo and Osaka. These centers house showrooms, office facilities, and information processing centers as well as distribution centers. As another example of this cooperative approach, 61 major textile wholesalers in Tokyo jointly agreed to construct a central distribution center in the fall of 1969.

The Ministry of International Trade and Industry has been encouraging the establishment of such centers since 1963 as a part of the government program to modernize Japan's distribution system, and has been providing management guidance as well as low-interest long-term loans to qualified parties. Between 1963 and 1968, 54 such centers either have been established or have been approved under the government assistance program. This program has been far more successful than similar efforts to move small retail stores into centrally located buildings.

Another form of joint effort is for a number of wholesalers to cooperate in developing their original product lines as well as common private brand merchandise. For example, 10 leading food wholesalers recently formed an association for such a purpose. Similar trends are notable among some wholesalers of soft goods. Some wholesalers have formed cooperative buying groups. For example, 38 major houseware wholesalers have recently formed such a group in order to obtain lower prices and to attain greater efficiency by undertaking cooperative buying, joint market studies, and common billing procedures. Efforts for rationalization have also taken the form of improvement of managerial practices. Traditionally, the great majority of wholesalers have been family-owned and family-managed concerns, and this fact has been reflected in their managerial practices. Now, however, a growing number of more progressive wholesalers actively are seeking opportunities to improve their managerial efficiency.

For one thing they are now actively recruiting college graduates instead of relying on the traditional hiring practice of taking young apprentices with a minimum of education. They also are making efforts toward systematic training and development of their junior and middle management. Some progressive wholesalers also are attempting to attain greater efficiency in such areas as delivery system, inventory control, sales management, and credit management. A few are utilizing computers in these efforts, with considerable effectiveness.

Perhaps most significant in this regard is that some progressive firms now have redefined their wholesaling functions. They have begun to view wholesaling not merely as buying and selling of merchandise but as providing a series of marketing services for customers as an integral part of their overall function. For example, a number of progressive wholesalers now extend a considerable amount of managerial assistance to their customers in such critical areas as merchandising, inventory control, advertising and sales promotions, and even training of their personnel. In addition, they attempt to provide up-to-date market and industry information. This redefinition of task has given new vitality and *raison d'être* to a number of wholesalers.

A recent survey undertaken by the MITI from a sample of some 200,000 retail and wholesale establishments reveals some interesting results in this regard. Among the wholesale establishments surveyed, only 19 percent reported that they extend any type of assistance to either their suppliers or customers. As might be expected, however, the percentage of those extending assistance grows significantly with an increase in size. For example, more than half of the establishments with 100 employees or more surveyed are reported to have some type of assistance programs. Details are presented in Table 5.6. Looking at the nature of the assistance, we

TABLE 5.6

Wholesale Establishments Extending Some Form of Assistance
to Manufacturers, Other Wholesalers, and Retailers
According to Size and Product Lines

| Size of Establishment and Product | Extending Assistance (%) | Not Extending Assistance (%) | Total (%) |
|---|---|---|---|
| No. of Employees | | | |
| 1–4 | 10 | 90 | 100 |
| 5–9 | 19 | 81 | 100 |
| 10–19 | 27 | 73 | 100 |
| 20–49 | 39 | 61 | 100 |
| 50–99 | 49 | 51 | 100 |
| 100 or more | 54 | 46 | 100 |
| Average | 19 | 81 | 100 |
| | | | |
| Product | | | |
| Textiles | 23 | 77 | 100 |
| Apparel and Sundry Items | 24 | 76 | 100 |
| Food and Beverages | 18 | 82 | 100 |
| Pharmaceutical and Cosmetic Goods | 27 | 73 | 100 |
| Machinery | 23 | 77 | 100 |
| Furniture | 18 | 82 | 100 |

Source: Adapted from *Wagakuni no Shōgyō, 1969 [Commerce in Japan, 1969]* (Tokyo: The Ministry of International Trade and Industry, 1970), p. 96.

find that the most popular form extended to manufacturers was technical and engineering aid in production, closely trailed by financial assistance and guidance in product designs. As expected, there are some notable variations according to product lines. Details are presented in Table 5.7. As to assistance extended to customers, the most important was managerial guidance. Details are presented in Table 5.8.

Another major step is toward vertical integration. A number of progressive wholesalers actively have been seeking to attain vertical integration, particularly of the downward type. This practice takes several different forms. Some are attempting to establish their own retail outlets. This practice is prevalent in such merchandise lines as men's ready-to-wear, in which wholesalers are still a dominant force. Reasons for their entry into retailing vary somewhat. In some cases it stems from their desire to obtain a better feel for consumers' needs in order to improve their wholesaling operations.

TABLE 5.7

WHOLESALERS EXTENDING VARIOUS TYPES OF ASSISTANCE TO MANUFACTURERS
ACCORDING TO SIZE AND PRODUCT LINE

(in percent*)

| Size of Establishment and Product | Equity Participation | Financial Assistance | Assignment of Senior Executives | Assignment of Regular Employees | Product Design | Technical and Engineering Assistance | Management Assistance | Guidance in Machinery and Equipment |
|---|---|---|---|---|---|---|---|---|
| *No. of Employees* | | | | | | | | |
| 1–4 | 10 | 25 | 1 | 7 | 27 | 31 | 18 | 3 |
| 5–9 | 14 | 24 | 5 | 12 | 24 | 27 | 19 | 7 |
| 10–19 | 17 | 26 | 5 | 16 | 25 | 25 | 21 | 8 |
| 20–49 | 24 | 30 | 7 | 15 | 25 | 23 | 20 | 8 |
| 50–99 | 34 | 30 | 12 | 14 | 23 | 25 | 21 | 11 |
| 100 or more | 37 | 40 | 18 | 22 | 27 | 29 | 28 | 18 |
| Average | 17 | 26 | 5 | 13 | 25 | 27 | 20 | 7 |
| *Product* | | | | | | | | |
| Textiles | 12 | 25 | 3 | 5 | 59 | 31 | 11 | 7 |
| Apparel and Sundry Items | 12 | 23 | 3 | 7 | 62 | 26 | 14 | 7 |
| Food and Beverages | 17 | 19 | 6 | 17 | 14 | 26 | 28 | 8 |
| Pharmaceuticals and Cosmetics | 25 | 12 | 4 | 25 | 9 | 20 | 29 | 2 |
| Machinery | 22 | 19 | 8 | 23 | 12 | 29 | 21 | 6 |
| Furniture | 10 | 25 | 2 | 6 | 56 | 22 | 15 | 3 |

* Percentage exceeds 100 because of duplications.

Source: Adapted from *Wagakuni no Shōgyō, Shōwa 1969* [*Commerce in Japan, 1969*] (Tokyo: The Ministry of International Trade and Industry, 1970), p. 96.

## TABLE 5.8

WHOLESALERS EXTENDING VARIOUS TYPES OF ASSISTANCE TO
WHOLESALE AND RETAIL CUSTOMERS ACCORDING TO SIZE AND PRODUCT

| Size of Establishment and Product | Wholesalers | | | | |
|---|---|---|---|---|---|
| | Equity Participation | Financial Assistance | Assignment of Senior Executives | Assignment of Employees | Management Assistance |
| *No. of Employees* | | | | | |
| 1–4 | 14 | 23 | 3 | 16 | 51 |
| 5–9 | 12 | 18 | 8 | 27 | 46 |
| 10–19 | 14 | 20 | 4 | 28 | 56 |
| 20–49 | 18 | 22 | 6 | 28 | 55 |
| 50–99 | 25 | 27 | 7 | 27 | 60 |
| 100 or more | 34 | 40 | 18 | 30 | 65 |
| Average | 16 | 22 | 6 | 25 | 53 |
| *Product* | | | | | |
| Textiles | 38 | 29 | 6 | 17 | 47 |
| Apparel and Sundry Items | 21 | 22 | 6 | 20 | 55 |
| Food and Beverages | 12 | 25 | 5 | 19 | 61 |
| Pharmaceuticals and Cosmetics | 8 | 15 | 5 | 30 | 69 |
| Machinery | 6 | 11 | 7 | 41 | 49 |
| Furniture | 20 | 23 | 4 | 31 | 36 |
| | Retailers | | | | |
| *No. of Employees* | | | | | |
| 1–4 | 6 | 26 | 1 | 15 | 66 |
| 5–9 | 8 | 23 | 2 | 27 | 58 |
| 10–19 | 10 | 27 | 3 | 31 | 59 |
| 20–49 | 14 | 30 | 3 | 33 | 62 |
| 50–99 | 16 | 33 | 4 | 42 | 68 |
| 100 or more | 19 | 36 | 7 | 41 | 66 |
| Average | 10 | 27 | 2 | 28 | 62 |
| *Product* | | | | | |
| Textiles | 20 | 38 | 1 | 27 | 56 |
| Apparel and Sundry Items | 16 | 24 | 1 | 39 | 56 |
| Food and Beverages | 8 | 30 | 1 | 21 | 66 |
| Pharmaceuticals and Cosmetics | 4 | 14 | 1 | 42 | 71 |
| Machinery | 9 | 23 | 4 | 31 | 67 |
| Furniture | 12 | 19 | 1 | 37 | 51 |

* Percentage exceeds 100 because of duplications.
Source: Adapted from *Wagakuni no Shōgyo, 1969* [Commerce in Japan, 1969] (Tokyo: The Ministry of International Trade and Industry, 1970), p. 96.

In some it is a means for diversification, while in others it is a deliberate effort to shift emphasis from wholesaling to retailing activities. Of course, wholesalers run a risk of alienating their retailer customers, as their new retail outlets are certain to come in direct competition with their old customers.

The second pattern is for large primary wholesalers to organize smaller secondary wholesalers on a selective basis into a loosely coordinated network of affiliates. They do so because they believe that, given the preponderance of very small retail establishments, small secondary wholesalers will continue to have a useful role to perform in the Japanese economy. The result is that a number of large primary wholesalers are now making deliberate efforts to strengthen their ties with selected secondary wholesalers and are organizing them into groups, with the primary wholesalers serving as the nucleus. The primary wholesalers extend various types of assistance, including financial and managerial participation, to the secondary wholesalers affiliated with the group.

The most common effort made by wholesalers to achieve downward vertical integration is through the organization of retailers in the form of voluntary chains. Since this is one of the most significant recent developments in the Japanese wholesaling sector, we shall examine it in some detail. Although the exact number of voluntary chains in operation is difficult to estimate, one good measure is the membership of the Japan Voluntary Chain Association. In 1969 the Association had 66 wholesaler-sponsored voluntary chains in its membership, with more than 22,000 member stores. As can be seen from Table 5.9, food stores dominate the scene, accounting for 24 out of 66 chains and over 50 percent of the total retail stores belonging to the chains. Interestingly, there were as many as 13 chains handling beds and related merchandise.

Voluntary chains in Japan were given initial impetus in 1963, when the Ministry of International Trade and Industry decided to give its official encouragement to the formation of such chains and began to provide financial and organizational guidance. It initiated an active educational campaign to disseminate knowledge of the concept of voluntary chains and their benefits to wholesalers as well as to retailers. Of course, the development of voluntary chains in Japan is still in its infancy. The total sales of stores belonging to cooperative or voluntary chains were estimated in 1968 to be about ¥100 billion, representing a mere 7 percent of all retail sales. Moreover, not all of the sales of the member stores are derived

TABLE 5.9

DISTRIBUTION OF WHOLESALER-SPONSORED VOLUNTARY CHAINS
ACCORDING TO MAJOR MERCHANDISE CATEGORIES, 1968

| Major Merchandise Categories | No. of Chains | No. of Retail Members |
|---|---|---|
| Food | 24 | 11,736 |
| Clothing | 14 | 2,746 |
| Sleeping Equipment and Bedding | 13 | 2,630 |
| Drugs and Cosmetics | 3 | 2,772 |
| Furniture | 2 | 469 |
| Household Goods | 4 | 550 |
| Stationery and Office Machines | 2 | 586 |
| Shoes | 1 | 318 |
| Watches | 1 | 445 |
| Others | 2 | 125 |
| Total | 66 | 22,454 |

Source: The Japan Voluntary Chain Association.

from merchandise bought through the voluntary or cooperative chains.

In order to have a closer look at the current status of voluntary chains, we shall now present the highlights of the previously cited study undertaken by the Research Department of the Tokyo Chamber of Commerce on cooperative and voluntary chains in Japan. The study investigated the practices of 38 wholesaler-sponsored voluntary chains. It revealed that the majority of voluntary chains were relatively small. Fifteen of the 38 chains studied had fewer than 100 member stores, and in only 4 chains did the membership exceed 500 stores. Also significant is the fact that 21 chains were sponsored by wholesalers with annual sales of less than ¥50 million.

For the majority of the sponsoring wholesalers, voluntary chains represent only a limited part of their operations. The study also revealed that retailers belonging to the chain represented a relatively small portion of the customers of the sponsoring wholesaler. In 12 chains the membership represented on the average less than 10 percent of the customers. Among 24 the membership represented less than 30 percent of their customers.

Among the total 38 chains surveyed only 3 were managed entirely by full-time employees (the average number of full-time employees was 20). In 18 chains the same personnel served voluntary chain accounts as well as nonaffiliated individual customers. In the remaining chains some full-time staff members were available to service voluntary accounts, but they required extensive assistance from other employees. The majority of member retail stores belonging to the voluntary chains included in this survey were small: 45 percent of them had fewer than four employees, and those with nine employees or less constituted more than 80 percent of the total membership.

The study also revealed that a third of the member stores surveyed bought more than half of their merchandise from the chain headquarters; another third of the stores, however, made less than 30 percent of their purchases through the chain, indicating a rather limited commitment on the part of the retail members. Interestingly, 22 of the 38 chains had their own private brands. The study also revealed that most of the voluntary chains were performing a number of services for their member stores, such as cooperative advertising and promotion programs, including issuing trading stamps, furnishing common store designs, and providing educational as well as consulting services.

As the foregoing survey reveals, most of the voluntary chains are still small and in the development stage, but there are a handful that are already functioning quite effectively. For example, Hiromaru grocery chain, sponsored by Hiroya, a large food wholesaler established in 1960, has a membership of some 460 and more than 50 full-time employees.

Largely because of the active educational efforts by the MITI and the Japan Voluntary Chain Association, the concept of voluntary chains is becoming widely disseminated. There is a growing awareness among wholesalers of its potential value as an effective means of meeting the competitive onslaught of large-scale retailing. However, the experience of the past several years has pointed to a number of major problem areas, the solutions of which are essential to the sound development of voluntary chains in Japan. Let us now examine them.

One serious problem is the lack of understanding as to the objectives and functions of a voluntary chain, on the part of both the sponsoring wholesaler and its retail members. Some wholesalers have established voluntary chains simply because it was a fashionable thing to do, while others have organized them merely as a convenient and eye-catching means of strengthening their ties with their customers. A number of wholesalers have been too zealous in their desire to increase the chain's membership and have indiscriminately recruited new member stores. This has led to serious problems of conflicting needs and interests among the membership. Similarly, some retail stores were induced to join a voluntary group merely out of their desire to obtain immediate advantages in the form of lower purchase prices.

Closely related to the inadequate understanding of the nature of the voluntary chain is the lack of commitment on the part of both sponsoring organizations and participating retailers. Frequently, neither the sponsoring wholesaler nor the retail members understand the fundamental fact that it requires considerable effort and commitment on the part of every participating store to make a voluntary chain a truly viable organization. Member stores do not give their support to the chain headquarters, particularly in its critical initial stage. As a result the sponsoring wholesaler complains about the lack of support from member stores, while retailers are dissatisfied since anticipated tangible benefits are often not immediately forthcoming.

Another problem area arises because wholesalers have not always been in a position to exert strong leadership due to their own limited financial and managerial capacities. Particularly serious has been the fact that a number of sponsoring wholesalers have failed to provide adequate merchandising service and guidance to their member stores.

We have examined a number of ways in which wholesalers are attempting to adapt themselves to the changing environment. It is a relatively small number, however, that share a strong sense of urgency and exert aggressive efforts for modernization and rationalization. The majority, particularly the smaller ones, have not done so, as is true of their counterparts in retailing. There appears to be a clear-cut dichotomy between those that are aggressively seeking modernization and those that are complacently drifting along. Those who are loath to innovate may survive for a time, but it is clear that their role and place in the nation's distribution structure will become increasingly precarious. Indeed, it is well for them to remember that while wholesaling functions always will have to be performed, there is no guarantee that they will be among the firms that will continue to perform these functions.

Adaptive Behavior of Department Stores

Until very recently department stores, as the only large-scale retailers, dominated Japan's retailing scene.[6] According to the Department Store Law, a department store is defined as a departmentalized store with at least 3,000 square meters (approximately 32,100 square feet) of sales space in the seven largest cities, and with a minimum of 1,500 square meters (approximately 16,050 square feet) in places other than those cities. In 1969 there were 243 department stores, with total annual sales of nearly ¥1.4 trillion, representing roughly 10 percent of the total retail sales in Japan (equivalent to roughly 5 percent of the total personal consumption expenditure).

The traditional preeminence of the department store now is being challenged by the rapid growth of large-scale mass merchandising firms. The traditional department stores, having enjoyed uncontested leadership for so long, have been slow to see the implications of the changing environment, particularly the emergence of large-scale mass merchandising chains. But they are now beginning to recognize these threats. Before considering specific ways in which traditional department stores are attempting to adapt, it would be well to review briefly the general characteristics of department stores in Japan.

Japanese department stores can be categorized into three major types. The first type are those growing out of traditional dry goods or apparel stores. These were the original department stores and traditionally have enjoyed the highest prestige. Many of them trace their origin to the Tokugawa era, during which they already had achieved prominence as the nation's leading retailers. The largest and most prestigious in this group are Mitsukoshi, Takashimaya, Matsuzakaya, and Matsuya. These stores are located in major metropolitan centers, particularly Tokyo. The second type are those that are owned and managed by private railroad firms in the metropolitan areas, notably in Tokyo, Osaka, and Nagoya. As a part of their diversification programs a number of private railroad firms with commuter lines have built department stores at their major terminals in recent years. The third type are those that are

---

6 For a succinct discussion of the changing role of department stores in Japan, see Hajime Sato and Sueaki Takaoka, *Gendai no Hyakkaten* [Department Stores in Contemporary Japan] (Tokyo: Nihon Keizai Shinbunsha, 1970), pp. 53–190.

commonly known as local department stores. They are located in large cities outside the metropolitan areas and are generally smaller than either of the first two types. Typically they are closely held family concerns.

A typical department store has annual sales of ¥5 billion, nearly 570 employees, and roughly 14,000 square meters (150,000 square feet) of sales space. Since the average retail store in Japan has annual sales of less than ¥7 million and only 3 employees, the difference is rather staggering. The sales of Mitsukoshi, the largest retail establishment in Japan, exceeded ¥14 billion in 1969, accounting for roughly 1 percent of the total retail sales in the nation.

Of the 246 department stores that existed in 1969, 46 are located in the major cities and the rest are scattered throughout Japan. As may be expected, the department stores in the six major cities are considerably larger than those located in other areas. The 46 metropolitan department stores in aggregate account for nearly 70 percent of the total department store sales and roughly half of the total floor space of all the department stores in Japan. In fact, among the metropolitan department stores, there are half a dozen or so that boast more than half a million square feet of sales space. With a few exceptions, traditional department stores had been single-establishment operations. Even among stores with branches, the number of outlets has seldom exceeded three or four.

Looking at the composition of sales by major merchandise categories, we find that in Japanese department stores, like their counterparts in the United States, soft goods constitute the single most important line of merchandise, accounting for roughly 43 percent of the total sales. Household furnishings, including home appliances, account for 15 percent, furniture for 13 percent, and sundry goods for 7 percent of the total sales. The remainder comes from miscellaneous sources.

Japanese department stores traditionally have placed much emphasis on extensive personal service and have been successful in creating a prestige-oriented and luxurious shopping atmosphere. In addition, a typical large department store contains an amusement center, theaters, restaurants, child care centers, and other customer service facilities. Indeed, Japanese department stores offer customers total shopping comfort. They also hold exhibits, concerts, and lecture series, and offer lessons in a wide variety of sports such as golf, bowling, and even skiing, and cultural and recreational activities such as flower arrangement and tea ceremony.

TABLE 5.10

FINANCIAL AND OPERATING RESULTS OF SELECTED DEPARTMENT
STORES, 1968

| | |
|---|---|
| Gross Margin as Percent of Sales | 21.6 |
| Selling and Administrative Expenses as Percent of Sales | 18.1 |
| Net Operating Income as Percent of Sales | 3.5 |
| Net Other Income as Percent of Sales | 0.7 |
| Net Profit Before Tax (percent) | 2.7 |
| Net Income After Tax (percent) | 1.6 |
| Annual Stock Turnover (times) | 22.6 |
| Annual Capital Turnover (times) | 2.4 |
| Before-Tax Return on Total Capital (perecnt) | 6.9 |
| Return on Equity (percent) | 24.4 |
| Percentage Equity is of Total Capital | 28.1 |

Source: *Hyakaten Tokei Nenpo: Showa 43 nen [Department Store Statistics, 1968]* (Tokyo: The Japan Department Store Association, 1969), p. 44.

Let us now examine the operating results of department stores. The National Association of Department Stores undertakes regular surveys of its members and makes public the composite of key operating data submitted by cooperating stores. A few major operating statistics are presented in Table 5.10.

Riding on the crest of the rapid expansion of the consumer market, the department stores have achieved a substantial growth

TABLE 5.11

INDEX OF THE TOTAL SALES OF DEPARTMENT STORES, 1960–1968

(1965 = 100)

| Year | Total Sales | Sales of Dept. Stores in Six Metropolitan Areas | Sales of Dept. Stores Located Outside of the Major Metropolitan Areas |
|---|---|---|---|
| 1960 | 47.3 | 51.0 | 39.6 |
| 1961 | 58.5 | 63.3 | 48.3 |
| 1962 | 68.3 | 73.6 | 57.0 |
| 1963 | 79.8 | 84.9 | 69.1 |
| 1964 | 90.8 | 93.6 | 84.9 |
| 1965 | 100.0 | 100.0 | 100.0 |
| 1966 | 112.2 | 110.4 | 116.1 |
| 1967 | 128.9 | 124.6 | 138.0 |
| 1968 | 150.4 | 142.2 | 167.6 |

Source: *Hyakkaten Hanbai Tokei Geppo, December 1968 [Monthly Report on Department Store Sales]* (Tokyo: The Ministry of International Trade and Industry, 1969), p. 4.

during the past several years. For example, as evidenced in Table 5.11, the total sales of department stores more than tripled between 1960 and 1968. Particularly remarkable has been the growth of department stores located outside the six major metropolitan areas.

Although the department stores have grown rapidly in the postwar years and have enjoyed supremacy in the Japanese distribution sector as the only large-scale retailers, there is growing evidence that their once-uncontested leadership is being challenged by the emerging mass merchandising chains. Ranked according to sales volume in 1969, the department stores occupied the first three places among the nation's large-scale retail establishments, and Daiei, the largest mass merchandising firm, came in fourth place. However, it is fully anticipated that by the early 1970s, Daiei will overtake the largest department store in Japan and will become the largest retail firm in the country.

Likewise, other mass merchandising firms are likely to dislodge department stores from their present top ranking. Moreover, according to a recent projection by the MITI's Committee on the Distribution Structure, by 1972 aggregate sales of regular chains will exceed those of department stores by a substantial margin. The projection indicates that the relative share of department store sales will remain at the present level of roughly 10 percent of total retail sales in 1972, but the share of the regular chains would increase from 5.7 percent in 1966 to 14.6 percent in 1972. Available evidence seems to point toward the accuracy of this projection.

According to the survey of the largest 102 stores undertaken by the *Japan Economic Journal* in 1969, large-scale retailing establishments account for exactly half of the total number. In terms of sales the department stores' share declined from 66 percent to 61 percent from the preceding year. Indeed, the department stores have been put on the defensive by the onslaught of the rapidly emerging mass merchandising firms. Several factors are responsible for this relative decline of the department stores. The most basic reason is the failure of the managements of traditional department stores to grasp the implications of consumption trends, particularly the emergence of the mass market and the geographic shift in the population. The department stores cater to the high-income class, as evidenced from Table 5.12. Given the seniority-related wage scale, it can be inferred from these data that the customers that regularly patronize department stores tend to be the older part of the consuming public.

TABLE 5.12

PATRONAGE PATTERNS OF DEPARTMENT STORES
ACCORDING TO INCOME CLASS, 1964

| Real Monthly Cash Income (¥) | Total Spent at Department Stores As % of Total Family Expenditure | Total Spent on Food at Department Stores As % of Total Family Food Expenditure |
|---|---|---|
| Less than 10,000 | 1.5 | 2.1 |
| 10,000–19,999 | 3.3 | 1.4 |
| 20,000–29,999 | 3.6 | 1.5 |
| 30,000–39,999 | 4.5 | 1.7 |
| 40,000–49,999 | 5.0 | 2.3 |
| 50,000–59,999 | 5.5 | 2.7 |
| 60,000–69,999 | 5.8 | 2.9 |
| 70,000–79,999 | 6.0 | 3.2 |
| 80,000–89,999 | 5.7 | 3.8 |
| 90,000–99,999 | 7.7 | 3.7 |
| 100,000–119,999 | 9.4 | 5.0 |
| 120,000–139,999 | 8.8 | 5.3 |
| 140,000–159,999 | 11.5 | 7.2 |
| 160,000 and over | 9.4 | 4.9 |

Source: Adapted from *1964 National Survey of Family Income and Expenditure*, Vol. 8 (Tokyo: The Office of the Prime Minister, 1966), p. 89.

Despite the tremendous increase in discretionary income enjoyed by the lower-income classes in recent years, department stores largely have failed to broaden their appeal to the emerging middle class. No doubt, department stores attract a large number of potential customers from this segment, but it is possible that their main appeal lies not in their merchandise but in their wealth of services and luxurious atmosphere. Many of these "customers" go to department stores to shop around in a luxurious atmosphere but do their actual buying at mass merchandising firms, where they can generally obtain lower prices. The increasing trend of urbanization and the rapid growth of suburbs have also contributed to the decline of department stores, which traditionally have concentrated in downtown business centers. Until recently, department stores largely had failed to keep up with this trend, whereas supermarkets and discount stores have been aggressively seeking the patronage of the rapidly growing and rather mobile surburban population (consisting largely of the newly emerging middle class) by establishing branch stores in key suburbs.

Since foodstuffs occupy such an important share in the total sales of Japanese department stores, the rapid rise of supermarkets in convenient locations has posed a major threat. Increasing traffic congestion has contributed further to worsening the plight of the department stores located in the heart of metropolitan centers. The so-called terminal department stores owned and managed by private railroad firms have not suffered nearly as much from this development as have those traditional department stores located in the heart of downtown shopping centers.

Along with the emergence of a middle class and the geographic shift in the population, there are two other important forces to be recognized. One is the rapid growth and penetration of national brands aggressively promoted by major manufacturers. This development has led to the decline in the relative importance of store prestige. Consumers have become more concerned over the reputation of manufacturers of the products and have become less conscious of where they buy particular brands. The other force is a growing labor shortage. The department stores, long known for their high-quality services, are now much concerned over rapidly rising wage rates, which naturally increase their operating expenses.

Department stores have enjoyed their preeminent position in the Japanese distribution system for so long that their managements have become complacent. In some ways the very power they wield has been a corrupting influence for the managements. For example, this attitude has been reflected in their dealings with their suppliers. For some time it has been customary for manufacturers and wholesalers selling to department stores to provide at least part of the sales personnel at their expense. A study conducted by the Fair Trade Commission among department stores in Tokyo in 1966 revealed that roughly 20 percent of the total sales personnel in the department stores were provided by wholesalers and manufacturers at their expense. In some extreme cases the percentage was reported to run as high as 50 percent. Department store management has come to expect these services. Manufacturers and wholesalers have been willing to provide such services because of the tremendous power that department stores wield in the Japanese distribution system. In addition, suppliers have extended liberal merchandise-return privileges. Indeed, department stores traditionally have shifted one of the major business risks to suppliers by being able to demand and obtain extremely liberal return privileges.

Of course, it is not entirely fair to attribute the failures of department stores to adapt to environmental changes solely to management's orientation; department stores have been somewhat constrained in their freedom to innovate because of the Department Store Law and other legal measures. The postwar version of the Department Store Law enacted in 1956 is designed primarily to protect small retailers against competition from large department stores. The Law requires, among other things, the approval of the Ministry of International Trade and Industry to establish new department stores, to expand existing stores, and to undertake mergers among the existing department stores. The Law also stipulates the number of days that department stores can operate in a month as well as the store hours. The Law also prohibits department stores from providing free transportation for customers to and from stores.

Particularly serious to the department stores is the need to obtain MITI approval for expansion of existing stores or the opening of new ones. Each application is screened by the Council on Department Stores, the advisory body to MITI. In examining each application, the Council seeks the opinion of the local business community in which the proposed store is to be located. Of course, it is not difficult to imagine that often the local business community is less than receptive to such a proposal. As a result, department stores, particularly large ones that are likely to pose a serious threat to the existing local business community, face some difficulties in undertaking an expansion program. For example, it is reported that during 1969 roughly one-third of the applications were approved with the condition that the proposed store size be substantially reduced.

Particularly detrimental to department stores is the fact that through legal loopholes mass merchandising firms have been virtually unaffected by the Law. Theoretically, any stores with 3,000 square meters of floor space in the seven major cities, or 1,500 square meters of floor space outside these cities, are subject to this Law. Mass merchandising firms, however, get around it by incorporating a number of nominal subsidiaries and by dividing sections of the store among them, so that no one company owns more than the legal limit. Obviously, the department stores are not allowed to follow this tactic.

Of course, the impact of the Law on department stores is far from certain. Between 1956 and 1969 the number of department stores increased by 80 percent, the total floor space more than doubled, and the total sales increased by nearly sixfold. It should be noted that to the extent that the Law has been effective, it has tended to benefit the existing department stores, particularly major ones, by restricting entry and competition.

In addition to the Department Store Law, the Anti-Monopoly Act prohibits department stores from engaging in eight specific practices, such as the use of premiums, unfair retaliatory actions against suppliers, and unfair demands for delivery of goods on consignment.

Confronted with the challenge of rapidly growing competitive forces, the managers of department stores have gradually become aware of the need to adapt their policies and strategies to meet the changing conditions. Progressive department stores are taking a series of steps toward this end, which we shall now examine.

First, a number of leading department stores in the major metropolitan areas have shifted to multiple-store operations by establishing branch stores in rapidly growing market areas to compete against mass merchandising chains. These branch stores are considerably smaller than the main store, typically ranging from 15,000 square meters (160,000 square feet) to 20,000 square meters (214,000 square feet). A number of new features have been incorporated, such as providing adequate parking facilities and following a merchandising policy that is consistent with the particular area that it serves. Thus some department stores are now departing from the traditional pattern of a single dominant establishment to that of a chain of smaller stores located in strategic market areas. Closely related to this trend are active efforts by department stores to develop shopping centers. The concept is still new in Japan, but a number of large department stores are taking the initiative in establishing shopping centers in attractive suburban markets.

Second, progressive department stores are now pursuing active diversification programs. While patterns vary widely among department stores, entry into supermarket operations has been particularly popular. Supermarkets present formidable competition to department stores, since the Japanese version of a supermarket carries a high proportion of nonfood items. This decision was based on the recognition that supermarkets hold such a basic appeal to the masses that efforts to arrest their growth would be fruitless. Rather, the managers of a number of department stores have come to recognize that they should capitalize on the super-market's growth potentials. There are, of course, obvious risks in their entry into supermarket operations, including the loss of prestige, but virtually all of the major metropolitan department stores, including the most prestige-minded Mitsukishi, have committed themselves to entering supermarket operations. In almost all cases supermarket operations are managed by a separate subsidiary. Other areas of diversification include entry into real estate, housing development, and leisure-related industries.

Third, leading department stores in the major metropolitan areas have been pursuing extensive expansion and improvement programs of their main stores. Remodeling and expansion of the main store are intended to facilitate the trend toward one-stop shopping and to make the store distinct enough to attract customers from suburbs who otherwise would prefer to shop in their own neighborhood. These expansion efforts have resulted in several department stores in Toyko with sales floor space of as much as 50,000 square meters, or roughly 535,000 square feet.

Fourth, leading department stores have been making innovative changes in their management practices. For example, a number of department stores are improving their buying practices, particularly in view of their entry into multiple-store operations. In the past, although department stores were large-scale in terms of their size, in their buying they often failed to take advantage of the potential benefits of volume purchases. This was due in part to the extremely wide merchandise assortment carried by a typical department store but stems largely from rather obsolete buying practices.

With the emergence of large-scale chains, however, this situation has undergone a radical change. Not only has it become necessary for department stores to rationalize buying procedures to obtain lower cost, but it is already discernible that some wholesalers and manufacturers have begun to place higher priority on sales to supermarket and discount chains because of their volume purchases. Department stores now find themselves, much to their dismay, in a position of having to compete with these new forms of large-scale retail institutions not only for customers but for sources of supply as well.

As a part of the rationalization of buying practices, some department stores have begun to engage in cooperative buying programs. While the volume of purchases made on this basis is still limited, half a dozen or so cooperative buying groups have been formed. One such buying group with 29 participating stores now buys ¥12 billion worth of merchandise per year, primarily soft goods. In early 1970 two leading department stores, Daimaru and Matsuzakaya, agreed to enter into a cooperative buying arrangement. This may well lead to an even closer relationship between the two stores in the future.

Closely related to cooperative buying practices is the development of unique merchandise lines to be sold under a store's private brand. This is being done on an individual store basis as well as through cooperative buying groups. Unlike private brand merchandise carried by discount stores, these represent high-quality original lines. Greater attention also is being paid to the further improvement of personal services. Particularly important in this regard is expansion of credit, including issuing credit cards, consumer consulting services, and a home sales program that typically accounts for 10 percent to 20 percent of total department store sales. Rationalization of management practices also includes growing emphasis on improvement in billing, inventory control, and credit evaluation, as well as on development of long-range plans and establishment of systematic management development programs.

Finally, a number of leading Japanese department stores are establishing close ties with well-known retailing institutions in the United States and Europe as a means of strengthening their distinct appeal and prestige. These cooperative ties have, up to the present, taken the form of the exchange of merchandise and trade information, but they may well develop into joint ventures as the current restrictions of entry of foreign capital into distribution activities are removed. In addition, leading department stores have entered into licensing agreements with well-known American and European manufacturers of high-fashion ready-to-wear merchandise and with famous designers to incorporate new fashions in their merchandise. These department stores not only sell this merchandise at their own stores but supply it to specialty stores as well as to smaller local department stores without direct access to foreign sources. Several leading department stores have also established branch stores overseas, including New York, Honolulu, Hong Kong, and Bangkok. Up until now, most of these branches have been rather small and intended primarily for publicity effect, but a number of leading stores have begun to undertake systematic efforts for overseas expansion programs.

As we have seen, a number of leading department stores, having recognized the rapidly changing environment, are now attempting to adopt new positions and strategies. In these attempts they have several major advantages that they can capitalize on. First, they have substantially more financial resources (primarily in the form of accumulated capital reserves) than have newly emerging large-scale retail institutions. For example, the aforementioned survey of the 102 largest retail firms conducted in 1969 revealed that the average capital employed by department stores was slightly over ¥10 billion (ranging from ¥100 million to ¥46 billion) in contrast to ¥4.6 billion (ranging from ¥700 million to ¥21.7 billion) for mass merchandising institutions. Moreover, many of the leading department stores have considerable real estate that is carried in their books at very nominal figures. In addition, they enjoy well-established banking connections, giving them ready access to additional funds. Since one of the chief problems now facing mass merchandising firms is the lack of funds to finance further growth, the department stores' ability to mobilize large sums of capital resources gives them a significant competitive edge.

Second, some department stores, notably those owned and managed by railroad interests, derive a significant competitive advantage from being a part of a well-diversified business. Most of the firms have a wide range of business interests in real estate development, home construction, sight-seeing, and other leisure-related industries. Many of these activities are located along their main railroad lines; thus the department stores owned and managed by these firms enjoy a number of advantages that come from being part of a well-diversified business enterprise whose activities are concentrated in a well-defined and fairly small geographic area.

Third, large department stores have excellent managerial resources. True, top management of many of the leading department stores has been rather conservative in its outlook, but they do have a potentially excellent cadre of managerial personnel. Until rather recently, large department stores have been the only retail institutions that regularly recruited college graduates and attempted to give them systematic training. Thus leading department stores have a pool of highly educated and well-trained managerial personnel. Finally, although it is rather intangible, department stores have a long-standing carry-over of the high prestige and reputation that they have traditionally enjoyed.

Thus far we have spoken primarily of large department stores in the major metropolitan areas, but what about smaller local department stores located outside the major metropolitan centers? These department stores are considerably smaller than those in major metropolitan areas, with substantially less financial and managerial resources at their command. Typically, they are owned and managed by family interests. Thus they are much more vulnerable to competition from new types of large-scale mass merchandising firms than are larger department stores located in the major urban centers.

In order to meet growing competitive pressure, some of these firms are pursuing, with varying degrees of success, similar strategies to those followed by their counterparts in the major metropolitan areas, such as diversifying into supermarket operations, expanding their stores, improving their services, and rationalizing their management practices. In addition, however, there are two unique strategies that smaller department stores have adopted in attempting to adapt to changing conditions.

One approach is for them to shift their policies to emphasize price appeal, departing from the traditional prestige and quality image of the department store. They are in essence attempting to transform themselves into mass merchandising firms. The other approach is to establish close management and financial ties with a major metropolitan department store. Such associations prove mutually beneficial. From the point of view of local department stores, this makes it possible to obtain much-needed managerial and financial resources, affording them better and broader access to sources of supply and opportunities to participate in cooperative buying. It also helps improve the image of a local store. To the large metropolitan department store, this approach makes it possible in a relatively painless way to expand its sphere of influence to new areas. These local stores may well prove to be good acquisition prospects in the future if the large metropolitan department stores should wish to expand into that particular market.

Despite these steps taken by small local department stores, their future outlook is far from bright. They now face increasing competition, not only from expansion-minded metropolitan department stores but from aggressive supermarket and discount chains as well. It is quite likely that less innovative local department stores will face a real battle for survival in years to come. Needless to say, the competitive environment of department stores is indeed a dynamic one. For one thing, there is already a trend for some of the mass merchandising firms, particularly those originally specializing in installment sales, to trade up in their merchandising and service policies. In fact, some have become virtually indistinguishable from traditional department stores.

### Adaptive Behavior of Trading Companies

One of the unique features on the Japanese business scene and certainly a dominant element in the nation's distribution system, are the trading companies. Trading firms perform such varied functions that they almost defy a clear and concise definition. Trading, in the narrow sense of the word, is but one of their functions. Some of the trading firms are extremely large. For example, the annual sales of the two leading trading firms—Mitsubishi Shoji and Mitsui Bussan—exceed ¥3 trillion ($8.5 billion). Large trading companies are active not only in the domestic market but in foreign trade as well. Among the ten largest trading companies, roughly 45 percent of total sales come from international transactions. In fact, it is estimated that 300 major trading firms are responsible for some 80 percent of the nation's imports and exports. The dominant status of trading companies in Japan's distribution scene can be understood easily from the fact that the combined domestic sales of the ten largest trading companies account for nearly 20 percent of the total wholesaling volume in Japan. It is impossible to examine the Japanese distribution structure without considering the role of trading companies. Moreover, trading companies, too, have been affected by the emerging trends discussed in Chapter 4. Our task in this section is to examine how they are responding to these environmental changes.

Although it is beyond the scope of our present analysis to undertake detailed examination of the functions of trading companies, a basic understanding of the nature and scope of their activities is essential if one is to understand their efforts to adapt their postures and policies to the needs of the emerging mass consumer market.

There are two basic types of trading firms. One type consists of those that handle diversified merchandise lines. As popularly described in Japan, these general-purpose trading firms handle anything from noodles to jet airplanes. The other is made up of firms that specialize in a given product category such as steel or textiles. Most notable among the first category are those that belonged to the major prewar Zaibatsu groups such as Mitsui, Mitsubishi, and Sumitomo. These trading companies, along with the groups' financial institutions, constituted the nucleus of these Zaibatsu. They acted as the primary sales and purchasing agents for their member firms, in both the domestic and foreign markets. In addition, these trading companies controlled a large number of smaller wholesalers and manufacturers through a variety of intricate means, extending credit and technical assistance as well as providing market contact. Thus, the Zaibatsu trading companies had literally thousands of small subcontractors and wholesalers under their direct or indirect control. These trading companies, therefore, occupied a pivotal position in the whole Zaibatsu system, playing an important coordinating and integrating role.

Understandably, the prewar Zaibatsu trading firms, notably, Mitsui Bussan and Mitsubishi Shoji, came under severe attack from the Occupation and were dissolved into numerous smaller firms as a part of the Occupation-sponsored Zaibatsu dissolution program; but soon after the Occupation was over, they became reunited once again.

Among the second type of trading company, particularly notable are those that began specializing in textiles and steel. In both cases they supply raw materials to major manufacturers from overseas and sell finished products in both foreign and domestic markets. Since the mid-1950s some of the large trading firms in the second category have been making conscious efforts to diversify into other lines, and thus in effect have become virtually indistinguishable from the first type. This trend has been particularly notable among trading companies specializing in textile products. For example, by the late 1960s the share of textile products in the total sales of C. Itoh & Co. and Marubeni Iida, two well-known trading companies that had previously specialized in textile products, declined to 40 percent and 25 percent, respectively. Although there are several thousand trading companies of varying sizes and descriptions, a handful of extremely large firms accounts for the dominant share of the sales volume of all trading firms. It is estimated, for example, that a dozen or so of the largest trading firms are responsible for nearly 60 percent of the total volume done by all trading firms.

Trading firms perform four major functions: (1) distribution of goods and services; (2) market development functions; (3) storage functions; and (4) financing functions. In addition, they provide ready market contacts, assume risks, disseminate market and trade information, and even provide technical support. Given the condition of capital scarcity, among Japanese firms the financial function is a particularly important one. Leading trading firms with close connections with the Japanese financial community enjoy considerable financial power, giving them a tremendous leverage in the Japanese distribution system. In overseas markets, in addition to ordinary foreign trade functions, trading companies are engaged in resource exploration, development of joint venture opportunities for their major customers, and construction projects of various types.

In recent years, with the changes taking place in the Japanese distribution scene, the role of trading companies has come under considerable controversy. Some argue that the days of trading companies are numbered, as large manufacturers have now begun to assume their own marketing functions and large retail chains have begun to emerge. Those who share this point of view argue that the conditions that gave trading companies their *raison d'être* are quickly disappearing. As evidence for this they point to the fact that trading companies are now almost totally excluded from distribution of such key consumer products as home appliances.

Others, however, point out that trading companies in the past have been flexible in their outlook and strategies, have shown remarkable ability in being able to identify new growth opportunities, and have been sensitive to changing conditions. They point to the evidence that the character and functions of trading companies have changed considerably in recent years to meet new challenges and opportunities. They predict that as long as these companies maintain this flexibility, they could indeed remain a formidable force in the nation's distribution system. There is no doubt that major trading companies have intensified their commitment to establish close ties with the mass consumer market. How, then, in order to assure their place in the changing distribution structure, are leading trading companies responding to newly created opportunities in the rising mass consumer market?

First, a number of major trading companies, having seen promising opportunities in mass merchandising, have entered this field, primarily in the form of supermarkets. This is a rather remarkable departure from the past pattern, since traditionally trading firms had not engaged in retailing activities themselves. As early as in 1963 Sumitomo Trading Company planned to establish a supermarket chain in Japan jointly with Safeway of the United States. In the face of stiff opposition from independent local retailers, the venture did not materialize. Subsequently, Sumitomo decided to enter this field on its own. Other leading trading companies that have established their own supermarket chains include Mitsui, C. Itoh, and Marubeni Iida, three leading trading firms in Japan. While none of these firms has yet firmly established itself in this field, given their resources, they have great potentials for developing into major national chains. In addition, as we have seen in Chapter 4, several leading trading companies are now planning to develop and manage shopping centers. Typically, to manage their retail operations trading firms have organized separate subsidiaries, a pattern that they traditionally have followed in entering into new fields.

Closely related to the foregoing is the entry of several major trading firms into the leasing of fully equipped supermarkets. Under this arrangement trading companies not only will construct store buildings but also will equip them and, for a fee, lease the fully equipped stores ready for operation. If desired by a lessee, the trading companies would also provide consulting service in designing the store layout, organization, and operations. Moreover, the lessee can obtain preferential treatment from the trading company if he wishes to purchase merchandise from it. This approach enables the trading company to enter into this field without having to assume day-to-day operating responsibility. In addition to the income obtained from leasing, these trading companies hope that through the leasing relationship they can increase their sales of merchandise to supermarkets. Mitsui Bussan has been the leader in this practice. It established a separate department specializing in leasing activities for supermarkets in 1967, and by 1969 had entered in agreements with some 20 supermarket chains, one of which was Seiyu, the second-largest chain in Japan. For the fiscal year 1968 the contract with the Seiyu chain alone amounted to over ¥500 million.

Another significant step that major trading firms have taken so far is to strengthen their ties with existing large retail chains. Most notable in this approach is the recent agreement between Seiyu and the Mitsubishi Trading Company. The agreement was announced in early 1969, and it stipulates that the trading company will extend to Seiyu ¥20 billion credit over the coming four years, and in return Seiyu has agreed that by 1972 it will purchase at least 20 percent of its total merchandise from the Mitsubishi Trading Company. The funds provided by the trading company will be used primarily to finance Seiyu's ambitious expansion program. What is most significant about this agreement is that it has gone considerably beyond what is considered a normal commercial relationship. A joint committee has been established consisting of managers at the operating level of both companies to coordinate the implementation of the agreements. The committee is charged with the responsibilities of coordinating production, processing, logistics, merchandise development, and import of foreign products.

This announcement was followed by other similar agreements. Even Daiei, Japan's leading supermarket chain, has entered a cooperative agreement with three large trading firms—Toyo Menka, C. Itoh, and Marubeni Iida. The agreement entered between Daiei and Toyo Menka, for example, is also quite broad in its scope. It stipulates, among other things: (1) that Toyo Menka will assist Daiei in its expansion efforts, including store leasing and marketing research; (2) that Toyo Menka will find foreign sources of merchandise; (3) that the two will cooperate in developing private brand merchandise for Daiei; and (4) that Daiei will increase its purchases from Toyo Menka.

Trading companies have also served as a link in creating formal cooperative relationships between major manufacturers and large supermarket chains. For example, in 1969 the Mitsubishi Trading Company was instrumental in linking Teijin Ltd., a major manufacturer of synthetic fibers, and Seiyu. Teijin will supply textiles to the Mitsubishi Trading Company, which, in turn, will convert them to finished ready-to-wear merchandise through their controlled subcontractors. The finished products then will be retailed by Seiyu. The three companies will also cooperate in developing original merchandise for Seiyu, and in this venture it is expected that the Mitsubishi Trading Company will play the chief coordinating role. A similar arrangement has been worked out among Toyo Rayon, Marubeni Iida, and Daiei.

Other firms have followed suit. In the fall of 1969, C. Itoh entered into an agreement to supply ready-to-wear merchandise to three major mass merchandising chains. What is significant in this arrangement is that the trading company and the three chains will cooperate in every stage of production, including deciding what and how much to produce. Actual manufacturing is performed by a network of C. Itoh's controlled manufacturers. Similarly, major trading companies are now attempting to develop new channels of distribution for certain types of fresh food, such as produce, eggs, meat, and fish, specifically for mass merchandising firms. Trading companies are now attempting to cast themselves in the role of rationalizing outdated channels of distribution for these products and developing more direct and efficient ones to assure supply of a large quantity of standard-quality merchandise to major chains. As a step toward this end, some trading companies have entered joint ventures with large chains to establish vertically integrated supply sources for meat from cattle or hog raising to its prepackaging. Mitsubishi Shoji established an egg farm that plans to supply fresh eggs directly to chains. Thus trading companies now have begun to mobilize their organizational skills to create new channels of distribution for a variety of products to meet the growing demand of the chains. This is particularly apparent in such fields as apparel and fresh foods, in which the traditional channels, dominated by a myriad of small production units, are inadequate to fill the need of the large chains.

In order to serve the needs of large retail chains better, trading companies have initiated other changes. These include establishment of a special organizational unit within the corporate structure to serve as the liaison between the company and the chains. They are also constructing merchandising and distribution centers to service chain accounts and are organizing special subsidiaries to supply only large-scale chains.

In addition to strengthening their ties with large supermarket chains, leading trading companies are also actively promoting organization of voluntary chains through their network of controlled wholesalers. The wholesalers, with assistance and guidance from trading companies, will organize their retail outlets into a voluntary chain to which the trading company will supply merchandise.

Other related activities by trading companies include entry into the distribution service field. Some trading companies, notably Mitsubishi Trading Company, have recently established a joint venture with Goldbond Stamp Company of the United States to sell trading stamps to retail outlets. As noted in Chapter 4, another major area of activities undertaken by leading trading companies is the development of shopping centers. Mitsubishi Shoji has entered into cooperative arrangements with a leading department store and two large mass merchandising chains to develop shopping centers. Mitsui Bussan announced plans in late 1969 to build three large shopping centers in the Toyko metropolitan area. The management of these trading companies feels that in the development of shopping centers it can effectively mobilize and combine a wide range of resources, including financial power, organizational skills, and the support of their related firms.

There are several reasons why the alliance between major trading companies and large supermarket chains is mutually attractive. From the point of view of the trading companies, this constitutes a relatively painless way of establishing direct linkage with the mass consumer market. Trading companies will have ready, if not captive, outlets for some of the more important merchandise they handle. The arrangement will also make it possible for the trading companies to bring to bear, in a most effective manner, their comparative advantages in the area of financial and managerial resources and well-established supply connections.

To supermarket chains, the alliance offers several advantages as well, not the least of which is access to the enormous capital resources that large trading companies have at their command. This will help finance their ambitious expansion programs, which, as we have seen, will require considerable amounts of capital. Moreover, these alliances assure the source of supply for two major lines of merchandise, food (fresh food in particular) and apparel. In soft goods, the manufacturing process goes through a series of stages, and trading companies are intricately involved in almost every stage. Their role is particularly important in converting textiles into ready-to-wear products. This process typically is performed by a large number of small establishments, and trading companies still maintain a firm control over them. Since soft goods have occupied a large share of the sales of mass merchandising firms in Japan, having dependable sources of supplies is extremely important.

With the growing size and number of supermarkets, the task has become increasingly difficult. Supermarkets have been confronted with a choice of undertaking their own manufacturing either through their own facilities or controlled subcontractors, or relying on trading companies with already established networks of manufacturers. To supermarket chains, the choice was an obvious one, since undertaking their own manufacturing would make further demands on their already strained managerial and financial resources. Moreover, the alliance with trading companies would be helpful in developing their own private brand merchandise. In fact, a number of original products already have been developed jointly and are being sold under existing brand names.

A similar situation is found for certain food items that are manufactured by a large number of small firms under the control of major trading companies. Moreover, with increasing volume, large-scale supermarket chains would need a more rational and efficient distribution system for food, including extensive development of frozen food and cold storage facilities. Here, too, the cooperation and assistance of trading companies could provide large chains with a ready-made source of supply. The closer relationships now evolving between large trading companies and large-scale supermarket chains have far-reaching implications.

Thus leading trading companies are making aggressive efforts to adapt their policies, strategies, and organizations to capitalize on the newly created opportunities in the mass consumer market. Of all the widely varied activities now being pursued by trading companies, particularly important has been the entry into the mass merchandising field—marking a new milestone for them. It is interesting, however, that trading companies were not an initiating force in promoting the growth of large-scale retailing. They have entered into this field only after its initial success has been all but proved.

Major trading companies have been making increasing efforts to find a niche in the mass merchandising field. As we have seen, they have much to offer to large chains, particularly in terms of financial and managerial resources and ability to provide an extensive network of procurement sources. Indeed, establishing close ties with mass merchandising firms offers promising potential to trading companies. To exploit these opportunities fully, however, there are a number of major problems to be overcome. Let us briefly consider the important ones.

First, it must be clearly recognized that entering into the mass merchandising field is a new experience to trading companies, and there is a limit to which their past experience, gained from large-scale trading of certain basic commodities at the wholesale level, is applicable to retailing operations. It is becoming increasingly clear that, to operate successfully in the mass merchandising field, trading companies must learn a great deal about retailing.

Second, dealing with the independent-minded and highly pragmatic management of mass merchandising firms poses a difficult problem to the management of major trading firms. Simply entering into a cooperative relationship in procurement, merchandise development, or store leasing does not always make the collaborating mass merchandising firms captive markets for their products. On the contrary, the pragmatic managers of these chains, anxious to maintain their independence and eager to maximize their unique competitive position, deliberately are trying to keep the relationship as fluid as possible. Taking advantage of the eagerness of trading companies to enter into this field, large chains often pit one against another to obtain better terms. Further complicating the relationship is the difference that exists in the very orientation and mentality of the managers of trading companies and those of chains. The former are professional managers and are the product of the nation's leading educational institutions, and as a group they tend to fit the mold of the "organization man." On the other hand, as we have already seen, the owners and managers of mass merchandising firms are highly individualistic, independent, self-made entrepreneurs with highly diverse backgrounds. In any case, although they see mutual advantages in collaboration, they are often suspicious of each other.

Finally, there is also some difference as to how each party perceives the emerging relationship. Trading companies naturally view the emerging cooperative relationship in store leasing, merchandise procurement, and so on, as a wedge to establish themselves in the mass merchandising field. On the other hand, mass merchandising firms assign to this relationship a much narrower role. To them it is only a means of achieving specific objectives, such as access to greater financial resources or dependable supplies of large quantities of standard quality merchandise. This difference is quite understandable. The relationship as of now is highly fluid, and there is every reason to believe that it will continue that way. Each party is certainly feeling its way. Only out of groping experiments and through constantly changing power relationships will the future pattern emerge.

Whether or not leading trading companies can make significant impact in the mass merchandising field still remains to be seen. There is considerable controversy as to the eventual role of trading companies in this field. Some predict that large trading companies, with their tremendous resources, will emerge as a dominant force even in this area. Some assign a more limited role to them.

In this chapter we have examined how traditional elements in the Japanese distribution system are responding to the innovative forces analyzed in Chapter 4. As we have seen, the degree of concern about the new developments varies widely among the traditional institutions, and there is also considerable diversity of concern within a given type of institution. Their response patterns also vary. Although some traditional institutions have gone a long way toward attaining new viability in the changing structure, others have been complacent. Of course, even those that are making intense efforts to adjust to the new conditions are not guided by a consistent clear-cut blueprint but rather are going through a series of groping experiments.There is no doubt that the interaction of the old and the new will become increasingly more dynamic, and the fate of those who fail to adapt will be all but certain.

# 6

# Development of Consumer
# Financing in Postwar Japan

One of the remarkable developments in the Japanese marketing system in recent years is the very rapid growth of consumer financing. In a very rudimentary form consumer financing has existed in Japan, as in other societies, for many centuries. Retailers extended credit to their customers on an informed basis; but it is only in recent years that consumer financing has become more formalized. Large manufacturers of consumer durables and certain retail outlets are now starting to recognize it as a valuable marketing tool.

Of the various types of consumer financing, particularly impressive has been the growth of installment credit. Because of its singular importance, much of this chapter will be devoted to the examination of its growth in postwar Japan. Another noteworthy development in this field is the recent increase in the use of credit cards. Although the extent of credit card use is still limited, in view of its potential importance we shall briefly examine its growth pattern.

## Installment Credit

### Growth Pattern

The use of installment credit, though in rather crude form, was first introduced in Japan in the early part of this century. By the 1920s it had gained some acceptance among certain types of Japanese consumers. A study conducted by the city of Tokyo in 1934 estimated that some 10,000 retail stores sold merchandise on installment credit, and the installment sales made by these stores accounted for about 8 percent of all retail sales in Tokyo.[1] Installment sales were employed extensively for such products as jewelry, sewing machines, furniture, pianos, radios, and clothing. The same survey investigated in greater detail the practices of 977 retail outlets engaged in installment sales and found that as high as 92 percent of the jewelry, 85 percent of the sewing machines, and 40 percent of the women's apparel handled by these stores were sold on the basis of installment credit.[2] Interestingly, the Singer Company introduced into Japan their installment credit program developed in the United States around the turn of the century. Likewise, Ford and General Motors established their own consumer financing companies in the early 1930s to help finance their exported automobiles.

The installment credit practices developed in prewar Japan had two dominant features.[3] One was that installment credit was used primarily as a means of selling products of inferior quality to low-income consumers. Thus, in the minds of most consumers, installment credit gained a rather negative image. The other feature was that credit was typically extended on an informal basis and was offered by retail stores rather than financial institutions or manufacturing firms. In most cases no formal contractual agreements were required.

It was not until the 1950s that installment credit as we know it today began to develop in Japan. Throughout the 1950s and 1960s consumer financing in Japan showed tremendous growth, as evidenced by the data presented in Table 6.1. The outstanding balance of installment credit was ¥38.6 billion in 1955; but 12 years later it reached nearly ¥662 billion, recording a seventeenfold growth. This rate of growth surpassed that of the country's GNP during the same period by a substantial margin. During the five-year period ending in 1967 the outstanding balance of consumer credit more than tripled. Table 6.2 provides further data on the magnitude of growth of installment credit in the 1960s.

---

[1] Japan Chamber of Commerce, "Wagakuni ni Okeru Kappu Hanbai no Genjo" ["Status of Installment Sales in Japan"], in Harumasa Yamaguchi and Kinosuke Miyashiro (eds.), *Shoshisha Kinyu Shu* (Tokyo: Nihon Sogō Shuppan Kikō, 1967), p. 128.

[2] *Ibid.*

[3] Noboru Kamakura, *Shohisha Loan [Consumer Loans]* (Tokyo: Chuokoronsha, 1966), pp. 15–16.

## TABLE 6.1

GROWTH OF INSTALLMENT CREDIT IN POSTWAR JAPAN, 1955–1967*

| Year | New Loans Made During the Year (¥ billion) | Percentage Increase over the Preceding Year | Outstanding Balance (¥ billion) | Percentage Increase over the Preceding Year |
|---|---|---|---|---|
| 1955 | 107.8 | – | 38.6 | – |
| 1956 | 147.4 | 36.7 | 54.8 | 42.0 |
| 1957 | 185.9 | 26.1 | 72.9 | 33.0 |
| 1958 | 213.2 | 14.7 | 86.3 | 18.4 |
| 1959 | 229.5 | 7.7 | 94.1 | 9.0 |
| 1960 | 267.1 | 16.4 | 120.2 | 27.0 |
| 1961 | 344.8 | 29.1 | 161.1 | 34.0 |
| 1962 | 415.7 | 20.6 | 205.3 | 27.4 |
| 1963 | 526.7 | 26.7 | 291.1 | 41.8 |
| 1964 | 641.8 | 21.9 | 379.6 | 30.4 |
| 1965 | 809.6 | 26.0 | 491.1 | 29.0 |
| 1966 | 906.4 | 11.0 | 551.9 | 12.0 |
| 1967 | 1,081.1 | 19.0 | 661.9 | 19.0 |

* The figures represent the combined outstanding balance of personal installment credit extended by financial institutions, manufacturers, and retailers for the purchase of consumer goods and services, but do not include credit extended for house purchase.
Source: The Bank of Japan.

Another indication of the rather widespread use of installment credit in Japan was revealed by a recent study conducted by the Ministry of International Trade and Industry. A variety of con-

## TABLE 6.2

THE OUTSTANDING BALANCE OF CONSUMER CREDIT, 1961–1966

| Year | Per Capita Balance of Consumer Credit Outstanding | Outstanding Balance of Consumer Credit / GNP | Outstanding Balance of Consumer Credit / Personal Consumption |
|---|---|---|---|
| 1961 | 1.7 | 0.9 | 1.6 |
| 1962 | 2.2 | 1.0 | 1.8 |
| 1963 | 3.0 | 1.2 | 2.2 |
| 1964 | 3.9 | 1.4 | 2.5 |
| 1965 | 5.0 | 1.6 | 2.9 |
| 1966 | 5.6 | 1.6 | 2.9 |

Source: *Shohisha Kinyu Jishi Jokyō Ichiran: Showa 42 nen [A Summary of the Current Status of Consumer Financing, 1967]* (Tokyo: Zenkoku Ginko Kyokai Rengokai, 1967), p. 5.

sumer goods was selected in which sales by means of installment credit were considered particularly important. The study investigated the practices of a nationwide sample of 10,432 retail outlets that carry these products. It revealed that installment sales are most widely used in the sale of sewing machines. Next come automobiles, for which roughly two-thirds of the total sales were made in this manner. Approximately half the total sales in men's clothing, television sets, washing machines, and stereo sets were made on installment credit. While these data are somewhat outdated, there is no evidence to suggest that the present pattern differs appreciably from that prevailing in 1966 (see Table 6.3).

What forces, then, have been responsible for this very rapid growth in installment credit? The single most important factor is, of course, the development of the mass consumer market. With postwar economic progress, consumers began to enjoy a growing

TABLE 6.3

SALES OF SELECTED MERCHANDISE ON INSTALLMENT CREDIT
BY THE STORES SURVEYED, 1966

| Item | Total Sales | Manufacturer or Retailer-Sponsored Installment Sales | Bank-Sponsored Installment Credit | Installment Credit Through Coupons | Cash Sales | Whole-sale |
|---|---|---|---|---|---|---|
| | (%) | (%) | (%) | (%) | (%) | (%) |
| Men's Clothing | 100 | 48 | – | 11 | 41 | – |
| Furniture | 100 | 24 | – | 4 | 72 | – |
| Television Sets | 100 | 49 | – | 3 | 47 | – |
| Electric Refrigerators | 100 | 48 | – | 4 | 48 | – |
| Electric Washing Machines | 100 | 47 | – | 4 | 49 | – |
| Stereo Sets | 100 | 48 | – | 4 | 47 | – |
| Sewing Machines | 100 | 84 | – | – | 16 | – |
| Pianos | 100 | 34 | 23 | 2 | 41 | – |
| Other Musical Instruments | 100 | 32 | 13 | 5 | 50 | – |
| Passenger Cars | 100 | 62 | 12 | – | 21 | 5 |

Source: *Kappu Hanbai Jittai Chosa Hokokusho: Dai Ikkan* [*A Survey of the Installment Credit Sales*, Vol. 1] (Tokyo: The Ministry of International Trade and Industry, 1967), p. 8.

discretionary income that allowed them to purchase items that were once considered to be luxuries. Suddenly consumers were confronted with many new possibilities that exceeded the fondest of their dreams a generation earlier. Postwar changes in consumer orientation reinforced their desire for immediate gratification of newly recognized wants. Their desires for material improvement were further stimulated by aggressive promotional efforts by large manufacturers. This meant that rather than postponing their purchase of expensive consumer goods and services until they had sufficient savings, they now wanted to possess them immediately by taking advantage of installment credit. In view of the ever-brighter future prospect of the economy, consumers were quite willing to make financial commitments for the future.

Another powerful force has been the active promotion of installment sales by large manufacturers of consumer goods, as well as by their distributors. In offering installment credit they saw an opportunity to expand the effective demand for their products and began to make concerted efforts to encourage its use.

Finally, active promotion of consumer financing by large financial institutions has been an important factor contributing to its growth. It is only in very recent years that financial institutions have entered into this field; but now virtually all city banks, provincial banks, and other types of financial institutions are involved actively.

### Types of Installment Sales Programs

Having looked at the growth pattern of installment credit and the major forces contributing to it, we shall now turn our attention to examination of the various types of installment credit now available. Although installment credit can be classified in various ways, a convenient categorization is on the basis of sponsorship. According to this classification, there are four major types: (1) retailer-sponsored programs, (2) the coupon system, (3) manufacturer- or dealer-sponsored programs, and (4) programs sponsored by financial institutions.

RETAILER-SPONSORED PROGRAMS. As we noted earlier, the supplying of credit by retail establishments is the oldest form of installment sale in Japan. The total amount of installment credit financed by retailers themselves is difficult to estimate accurately, but for certain types of products, such as clothing, furniture, jewelry, and musical instruments, it plays a major role. In retail-sponsored programs retailers assume the entire risk, and they perform all the necessary functions associated with installment sales, including credit investigation, contract preparation, and collection. Because of their small size the amount that most of these stores can commit to financing installment sales is rather limited. According to the MITI study mentioned earlier, the average outstanding balance of installment credit of the stores surveyed ranges from ¥2.6 million, or roughly $7,000, for clothing stores, to ¥3.78 million, or slightly over $10,000, for stores selling musical instruments. As indicated in Table 6.4, for working capital out of which installment

TABLE 6.4

AMOUNT AND SOURCE OF WORKING CAPITAL OF RETAIL
ESTABLISHMENTS, 1967

| Type of Store | Working Capital | | Sources of Working Capital (in percent) | | | |
|---|---|---|---|---|---|---|
| | Average Amount (¥1,000) | Percent of Annual Sales | Own Funds | Trade Credit | Debts from Financial Institutions | Total |
| Clothing | ¥ 5,970 | 38 | 28 | 36 | 36 | 100 |
| Furniture | 9,510 | 27 | 27 | 34 | 39 | 100 |
| Home Appliances and Equipment | 7,330 | 38 | 27 | 44 | 29 | 100 |
| Musical Instruments | 15,460 | 21 | 28 | 37 | 35 | 100 |

Source: *Kappu Hanbai Jittai Chosa Hokokusho: Dai Ikkan [A Survey of the Status of Installment Credit Sales,* Vol. 1] (Tokyo: The Ministry of International Trade and Industry, 1967), p. 20.

sales are generally financed, the stores surveyed rely heavily on inventory credit extended by wholesalers and manufacturers as well as borrowing from financial institutions. It is important to note that for none of the merchandise did the merchants' own funds exceed 28 percent of their total working capital.

The terms of retail-sponsored installment credit vary according to product categories, but typically 20 percent of the purchase price is required for down payment, and the repayment period seldom exceeds one year. According to the MITI study, the average ratio of bad debts to sales on an annual basis runs 1.1 percent for clothing stores, 0.7 percent for furniture stores, 0.9 percent for home appliance stores, and 0.2 percent for stores handling musical instruments.[4] The ratio for stores selling home equipment (mainly sewing machines) was the lowest, at 0.04 percent of total sales.

In 1966 there were some 11,000 retail outlets with five employees or more that derived at least 50 percent of their total sales from installment sales. These stores, representing but 0.8 percent of the total number of retail stores, were responsible for 4.2 percent of total retail sales for that year. It is interesting to note that among stores with 30 to 49 employees, these stores represented 16.1 percent of the total number of stores in this category. Details are presented in Table 6.5. Particularly prominent among these stores

TABLE 6.5

RETAIL STORES ENGAGED IN INSTALLMENT SALES, 1966*

| Size of Firm (no. of employees) | No. of Stores | Percentage of Total Retailers | Percentage of Total Retail Sales |
|---|---|---|---|
| 5–9 | 2,245 | 5.6 | 5.4 |
| 10–19 | 2,603 | 8.7 | 7.8 |
| 20–29 | 1,075 | 14.7 | 10.9 |
| 30–49 | 722 | 16.7 | 11.8 |
| 50–99 | 274 | 14.5 | 12.7 |
| 100 or more | 74 | 9.3 | 4.6 |
| Total | 10,993 | 0.8 | 4.2 |

*Stores with five employees or more deriving at least 50 percent of total sales from installment sales.

Source: Adapted from *Waganuki no Shōgyō, 1969 [Commerce in Japan, 1969]* (Tokyo: The Ministry of International Trade and Industry, 1970), p. 76.

are so-called installment credit department stores that specialize in installment sales. This is a rather unique retail institution in Japan. Its origin goes back to the 1920s, and these stores became well established by the 1930s. While their operations were totally suspended during World War II, they became popular once again in the 1950s. At the time of this writing there were more than 450 firms of this type, with some 760 stores. They are estimated to account for slightly less than 3 percent of total retail sales in Japan. While the majority of these stores are small, there are a few very large ones. The largest firm of this type has more than 40 stores,

[4] *Kappu Hanbai Jittai Chosa Hokokusho: Dai Ikkan [A Survey on the Status of Installment Credit,* Vol. 1] (Tokyo: Ministry of International Trade and Industry, 1967), p. 19.

with annual sales of ¥38 billion, and ranks among the top 20 retail firms in Japan.

The aforementioned MITI study investigated practices of 180 of these installment credit stores and revealed some significant operating characteristics, the highlights of which we shall present here. In 1966 the installment credit stores surveyed averaged around ¥438 million in sales, of which ¥383 million, or roughly 87 percent, were made on installment credit.[5] Eighty-seven percent of the stores included in the survey had sales of less than ¥300 million, and only 5 percent had sales exceeding ¥1 billion. Slightly over half of the stores surveyed had sales space of less than 300 square meters (roughly 3,200 square feet) and three-quarters of them had fewer than 50 employees. The study also revealed that a typical installment credit store derived half of its total sales from apparel and related items, 15 percent from furniture, 13 percent from home appliances, and the remainder from assorted other merchandise.

The MITI study also revealed that 71 percent of the stores surveyed required a down payment ranging from 10 percent to 15 percent, and typically the repayment period did not exceed one year. As in the case of ordinary retail outlets, installment credit stores rely heavily on borrowing for financing their installment credit sales. The MITI survey revealed that the working capital of the participating stores averaged around ¥26.5 million, of which 79 percent was derived from debt sources (47 percent from trade credit, and 30 percent from financial institutions).[6]

These stores have grown rather rapidly by being able to fill a particular consumer need. It appears, however, that they have now reached a turning point and are confronted with a number of serious problems. For one thing, competitive pressure is mounting. In recent years the number of installment credit stores has proliferated, leading to keen price competition as well as to the offering of liberalized credit terms, thus increasing operating costs. It is estimated that expenses incurred on collection alone now run about 3 percent of sales, and the bad-debt ratio is also increasing, in some cases running as high as 5 percent of total sales. The fact that these stores must finance installment sales at their own risk also limits their ability to expand their sales. Their already heavy

---

5 *Ibid.*
6 *Ibid.*, p. 18.

dependence on debt financing makes the problem even more serious. Many have exhausted their debt capacity and are saddled with high finance charges from past borrowing.

Another competitive threat comes from regular department stores, which now have begun to extend installment credit. A number of installment credit stores have been unable to respond to these changing competitive conditions effectively and have been forced out of business. The competitive impact has been particularly serious among smaller stores. Increasingly, the more aggressive installment credit stores are shifting their emphasis to cash discounting operations.

THE COUPON SYSTEM. Another rather unique method of installment credit sales in Japan is what is commonly known as the coupon system. The objective of this program is again to permit small independent stores to engage in installment credit sales. Basically, there are two types. One is a cooperative arrangement organized and managed by the retailers themselves. It is usually organized by neighborhood shopping centers or a group of specialty stores that are in the same line of business. There are some 1,200 such retailer-sponsored groups.

The second type is sponsored and managed by independent organizations that provide their service to retailers on a fee basis. It is estimated that there are some 90 of these organizations. While sponsorship differs, the functions performed by these organizations are basically similar. To qualified customers they issue coupons, which can be used for the purchase of merchandise at any of the subscribing stores. The consumers then make regular monthly payment to the sponsoring organization; this sponsor, in turn, makes periodic settlements with its member stores. To facilitate credit investigation and collection, membership is generally drawn from organized groups such as labor unions, other employee groups, and professional organizations.

This form of installment sales has shown a steady growth during the past several years. A recent study by the Small–Medium-Size Enterprise Agency, an arm of the Ministry of International Trade and Industry, reports that the total amount of coupon sales runs around ¥150 billion, or 1.5 percent of total retail sales, and has been growing at the rate of 10 percent annually. Coupon programs is general are not nearly as important as installment sales programs sponsored by manufacturer or retailers, but for certain product lines they are extensively used. For example, according to the MITI study, 11 percent of the total sales of men's clothing stores surveyed came from this source.

According to the MITI study, the majority of these organizations are relatively small, as evidenced by the following statistics. Of 695 organizations studied, 41 percent issued less than ¥30 million worth of coupons in 1966, and 77 percent issued less than ¥100 million. Forty percent of the organizations studied had fewer than 50 member stores; 37 percent had between 50 and 99 stores, and only 2 percent had more than 500 stores subscribing to their service.[7] Typically, these organizations extend credit from four to ten months and charge fees to both member stores and subscribing consumers. For the payment period of up to ten months the charge to stores is about 5 percent of the sales; for consumers, the fee ranges from 4 percent to 7 percent.[8]

MANUFACTURER-SPONSORED PROGRAMS. In Chapter 3, we made reference to the fact that large manufacturers of consumer durables are now actively engaged in extending installment credit. In the process several different patterns of credit arrangement have emerged. The first type is a program whereby manufacturers, at their own risk, extend installment credit directly to consumers. Under this arrangement manufacturers undertake all the necessary functions associated with installment sales, including credit investigations and collection. This pattern is found primarily in the sale of products such as musical instruments and sewing machines, which are distributed through the manufacturers' own retail outlets. The second pattern is one in which dealers, on a fee basis, perform essential functions related to installment sales on behalf of the manufacturer. For reasons of cost and convenience, manufacturers generally prefer to let their dealers undertake credit investigation and collection, since these functions can best be performed at the level where sales are actually consummated. Even under this arrangement, manufacturers still assume financial as well as legal obligations.

The third type is a program in which manufacturers supply most of the funds needed for financing installment sales but their dealers perform all the necessary auxiliary functions, including the assumption of risk. This pattern has been followed in the sale of

---

[7] *Kappu Hanbai Jittai Chosa Hokokusho: Dai 4 Kan [A Survey on the Status of Installment Credit, Vol. 4]* (Tokyo: The Ministry of International Trade and Industry, 1967), p. 12.

[8] *Ibid.*, p. 18.

automobiles. In the fourth program the manufacturers establish a subsidiary specializing in the extension of installment credit. These subsidiaries are generally known as installment credit companies, and they are either entirely financed by the parent company or jointly financed with affiliated wholesalers and retailers. This approach is most common in electric home appliances. For example, Matsushita Electric, the leading manufacturer of home appliances, has a subsidiary specializing in installment financing, which, in turn, has some 72 satellite firms located throughout Japan. These companies do not engage in sales activities but provide necessary financial and administrative support to dealers in making installment credit sales. The individual dealer turns over his installment sales contracts to the affiliated installment sales company in his territory, from which he in effect receives immediate payment for the merchandise. Thus, as far as dealers are concerned, sales on installment are little different from cash sales. Although there are considerable variations in the mode of operations, large manufacturers of consumer durables now place major emphasis on installment sales as an effective marketing tool.

There is another type of manufacturer-oriented installment sales program that is basically different from those that have been described. This is a plan whereby consumers make a series of regular prepayments to manufacturers or dealers before they actually receive the merchandise. In some cases payment must be completed, while in others a certain portion of the total price must be prepaid, before a purchaser can take possession of the goods. The major inducement to consumers is a substantial discount in price. For obvious reasons this program is regulated, and only licensed manufacturers or dealers can engage in it. There are more than 230 authorized manufacturers and dealers serving some 10 million consumers, and the outstanding balance of such prepayment is estimated to run as high as ¥50 billion. This plan is particularly popular in the purchase of sewing machines, home appliances, and furniture.

PROGRAMS SPONSORED BY FINANCIAL INSTITUTIONS. In the postwar development of consumer financing in Japan, financial institutions have played a key role as a major supplier of funds. We have noted in the preceding discussion how heavily firms that engage in consumer financing rely on such credit. As of December 1969 the outstanding balance of the loans that financial institutions had extended to various types of firms engaged in installment sales amounted to ¥1,373 billion, representing roughly 3 percent of the total loan balance. The amount nearly doubled between 1965 and 1969. Approximately 80 percent of the outstanding loans have been made to automobile sales companies. Details are presented in Table 6.6.

In addition to this indirect form of participation, commercial banks in recent years have become directly involved in consumer financing, particularly with installment credit. This has been a major innovation for Japanese banks, which traditionally confined their activities to large industrial clients. It was around 1960 when Japan's major city banks became interested in consumer financing. Japanese financial institutions entered into consumer financing for quite different reasons than those of their American counterparts. The latter entered this field in their aggressive search for more lucrative avenues for investing their funds, whereas Japanese city banks have done so for defensive reasons.

As a result of the very rapid development of securities markets in the late 1950s, Japan began to witness a major change in the flow of investment funds. Unlike in prewar Japan, ownership of securities became widely diffused among the people, thus competing with commercial banks for personal savings, which had been the prime source of funds for major banks. Between 1956 and 1961 the percentage of personal savings in the form of bank deposits declined from 64 percent to 55 percent, and during the same period the percentage of savings in the form of securities increased from 25 percent to nearly 32 percent. A relative decline of bank funds also can be seen from the fact that up until the late 1950s financial institutions supplied 90 percent of the financial requirements of Japanese industries, but by the early 1960s the percentage declined to about 76 percent.[9] Particularly seriously affected were the city banks, Japan's major financial institutions, whose relative importance continuously declined during these years. The funds supplied by the city banks as a percentage of the total provided by all financial institutions declined from 54 percent in 1956 to 43 percent in 1962.[10] This obviously had far-reaching implications for major commercial banks.

Faced with these situations, the city banks turned to consumer

[9] Hisao Aoki, *Ginko no Shohisha Kinyu [Consumer Financing by Banks]* (Tokyo: Toyo Keizai Shinpo Sha, 1964), p. 4.
[10] *Ibid.*, p. 15.

financing as a defensive strategy to attract a greater share of personal savings, the all-important source of funds. It was felt that consumer financing would be an effective tool to establish closer relationships with the masses and to "popularize" the city banks so that they would be in a better position to compete for personal savings. Another motivating force for the city banks stemmed from their view that entering into this field in cooperation with their major client firms would contribute to cementing their ties with them. This was one of the reasons why the city banks initially developed their installment programs in cooperation with specific large manufacturing enterprises. Sumitomo Bank, a well-known former Zaibatsu bank, pioneered this program in 1960 by developing a program for automobile financing in cooperation with the Prince Motor Company. Other city banks soon followed suit. Under this arrangement, the banks typically required the guarantee of their loans by the particular manufacturing firm or its dealers; thus, in a very strict sense, this cannot be considered as bank-sponsored installment credit. The products commonly sold under this plan include automobiles, home appliances, and musical instruments.

In recent years, however, the banks have begun to make personal loans directly to consumers, not tied to the purchase of any specific product and without requiring the guarantee of a manufacturer. In some cases not even collateral is required. To illustrate the consumer financing programs of a typical city bank, we shall examine the case of Mitsubishi Bank, one of the leading city banks. The bank has consumer loan arrangements with seven automobile manufacturers, seven manufacturers of home appliances, two manufacturers of musical instruments, and eleven construction firms engaged in home building. In the case of automobiles the bank loans from ¥100,000 to ¥1 million, with the repayment period ranging from six months to two years, and requires the guarantee of the manufacturer or dealer. In the cases of home appliances and pianos the amount loaned ranges from ¥40,000 to ¥1 million. For home loans the amount ranges from ¥600,000 to ¥10 million and is made for a period of up to 15 years.

The bank has two types of consumer loans that are not tied to a particular firm or product. One type is based on a savings plan. To be eligible, customers must make a deposit of a stipulated sum each month for ten consecutive months, and the maximum amount to be loaned under this plan is twenty times the monthly deposit.

## TABLE 6.6

### LENDING OF OPERATING FUNDS TO "RETAILERS OF INSTALLMENT PAYMENT"

(¥ million)

| Type of Bank | Year (as of 12/31) | Total | Retailers of Installment Payment | | | | Organizations Issuing Coupons | | | | Lending Secured by Installment Payment Bills |
|---|---|---|---|---|---|---|---|---|---|---|---|
| | | | Sub-total | Automobile Sales Cos. | Inst. System Dept. Stores | Others | Sub-total | Credit Sales Cos. | Assoc. of Specialty Stores, etc. | Construction Cos. | |
| All Banks | 1965 | 500,901 | 463,852 | 405,035 | 13,880 | 44,927 | 21,563 | 6,993 | 14,570 | 15,496 | 318,888 |
| | 1966 | 633,266 | 580,079 | 508,205 | 19,520 | 52,353 | 26,672 | 9,936 | 16,735 | 26,514 | 400,648 |
| | 1967 | 754,798 | 689,974 | 607,856 | 20,178 | 61,940 | 31,734 | 12,010 | 19,724 | 33,089 | 471,283 |
| | 1968 | 893,601 | 813,951 | 717,888 | 24,648 | 71,415 | 36,806 | 14,643 | 22,162 | 42,843 | 554,883 |
| | 1969 | 1,066,956 | 938,850 | 819,512 | 26,522 | 92,815 | 47,260 | 20,082 | 27,177 | 80,846 | 625,112 |
| City Banks | 1965 | 238,601 | 225,995 | 189,586 | 7,419 | 28,990 | 7,878 | 4,472 | 3,406 | 4,728 | 148,080 |
| | 1966 | 272,801 | 258,971 | 214,424 | 10,382 | 34,164 | 9,787 | 5,986 | 3,801 | 4,042 | 173,861 |
| | 1967 | 303,061 | 289,163 | 242,429 | 9,645 | 37,089 | 10,616 | 6,229 | 4,386 | 3,283 | 192,310 |
| | 1968 | 368,841 | 351,731 | 295,793 | 12,476 | 43,461 | 12,406 | 7,536 | 4,869 | 4,703 | 230,182 |
| | 1969 | 472,356 | 440,504 | 369,208 | 14,364 | 56,930 | 18,960 | 10,385 | 8,575 | 12,891 | 279,596 |
| Local Banks | 1965 | 186,099 | 169,967 | 150,204 | 4,968 | 14,795 | 13,246 | 2,132 | 11,114 | 2,886 | 121,181 |
| | 1966 | 244,573 | 223,970 | 200,294 | 6,614 | 17,060 | 15,724 | 2,860 | 12,855 | 4,878 | 156,252 |
| | 1967 | 298,933 | 274,934 | 244,932 | 7,941 | 22,060 | 18,669 | 3,403 | 15,265 | 5,330 | 192,605 |
| | 1968 | 350,029 | 324,005 | 289,464 | 9,369 | 25,170 | 21,117 | 3,917 | 17,200 | 4,907 | 229,838 |
| | 1969 | 376,204 | 347,123 | 306,775 | 9,734 | 30,613 | 24,126 | 5,883 | 18,242 | 4,954 | 243,710 |

| | | | | | | | | | | |
|---|---|---|---|---|---|---|---|---|---|---|
| Trust Banks, Long-Term Credit Banks, and Trust Accounts of All Banks | | | | | | | | | | |
| 1965 | 76,201 | 67,880 | 65,245 | 1,493 | 1,142 | 439 | 389 | 50 | 7,882 | 49,627 |
| 1966 | 115,890 | 97,137 | 93,486 | 2,521 | 1,128 | 1,160 | 1,081 | 79 | 17,593 | 70,535 |
| 1967 | 152,804 | 125,878 | 120,495 | 2,592 | 2,791 | 2,450 | 2,337 | 73 | 24,476 | 86,368 |
| 1968 | 174,730 | 138,215 | 132,630 | 2,801 | 2,783 | 3,282 | 3,189 | 93 | 33,232 | 94,861 |
| 1969 | 218,396 | 151,222 | 143,528 | 2,422 | 5,271 | 4,172 | 3,813 | 359 | 63,000 | 101,804 |
| Mutual Loan and Savings Banks | | | | | | | | | | |
| 1965 | 112,058 | 103,345 | 91,753 | 2,953 | 8,639 | 2,479 | 1,027 | 1,452 | 6,234 | 70,873 |
| 1966 | 138,324 | 126,172 | 112,726 | 3,888 | 9,557 | 2,986 | 1,177 | 1,808 | 9,165 | 84,978 |
| 1967 | 164,470 | 147,991 | 132,815 | 3,991 | 11,185 | 3,677 | 1,610 | 2,067 | 12,802 | 109,911 |
| 1968 | 178,713 | 159,084 | 144,149 | 4,245 | 10,689 | 3,453 | 1,793 | 1,649 | 16,175 | 115,176 |
| 1969 | 221,922 | 189,150 | 172,146 | 4,046 | 12,957 | 5,013 | 2,894 | 2,119 | 27,758 | 141,864 |

Source: *Annual Economic Statistics, 1969* (Tokyo: The Bank of Japan, 1970), pp. 39–40.

The other type is a straight personal loan, ranging in amount from
¥30,000 to ¥2 million. Repayments are made on a monthly installment basis for a maximum of three years. The bank loans up to ¥1
million without security but does require two cosigners, who must
guarantee the loan.

At the time of this writing, 12 of the 13 city banks were engaged
in consumer financing. With the entry of the major city banks into
the consumer financing field, other types of financial institutions
quickly followed their example. Now virtually all 63 provincial
banks are engaged in consumer financing, and others, such as trust
companies, long-term credit banks, mutual loan and savings banks,
and credit associations, have also entered this field.

From a rather modest beginning, financial institutions have entered the consumer financing field at a very rapid rate. Particularly
noteworthy are the inroads made by the provincial banks. The outstanding balance of installment credit extended by provincial banks
exceeded ¥160 billion in 1968, accounting for roughly 42 percent
of total consumer installment loans. Aware of further growth opportunities, the banks are increasing their commitments to consumer financing. A number of city and provincial banks recently
have established a separate organizational unit specializing in consumer financing.

*Consumers' Attitudes toward the Use of Installment Credit*

We shall now turn our attention to the consumers' attitudes toward the use of installment credit. The importance of the consumers' reactions cannot be overemphasized, inasmuch as it is
consumers who hold the key to the ultimate success of installment credit.

Let us first present a profile of consumers who buy on the installment plan. The quarterly survey on consumption and savings
conducted by the Economic Planning Agency provides an excellent
source of data. The survey was based on a carefully chosen nationwide sample of more than 5,000 households. As to the extent of
consumer acceptance of installment purchase, the latest survey
reveals that 36 percent of the households included in the sample
were buying on installment. The fact that more than one-third of
all households surveyed were engaged in installment purchases at
the time of the survey is indicative of their wide acceptance.[11]

11 *Shohisha Doko, Showa 44 nen [Consumer Trends, 1968]* (Tokyo: Shohisha Doko Kenkyukai, 1969), p. 178.

## TABLE 6.7

INSTALLMENT PURCHASES BY HOUSEHOLDS
IN VARIOUS OCCUPATIONAL CATEGORIES, FEBRUARY 1968

| Occupational Category of Household Head | Percentage of Households Buying in Installments | Average Outstanding Balance of Loan (¥) |
|---|---|---|
| Agricultural Households | 28.7 | 12,100 |
| Pure Agricultural Households | 17.1 | 6,700 |
| Semiagricultural Households* | 37.6 | 16,300 |
| Nonagricultural Households | 38.3 | 17,400 |
| Wage Earners | 42.1 | 17,000 |
| Individual Proprietors | 31.1 | 18,200 |
| All Households | 36.2 | 16,300 |

* Those households which derive a portion of their income from nonagricultural sources.

Source: *Shohisha Doko [Consumer Trends]* (Tokyo: Shohisha Doko Kenkyukai, 1969), pp. 178–179.

Scrutiny of the occupational category of the users reveals that installment purchase is most widely practiced by wage earners. As indicated in Table 6.7, it is least popular among agricultural families, particularly those that derive their entire income from agricultural sources. The survey further revealed that the amount of outstanding installment credit per family averaged ¥16,300, ranging from ¥6,700 for farmers' households to ¥18,200 for individual

## TABLE 6.8

THE USE OF INSTALLMENT CREDIT ACCORDING TO INCOME CLASSES, 1967

| Annual Income of Households (¥1,000) | Percent of Households Using Installment Purchase | Average Outstanding Balance per Household (¥) |
|---|---|---|
| Less than ¥300 | 22.2 | 3,000 |
| ¥300–599 | 34.4 | 10,600 |
| ¥600–899 | 39.7 | 16,800 |
| ¥900–1,199 | 38.6 | 18,200 |
| ¥1,200–1,499 | 38.2 | 21,800 |
| ¥1,500–1,800 | 33.9 | 23,900 |
| More than ¥1,800 | 21.1 | 19,800 |

Source: *Shohi to Chochiku no Doko [A Trend on Consumption and Savings]* (Tokyo: The Economic Planning Agency, 1967), p. 102.

proprietors.[12] It is interesting to note that among individual proprietors, those who were buying on installment represent a relatively small percentage in comparison with wage earners and farmers, but their average loan amount was substantially higher than that of the other occupational groups.

The survey also shows the extent of installment purchases according to various income categories. As is evident in Table 6.8, the use of installment credit is widely diffused throughout the range of income classes. While the highest percentage of users were found in the income bracket between ¥600,000 and ¥900,000, it is significant to note that more than a fifth of those surveyed in the highest income bracket were also buying on installment.

In 1966 the Ministry of International Trade and Industry investigated the use of installment credit among a nationwide sample of 2,000 housewives. Since this study contains data not included in the quarterly survey on consumption and savings, its key findings will also be presented.

Significantly, 74 percent and 53 percent, respectively, of the housewives surveyed were familiar with the coupon system and consumer loan programs of financial institutions. As Table 6.9 indicates, 30 percent of those surveyed used the coupon system, and about 5 percent had obtained consumer loans from banks during

TABLE 6.9

HOUSEWIVES' USE OF INSTALLMENT CREDIT BY MAJOR TYPE, 1965

| Type of Installment Program Used by Respondents | Percentage Using Particular Program |
|---|---|
| All Three Types of Programs (coupons, bank loans, and regular installment) | 0.2 |
| Coupons and Bank Loans | 0.3 |
| Coupons and Regular Installment Credit | 3.6 |
| Bank Loans and Regular Installment Credit | 1.4 |
| Coupons Only | 4.0 |
| Bank Loans Only | 2.6 |
| Regular Installment Credit Only | 33.1 |
| No Form of Installment Credit | 54.8 |
| | 100.0 |

Source: *Shohisha Shinyo no Riyo ni Kansuru Seron Chosa [A Survey of Public Opinion on the Use of Consumer Financing]* (Tokyo: The Ministry of International Trade and Industry, 1966), p. 20.

[12] *Ibid.*, pp. 178–179.

the preceding year.[13] For purposes of this study loans sponsored by manufacturers and retailers were designated as regular installment programs. In terms of usage they were the most popular. As high as 38 percent of respondents reported that they used some form of this plan during the preceding year. Of the 62 percent of the respondents who had not used regular installment credit during the previous year, 28 percent said they had used it during the preceding ten years.

The foregoing MITI survey reveals some interesting data concerning the uses to which various types of installment credit programs are put. The majority of respondents who use the coupon system (67.5 percent) said that they used it to purchase apparel.[14] Consumer loans obtained from banks were most frequently used for purchase of a house or for home remodeling (43 percent of the users gave this as the reason). Slightly over 18 percent used bank loans to purchase automobiles.[15] According to this survey, the regular installment program was used most extensively for the purchase of home appliances (60.4 percent) and other consumer durables such as pianos, organs, motorcycles, and automobiles.[16]

The study also showed the socioeconomic characteristics of persons using the three major forms of installment credit. The user profile is presented according to area of residence, occupation, and income. The data are shown in summary form in Table 6.10. On the basis of these two surveys, we can conclude that purchases on installment credit are widely accepted and that users cut across various socioeconomic strata. This is a significant departure from the prewar pattern, in which the use of installment credit was largely confined to the lower-income classes.

Let us now examine the consumers' attitudes toward the use of installment credit. The aforementioned MITI study again gives a useful insight into this question. The survey asked the respondents (both users and nonusers) whether or not they felt or would feel embarrassed to purchase on installment credit. This question is particularly relevant in view of the negative image traditionally associated with installment buying. This practice was in the past

[13] *Shoshia Shinyo no Riyo ni Kansuru Seron Chosa [A Survey of Public Opinion on the Use of Consumer Financing]* (Tokyo: The Ministry of International Trade and Industry, 1966), p. 13.

[14] *Ibid.*

[15] *Ibid.*, p. 16.

[16] *Ibid.*, p. 18.

## TABLE 6.10

USER PROFILES OF THREE MAJOR TYPES OF INSTALLMENT CREDIT BY
RESIDENCE, OCCUPATION, AND MONTHLY HOUSEHOLD EXPENDITURE, 1965

| Socioeconomic Characteristic | Total | | Used Regular Install- ment Credit | Used Coupon System | Used Consumer Bank Loans |
|---|---|---|---|---|---|
| | No. of Cases | Per- cent | | | |
| I. Residence | | | | | |
| Seven Urban Centers | 563 | 100.0 | 40.3% | 8.9% | 3.9% |
| Other Cities | 1,230 | 100.0 | 37.2 | 9.3 | 5.4 |
| Towns and Villages | 807 | 100.0 | 38.8 | 5.8 | 3.7 |
| II. Occupation | | | | | |
| Self-employed: | | | | | |
| Farmers and Fisher- men (100 percent) | 503 | 100.0 | 27.6 | 2.8 | 2.8 |
| Farmers and Fisher- men (less than 100 percent) | 111 | 100.0 | 40.5 | 3.6 | 0.9 |
| Others | 548 | 100.0 | 35.9 | 6.9 | 9.7 |
| Employees: | | | | | |
| Managers and Professionals | 79 | 100.0 | 35.4 | 10.1 | 10.1 |
| Specialists | 143 | 100.0 | 44.8 | 12.6 | 4.2 |
| Clerks | 467 | 100.0 | 38.3 | 13.3 | 4.3 |
| Laborers | 659 | 100.0 | 48.3 | 10.0 | 2.4 |
| III. Monthly Household Expenditures (¥) | | | | | |
| Less than 20,000 | 349 | 100.0 | 33.0 | 3.2 | 2.3 |
| 20,000–29,999 | 656 | 100.0 | 39.0 | 7.5 | 2.3 |
| 30,000–39,999 | 693 | 100.0 | 40.5 | 7.8 | 3.6 |
| 40,000–49,999 | 394 | 100.0 | 44.2 | 12.7 | 5.6 |
| 50,000–59,999 | 179 | 100.0 | 36.3 | 11.2 | 8.4 |
| 60,000–69,999 | 76 | 100.0 | 36.0 | 8.0 | 12.0 |
| 70,000–79,999 | 33 | 100.0 | 33.3 | 12.1 | 21.2 |
| 80,000 and over | 600 | 100.0 | 36.1 | 16.4 | 14.8 |
| Total | 2,600 | 100.0 | 38.4 | 8.2 | 4.5 |

Source: *Shoshia Shinyo no Riyo ni Kansuru Seron Chosa [A Survey of Public Opinion on the Use of Consumer Financing]* (Tokyo: The Ministry of International Trade and Industry, 1966), p. 41.

often thought of as buying beyond one's means and was considered to be less than prudent and acceptable behavior. The study revealed that this previous attitude is now shared by only a small proportion of the respondents (3.9 percent among users and 11 percent among nonusers).[17] While the overwhelming majority did not feel embarrassed to use installment credit, a substantial number objected to some aspects of it. For example, 40 percent of respondents objected on the ground that credit investigation was somewhat distasteful to them.[18]

The most serious objection to the use of consumer credit was, however, high cost. As many as 64 percent (59.9 percent among users and 66.6 percent among nonusers) singled out this aspect as the most undesirable. Significantly, nearly 35 percent of all respondents (38 percent among users and 32.4 percent among nonusers) voiced an opinion that installment buying tended to encourage buying beyond their means.[19] One out of four felt that the procedures involved in buying on installment credit were excessively cumbersome.

Despite these specific objections it is extremely interesting to note that the vast majority of respondents had a favorable overall attitude toward the use of installment credit. As high as 81 percent felt that the installment credit system was beneficial to consumers; only 5 percent of the respondents felt that it was detrimental. As might be expected, there was, however, a significant variation in the response to this question between users and nonusers. Nearly 90 percent of those who had used some form of installment credit program during the past year felt that it was beneficial, and 82.5 percent of those who had used it sometime during the preceding ten years agreed with this point of view.[20] However, among nonusers only 67.5 percent agreed with this statement, and 8.1 percent of nonusers (in contrast to 3.0 percent and 4.5 percent of the current and past users) felt that installment buying was definitely harmful to the consumers' welfare.

The acceptance of consumer installment credit has shown a tremendous growth in postwar Japan. Installment purchase is widely diffused among broad segments of the population, and it has largely overcome the negative image that had been traditionally associated with it. It has, in fact, become extremely important in the sale of a number of consumer durables, as evidenced by the statistics cited earlier. Despite its rapid growth in terms of absolute amount the development of installment credit in Japan is still in

17 *Ibid.*, p. 27.
18 *Ibid.*, p. 50.
19 *Ibid.*, p. 23.
20 *Ibid.*, p. 59.

its infancy, as demonstrated by the following comparative data. In 1967 the outstanding per capita balance of installment credit in Japan was just over $18, while in the United States the amount was nearly $380, or roughly 25 times that of Japan. Also in the same year the outstanding balance of consumer credit in Japan was less than 2 percent of the country's Gross National Product, while the comparable ratio for the United States and for Great Britain was 10 percent and 3.4 percent, respectively. As we have noted, Japan's financial institutions have been intensifying their efforts to expand into consumer financing; but in 1967 the amount of loans made directly to consumers represented less than 1 percent of the total outstanding loans. Even if the loans made to enterprises engaged in installment sales are included, the amount was less than 4 percent of the total loans outstanding.[21]

*Major Problem Areas*

When examined in this perspective, installment credit in Japan is still in its infancy. Although its future looks rather promising, there are several major problem areas, the solution of which is essential to its further growth. Let us now examine these problems.

One serious impediment for future growth is the high cost of installment credit to ultimate users. Consumers must pay considerably more for the same merchandise if they buy it on installment. Installment credit stores, for example, charge 10 percent to 15 percent more for merchandise bought on credit. In the previously cited MITI study on consumers' attitudes toward installment credit, the reader will recall that 64 percent of the respondents complained about the high cost.

The interest rate charged by financial institutions on consumer loans averages about 6 percent. Since interest is not calculated on the declining balance of the loan, the real cost is considerably higher than the nominal interest rate. Two major factors contribute to this high cost. One is that in view of the capital shortage relative to the demand, the interest rate is generally high in Japan. Second, installment credit, consisting of a multitude of small loans, is inherently expensive to manage. In the case of Japan, this is further compounded by institutional inadequacies, which we shall examine briefly.

First, credit investigation is difficult to perform. Some semblance

---

21 *Shohisha Kinyu Jishi Jōkyō Ichiran [A Summary of Current Status of Consumer Financing]* (Tokyo: Zenkoku Ginko Kyokai Rengokai, 1968), p. 5.

of credit clearing facilities does exist, but in terms of both availability and quality of services provided the facilities are deplorably inadequate, particularly considering the demands placed upon them. The aforementioned MITI study conducted among a nationwide sample of 10,432 retail stores carrying products that are commonly purchased on installment credit asked the responding firms the extent to which they investigate the credit standing of potential borrowers. As might be expected, there is considerable difference in the degree to which credit investigation is undertaken according to the products carried, ranging from 42 percent for men's clothing stores to 96 percent for automobile dealers. Of course, it must be recognized that credit investigation is not always necessary, since at least in some cases the customer's credit standing is already known to the management of the particular store.

The survey also inquired of those regularly requiring credit investigation as to who performs this function. With the exception of the automobile dealer category, in which 40 percent of the respondents reported the regular use of specialized agencies, the participating stores relied primarily on their own personnel in investigation of customers' credit standings.[22] The survey also revealed that most stores did not have trained investigators but used their sales personnel for this purpose. Clearly, this approach has serious disadvantages.

There are several reasons for inadequate development of professional facilities for credit investigation. It is partially due to the relative immaturity of consumer financing in Japan. For centralized credit clearing facilities to be truly useful, they must have a considerable amount of accumulated data. Another reason lies in the difficulty of obtaining highly personal information in a society in which the need for credit investigation is not always fully appreciated. Finally, cooperation among rather individualistic retail establishments in supplying credit information has been difficult to achieve. Many stores are reluctant to turn over what they consider their customer's confidential information, or what they have come to view as their proprietary data, to a central clearing house for use by others.

Inadequate credit investigation increases the risk of credit extension, thereby raising the cost. To compensate for incomplete

---

[22] *Kappu Hanbai Jittai Chosa Hokokusho: Dai Ikan [A Survey on the Status of Installment Credit, Vol. 1]*, p. 15.

credit investigations, sellers often require a cosigner to the note, a practice that more often than not is resisted by the customer. It is not only troublesome to find someone willing to become a cosigner, but the customer may feel that this is embarrassing. All these factors tend to inhibit the sound development of installment credit.

Another source of inadequacy is found in the legal framework. This subject is rather complicated, and it is beyond the scope of this chapter to consider it in detail. In essence, the problem lies in the legal enforceability of installment sales contracts. In case of default the installment credit contract under the present legal system lacks absolute legal enforceability. This legal inadequacy forces the seller to use promissory notes with specific due dates, which means that each installment sales agreement must be accompanied by a number of promissory notes, a process that is not only cumbersome but costly.

The present collection method also adds to the cost. As revealed in the MITI survey, with but few exceptions sponsoring organizations must send their own personnel to collect, rather than users' taking the initiative in making payments, as is customary in the United States. One major reason for this is that the use of personal checks is still very limited in Japan. The collection of a large number of small accounts at regular intervals is, needless to say, an expensive and cumbersome undertaking.

Another major problem stems from the fact that the bulk of installment credit must be financed by manufacturers, dealers, or retailers themselves at their own risk. Because their own financial resources are very limited, wholesalers and retailers tend to shift this burden to the manufacturers, who are already saddled with large debt obligations themselves. This is particularly serious in the case of consumer durables for which the unit price is high and the payment period tends to be longer. Nowhere is this problem more acute than in the automobile industry. Floor financing practice, which is common in the United States, is totally absent in Japan, and moreover, dealers are on the whole inadequately financed.

According to the MITI study, an average automobile dealer finances 91 percent of his total working capital with some form of debt.[23] The breakdown of the debt sources is even more revealing. Forty-two percent of the 91 percent debt-financed working

[23] *Ibid.*, p. 20.

capital is in the form of inventory credit extended by manufacturers, and the remaining 49 percent is derived from various types of loans from financial institutions and the particular manufacturer. In fact, on the average, 8 percent of the 49 percent takes the form of outright loans made by the manufacturer. In other words, the average dealer draws roughly half of his working capital from the manufacturer in the forms of inventory credit and outright loans, a substantial portion of which is used for financing installment sales.

This creates a very serious financial burden on the automobile manufacturers. In 1968, for example, the automobile industry manufactured some 2.5 million automobiles of various types, roughly 80 percent of which were sold on installment credit. This meant that approximately ¥1,600 billion were required to finance these installment credit sales. The bank-sponsored installment credit program mentioned earlier has somewhat alleviated this problem, but in terms of absolute amount it has been relatively insignificant, representing only 7 percent or 8 percent of total installment sales. It is estimated that manufacturer- and dealer-sponsored installment credit is about 14 times the amount financed directly by financial institutions.[24] Moreover, even the bank-sponsored loans generally require guarantee by the manufacturer or the dealer. In fact, some automobile manufacturers have established a subsidiary to perform this function. Thus the manufacturers find themselves in a position of having to underwrite a substantial portion of dealers' working capital as well as to provide much of the funds for consumer financing. There is a growing concern among Japanese automobile manufacturers that unless a solution is found to this problem, their ambitious efforts for market expansion will be seriously retarded. At the time of this writing, a number of alternative plans designed to solve this problem were under consideration.

We have identified some major problem areas that are inhibiting the further development of installment credit in Japan. A number of steps are now being taken to alleviate these problems.

### Some Possible Solutions

A most encouraging development in this regard is the increasingly active interest shown by the government in the development

---

[24] *Kokumin Seikatsu Hakusho: Showa 43 nen ban [White Paper on National Life, 1968]* (Tokyo: The Economic Planning Agency, 1968), p. 28.

of consumer financing in general and installment credit in particular. This growing government concern stems from two considerations. One factor is that in the face of the increasing importance of consumer credit in the national economy, its sound development and management will be critical from the point of view of national economic policy. The other motivating force behind the government's growing concern relates to liberalization of the restriction on foreign direct investment now in progress. As we have noted, Japan has been undertaking step-by-step capital liberalization since the summer of 1967. It is fully expected that current restrictions on the entry of foreign firms into the distribution sector will be relaxed in the near future.

The Japanese government feels that the distribution sector is very vulnerable to foreign competition; therefore, it is extremely anxious to take steps to enhance its competitive capacity. Government officials are keenly aware that consumer financing is an area in which Japanese firms are particularly at a disadvantage, in view of the tremendous financial resources and managerial expertise that large multinational firms command in this critical field. Government concern is particularly keen in the area of consumer durables such as automobiles and home appliances, in which installment credit plays a very vital role.

The Ministry of International Trade and Industry, under whose jurisdiction this matter falls, recently established a special committee on installment credit whose membership includes senior bureaucrats, prominent academicians, and representatives of the private sector. The committee's chief function is to make appropriate policy recommendations to the Minister in the field of consumer financing. With the active encouragement of the government, two noteworthy developments are now under way. One is that in the fall of 1969 15 large firms representing those industries that are engaged in extensive installment sales (home appliances, musical instruments, and sewing machines) decided to establish jointly a new corporation specifically designed for credit investigation. Another noteworthy effort is the recent announcement that the Japan Installment Credit Association formulated a six-year plan to establish a nationwide mechanism for effective credit investigation. Also under consideration is the establishment of a quasi-public corporation specializing in consumer financing. This organization as envisioned now will be financed partially by the government and will serve as a major supplier of much-needed funds. It is felt that this will be a significant step forward, since the shortage of funds, as we have noted, is a very serious impeding factor.

A proposal has also been made to establish an independent corporation, organized on an industry basis, whose chief function would be to guarantee consumer loans made by financial institutions rather than leaving each firm to perform this function on its own. Another proposal is to extend government loans at attractive interest rates to small establishments engaged in installment credit sales. As a first step, the Small–Medium-Size Enterprise Agency has recently committed itself to making loans to firms issuing credit coupons.

### Growth of Credit Cards

Another rapidly growing form of consumer financing is the use of the credit card. Although its objectives and functions differ from those of installment credit, it has a number of attractive features and can be a potent marketing tool, as proved in the United States. The use of the consumer credit card is still in its infancy in Japan, but because of its potential usefulness as a marketing tool and its apparently bright prospects, we shall briefly examine its growth pattern during the last several years.

The concept of the credit card was first introduced into Japan in 1960 by Japan Diners Club, a three-way joint venture formed by Diners Club International, the Fuji Bank, and the Japan Travel Bureau. In the following year the Sanwa Bank, in cooperation with Japan Credit Sales Company, established the Japan Credit Bureau. In the first several years both firms experienced considerable difficulty in selling the new concept; but in the late 1960s the concept gained considerable impetus, and by 1969 eight different types of credit card were available, with an estimated membership of 1.5 million. Total sales using credit cards were estimated to be about ¥60 billion for 1969. Some 100,000 outlets now honor credit cards. According to a recent estimate, in 1969 compared with 1968, the number of stores honoring credit cards and the number of subscribers grew fivefold, while the sales made through credit cards increased 2.6 times.

Chiefly responsible for their rapid growth during the past year or two is active entry of major city banks into this field. We have noted earlier that city banks have become increasingly interested in consumer financing. Their interest in credit cards was further reinforced by the success that major commercial banks in the United States have recently enjoyed in this field. The Fuji Bank, the largest city bank in Japan, now owns controlling interest in Japan Diners Club, which now claims membership of some 6,500 stores and some 56,000 cardholders, with total annual sales of roughly ¥6 billion. The Japan Credit Bureau, originally established by the Sanwa Bank, was reorganized in 1968. The newly formed company is now owned by 5 city banks, including Sanwa, and 18 other major Japanese corporations. The Japan Credit Bureau, with some half a million members and roughly 25,000 subscribing stores, is now the largest bank-sponsored credit card operation in the country. The annual sales are reported to be around ¥15 billion.

In late 1967 two other leading city banks also entered this field. Mitsubishi Bank, with the strong backing of 16 member firms, established the Diamond Credit Service Company. Characteristic of Mitsubishi operations, it mobilized strong group ties among the member firms, and by 1969 the membership reached 130,000, roughly 25 percent of whom were believed to be associated with the Mitsubishi group. It is subscribed to by some 10,000 retail outlets, including all 2,400 Mitsubishi Oil Service Stations. Annual sales are estimated to be around ¥5 billion. Also in late 1967 Sumitomo Bank, another major city bank in Japan, began its own credit card operations in cooperation with the Bank of America. In 1968 Tokai Bank, a city bank headquartered in Nagoya, followed suit. In addition to these financial institutions Credit Sales Corporation has recently entered credit card operations as a part of its multifarious activities in the area of consumer financing. It now claims nearly half a million members, with some 5,000 subscribing retail outlets. Its total sales are estimated to be about ¥15 billion, considerably larger than bank-sponsored programs, with the exception of the Japan Credit Bureau.

Although the use of credit cards in Japan has gained momentum in recent years, it is still in its infancy, and considerable promotional and educational efforts are needed for its expansion, among both consumers and retail outlets. Three major obstacles exist, the removal of which is essential to further progress. First, all the familiar problems in regard to credit investigation discussed earlier also apply to the credit card. The ability to obtain up-to-date and accurate credit information is essential to the successful dissemination of this service. Second, the high cost of credit card arrangements to subscribing retail outlets is considered to be a deterrent, since the charge made to subscribing stores ranges from 3 percent to 10 percent. Many potential subscribers object to this seemingly high service charge, particularly when they are not certain of the extent to which the availability of credit cards will bring new business. Finally, unclear government jurisdiction over credit cards can be a serious deterrent to future growth. Bank-sponsored services come under the jurisdiction of the Ministry of Finance, which supervises all banking activities, whereas the services sponsored by nonfinancial institutions, such as Japan Credit Sales Corporation, are under the jurisdiction of the Ministry of International Trade and Industry, with its own set of restrictions and regulations.

In this chapter we have examined two major types of consumer financing. Though still in its infancy compared with the United States and even with some European countries, consumer financing in Japan has experienced a very rapid growth in recent years. As we have seen, consumer financing, particularly installment credit, is widely diffused among the masses and has made it possible for an average consumer to acquire durable goods and expensive services in anticipation of future earnings. It is fully expected that the demand for this service and for credit cards will continue to grow in the future. The challenge now is to develop a sound institutional framework to assure continuing growth.

# 7

# Government Policies toward
# the Distribution Sector

Throughout Japan's modern history the government, particularly
the state bureaucracy, has exercised strong influence on the nation's
business community. In the early days of Japan's industrialization
the government was the promoter, owner, and administrator of
modern strategic industries. Most of these industries initiated by
the government were subsequently turned over to private interests.
Throughout prewar Japan, however, the government continued to
exercise strong influence, albeit informal, over the Zaibatsu-dom-
inated business community.

In the aftermath of World War II both the government and the
business community became subject to extensive Occupation-
sponsored reforms. Although the political and economic systems
that have subsequently emerged are different from those that
existed prior to the war, the government, even in contemporary
Japan, still plays a very important role in guiding activities of the
Japanese business community. William Lockwood, a noted authority on the Japanese economy, succinctly describes the pervasive
influence of the government on Japanese business as follows:

> The hand of government is everywhere in evidence, despite its limited
> statutory powers. The Ministries engage in an extraordinary amount of
> consultation, advice, persuasion, and threat. Industrial bureaus of
> MITI proliferate sectoral targets and plans; they confer, they tinker,
> they exhort. This is the "economics of admonition" to a degree incon-
> ceivable in Washington or London.[1]

[1] William W. Lockwood, "Japan's 'New Capitalism,'" in William W. Lock-

It should be noted, however, that throughout Japan's modern history the government has always been oriented toward big business, and until very recently it paid virtually no attention to the needs of small- and medium-size business establishments, except to the extent that they affected the operations of large enterprises. This is so despite the fact that small- to medium-size enterprises were much more numerous than were large firms—in fact, relatively small firms transacted most of Japanese business. It is also noteworthy that traditional government policy had been oriented toward the manufacturing sector. This is not without justifications in light of the circumstances under which Japan's industrialization was initiated and subsequently carried out. It should be recalled that the major concern of the ruling elite in the initial days of Japan's industrialization was that of *"Fukoku Kyohei"* or "building a wealthy nation and strong army." To achieve this overriding national goal, the political elite spared no effort, and this political philosophy essentially continued throughout the pre-World War II era. Although the postwar reforms repudiated the prewar national ideology, the government industrial policy has still been geared primarily toward assisting large-scale manufacturing industries.

The primary concern of the government in the early postwar years was to rebuild Japan's industrial base from the great devastation wrought by the war. Given the very pressing needs of that period and the tradition of the Japanese government, it is understandable that it gave priority to rebuilding large-scale industrial firms in its economic recovery program. The government not only sought to protect large strategic industries from foreign competition but extended generous assistance to large business establishments, including channeling a huge sum of low-interest capital to these firms. Indeed, these aggressive government efforts contributed importantly to Japan's postwar industrial success.

In the last several years, however, the government gradually has become more responsive to the needs of the distribution sector. Although its involvement is still on a limited scale, it is nevertheless a significant departure from tradition. In this chapter we shall attempt to examine the government's policy toward the distribution sector as it has evolved during the past several years. In so

---

wood (ed.), *The State and Economic Enterprise in Japan* (Princeton, N.J.: Princeton University Press, 1965), p. 503.

doing, we shall first review the background leading to the growing government concern in this area, then examine specific programs proposed and implemented by different government agencies. Finally, we shall attempt to evaluate their effectiveness.

## Underlying Forces

There are several reasons why the government has become increasingly interested in problems of the distribution sector. First, this interest stems in part from a growing concern for the general welfare of small- to medium-size establishments among which, of course, marketing intermediaries comprise an important share. Even in the early postwar years, while the government's policies predominantly were oriented toward large business, it did take some steps to promote the interest of small- to medium-size firms. Tangible evidence of this was the establishment of the Small-Medium-Size Enterprise Agency in 1948 as a semiautonomous body within the Ministry of International Trade and Industry. The agency has been charged with the responsibilities of developing and implementing government policy toward small business. In the 1950s the government also took steps to establish or reestablish several public or quasi-public financial institutions designed to aid small- to medium-size firms. The most significant postwar development in this regard, however, was the passage of the Small–Medium-Size Enterprise Act in 1963. The Act sought two basic objectives: (1) the modernization and rationalization of small- to medium-size enterprises, and (2) the strengthening of their international competitive ability. The Act committed the government to take positive steps toward these objectives.

Contributing directly to the passage of this Act were two important factors. One was a growing disparity in size, as well as financial, technical, and managerial capacities, between large-scale firms on one hand and small- to medium-size firms on the other. During the late 1950s and early 1960s large-scale manufacturing firms in strategic industries achieved a tremendous growth with active support from the government. Of course, small firms, particularly those that were closely tied as subcontractors to large firms, did share in the phenomenal economic progress, but not nearly to the degree enjoyed by large industrial firms. The gaps between large and small firms that have always existed widened, and their political and economic implications became increasingly serious. It became evident that some governmental actions were needed to correct this situation.

The other reason prompting the government's concern for the welfare of small firms was the anticipation of growing international competition. By the early 1960s the Japanese government became subject to increasing foreign pressure to liberalize its restrictions on foreign trade. It became increasingly clear to the government policy planners that no longer could Japanese business operate in a highly protected environment. It was felt that small- to medium-size firms with limited resources and outdated management practices would be most vulnerable to foreign competition.

It is important to note here that owners of small businesses and their workers by their sheer number wield considerable political power in contemporary Japan. Those employed in small- to medium-size firms represent about 65 percent of the total work force employed in all industries—manufacturing, commerce, and services. In the distribution sector alone, as we have seen, there are more than 1.3 million retail shops and 281,000 wholesalers, with some 7.3 million workers. The overwhelming majority of these establishments are small enterprises of fewer than five employees. Moreover, owners and managers of small- to medium-size firms, along with farmers, constitute the backbone of the Liberal Democratic Party, Japan's ruling conservative party.

It is highly signficant to observe that the government's interest in the distribution sector, at least initially, came about as a result of its concern for small- to medium-size enterprises rather than from its recognition of the need to improve the efficiency of the distribution sector. This set the tone for the initial government policy toward the distribution sector. In fact, at least in the beginning, the government's programs for small- to medium-size firms were production-oriented in that the primary emphasis was directed to small- to medium-size manufacturing firms. The passage of the Small-Medium-Size Enterprise Act, however, marked a turning point, and gradually the government began to show increasing concern for the protection and modernization of small-scale marketing intermediaries. Once it became involved with the distribution sector, it became increasingly aware of the rather serious strains now being experienced by this sector in the face of the major environmental changes described earlier.

The government's concern for the distribution sector also stemmed from the rapidly rising consumer prices of the last several years. As we saw in Chapter 1, the wholesale price index has remained relatively stable during the last several years, but the consumer price level has experienced a considerable rise. The growing disparity between the wholesale and consumer price indexes is telling evidence that the traditional distribution system is less than effective in performing its functions efficiently in an emerging mass consumer market. Rising consumer prices have developed into one of the most sensitive political issues in Japan, and much pressure is now being exerted on the government to arrest this tide. This issue provides an immediate, if not the most compelling, reason prompting the Japanese government to modernize the outmoded distribution system.

Another reason for growing government concern for the distribution sector has been based on its realization that the obsolete and highly fragmented distribution sector would be particularly vulnerable to foreign competition in the event of capital liberalization. The Japanese government officials, concerned with this competitive vulnerability of the Japanese distribution system, are most anxious to take any steps necessary to promote the modernization of this sector. Thus the recent government interest in the distribution sector has stemmed from a variety of reasons, and this fact, as we shall see later, has some important implications in determining the overall effectiveness of the government's policies and programs in this area.

### The Government's Policy toward the Distribution Sector

During the past two decades government policies toward the distribution sector have gone through three clearly indentifiable evolutionary stages. The first stage, covering the period roughly between 1948 and 1962, may be called the protection stage. During this phase the government's main concern was to protect small independent wholesale and retail establishments, particularly the latter, from unfair competition from large establishments such as department stores as well as from special types of retail institutions such as cooperatives, and to make available various types of assistance in the forms of low-interest loans, management consulting, and educational services to improve their competition position. This stage had two noteworthy characteristics. One is that the programs were designed not for the purpose of improving efficiency of the total distribution system but for the protection of existing small-scale marketing intermediaries. The other feature is that the programs were formulated as part of the government policy toward small- to medium-size enterprises in general. In other words, small marketing intermediaries were believed to deserve protection and assistance not because they were engaged in distribution activities but because they were small. This distinction, although it may appear rather subtle on the surface, is nevertheless important in setting the tone of government policy in the first stage.

Only in the second stage did the programs specifically designed for marketing intermediaries emerge. This stage, which covers a brief period between 1962 and 1968, retained one of the main features of the first stage; that is, the programs were designed to promote the interest of existing small marketing intermediaries. It differed, however, from the first stage in that it stressed positive actions rather than passive protective measures and maintenance of the status quo. A number of specific programs were formulated to assist small retailers and wholesalers in achieving modernization and rationalization to improve their competitive ability. The second stage was still characterized, however, by uncoordinated and fragmented programs designed for a rather limited segment of the distribution sector.

The third stage, which began in 1968, departed from the preceding stage in a very significant way in that its major objective was to improve the efficiency of the total system. For the first time, the basic goal shifted from protecting and promoting only certain segments of the distribution sector to improving the total system. The basic objective clearly has become the welfare of the entire national economy.

While government policies toward the distribution sector have gone through three rather distinct stages in their philosophy, practical considerations dictated the retention of most of the programs initiated in each of the earlier stages. What is important in distinguishing these stages is not so much the content of specific programs but rather the basic orientations and objectives. Now let us examine in some detail the programs formulated in each stage.

### The First Stage: Protection of Small Enterprises

Among a number of protective measures for small independent establishments, the most significant is the Department Store Law enacted in 1956. The Law imposes several restrictions on the operations of department stores in Japan. They include (1) requiring government approval for establishment of a new department store and for mergers, as well as for expansion of the existing store; (2) placing restrictions on the number of operating days in the month and on store hours; (3) prohibiting certain business practices such as provision of free transportation for customers to and from stores; and (4) requiring department stores to submit their operating results to the Ministry of International Trade and Industry at regular intervals.

The second legal action was taken in 1959 in the form of the Special Act for Retailers. The Act placed restrictions on the operating freedom of company stores. It is customary for large Japanese firms to maintain company stores for employees where they can purchase a variety of merchandise at a substantial discount. Provision of such services is considered part of rather extensive benefits provided by large Japanese corporations. These stores pose serious competitive threats to small independent retailers in the area. To minimize this negative effect, the Act prohibits company stores from serving customers who are not eligible for such services. The Act also requires approval for manufacturers and wholesalers to enter into retailing. Approval is also necessary when manufacturers and wholesalers engaged in retailing want to discontinue their retailing operations. Finally, the Act authorizes the prefectural governors to serve as arbitrators upon the request of parties involved in conflicts between certain manufacturers and retailers, between wholesalers and retailers, or among retailers themselves.

Another legal protection for small retail establishments is found in the Consumer Cooperative Act, which prohibits consumer cooperatives from selling merchandise to nonmembers unless specific permission is obtained.

There is a widely shared view that the protective measures have been less than effective in achieving the initial objectives. The Department Store Law has been particularly unpopular. The managers of department stores naturally find the Law excessively restrictive, while in the opinion of an average small merchant the Law is only of marginal value in protecting him against competition from large department stores. With the rapid emergence of mass merchandising firms that for all practical purposes operate outside the Law, it has become even more archiac.

In the mid-1960s MITI's policy toward small- to medium-size wholesalers and retailers began to undergo some changes. It became increasingly apparent to MITI policy planners that the past policy, designed merely to protect (inadequately, at best) small independent merchants, was neither sufficient nor even appropriate in view of the rapidly changing conditions. We should recall that this was the time when a truly viable mass consumer market began to evolve, and marketing-oriented large-scale manufacturing firms began to emerge in a number of consumer industries. This was also the time when we began to witness the rapid rise of aggressive mass merchandising firms. Indeed, this was the beginning of the widely talked about "*Ryutsu Kakumei*" or "distribution revolution." The prospect of liberalization of foreign capital also became increasingly imminent in the mid-1960s. Government policy planners became increasingly aware of the fact that more immediate and drastic actions were needed.

### The Second Stage: Rationalization of Small- to Medium-Size Wholesalers and Retailers

It was against this background that the Committee on Distribution was formed within the Council on Industrial Structure. The Council is a blue-chip standing committee established to advise the Minister of International Trade and Industry on matters relating to the nation's industrial policy. It is composed of leading business executives, scholars, and prominent citizens, and has a number of committees to deal with problems in specific fields and industries. The Committee on Distribution, like its counterparts in other industries, consists of marketing experts drawn from academic and business communities as well as representatives of the public. The Committee's main function is to advise the Minister of International Trade and Industry in formulating national policies toward the distribution sector. The organization of the Committee marked the entry into the second stage of MITI policy toward the distribution sector. The policy emphasis shifted from protection and maintenance of the status quo to a definite commitment to modernize the traditional distribution sector and to strengthen its competitive capacity. To implement this new philosophy, MITI, upon the advice of the Committee on Distribution, formulated a number of new programs, which we shall briefly examine.

RELOCATION OF WHOLESALERS TO A PLANNED WHOLESALE CENTER. As we have observed, the Japanese wholesaling structure is extremely complex, consisting of a large number of small establishments. It may be recalled from our earlier discussion that nearly half the wholesalers in Japan consist of establishments with fewer than five employees. With increasing volume of merchandise and with worsening traffic congestion, wholesalers located in the traditional wholesale district have become less and less capable of performing their functions. Moreover, many of the buildings that are now occupied by wholesalers were built in the prewar era. They are poorly laid out and have limited warehouse space. The wholesalers, in order to handle a greater volume of merchandise, have steadily increased the number of delivery automobiles. For example, between 1956 and 1964 the average number of automobiles, including passenger cars owned by wholesalers, increased from 0.75 per store to nearly 2.5. This alone has contributed significantly to urban traffic congestion in major wholesaling centers. Because of the increasingly serious traffic congestion and typically high land value in the usual wholesale districts, expansion and modernization of existing physical facilities are usually prohibitively expensive.

In order to improve the wholesalers' capacities to perform their functions more effectively, the government set out to assist interested wholesalers in establishing cooperatively a planned wholesale center in a suburb or in a high-rise building in the center of a city, and to move at least part of their operations to such a center. For this purpose, the government, through the Small–Medium-Size Enterprise Promotion Agency, together with the prefectural government, extended a low-interest (2.2 percent), long-term loan to cover a maximum of 65 percent of the total cost related to the construction of such a center. The loan stipulates a maximum repayment period of 15 years, which is to commence no later than 3 years after the loan is made.

Not only will the program help solve the immediate problems of transportation and storage but it is also hoped that this will open the way for more cooperation among wholesalers, which may well lead to eventual mergers. In order to qualify for government assistance under this provision, the following conditions must be satisfied:

1. There must be at least 20 wholesale establishments and they must organize a cooperative association. All participants must be wholesalers; however, when proved desirable, up to 20 percent of

the firms in the center can be establishments engaged in manufacturing or transportation activities closely related to wholesaling.

2. The site for the proposed center must be consistent with local municipal development plans.

3. At least two-thirds of the participants must agree to relocate all or at least part of their facilities to the proposed site.

4. The proposed center must include some common facilities to be used by all participating organizations.

5. The proposed center must be constructed in such a way as to result in substantial improvements of managerial practices of the participating organizations.

6. Each individual store within the center must be constructed with maximum safety and durability.

This program was initiated in 1963, and the first proposal approved was a plan submitted by some 145 wholesalers in the city of Takasaki, located approximately 130 miles northwest of Tokyo. By the end of fiscal year 1968 a total of 44 such plans had been approved; as of 1969, 15 of these centers were in operation.

PROGRAMS DESIGNED FOR RETAILERS. As part of the modernization program, MITI policy planners, keenly concerned with the condition of the retailing sector, developed several different types of programs to assist the small retailers. Among several programs designed, the first to be proposed was the establishment of cooperative supermarkets and department stores. Since the objectives of this program were discussed in some detail in Chapter 5, they will not be repeated here. To qualify under this program, the prospective participants must meet the following conditions:

1. There must be more than five participating retail stores.

2. At least 70 percent of the participants must be small- to medium-sized retail stores (those with fewer than 50 employees).

3. The proposed store must have at least 200 square meters, or 2,140 square feet, of floor space.

4. The proposed building must be designed to meet minimum standards of durability and safety.

To those who qualify under this plan, MITI, through the Small–Medium-Size Enterprise Promotion Agency, in cooperation with the prefectural government, will extend a loan of up to 65 percent of the cost of construction of the store and purchase of equipment at 2.2 percent interest. The maximum repayment period is 15 years, which is to be started within 3 years after the loan is made. The program was initiated in 1963, and between 1963 and 1968, 103 loans for cooperative department stores and 52 cooperative supermarkets were approved. However, for the reasons noted in Chapter 5, the program fell far short of its original expectations.

ASSISTANCE IN MODERNIZATION OF SHOPPING DISTRICTS. This program is designed to encourage a group of stores located in a given area cooperatively to renovate and modernize the entire shopping district to enhance its appeal to customers. This program grew out of recognition that the modernization of a single store often was not sufficient; in order to achieve the maximum impact, the modernization of an entire neighborhood shopping district was in order. Modernization programs call for renovation of existing facilities as well as addition of some common facilities such as parking accommodations. To be eligible for government assitance under this program, participating firms must satisfy the following conditions:

1. At least 80 percent of the participating stores will have to maintain a store in a proposed shopping district.
2. There must be 30 participants, at least 75 percent of whom must be small- to medium-size retail establishments.
3. The proposed center must have some common facilities to be used by participating establishments.

Government assistance is made on the same basis as for the previously described programs. This program began in 1964, and during the five-year period ending in 1969 five such centers have been approved.

FORMATION OF VOLUNTARY AND COOPERATIVE CHAINS. The aforementioned programs, although their objectives are highly laudable, have had only limited impact (for the reasons discussed in Chapter 5). The less than enthusiastic response by the average retail store is not difficult to understand. As the MITI officials became aware of the limitations of these programs, and in the face of the rapidly rising consumer price index, they came under increasing pressure to devise a program with a much broader appeal that could produce immediate results.

Confronted with this need, MITI devised a program to promote the formation of voluntary and cooperative chains among existing independent retailers. To provide adequate encouragement to the formation of such chains, MITI extends its assistance in a number of different forms. The Small–Medium-Size Enterprise Promotion Agency makes loans for the construction of the headquarters facilities and central warehouses. The Japan Development Bank, a major public financial institution, will also make loans for the construction of central warehouses by medium-size enterprises. In addition, provisions have been made for two financial institutions serving small- to medium-size firms to make long-term loans to help finance the initial organization and subsequent development of both voluntary and cooperative chains. Between 1966 and 1968, nine loans had been made by the Japan Development Bank, and eight loans for this purpose have been granted by the Small–Medium-Size Enterprise Promotion Agency.

The government also has begun an extensive campaign to educate retailers on potential benefits of voluntary and cooperative chains. These efforts include distributing pamphlets, inviting foreign experts on voluntary chains, sponsoring paid radio and TV commercials on the concept of voluntary and cooperative chains, holding lectures by Japanese experts throughout the country, and finally organizing study teams to the United States and Western Europe to learn more about the operations of voluntary and cooperative chains in these countries. In addition, the government has held training programs to develop supervisors of voluntary and cooperative chains and consultants through the Small–Medium-Size Enterprise Promotion Agency. Another major incentive for organizing voluntary and cooperative chains takes the form of accelerated depreciation for warehouses and other installations of the central headquarters of the chain.

Quite apart from specific assistance programs designed for small retailers and wholesalers, there are a number of programs that are designed for small- to medium-size firms regardless of the particular industry in which they operate. Small wholesalers and retailers, as small enterprises, are eligible for such assistance. We shall now describe briefly the major programs in this area. Particularly noteworthy are two types of management guidance or consulting services and financial assistance.

In 1967 the Japanese government expanded considerably the scope of the previous efforts in these areas and combined two agencies in order to coordinate government programs for the pro-

motion of small- to medium-size enterprises better. The Small–
Medium-Size Enterprise Agency maintains management guidance
centers in each prefecture and in the six major cities in cooperation
with the prefectural and municipal governments. They provide
consulting services to small- and medium-size firms, including
small independent retailers and wholesalers. During the fiscal year
1967 nearly 4,000 such consulting services were performed on behalf of small wholesalers and retailers.

In addition, these centers sponsor two types of training programs
for owners and managers of small retail and wholesale establishments. One is a 95-hour program covering virtually every topic of
importance in the management of small wholesale and retail establishments. For the fiscal year 1968 some 2,700 owners and managers participated in this program. The cost of the program is
borne equally among the three parties: the national government,
the prefectural government, and the individual participants themselves. There is also a shorter version (36 hours) of a similiar program designed primarily for employees of small retail establishments. In addition, the Agency has a program to train consultants
for small businesses.

Another major government program is to subsidize provision of
consulting and educational services by the Local Federation of
Small Businesses. Only wholesale and retail enterprises with fewer
than four employees are eligible for this service, and programs are
coordinated in conjunction with the local Chamber of Commerce.
There are nearly 2,500 such consulting associations throughout
Japan, and in 1967 alone they handled more than 2.8 million cases.
In addition, these organizations sponsor lectures and seminars on
topics of special relevance to owners and managers of small firms.
For these activities the government paid a subsidy of ¥2.9 billion
in 1968.

Looking now at the financial aspects, we see that there are three
public or quasi-public financial institutions specifically designed to
extend loans to small- to medium-size firms. Most such firms in
Japan suffer from serious capital shortage, and further, they are at
a serious disadvantage in obtaining loans from commercial banks
and other private financial institutions. These public or quasi-
public financial institutions have been established to compensate
for these handicaps. Although the specific purposes of these institutions vary, only enterprises with fewer than 50 employees that

are capitalized at less than ¥10 million are eligible to obtain loans from them. These institutions extend loans for working capital as well as for capital investment.

The objectives of the programs designed in the second stage, as we have just discussed, were to seek modernization of existing small wholesale and retail establishments to increase their competitive capacity vis-à-vis mass merchandising firms. It is noteworthy, however, that these programs were not aimed at improving the total efficiency of the nation's distribution system. It is true that the programs proposed in the second stage sought to take positive actions rather than simply to protect small- to medium-size firms; but the emphasis, nevertheless, was placed on modernization of only a certain part of the Japanese distribution sector. These programs tended to be highly fragmented, and the overall needs of the total distribution system were not carefully assessed.

### The Third Stage: The Total System Approach

In the late 1960s MITI officials who were concerned with the distribution sector as well as members of the Committee on Distribution began to see that a basic reassessment of the past approach was in order. They came to recognize that government policies and programs for the distribution sector should be designed to build a viable and efficient national distribution system; the programs had to be more comprehensive than those in the past and should be designed to meet this overriding objective. Moreover, the emphasis had to be placed on achievement of coordinated efforts to obtain the maximum benefits.

Reflecting the basic changes in the thinking of key policy-makers, the Committee on Distribution was charged with the responsibility of developing well-coordinated and viable programs to modernize the entire distribution sector. The Committee, working closely with MITI policy-makers, called a number of public hearings, consulted with a large number of experts, and held a series of careful deliberations of their own. In the summer of 1968 it submitted an interim report to the Council on Industrial Structure. The report was appropriately entitled *A Perspective and the Challenge of Modernization of the Distribution Sector*. This was the very first attempt to examine the problems of the distribution sector from the point of view of the entire national economy, and as such it heralded a new era. Since this report is likely to have profound influence in shaping

MITI's future policies and programs in this area, it would be worthwhile to review the major points and recommendations it proposed.

INTERIM REPORT OF THE COMMITTEE ON DISTRIBUTION. The report begins with a brief examination of the dynamic changes that have been taking place in the environment in which the Japanese distribution system must now function. The major environmental changes are summarized as follows: rapid postwar economic growth; the emergence of a mass consumption economy; extensive adoption of the mass production system; labor shortage; accelerating urbanization technological advance in the areas of transportation, communication, and information processing; and finally, impending liberalization of restrictions on direct foreign investment in Japan.

MAJOR CHALLENGES. The report then identifies four major challenges that lie ahead in achieving modernization of Japan's distribution system. The most serious challenge is a basic assessment of the role and functions of each of the key institutions in the distribution sector in a rapidly changing environment. The report emphasizes that, rather than merely continuing to provide traditionally defined functions, each marketing institution must now identify new needs and develop capabilities to fulfill these needs. Particularly important, according to the report, is the information function of the marketing intermediaries—that is, the ability of marketing intermediaries to assess the demand quickly and accurately and to convey this information to suppliers of goods and services.

The second challenge, according to the report, is the development of proper market conditions and a good competitive atmosphere. To modernize the distribution sector, it is essential to encourage entry and growth of innovative marketing institutions and to promote healthy competition among different types of marketing intermediaries and channels. The report stresses the importance of creating and maintaining an environment conducive to fair competition.

The third challenge is creation of an effective and efficient physical distribution system, including packaging, storage, transportation, and material handling. These functions are believed to be responsible for over 50 percent of the entire distribution cost in a number of major merchandise categories. Present facilities for physical distribution in Japan are extremely inadequate.

As a final challenge, the report stresses the importance of creating infrastructures and institutional framework to promote the modernization of the distribution sector. This includes promoting regional and urban planning, improving communication and transportation systems, and strengthening institutional framework to encourage the flow of capital to the distribution sector. In these areas, the report points out, government—both national and local—has a major role to play.

Having identified the four challenges facing the Japanese distribution system, the report then attempts a five-year projection of the scale of the distribution sector, which we have already examined in Chapter 4.

CRITERIA OF NATIONAL POLICY. The report then sets forth the following criteria to be applied in formulating national policy on the distributing system.

1. The policy must seek maximum impact and must contribute to the improvement of significant segments of the nation's distribution sector. Given the number and diversity of establishments engaged in distribution activities, the first step should consist of educational programs designed to create awareness of the implications of relevant environmental changes and the changing role and functions of distribution institutions in a dynamically evolving environment.

2. The policy must be designed to encourage small retailers and wholesalers to take the initiative in attempting their own rationalization and modernization rather than complacently depending on government assistance.

3. The policy should encourage development of model projects with the maximum demonstration effect.

4. Each program should be designed from the point of view of the total distribution system and must be carefully coordinated with other programs. Utmost attention should be given to the protection of consumer interests.

5. The policy should be formulated in close consultation between the government and the private sector.

6. To facilitate the implementation of specific programs, maximum cooperation should be obtained from trade associations and regional and local voluntary associations of commercial establishments.

POLICY RECOMMENDATIONS. Against the foregoing considerations, the report made the following policy recommendations:

1. *To encourage cooperative actions among wholesale as well as retail establishments.* This is a confirmation of the previous programs designed to promote reorganization of highly fragmented small establishments through a variety of cooperative efforts with government assistance.

2. *To improve operating efficiency and managerial practices.* The report recognizes the importance of improving the operating efficiency and managerial practices of each establishment as a means toward rationalization of the entire distribution system. Areas specifically cited in this report include improvement of merchandising techniques and information processing, adoption of self-service techniques, and establishment of distribution centers. The report recommends programs to encourage cooperative efforts among small wholesalers and retailers to centralize clerical functions such as billing in order to achieve a more effective and efficient use of manpower.

3. *To reorganize labor policy in consideration of the acute labor shortage.* Particularly important in the distribution sector, the report recommends programs to promote the introduction of labor-saving management concepts and techniques by those engaged in distribution activities. It urges better utilization of unskilled workers such as part-time employees, housewives, and older workers. The report also recognizes the importance of training management personnel in view of the rapidly growing demand for middle management in distribution firms. It also urges expansion and improvement of college-level training for those who aspire to a management career in distribution.

4. *To rationalize trade customs and relationships.* The report notes that the traditional Japanese distribution sector is characterized by complex trade practices, including the extension of extremely liberal credit terms, extensive use of highly individualized rebates and discounts, frequent sales in small quantities, and liberal return privileges. These trade practices, having grown out of many years of tradition, have even worsened in recent years because of strong competitive pressure and are contributing to higher distribution costs. The report recognizes the difficulty of correcting these practices immediately, but as the first step it urges use and promotion of standard trade terms for key merchandise.

5. *To rationalize physical distribution.* The report recognizes the importance of improving the effectiveness of the physical distribution system. Recognizing the importance of the role that manufacturers play here, it urges their cooperation in this effort. Particularly important is the development of an efficient integrated national network of physical distribution through standardization and mechanization: adoption of unit control, construction of warehousing facilities in strategic locations, and coordination among various modes of transportation.

6. *To promote coordinated development of large-scale distribution facilities.* The report recognizes the importance of preventing unplanned and haphazard development of newly emerging large-scale distribution facilities such as planned shopping centers, wholesale centers and warehouse and distribution centers. The report urges individual firms to give appropriate consideration in selecting sites for these large-scale distribution facilities to the optimum allocation of resources for the benefit of the national economy. Their locations should be consistent with urban and regional plans. In order for these enterprises to select appropriate locations for their large-scale distribution facilities, it is essential for them to obtain detailed information on salient aspects of the market under consideration. This would include size of the trading area, price of the land, availability of transportation, economic and social profiles of consumers, and so on. The report suggests that in order to assist private enterprises in locational decisions, it would be highly desirable for the government to gather up-to-date detailed market information on a continuing basis and to make it available to all concerned through a central data bank.

7. *To improve collection of commercial statistics.* Recognizing the importance of ready access to detailed commercial statistics to serve as a basis for better planning by individual firms as well as by the entire distribution sector, the report recommends improvement of the collection, tabulation, and presentation of more comprehensive statistics on commercial activities, and urges the establishment of a computer-based information storage and retrieval system in order to make the statistics easily and speedily accessible to potential users.

8. *To provide needed capital.* The report recognizes that the modernization of the distribution sector requires substantial capital investment, particularly in view of rising real estate costs. The report suggests that, to the maximum extent possible, moderniza-

tion of the distribution sector should be financed by private capital. It does recognize, however, that the past tendency has been for the bulk of the private capital to flow into the manufacturing sector, particularly to large firms, and that the distribution sector has suffered from chronic capital shortage. The report recommends that as a means to encourage the flow of private capital into the distribution sector, the government should finance its large-scale basic projects. Recognizing the limited availability of private capital, the report also stresses the importance of assuring adequate provision of public funds to assist small- to medium-size retail and wholesale establishments in their modernization efforts. It then urges appropriate institutional reforms to assure provision of adequate working capital to these small firms. These steps, it states, will contribute considerably toward bringing about desired changes in traditionally highly complex trade practices, since these practices largely had evolved to compensate for insufficient working capital. In addition to providing adequate capital to those engaged in distribution activities, the report recognizes the importance of sound development of the installment credit system for both industrial and consumer products, and urges that necessary steps be taken to promote its development.

These policy recommendations are now being translated into specific programs. Although still in a rather preliminary stage, a number of steps are already being taken.

First, a program is now under way to improve distribution functions in a number of major metropolitan areas. Plans for systematic development of wholesale centers, trucking terminals, packaging facilities, and central markets are now being formulated. The necessary legal framework has been established, and a small budget has been made available for the initial planning.

Another step has been initiated in the area of modernization of trade practices. During fiscal year 1968 trade customs and practices of six major merchandising categories were investigated, and out of these studies emerged recommended trade terms and practices. For fiscal year 1969 similar studies were being undertaken for five other product categories. Also under study were suggested terms for installment credit for a number of major consumer durables.

To modernize physical distribution activities, a program is now under way in cooperation with the Japan Chamber of Commerce to promote standardization and mechanization of the physical distribution process. A small budget has also been made available for the initial planning and provision for loans from the Japan Development Bank. Also, to promote the efficient flow of information and to encourage savings in labor cost. MITI has made available loans through the Small–Medium-Size Enterprise Agency. A similar arrangement is being developed to encourage establishment of central computer facilities to be used by a number of retailers and wholesalers in a given area. In this connection a small budget was also allocated to help promote standardization of billing procedures.

Other specific actions have been implemented, of which two are particularly noteworthy. Beginning in fiscal year 1968, the government established through two public financial institutions a low-interest, long-term loan program to help finance certain types of modernization programs, including construction of distribution centers, self-service stores, and model stores for voluntary chains. The program also is designed to extend loans to help the independent wholesaler and retailer to move to planned wholesale centers or shopping centers.

The other program that is now being implemented on a small scale is an attempt to promote rationalization of the distribution sector on a regional basis. The program will be undertaken in cooperation with the Japan Chamber of Commerce. The major objective of this program is to attempt to integrate a modernization program of the distribution sector with regional development and urban renewal programs. The initial stage calls for the selection of four cities for which a ten-year integrated development plan will be formulated.

In addition to the programs already mentioned, several others are now under consideration. Particularly important are recommendations under study in the area of consumer financing. These recommendations include the establishment of quasi-public financial institutions to provide much-needed capital and to improve credit investigation facilities. Also under consideration is the establishment of a specialized educational institution to train future managers of the distribution industry.

The recommendations included in the interim report have come a long way from the previous rather fragmented approach. The report has made a systematic analysis of the problems confronting the nation's distribution sector and has made a number of suggestions and recommendations that, if carried out successfully, will have a major impact in shaping the nation's distribution system in the future.

In July 1969 the Committee on Distribution submitted another series of recommendations to the MITI. The report, prepared by the Subcommittee on Distribution Policy under the chairmanship of Professor Shuji Hayashi, stressed application of the systems concept to achieve modernization of the distribution sector. The report states that the application of the systems concept will contribute significantly to upgrading efficiency and improving productivity of the nation's distribution sector. It stresses that the successful implementation of the systems concept can be done only through the cooperation of both the public and private sectors. The report goes on to suggest certain actions that the government should take to implement the systems concept. The recommended steps include establishing a central coordinating administrative body, identifying a series of guidelines for the private sector, providing vital information on distribution activities, improving information flows in the distribution sector, and providing loans and tax incentives to encourage the adoption of the systems concept. For effective implementation of these policy recommendations in both the 1968 and 1969 reports, however, several major problems must be recognized.

## Major Remaining Problems

First, recommendations of the Committee are stated in rather vague terms. This is consistent with the Japanese bureaucratic tradition, in which such a report typically sets the basic tone and direction and formulation and implementation of specific programs are left to bureaucratic functionaries. The real test, then, depends on how successfully the Ministries, particularly the Ministry of International Trade and Industry, can translate these recommendations into a series of viable action programs and implement them in such a way as to maximize their impact.

In this context alone there are several serious problems. First, understandably, the MITI policy planners must operate within the overall framework of the priority ranking established within the government for budget allocations. Thus the successful implementation depends, to an important degree, on the formal and informal power that officials in charge of these programs can command within MITI, and on their influence with the Ministry of Finance, which has all-important authority for budget allocations.

Given the strong traditional orientation toward large-scale manufacturing firms, it is by no means certain that those charged with the distribution programs will enjoy the most influential position, even within MITI.

Another potentially serious problem in this connection is the extent to which MITI officials can adhere to the lofty goals expressed in the report in developing specific programs. The report explicitly states that the ultimate objective of government policy in this area is the modernization of the nation's entire distribution structure and the good of the entire national economy. But it is important to note that there is mounting pressure for achieving immediate results in such areas as stabilization of consumer prices and protection of small establishments against giant firms as well as against foreign competition. These tangible and immediate objectives may well compete for priorities in MITI policy planning. As bureaucrats, MITI officials cannot be entirely free from political influence, and there may well be temptations to emphasize those programs and policies that are politically expedient and those that are likely to produce immediate results, even though judged in terms of their total contribution to the stated objectives they may be marginal at best.

The third major problem is that the statutory power of the government in this field is severely limited. Of course, MITI officials, despite their limited legal power, have been able to exercise pervasive influence vis-à-vis large manufacturing firms. The policymakers should assess carefully the extent to which the government can, in fact, guide the modernization of the distribution sector. It is well known that in Japan the traditional relationship between big business and government has been an extremely close one. From this long-established tradition, the bureaucrats know how to deal with management of large industrial and financial concerns. Big business is very aware of the power of the state bureaucracy and is generally responsive to its guidance. High-ranking bureaucrats and today's professional executives of large industrial and financial firms have much in common in their backgrounds Both formal and informal communication links between the two are readily available. To be sure, there are some differences between the two groups, but they are similar in their basic orientations.

In dealing with small shopkeepers, however, bureaucrats face an entirely different situation. The sheer number alone presents a formidable problem of communication. More basically, however, there is an almost unbridgeable gap in orientation and outlook between the elite bureaucrats and independent-minded small merchants. On the one hand, bureaucrats find it difficult to understand the merchants' outlook and point of view; on the other hand, merchants are highly individualistic and are suspicious of the government.

In dealing with these merchants, short of outright control the government lacks absolutely effective means to enforce its guidelines. It certainly lacks the strong incentives and potential threats that the state bureaucracy can bring to bear on large businesses. The power of the Ministries is essentially limited to providing various forms of incentives and moral persuasion. Of course, the bureaucrats are not unaware of this problem. This is the very reason why they emphasize educational programs, model projects, and working with trade associations and other types of local organizations. Even then, the task is a formidable one, indeed, and implementations of the programs will pose considerable difficulty.

Another closely related problem is that many merchants simply are indifferent to the government measures to improve the efficiency of distribution. Some are too preoccupied in attempting to make a meager daily living, while others, assured of a reasonably satisfactory standard of living, are not motivated to innovate. Indeed, the government has not been very successful in kindling among a large number of individualistic merchants a sense of urgency as to the need to take some action.

Finally, one of the most central factors in determining the success of the recommendations included in this report is the degree to which MITI can obtain cooperation from other Ministries in developing and implementing specific programs. The jurisdictions over the distribution sector are widely diffused among a number of government agencies, and each is attempting to develop its own sets of policies and programs. For example, food distribution comes under the jurisdiction of the Ministry of Agriculture. It is establishing its own set of policies and programs to improve a rather archaic food distribution system. These programs include the development of cold storage facilities, rationalization of a traditional central market system, and so on. Programs relating to transportation and logistics are under the jurisdiction of the Transportation Ministry, whereas road construction, urban and regional planning, and related activities are under the Ministry of Construction. The Economic Planning Agency, the MITI, the Fair

Trade Commission, and the Ministry of Welfare share responsibilities in the area of consumer protection. Above all, the Finance Ministry to a large measure controls the allocation of the national budget.

The report urges the cooperation of the various government agencies concerned with the problems of distribution. Clearly, mere exhortation to cooperate will not be sufficient. Typical of government agencies elsewhere, inter-Ministry rivalry is strong in the Japanese bureaucracy, each with a powerful vested interest. How to coordinate their activities in implementing the integrated programs of modernization and rationalization remains a very serious problem. In fact, the effectiveness of almost every phase depends, to an important degree, on this issue.

In summary, the recent efforts by the government to improve the efficiency of the distribution sector, though highly admirable, mark only a beginning. Thus far, they have had only limited impact. In judging the government programs, however, it is only fair to recognize the relative inexperience of the government in these matters as well as the inherent difficulties involved in formulating effective programs. Given these conditions, it is likely that viable policies will be formed through a series of groping experiments rather than through a well-thought-out and systematic approach. It is highly significant to note, however, that when the need for modernization of the distribution sector became apparent, the government stepped in to assume an active role in this field to encourage, supplement, and coordinate the efforts that are made by the private sector. The characteristically pragmatic and close cooperative approach between the public and private sectors has again merged in the solution of one of the most serious national problems in contemporary Japan.

# 8

# Some Tentative Observations

Broadly conceived, marketing is a process designed to satisfy certain basic human needs. Its functions are far more than a simplistic mechanical process of distributing goods and services from producers to consumers. It is a basic component of social systems in all but the most primitive societies. As such, marketing is deeply imbedded in the social system. This rather broad conceptualization of marketing has several important implications, of which the following are particularly noteworthy. First, although the marketing system seeks to satisfy basically the same human needs in various societies, the manner in which it performs its task varies widely, and the pattern is determined, to a large measure, by the environment in which the system operates. Second, the marketing system, in order to remain as an effective socioeconomic institution, must maintain its viability in terms of the environment and must be responsive to environmental changes, adapting to meet the different needs created by new environmental developments. Third, although the marketing system in a society is shaped by other institutions in that society, the influence is by no means one-sided. As a dynamic institution, the marketing system is capable of generating changes on its own, which in turn will have significant impact on the entire society.

This study has sought to examine empirically in the Japanese context the concepts that just have been postulated. Having examined in some detail each of the major aspects of the rapidly changing Japanese marketing system, in this chapter we shall attempt (1) to summarize major findings of this study, (2) to offer some intriguing but tentative observations concerning the behavior of a marketing system in a very dynamic environment, and (3) to suggest possible patterns of development that the Japanese marketing system is likely to follow in the foreseeable future.

## Summary of Research Findings

Having examined salient characteristics of the nation's traditional distribution structure, we have sought to identify major environmental changes that are placing serious strains on the contemporary Japanese marketing system. The most basic and significant environmental change is the nation's sudden entry into a mass consumption economy created by the interacting forces of postwar social reforms and dynamic economic growth. As one of the most far-reaching consequences of this development, we have witnessed in postwar Japan the rapid rise of a truly viable middle class. In fact, contemporary Japan can be characterized as a middle-class-dominated society. Consumer orientation and life style, as we have seen, have undergone considerable change during the last decade and a half.

The manufacturing sector aggressively sought opportunities in this rapidly growing consumer market. Particularly significant was the entry of large-scale manufacturing firms into the consumer market, leading to the development of broad consumer industries employing mass production techniques. This has resulted in a tremendous increase in the output of consumer goods. The very aggressive efforts of large manufacturers to introduce new products has widened substantially the range of products that are available to an average consumer. Other environmental changes impinging directly on the nation's marketing system included a growing labor shortage and an accompanying rise in the wage level; the prospect of intensifying foreign competition; and significant technological advancement in the areas of transportation, storage, and information handling.

In light of these new environmental developments, a number of significant changes have taken place in the Japanese marketing system during the past decade and a half. We shall summarize them briefly. Departing radically from the prewar pattern, the large manufacturers of consumer goods have become cognizant of the importance of marketing as a key business function. They have made a series of organizational realignments to give increasingly greater weight to marketing functions and to sharpen their marketing capabilities. They now recognize the need for marketing research, and most large consumer goods manufacturers rely extensively on marketing research to guide their decisions. These manufacturers now make large financial commitments to advertising and sales promotion. Also large consumer goods manufacturers in certain industries have emerged as captains of the channels of distribution by successfully creating a vertically coordinated and controlled system.

The environmental changes we discussed earlier and the rise of marketing-oriented manufacturers have had significant impact on marketing intermediaries. But, of course, considerable differences are found in the manner in which different elements in the distribution sector have perceived the changing environment and how they are attempting to adapt to it. In terms of the response patterns, they can be broadly categorized into three basic groups. The first category is represented by those that are either incapable of comprehending or unwilling to recognize implications of the rapidly changing environment. This group consists of a relatively large segment of very small wholesalers and retailers. The second group is made up of new types of marketing institutions, particularly mass merchandising firms, that have recently emerged. While these firms are relatively few numerically, they are highly visible, aggressive, and innovative elements in Japan's contemporary marketing scene. These mass merchandising firms literally have revolutionized Japan's traditional distribution structure. In a decade or so they have become a formidable force.

Between tradition-bound elements and the highly innovative new ones, there is a segment within the traditional sector that has not lost vitality but is developing defensive or counterstrategy to gain a new viability in the dynamically changing environment. Specific strategies pursued by these institutions differ, of course, among individual firms, and so does their effectiveness. New techniques include cooperative approaches among small retailers and wholesalers in the form of voluntary or cooperative chains; reassessment of the traditional role and redefinition of the functions of wholesalers; defensive strategies developed by department stores; and increasingly more active involvment of large trading firms in the mass merchandising field.

Also noteworthy is the fluidity that characterizes the more dynamic segments of the distribution system in Japan. Intercorporate ties among mass merchandising firms, through mergers, acquisitions, and cooperative relations of various types, are now being forged. Also, close ties between the mass merchandising firms and large trading firms are swiftly evolving. We are also witnessing groups such as banks, real estate developers, life insurance companies, and others entering the distribution field, as is well evidenced in the development of shopping centers. Another area that is highly fluid encompasses the shifting power relationships in the distribution sector. Large-scale consumer goods manufacturers in a number of major product lines have recently emerged as captains of the channel. Rapidly growing mass merchandising firms, however, are challenging the preeminence of large manufacturers in this area; the struggle for leadership between these two powerful elements is already evident.

Another major development on the Japanese marketing scene is the very rapid growth of consumer financing, particularly in the form of installment credit. As we have seen, the use of installment credit is now widely diffused among various income and occupational groups. It has successfully overcome the negative image traditionally associated with it and has become an important marketing tool. It has contributed significantly to the wide diffusion of consumer durables. We also are witnessing the rapid growth of the use of credit cards in Japan.

Having analyzed dynamic changes that are taking place in the nation's distribution system, we then examined the increasingly active role now being played by the government in the modernization of the distribution sector. Despite the fact that the government has been a dominant force in Japanese business during the past century, it had until recently all but neglected the distribution sector. Government policy characteristically had been geared to the large strategic industries and was production-oriented. During the 1950s the government did develop several major programs to assist small marketing intermediaries, but they were formulated as a part of the government program for the protection of small-scale enterprises of all kinds.

Then the government began to show an increasing concern for modernization of the distribution sector. It developed a number of specific measures in the early 1960s to promote rationalization of small marketing intermediaries, but they were formulated as a ever, these programs were largely piecemeal; a coordinated approach was conspicuously absent. Only in recent years did the government begin to recognize the need for the systematic development of well-coordinated policies for the modernization of the distribution sector. As we have seen, the programs are still in the formative stage. There are reasons to suspect, however, that government programs to assist the modernization of the distribution sector, though their objectives are laudable, may not enjoy the same degree of success that characterized programs designed to guide and assist strategic manufacturing industries dominated by a small number of giant firms.

## Some Generalizations about Current Innovative Processes

Examination of the Japanese marketing system has illuminated several intriguing aspects of its adaptive processes in the very dynamic and rapidly changing environment. Let us now consider them.

First, the Japanese case clearly demonstrates the dynamics of a marketing system. We have noted that the Japanese marketing system traditionally had lagged behind the nation's economic development and had been characterized as a backward element of the Japanese economy. Clearly, however, even this seemingly conservative and tradition-bound marketing system had a latent capacity for innovation. It has been able to respond to rapid environmental changes. True, the adaptive process has not been free from serious tensions and strains; but within a rather short period of time the system, as we have seen, has responded to the changing environment. Not only have a number of new marketing concepts, techniques, and institutions been successfully introduced, but at least certain elements in the traditional institutions, whose survival was threatened by these changes, have lost little time in developing effective counterstrategies to maintain their functional viability in the changing environment.

Also significant is the fact that these innovations have been so rapidly accepted and widely diffused. It must be remembered that these concepts differed radically from the traditional approaches, yet they were introduced and promoted initially by literally a handful of entrepreneurs with limited resources. This is a rather dramatic illustration of the dynamics of social change, in which strong latent needs simply thrust forward when appropriate institutional mechanisms were introduced.

The history of Japan's economic development during the past century has demonstrated that the Japanese social system possesses an enormous capacity to initiate and sustain rather dynamic changes with a minimum of disruptive effect. Apparently, being a part of this dynamic social system, the marketing system also possessed this latent capacity to adapt to rapid environmental changes. The experience of the past decade clearly indicates that the Japanese marketing system is flexible enough to allow changes and accommodate innovative forces.

Second, it is noteworthy in the case of Japan that, at least initially, changes in the marketing system have come as a result of the system's response to environmental changes. In other words, the marketing system itself was not the initiating force in triggering environmental changes, but once the changes in the marketing system were initiated, they in turn began to exert profound influence on the environment. Out of this began a process of interaction between the marketing system and the environment, which accelerated the very environmental changes that had originally caused the marketing system to respond. The cause-and-effect relationship was clear in the initial stage, but the pattern emerging subsequently was that of two forces vigorously interacting and reinforcing each other. Closely related to the foregoing is the presence of a time lag in response patterns between the manufacturing and distribution sectors. Manufacturers, particularly large consumer goods manufacturers, were the first to recognize the implications of the growing mass consumption market and develop appropriate strategies to capitalize on it.

Third, the innovations in the Japanese marketing system came as a result of groping experiments of enterprising entrepreneurs in both the manufacturing and distribution sectors who saw profitable opportunities for innovation in the traditional system in the rapidly changing environment. These innovations did not come about as a result of organized and systematic plans that were well thought out in advance. They were uncoordinated trial-and-error experiments.

Fourth, the Japanese case dramatically illustrates the importance of cultural borrowings in the marketing field. True, the marketing innovations we have examined throughout this book have been introduced by the Japanese themselves, and with few exceptions foreign firms have played no direct role. Nevertheless, it is important to point out that the foreign, particularly American, influence has indeed been profound in shaping the pattern of innovations in the Japanese marketing system. American marketing literature has been read widely by the Japanese. Much American literature on marketing is translated into Japanese with a minimum time lag and, hence, is widely available almost immediately. Large manufacturers of consumer goods have looked to their American counterparts in designing their marketing organizations, policies, and strategies. Marketing executives of most of these large consumer goods manufacturers have come to the United States to observe American marketing practices personally.

The American influence has been even more profound on those entrepreneurs who successfully have introduced mass merchandising retail institutions into Japan. They have carefully studied the American pattern and have drawn heavily from the American experience. Most of them continue to keep up with the latest developments in the United States through extensive reading of American literature and regular visits. In fact, for a number of entrepreneurs their first trip to the United States marked a turning point in their careers, providing fresh ideas and insights, which they capitalized on after their return. Thus, in the Japanese case, we see a marketing system serving as an agent of cross-cultural transmission of ideas and practices.

Although the American model undeniably has had an enormous influence in shaping the patterns of innovation in the Japanese marketing system, it should be clearly noted that the process required far more than simple copying. And even though environmental differences between the two nations have been gradually narrowing, they are still substantial, requiring considerable modification if American concepts are to be successful. The entrepreneurs have introduced American techniques, concepts, and institutions selectively, and they have been largely successful in adapting them to fit the needs of the Japanese environment. Surely the presence of the American model has simplified the task, but they do deserve full credit for identifying the need for innovation in the rapidly changing environment, seeking appropriate concepts, modifying them to fit the Japanese condition, and finally successfully implementing them. The fact that these enterprising entrepreneurs have drawn heavily upon American experience should in no way discredit or discount their valuable contributions.

It is highly relevant to note here that the pattern followed by these marketing innovators is quite consistent with the Japanese tradition and is closely parallel to the strategy pursued in the earlier days of Japan's industrialization slightly more than a century ago. While emerging from the feudal past the leadership, intensely committed to Japan's industrialization and modernization, eagerly turned to the West for advanced technology as well as for a framework for social and political reform. The ruling elite, after some groping experiments, soon became highly selective in borrowing Western methods and ideas and developed a capacity to fit them to the environment and needs of Japanese society. Moreover, while extensively borrowing from the West, they successfully kept foreign dominance and control to a minimum. Initiative and leadership in the innovative process remained in the hands of the Japanese themselves. The prevailing spirit was aptly expressed in a popular slogan of the era, "*Wakon Yosai*"—"Japanese spirit and Western technology."

Japan followed a similar strategy in rebuilding her industrial base in the post-World War II period and in achieving her rapid economic growth in the subsequent years. Once again, a similar pattern is being followed in the modernization of the marketing system. The circumstances are different and so are the objectives to be achieved and the individuals involved, but the pattern is the same blending of Western technology, broadly conceived, and the Japanese spirit and ingenuity. Clearly, the Japanese are following a time-tested formula for their marketing modernization.

Finally, it is significant to note that the postwar marketing innovations—particularly the introduction of mass merchandising concepts, institutions, and technologies—have been undertaken by a rather small number of enterprising innovators. Literally a handful of men were responsible for triggering "*Ryutsu Kakumei*," or the "distribution revolution." Although the individual backgrounds and origins of these innovators differ, many of them share a number of common personal characteristics. Let us consider their salient traits.

First, the majority of the innovative merchants responsible for the introduction of mass merchandising concepts have come from outside the established power structure in the traditional distribution system. They have emerged from relative obscurity. They did not come from large prestigious department stores, well-known specialty stores, or large trading companies, despite the fact that they all had been familiar with recent developments in the American marketing scene. The majority of the innovators came from the traditional small-scale retailing sector. For a variety of reasons, these men were able to see the implications of rather significant changes that were taking place in the environment. In the innovative process, having little to lose, these men were willing to take high risks. To them, the potential benefits of innovation far outweighed the possible loss associated with failure.

Closely related to the foregoing is the fact that most of these retail entrepreneurs did not come from the elite of Japanese society. Their educational background, an all-important determinant of social status in contemporary Japan, varies widely. Some had only a minimum of education, while others had college degrees. With few exceptions, even those with college degrees did not graduate from one of the half-dozen highly esteemed universities. The second widely shared characteristic is that they are relatively young; many are in their thirties and forties. Also, in many cases their lives were significantly affected by World War II and events that took place in the immediate postwar period. The war and its aftermath disrupted their education and their career plans and aspirations, forcing them to change their career goals and ambitions,

The third common feature is that many of the innovators have been highly flexible and pragmatic in their attitudes. They have been very methodical in their approaches and deliberate in their choices. As might be expected, they have shown little attachment to tradition and no hesitation to change, if such change is perceived to be profitable. Finally, these men show a strong emotional commitment to the concepts they espouse. The mass merchandising concept to many of them is far more than a simple marketing technique. To them, it is a philosophy of business or even a way of life. In fact, many of these men propagate their newly espoused merchandising concepts with evangelical fervor.

Examination of the innovative process of the contemporary Japanese marketing system is incomplete without considering whether or not the emerging system is becoming increasingly similar to patterns found in other mass consumption societies, particularly in the United States. This question is a highly significant one, since it has considerable relevance to the "stages of development" concept in marketing, as proposed by a number of marketing scholars. In brief, this theory postulates that there exist discernible levels of development in marketing to which each marketing system can be assigned, and within each stage there are clearly identifiable similarities. This theory also implies that marketing in a given society evolves in a somewhat orderly fashion through these stages.

As we have seen throughout this book, with Japan's entry into the mass consumption economy the marketing system has been undergoing significant changes. These changes include the following:

1. Emergence of marketing-oriented large manufacturing firms, particularly those specializing in consumer products.
2. Greater importance attached to marketing research and demand-creation activities.
3. Rapid growth and diffusion of mass merchandising retail institutions.
4. Attempts by traditional wholesale and retail institutions to adopt counterstrategy to regain their functional viability.
5. Dynamic and shifting power relationships among various elements in the distribution structure.
6. Significant growth of consumer financing, particularly installment credit.

Review of these developments leads one to conclude that, as it evolves to meet the demands of a rapidly growing mass consumption society, the Japanese marketing system is becoming increasingly similar to that of the United States. Thus, to the extent that these characteristics are emerging, the Japanese experience tends to confirm the "stages of development" concept or the "convergence" theory.

The Japanese marketing system no doubt is becoming increasingly similar to its American counterpart in a number of important aspects, and this development has not been independent or accidental. On the contrary, the "demonstration effect" of the American system has been most profound. As we have repeatedly observed throughout this book, those seeking innovations for the Japanese marketing system have made conscious efforts to draw from American experience. It is extremely interesting to note that progressive Japanese marketing executives and innovative merchants believe intuitively that, with a certain time lag, the Japanese marketing system will develop along the lines of the American system. They share a view that present developments in the American marketing system will be a good precursor of future patterns of the Japanese system. They are most anxious to identify those concepts, institutions, and techniques that may be effectively adapted to the Japanese economy.

Thus the convergence now taking place between the Japanese and American marketing systems is not an independent development. Rather, it should be viewed as a case of cross-cultural diffusion. In the contemporary world in which barriers to international communication have been significantly reduced, it would be unrealistic to expect that major innovations in a marketing system can be totally indigenous to a particular society. Especially in mass consumption economies, the American experience has been so dramatic that its influence is likely to be very pervasive.

### Impact of Marketing Innovations on the Society

Earlier in this chapter we reemphasized that the innovative changes in the Japanese marketing system originally came about as a response to sweeping environmental changes, but once the innovations in the marketing system occurred, they, in turn, began to exert a powerful influence on the society. Throughout this book we have alluded to the forceful impact of these changes in the marketing system on the society as a whole. We shall now briefly expand upon this aspect.

First, the new marketing policies pursued aggressively by large manufacturers of consumer goods in response to the burgeoning consumer market have contributed much in accelerating the growth of that market. The introduction of the mass production system in consumer industries has resulted in considerable cost saving in the production of these goods. Because of intense competitive pressure, much of the cost reduction thus achieved has been passed on to consumers in the form of lower prices. This fact has been particularly significant in bringing heretofore prohibitively expensive consumer durables within the reach of an average consumer. The widespread ownership of consumer durables, which has important social implications, has been promoted further by the rapid growth of installment credit, in the development of which large manufacturers of consumer durables have played an important role.

Large manufacturers have also undertaken extensive product development in the consumer field. In this, they have served as an effective agent of international technological transfer. To fill the technological gap in consumer industries, large Japanese manufacturing firms have searched for advanced technology in the

United States and Europe and have adapted it to meet the needs and tastes of Japanese consumers. Large manufacturing firms have also made extensive market development efforts to persuade consumers of the utility of these products. These manufacturers' efforts certainly have contributed to the enrichment of the material well-being of average consumers and have helped bring about important changes in their life style.

Aggressive promotional efforts undertaken by large consumer goods manufacturers have also had profound impact on shaping the consumer mentality. Extensive mass-media advertising has contributed much toward the rapid diffusion of a new life style, raising the consumer's aspirations for material well-being and promoting middle-class values and orientations. Extensive use of mass-media advertising by large manufacturers has facilitated the development of the mass media, which, of course, have had rather profound impact on the economic and political development in contemporary Japan.

Rapidly growing mass merchandising firms have also made important contributions in promoting social change. Mass merchandising institutions have offered consumers radically different alternatives to the merchandising approach followed by the traditional retail institutions. They have provided the masses with a viable institutional mechanism whereby they can better satisfy their rapidly rising aspirations for material goods. The introduction of mass merchandising methods has also improved the efficiency of the distribution system.

In addition, these newly emerging mass merchandising firms have provided a rather significant fresh outlet for entrepreneurial talents as well as new employment opportunities for a substantial number of individuals, leading to greater social mobility. This has been an extremely important contribution because, traditionally, opportunities for managerial careers within major industrial and financial corporations and government service have been closely restricted in Japan. The elite in the government service and large industrial or financial organizations customarily have been recruited from among graduates of half a dozen leading universities. Those who do not have a degree from the right university, let alone those without college degrees, have been generally excluded from entry into these organizations. Even if they were hired, they had only limited opportunities for career advancement. Although this practice has been undergoing a gradual change, the traditional pattern is still rather pervasive. Mass merchandising institutions have provided an entirely new and very attractive alternative of managerial careers for persons who had been all but denied opportunities in large public or private bureaucratic organizations.

The mass merchandising firms, as we have seen earlier, now actively recruit college graduates to their managerial ranks. These stores hold little appeal to graduates of the leading universities, who still prefer to seek secure and promising careers with government bureaus or large industrial or financial institutions. These men typically are not interested in retailing as a career. The only retailing career they would even consider is employment with prestigious department stores. In contrast, graduates of less prominent universities, and those with only a high school education, find career opportunities in mass merchandising highly attractive. It is among these students that large mass merchandising firms have been recruiting their potential managers.

It is interesting that personnel practices of rapidly growing mass merchandising firms offer further contrast to those typically followed by large industrial or financial concerns. The latter, in recruiting their personnel, have tended to seek out bright but stable and conforming young men with the right credentials and background. On the other hand, newly emerging mass merchandising firms tend to seek out more individualistic and aggressive men. Also, despite security and prestige, career advancement in large industrial firms has been a slow and tedious process, largely based on one's educational background and seniority. In contrast, mass merchandising firms place considerably greater emphasis on ability and demonstrated performance in their personnel reward system. Because of their very rapid growth and expansions during the past decade, mass merchandising firms have been able to promote their managers considerably more rapidly than have established large enterprises. It is not unusual to find men in their thirties in key managerial positions in mass merchandising firms. Although employment with such firms may be quite demanding, an increasing number of college graduates are now being attracted to mass merchandising firms because of the opportunities they offer.

**Future Outlook**

Given the dynamism that characterizes the Japanese business environment, an attempt to predict future developments in the marketing system is indeed hazardous. We shall nevertheless attempt to identify several salient patterns that are likely to continue or emerge, and predict challenges that each major element in the distribution system is likely to face in the near future.

Looking first at the nature of the market, we have every reason to believe that the trends we noted in Chapter 2 are likely to continue. At least for the foreseeable future, the GNP is likely to continue to grow at a rapid rate. A recent forecast of the Japanese economy prepared by the prestigious Japan Economic Research Center reveals that the nation's GNP will experience roughly 70 percent real growth during the first half of the decade of the 1970s. By 1975 it is projected that Japan's GNP will reach $418 billion, roughly equivalent to the combined GNP of the four major European countries (England, West Germany, France, and Italy) in 1968. Further details are presented in Table 8.1. According to this forecast, Japan's GNP in 1975 will be almost one-third of the projected GNP of the United States for that year and will be even greater than the *combined* projected GNP of West Germany and France for the same year. This is indeed amazing, since only in 1968 did Japan surpass West Germany's GNP.

A longer-term forecast of the Japanese economy has also been prepared by the same institution; a few salient figures are presented in Tables 8.2 and 8.3. One of the most significant aspects of this

TABLE 8.1

PROJECTED GNP FOR SELECTED COUNTRIES, 1969–1975

(in billions of current dollars)

| Year | Japan | U.S.A. | West Germany | France | England | E.E.C. |
|------|-------|--------|--------------|--------|---------|--------|
| 1969 | 166.4 | 920.8 | 141.3 | 125.2 | 107.0 | 393.7 |
| 1970 | 193.1 | 985.3 | 150.5 | 134.6 | 112.9 | 424.6 |
| 1971 | 225.7 | 1,054.2 | 160.3 | 144.7 | 119.1 | 456.1 |
| 1972 | 262.9 | 1,128.0 | 170.7 | 155.6 | 125.7 | 490.0 |
| 1973 | 306.6 | 1,207.0 | 181.8 | 167.2 | 132.6 | 526.4 |
| 1974 | 357.8 | 1,291.5 | 193.6 | 179.8 | 139.9 | 565.7 |
| 1975 | 418.3 | 1,318.9 | 206.2 | 193.3 | 147.6 | 605.8 |

Source: The Japan Economic Research Center.

TABLE 8.2

LONG-TERM PROJECTION OF THE JAPANESE ECONOMY

| | 1967 | | 1975 | | 1980 | | 1985 | |
|---|---|---|---|---|---|---|---|---|
| | Value | Projected Average Annual Growth Rate (%) 1961–67 | Projected Value | Projected Average Annual Growth Rate (%) 1968–75 | Projected Value | Projected Average Annual Growth Rate (%) 1976–80 | Projected Value | Projected Average Annual Growth Rate (%) 1981–85 |
| Gross Domestic Product* | 40,235 | 10.4 | 102,300 | 12.4 | 176,580 | 11.0 | 297,720 | 11.0 |
| The Primary Sector* | 3,673 | 3.0 | 4,005 | 1.1 | 4,448 | 2.1 | 4,915 | 2.0 |
| The Secondary and Tertiary Sectors* | 36,562 | 11.5 | 98,295 | 13.2 | 172,132 | 11.9 | 292,805 | 11.2 |
| Private Capital Investment | 7,126 | 9.4 | 21,685 | 14.9 | 34,454 | 9.7 | 56,709 | 10.5 |
| Index of Manufacturing Output (1965 = 100) | 136.0 | 12.1 | 371.1 | 13.4 | 655.7 | 12.1 | 1,121.3 | 11.3 |
| Per Capita Income ($) | 877 | 8.7 | 2,061 | 11.3 | 3,379 | 10.4 | 5,480 | 10.1 |
| Rate of Savings | 31.8 | – | 40.0 | – | 38.6 | – | 37.2 | – |
| Labor Force (10,000 persons) | 4,930 | 1.5 | 5,408 | 1.2 | 5,624 | 0.8 | 5,834 | 0.7 |

*Values are in ¥ billion in 1965 prices.
Source: "Jishitsu 11–12% no Senzai Seichō Ryoku" ["11–12% Real Annual Growth Potentials"], *Nihon Keizai Shinbun* [*The Japan Economic Journal*], September 20, 1969, p. 10.

## TABLE 8.3

Projected Growth Rate (Value Added) by Major Industry

(index: 1965 = 100; ¥ billion in 1965 prices)

| | 1975 | | | 1980 | | | 1985 | | |
|---|---|---|---|---|---|---|---|---|---|
| | Index | Pro-jected Value | Average Annual Growth Rate (%) 1971–75 | Index | Pro-jected Value | Average Annual Growth Rate (%) 1976–80 | Index | Pro-jected Value | Average Annual Growth Rate (%) 1981–85 |
| *Value Added* | | | | | | | | | |
| Agriculture and Fishing | 143.3 | 4,005.0 | 1.8 | 159.1 | 4,448.0 | 2.1 | 175.8 | 4,915.9 | 2.0 |
| Construction | 425.4 | 7,932.9 | 14.3 | 742.6 | 13,848.0 | 11.8 | 1,310.8 | 24,443.8 | 12.1 |
| Tertiary Sector | 372.2 | 48,653.0 | 12.1 | 636.1 | 83,147.0 | 11.3 | 1,050.9 | 137,361.0 | 10.6 |
| *Value of Shipment* | | | | | | | | | |
| Fibers and Textiles | 253.6 | 5,516.8 | 8.4 | 383.0 | 8,331.8 | 8.6 | 584.0 | 12,704.3 | 8.8 |
| Chemicals | 371.8 | 9,434.8 | 14.5 | 709.5 | 18,004.3 | 13.8 | 1,336.5 | 33,915.0 | 13.5 |
| Iron and Steel | 379.8 | 8,308.1 | 11.9 | 650.0 | 14,218.8 | 10.0 | 1,115.2 | 24,395.0 | 11.4 |
| Machinery | 454.5 | 22,838.6 | 15.5 | 886.2 | 44,531.6 | 14.3 | 1,691.4 | 84,972.9 | 13.8 |

Source: "Jishitsu 11–12% no senzai Seichō ryoku" ["11–12% Real Annual Growth Potentials"], *Nihon Keizai Shinbun* [*The Japan Economic Journal*], September 20, 1969, p. 10.

projection and others is the rapid growth of per capita income. As shown in Table 8.2, per capita income of Japan will reach the current European level by 1975 (projected to be slightly over $2,000), and by 1980 it is projected to reach the current United States level. By 1985 Japan's per capita income ($5,480) will reach an amount only slightly below the projected United States per capita income for that year. Thus, by 1985, if these projections prove correct, Japan will rank second only to the United States, even in terms of per capita income. Like any long-term forecast, this one is by no means infallible and is subject to many assumptions and conditions, but it does indicate the potentials of the Japanese economy.

The population is projected to increase to 108.6 million and 116.5 million by 1975 and 1980, respectively. The composition of the population by age group also will undergo some change. Particularly noteworthy is that by 1975 persons over 60 years of age will account for 14 percent of the entire population (in contrast to 10 percent in 1967). The current trend toward decreasing family size is likely to continue. By 1975 it is expected that the average family size will be 3.5 (4.08 in 1965), and by 1980 it will decline further to 3.2. It is also projected that by 1975 wage earners will reach 70 percent of the total labor force.

The current trend toward urbanization will continue. It is projected that by 1975 over 75 percent of Japan's total population will live in cities, and half the nation's population will be concentrated in the narrow belt of the densely populated area stretching between Tokyo and Osaka.

Qualitative changes in consumers' value orientations will continue in the future, and there is every reason to believe that the middle-class orientation will receive even further emphasis. The areas that deserve particularly close attention will be the accelerating trend toward the increasing desire for material wants, Westernization of life style, growing family orientation (not the traditional but a modern variety), and increasing leisure time. These trends, acting individually and in concert, will result in complex interactions and generate pressures that conceivably could alter the life style and consumption patterns still further.

Marketing orientation among large consumer goods manufacturing firms shows every sign of continuing to grow. The impending capital liberalization program will encourage the entry of multinational corporations into Japan, further intensifying the already keen competition in the consumer market. Demand-creation by large manufacturers of consumer goods thus will become increasingly critical. These manufacturers will find that the consumer will become increasingly more demanding and discriminating. They must also be prepared for the growing countervailing power of rapidly emerging mass merchandising firms. In certain product lines, such as home appliances and processed foods, large manufacturers will likely experience a gradual erosion of their power over the channels of distribution.

To cope with these developments, the manufacturers of consumer goods will find it necessary to undertake further improvements and refinements in several critical areas. A greater emphasis should be placed on marketing research to assess increasingly affluent consumers' tastes and wants, which undoubtedly will become even more complex and diverse. The precise measurement and prediction of consumer behavior will become ever more difficult, requiring large consumer goods manufacturers to sharpen their marketing research skills. Even more critical is the need to relate research findings to the formulation of marketing strategies, policies, and programs. A rather wide gap is currently found, even among Japan's leading manufacturers of consumer goods, between marketing research and formulation of marketing strategies. Throughout this study it has been observed that detailed findings of rather elaborate and well-conceived research studies often did not receive the attention they deserved in the process of strategy formulation. Too often key marketing decisions are made primarily on an intuitive basis. The familiar problems of differences in outlook between line marketing managers and marketing research specialists are also vividly observed in major Japanese corporations.

Closely related to the foregoing point is the importance of establishing clear-cut marketing goals and formulating appropriate strategies to achieve these goals, through assigning proper weights to each element of the marketing mix and ensuring proper coordination among them. The greatest challenge in marketing facing Japanese manufacturing firms lies in these areas. There has been a strong tendency for Japanese marketing executives of large consumer goods manufacturers to be preoccupied with decisions of a tactical nature without devoting adequate attention to marketing strategy.

With regard to the distribution sector, the polarization that had begun earlier between the aggressive innovative firms and tradition-bound ones is likely to intensify. Of course, it is not likely that tradition-bound small-scale wholesalers and retailers will totally disappear from the scene. Given the structure of the Japanese distribution system, they will remain dominant at least numerically for some time. However, it is not difficult to predict that their importance will decline.

Mass merchandising institutions will continue to grow in size and number, and by the end of the 1970s they are likely to become the dominant retail institution in the nation's distribution system. While their future appears all but assured, they, too, will face several severe challenges. One is a question of management. A key to their continued growth is the degree to which the successful entrepreneurs can transform themselves and their immediate subordinates into an effective management team capable of managing a large, diversified enterprise. The second major challenge is that of growing competition among large mass merchandising firms themselves. We have just begun to witness this trend, and there is every reason to believe that it will continue. This trend undoubtedly will lead to mergers and acquisitions among some of these firms.

The third challenge lies in the area of diversification. In order to increase their size, mass merchandising firms are under great pressure to undertake active diversification programs. In so doing, they must answer such questions as: Should they, in fact, diversify? And if so, to what activities? Should they view their primary mission as that of mass merchandising or should they consider themselves in the broadly defined consumer service field? The answers to these questions will obviously vary among firms. What is critical, however, is that these decisions are made in a deliberate, well-thought-out manner. Closely related to the foregoing is whether it will be possible for them to achieve their rather ambitious growth objectives and still maintain their autonomy and independence from financial institutions and trading companies. The fourth question to be raised is whether or not they will trade up and thereby depart from the very mass merchandising concept that has made them successful. Will they make room for emergence of still newer types of institutions, essentially repeating·a rather common evolutionary pattern of retailing institutions in the United States?

Finally, another critical challenge facing innovative entrepreneurs is the need for a more refined approach in drawing from American experience. There has been a tendency, at least among some firms, to be preoccupied with importing the latest American developments. This is quite understandable, since these firms are anxious to gain even a temporary edge over competitors by being the first to adopt advanced American marketing techniques. This aggressiveness has been an important factor contributing to rapid introduction of innovations in certain aspects of Japan's marketing system.

This "latest development" syndrome, however, has not been without its problems. Overly anxious entrepreneurs have sometimes imported new concepts and techniques without adequately evaluating their appropriateness to the Japanese environment. They also have often neglected to examine American developments in historical perspective or to identify carefully why a particular concept has proved successful in the United States. Unlike in the past, in the light of growing competition the trial-and-error approach of drawing from the American model will be less acceptable.

Progressive elements among the more traditional distribution establishments will place further emphasis on developing strategies to maintain their viability, or even to wrestle the initiative away from the newly emerged mass merchandising firms. Major trading companies with abundant financial and managerial resources undoubtedly will become a formidable force in the mass merchandising field. Judging from their orientation, they are likely to place their primary emphasis on developing close ties with existing mass merchandising chains through supplying merchandise, undertaking joint merchandising developments, extending loans for expansion, and leasing physical facilities, including fully equipped stores.

Department stores, another major traditional retail institution, are likely to encounter very intense competitive struggles. In particular, smaller department stores will face a very serious test for survival in the future. During the next decade we may well witness substantial restructuring of the department store industry. Some of the smaller ones undoubtedly will be forced to change their *modus operandi*. Some may decide to enter into the mass merchandising field. A number of them may be absorbed by larger department stores or mass merchandising firms. Mergers among smaller department stores will be a distinct possibility.

Consumer financing is likely to grow at even an accelerating rate. According to one projection, the outstanding balance of installment credit will reach over ¥982 billion by 1975. In addition, other types of consumer financing, particularly the use of credit cards, will continue to increase.

It is quite likely that the government will play an increasingly active role in the attempt to modernize the Japanese distribution sector. For the reasons noted earlier, it is highly questionable, however, whether the government efforts in this direction will be truly meaningful and effective. One area that deserves close government attention is the whole issue of consumerism. Various Ministries and commissions have begun to show some concern for consumer protection and education, but the current measures are still fragmented and inadequate. With the emergence of a mass consumer market, the government's role in developing strong and well-coordinated consumer programs will become extremely critical.

Prediction of future developments in the Japanese marketing system is indeed incomplete without examination of one additional major issue: the possible entry of foreign, particularly American, large-scale retail institutions into the Japanese market. This possibility is of great concern to those engaged in marketing in Japan. This concern is quite understandable because of the potential threat that these firms would pose to the still comparatively small mass merchandising firms in Japan. Without question, Japan presents an attractive market to large American mass merchandising firms for a number of reasons.

First, Japan is now the second largest mass market in the world. Nearly 100 million consumers with rapidly growing discretionary income are concentrated in a total land mass smaller than the state of California. Moreover, the high population density makes it possible for American mass merchandising firms to maximize their impact. To reach this highly concentrated market, Japan also offers one of the best-developed networks of mass communication media that can be readily mobilized for promotional purposes.

Second, the Japanese consumer market is becoming increasingly similar to the American market. American mass merchandising firms can draw from their vast knowledge gained from successfully operating in the largest mass consumer market in the world. Since Japanese mass merchandising firms are drawing heavily from the American model, this would give American firms considerable advantage in dealing with the Japanese consumer.

Third, local procurement of merchandise presents no problem in Japan. It is axiomatic that for mass merchandising concepts to succeed they must be supported by a mass production system. The Sears experience in Mexico demonstrates how essential the presence of a mass production system is to the success of American-type mass merchandising firms.[1] In Japan, with an extensive mass production system, procurement of merchandise presents no problem. In fact, a number of major American retailing firms already maintain their buying offices in Japan to procure merchandise for their stores in the United States.

To offset these attractive aspects, American firms are likely to encounter several major problems in their attempt to enter Japan. First, they will face keen competition from local mass merchandising firms. By the time American mass merchandising firms are allowed to enter Japan, Japanese firms will have become sufficiently large and powerful that they will be a formidable competitive force. The situation in Japan, then, will be quite different from that prevailing in such countries as Mexico, Brazil, and Peru, where Sears and other American mass merchandising firms have enjoyed considerable success. In these countries, no local mass merchandising firms of any significance had existed when the American firms first entered these markets.

Second, there are likely to be a number of serious constraints in the Japanese business environment which will reduce the American firms' competitive advantages. As we have seen, the distribution channels are still quite complex and so are the trade practices, not to mention some basic differences in the ways of doing business in Japan.

Third, if American retailing firms should enjoy any degree of success, they may well become subject to retaliatory pressures from the local business community. There is already a precedent for this. An organized group of retailers successfully blocked the entry of Safeway of the United States into Japan in the early 1960s. Retail merchants, if properly organized, could become a potent force with considerable political influence.

Finally, the government has singled out the distribution sector as one of the most crucial areas in formulating its policy of capital liberalization, and the government is likely to keep its watchful eyes on American mass merchandising firms in Japan. If the government perceives that American firms pose a sufficient threat to the welfare of the Japanese retailers, it will be quite likely to step in

---

[1] Richardson Wood and Virginia Keyser, *Sears, Roebuck de Mexico, S.A.* (Washington, D.C.; National Planning Association, 1953) pp. 10–15.

through informal administrative guidance to restrain their competitive strength.

For these reasons and others, despite the presence of promising market opportunities and seemingly effective competitive advantages, it will by no means be easy for large American mass merchandising firms to enter successfully into Japan and to attain a viable position in that market. Moreover, even after the present capital liberalization program is completed, it is likely that the maximum foreign ownership to be allowed in this field will be 50 percent. Thus, for legal as well as practical reasons, joint ventures with Japanese partners may well be the only feasible way for American retail firms to enter the Japanese market.

As potential partners in joint ventures, two types of Japanese institutions are often mentioned. One is the trading company. Large trading companies have participated in a number of international joint ventures, and with their extensive international contacts and knowledge of the domestic market they will be attractive candidates for joint ventures. Safeway, for example, sought to enter Japan through a joint venture with Sumitomo Trading Company. With growing interest in the mass merchandising field, such an arrangement may appeal to trading companies as well. There is, however, one important consideration; that is, major trading companies may be sufficiently committed to existing Japanese mass merchandising institutions through a variety of relationships as described earlier that they may not wish to take the serious risk of being alienated from them by entering into joint ventures with foreign firms.

The other potential partners for joint ventures are those small mass merchandising firms whose existence is being threatened by intensifying competitive pressure. These marginal mass merchandising firms likely will face a real test of survival in the near future and may well consider seriously the prospect of entering into joint ventures with American firms. Of course, three-way joint ventures among American mass merchandising firms, Japanese retailing firms, and trading companies are also within the realm of possibility.

Although the strength of American mass merchandising firms should not be underestimated, sudden large-scale entry of American mass merchandising firms into Japan, immediately upon completion of the present round of capital liberalization, would be unlikely. Perhaps a more immediate threat to the Japanese distribution sector is possible entry of franchised chains of specialty stores. Franchise operations in certain types of prepared foods, drive-ins, and restaurants have already shown a considerable interest in the Japanese market, and the very nature of franchise operations makes it possible to overcome, at least in part, the local resistance that is likely to be associated with entry of mass merchandising firms. Since franchise operations are relatively small in scale and serve a rather limited segment of the market, their impact on competitors is likely to be minor, and as a result they may experience less difficulty in positioning themselves in the Japanese market.

### Concluding Remarks

As we have seen, marketing penetrates the basic fabric of a society, and it can be considered an important mechanism in providing for social change. It is indeed through the marketing system that consumers articulate some of their very basic values. Therefore, the goals, ethics, and welfare of the marketing system are inseparable from the goals, aspirations, and welfare of the society at large. As an active adaptive agent of the society, the marketing system can have a profound influence in shaping the values of the society. The role of the marketing system is particularly influential in affluent mass consumption societies. In fact, in these societies the marketing system can be a major force in shaping the values and quality of life of the entire society.

The research upon which this book is based addressed itself to the dynamic adaptive behavior of Japan's marketing system, one of the most remarkable but often neglected aspects of the nation's postwar economic growth. Notwithstanding the limitations of this research, it is hoped that the detailed investigation of a marketing system in a highly dynamic environmental setting has illuminated some of the basic issues we have set out to examine. These issues are far from being resolved; on the contrary, the study undoubtedly has raised questions more than it has provided definitive answers.

It is appropriate to conclude this summary by noting that many of the problems being faced by Japanese marketers are not unique to Japan; most of them will be commonly faced by others in similar environments. Viewing their problems as uniquely Japanese will limit the horizon of the Japanese marketers. Indeed, the challenge of evolving a marketing system that is viable in an affluent mass consumption society rests squarely on those engaged in marketing in any highly developed mass consumption society, including Japan. It is the author's earnest wish that all those concerned with marketing will join him in the further exploration and solution of these exciting issues.

# Bibliography

## Sources in English

### Books

Abegglen, James C. *The Japanese Factory: Aspects of Its Social Organization* (Glencoe, Ill.: The Free Press, 1958), 142 pp.

Allen, G. C. *Japan's Economic Expansion* (London: Oxford University Press, 1965), 296 pp.

Ayukawa, Iwao F. *A History of Labor in Modern Japan* (Honolulu: East-West Center Press, 1966) 406 pp.

Bartels, Robert (ed.). *Comparative Marketing: Wholesaling in Fifteen Countries* (Homewood, Ill.: Richard D. Irwin, Inc. 1963), 350 pp.

Bellah, Robert N. *Tokugawa Religion: The Values of Pre-Industrial Japan* (Glencoe, Ill.: The Free Press, 1957), 249 pp.

Belshaw, Cyril S. *Traditional Exchange and Modern Markets* (Englewood Cliffs, N.J.: Prentice-Hall, Inc., 1965), 192 pp.

Benedict, Ruth. *The Chrysanthemum and the Sword: Patterns of Japanese Culture* (Boston: Houghton Mifflin Company, 1946), 324 pp.

Bisson, T. A. *Zaibatsu Dissolution in Japan* (Berkeley: University of California Press, 1954) 314 pp.

Boddewyn, J. *Comparative Management and Marketing* (Glenview, Ill.: Scott, Foresman & Company, 1969), 302 pp.

Cook, Alice. *Japanese Trade Unionism* (New York: New York State School of Industrial Relations, Cornell University, 1965), 216 pp.

De Bary, William T. *Sources of Japanese Tradition* (New York: Columbia University Press, 1964), 202 pp.

Dore, R. P. (ed.). *Aspects of Social Change in Modern Japan* (Princeton, N.J.: Princeton University Press, 1968), 474 pp.

———*City Life in Japan: A Study of a Tokyo Ward* (Berkeley and

Los Angeles: University of California Press, 1958), 472 pp.

Fayerweather, John. *International Marketing* (Englewood Cliffs, N.J.: Prentice-Hall, Inc., 1965), 120 pp.

Goldman, Marshall J. *Soviet Marketing: Distribution in a Controlled Economy* (New York: The Free Press of Glencoe, 1963), 261 pp.

Hagen, Everett. *On Theory of Social Change* (Homewood, Ill.: Dorsey Press, 1962), 557 pp.

Hall, John Whitney, and Richard K. Beardsley. *Twelve Doors to Japan* (New York: McGraw-Hill Book Company, 1965), 649 pp.

Katona, George. *The Mass Consumption Society* (New York: McGraw-Hill Book Company, 1964), 343 pp.

Kindleberger, Charles P. *Economic Development* (New York: McGraw-Hill Book Company, 1965), 425 pp.

Levine, Solomon B. *Industrial Relations in Postwar Japan* (Urbana, Ill.: University of Illinois Press, 1958), 200 pp.

Lockwood, William W. *The Economic Development of Japan: Growth and Structural Change, 1868–1938* (Princeton, N.J.: Princeton University Press, 1954), 603 pp.

————(ed.). *The State and Economic Enterprise in Japan* (Princeton, N.J.: Princeton University Press, 1965), 753 pp.

Maki, John M. *Government and Politics in Japan: The Road to Democracy* (New York: Frederick A. Praeger, 1961), 275 pp.

Marshall, Byron K. *Capitalism and Nationalism in Prewar Japan: The Ideology of the Business Elite* (Stanford, Calif.: Stanford University Press, 1967), 163 pp.

Moyer, Reed, and Stanley C. Hollander (eds.). *Markets and Marketing in Developing Economies* (Homewood, Ill.: Richard D. Irwin, Inc., 1968), 264 pp.

Nakamura, Hajime. *Ways of Thinking of Eastern Peoples: India, China, Tibet and Japan* (Honolulu: East-West Center Press, 1964), 712 pp.

Nakayama, Ichiro. *Industrialization of Japan* (Honolulu: East-West Center Press, 1964), 73 pp.

Norman, E. Herbert. *Japan's Emergence as a Modern State: Political and Economic Problems of the Meiji Period* (New York: Institute of Pacific Relations, 1940), 254 pp.

Palamountain, Joseph C., Jr. *The Politics of Distribution* (Cambridge, Mass.: Harvard University Press, 1955), 257 pp.

Plath, David W. *The After Hours: Modern Japan and the Search for Enjoyment* (Berkeley and Los Angeles: University of California Press, 1964), 222 pp.

Reischauer, Edwin O. *The United States and Japan* (3rd ed.; Cambridge, Mass.: Harvard University Press, 1965) 396 pp.

Sansom, G. B. *Japan: A Short Cultural History* (New York: D. Appleton-Century, Inc., 1943), 554 pp.

Scalapino, Robert A. *Democracy and the Party Movement in Prewar Japan: The Failure of the First Attempt* (Berkeley: University of California Press, 1962), 471 pp.

Sheldon, Charles David. *The Rise of the Merchant Class in Tokugawa Japan, 1600–1868: An Introductory Survey* (Locust Valley, N.Y.: J. J. Augustin, Inc., 1958), 206 pp.

Smith, Thomas C. *Political Change and Industrial Development in Japan: Government Enterprise, 1868–1880* (Stanford, Calif.: Stanford University Press, 1955), 126 pp.

Vogel, Ezra F. *Japan's New Middle Class: The Salary Man and His Family in a Tokyo Suburb* (Berkeley and Los Angeles: University of California Press, 1963), 299 pp.

Wood, Richardson, and Virginia Keyser. *Sears, Roebuck de Mexico, S.A.* (Washington, D.C.: National Planning Association, 1953), 171 pp.

Yoshino, M. Y. *Japan's Managerial System: Tradition and Innovation* (Cambridge, Mass.: The M.I.T. Press, 1968), 292 pp.

*Articles*

Dore, R. P. "Mobility, Equality, and Individuation in Modern Japan," in R. P. Dore (ed.), *Aspects of Social Change in Modern Japan* (Princeton, N.J.: Princeton University Press, 1967), pp. 113–150.

Dowd, Laurence P. "Wholesale Marketing in Japan," *Journal of Marketing*, 23 (October 1959), 251–260.

Gleason, Alan H. "Economic Growth and Consumption in Japan," in William W. Lockwood (ed.). *The State and Economic Enterprise in Japan* (Princeton, N.J.: Princeton University Press, 1965, pp. 291–346.

Horie, Yasuzo. "Entrepreneurship in Meiji Japan," in William W. Lockwood (ed.), *The State and Economic Enterprise in Japan* (Princeton, N.J.: Princeton University Press, 1965), pp. 183–208.

Lockwood, William W. "Japan's 'New Capitalism,' " in William W. Lockwood (ed.), *The State and Economic Enterprise in Japan* (Princeton, N.J.: Princeton University Press, 1965), p. 447–522.

Nicosia, Francesco M., and Charles Y. Glock. "Marketing and Affluence: A Research Prospectus," in Robert L. King (ed.), *Marketing and the New Science of Planning* (Chicago: American Marketing Assoc., 1968), p. 561.

"Report of the Definition Committee." *Journal of Marketing*, 13 (October 1948), 209.

## Sources in Japanese

*Books*

Abe, Mikio. *Seicho Shohin* [*Growth Products*] (Tokyo: Nihon Keizai Shinbunsha, 1968), 214 pp.

Aoki, Hisao. *Ginko no Shohisha Kinyu* [*Consumer Financing by Banks*] (Tokyo: Toyo Keizai Shinpo Sha, 1964), 198 pp.

Arakawa, Yukichi. *Kouri Shogyo Kozoron* [*Theory of Retail Structure*] (Tokyo: Chikura Shobo, 1967), 480 pp.

————*Shogyo Kozo to Ryutsu Gorika* [*Commercial Structure and Rationalization*] (Tokyo: Chikura Shobo, 1967), 350 pp.

*Dentsu Kokoku Nenkan, 1969* [*The Dentsu Advertising Annual, 1969*] (Tokyo: Dentsu Advertising Agency, 1969) 650 pp.

Fukami, Giichi (ed.). *Marketing Koza: Hanbai Kinyu* [*Consumer Finance: Marketing Series*] (Tokyo: Yuhikaku, 1967), 309 pp.

————(ed.). *Marketing Koza: Ryutsu Mondai* [*Distribution Problems: Marketing Series*] (Tokyo: Yuhikaku, 1966), 420 pp.

————*Supermarket* (Tokyo: Chikura Shobo, 1967), 236 pp.

Hayashi, Shuji. *Ryutsu Kakumei* [*Revolution in Distribution*] (Tokyo: Chuokoransha, 1962), 206 pp.

————*Ryutsu Keizai no Kadai* [*Challenges in the Economics of Distribution*] (Tokyo: The Japan Productivity Center, 1968), 345 pp.

————, and Chikashi Nakanishi (eds.). *Gendai no Butteki Ryutsu* [*Physical Distribution in the Contemporary World*] (Tokyo: Nihon Keizai Shinbunsha, 1968), 376 pp.

Kamakura, Noboru. *Shoshia Loan* [*Consumer Loans*] (Tokyo: Chuokoronsha, 1966), 187 pp.

Kojima, Satohiro. *Korekara no Shohishazo* [*Profiles of Consumers in the Future*] (Tokyo: Diamond Publishing Co., 1966), 248 pp.

*Kokumin Seikatsu Tokei Nenpō, Showa 43 nen ban* [*Annual Statistics on National Life, 1968*] (Tokyo: Kokumin Seikatsu Kenkyūjo, 1969), 260 pp.

*Kokuminsei no Kenkyu, 1965* [*A Study of Japanese National Character, 1965*] (Tokyo: Tokei Suri Kenkyūjo, 1966), 116 pp.

Matsuki, Yozo (ed.). *Butsuryu Kakumei* [*Revolution in Physical Distribution*] (Tokyo: Nihon Noritsu Kyokai, 1969), 248 pp.

Mikami, Tomisaburo. *Shogyo Kakushin* [*Commercial Revolution*] (Tokyo: Chuo Keizaisha, 1967), 263 pp.

Minami, Hiroshi, and Mitsuru Inuta. *Shohi no Shiso* [*Consumption Ideology*] (Tokyo: Nihon Keizai Shinbunsha, 1967), 180 pp.

Miyamoto, Mataji. *Kinsei Shōnin Ishiki no Kenkyu* [*Studies in the Merchant Mentality of the Early Modern Period*] (Tokyo: Yuhikaku, 1941), 370 pp.

————*Nihon Shōgyō Shi* [*Commercial History of Japan*] (Tokyo: Ryuginsha, 1943), 382 pp.

Nihon Keiei Seisaku Gakkai (ed.). *Shohisha Kinyushu* [*Consumer Financing*] (Tokyo: Nihon Sōgō Shuppan Kiko, 1967), 350 pp.

Sakisaka, Masao (ed.). *Nihon Sangyo Zue* [*An Overview of Japanese Industries*] (Tokyo: Toyo Keizai Shinpo Sha, 1968), 182 pp.

Sato, Hajime, and Sueaki Takaoka. *Gendai no Hyakkaten* [*Department Stores in Contemporary Japan*] (Tokyo: Nihon Keizai Shinbunsha, 1970), 108 pp.

*Seikatsu Ishiki ni Kansuru Kenkyu* [*A Study of Views on Life*] (Tokyo: Kokumin Seikatsu Kenkyūjo, 1969), 262 pp.

Shizawa, Yoshio. *Voluntary Chains: Riron to Jissai* [*Voluntary Chains: Theory and Practice*] (Tokyo: Dobunkan, 1968), 526 pp.

*Shohisa Kinyu Jishi Jōkyō Ichiran* [*A Summary of Current Status of Consumer Financing*] (Tokyo: Zenkoku Ginko Kyokai Rengokai, 1968), 16 pp.

*Shohosha no Seikatsu Ishiki to Shohi Chochiku Kodo ni kansuru Kenkyu* [*A Study of Consumers' Attitudes Toward Consumption and Savings*] (Tokyo: Kokumin Seikatsu Kenkyūjo, 1967), 269 pp.

*Super Chain 100 Sha no Jittai Chosa* [*A Report on Operating Characteristics of 100 Chains*] (Tokyo: Nihon Sen-I-Kenkyūjo, 1969), 121 pp.

Tajima, Yoshihiro. *Nihon no Ryutsu Kakumei* [*Distribution Revolution in Japan*] (Tokyo: Nihon Noritsu Kyokai, 1962), 202 pp.

Takebayashi, Shotaro. *Shōgyō Keei no Kenkyu* [*Research on Management of Commercial Enterprises*] (Tokyo: Yuhikaku, 1955), 280 pp.

Tanimoto, Taniichi. *Daitoshi ni Okeru Butteki Ryutsu no Shomondai* [*Problems in Physical Distribution in Large Cities*] (Tokyo: Kotsu Nihonsha, 1969), 188 pp.

*Tokyo ni Okeru Supermarket no Genjo, Showa 42 nen* [*The Status of Supermarkets in Tokyo, Fiscal year 1967*] (Tokyo: The Tokyo Chamber of Commerce, 1968), 180 pp.

*Toshi ni Okeru Shohisha no Ishiki to Kodo* [*Consumers' Orientation and Behavior in Large Cities*] (Tokyo: Kokumin Seikatsu Kenkyūjo, 1965), 285 pp.

Tsuchiya, Takao. *Nihon Keei Rinenshi* [*A History of Japanese Managerial Ideology*] (Tokyo: Nihon Keizai Shinbunsha, 1964), 362 pp.

Uno, Masao. *Nihon no Marketing* [*Marketing in Japan*] (Tokyo: Dobunkan, 1968), 475 pp.

*Wagakuni ni Okeru Meika no Hanbai Katsudo* [*Marketing Activities by Manufacturers in Japan*] (Tokyo: The Japan Chamber of Commerce, 1966), 182 pp.

*Wagakuni no Voluntary Chain no Genkyo* [*Current Status of Voluntary*

*Chains in Japan*] (Tokyo: Research Department, The Tokyo Chamber of Commerce, 1968), 170 pp.

Yano Kotaro Kinen Kai (ed.). *Nihon Kokusei Zue, 1968* [*National Profiles of Japan, 1968*] (Tokyo: Kokusei Sha, 1968), 240 pp.

*Zude Miru Kokumin Seikatsu* [*Pictorial Analysis of National Life*] (Tokyo: The Japan Productivity Center, 1967), 235 pp.

### Articles

Japan Chamber of Commerce, "Wagakuni ni Okeru Kappu Hanbai no Genjo" ["Status of Installment Sales in Japan"], in Harumasa Yamaguchi and Kirosuke Miyashiro (eds.). *Shohisha Kinyu Shu* (Tokyo: Nihon Sogō Shuppan Kikō, 1967), pp. 128–140.

"Kouri Kyodaika no Honryū ["Entry of Retailing into Large-Scale Business"], *Nihon Keizai Shinbun*, January 4, 1970, p. 8.

"Kyodai Jidai ni Totsunyū Suru Kourigyō ["Entry into an Era of Large Business in Retailing"], *Nihon Keizai Shinbun*, April 30, 1968, p. 7.

"Masu masu Fueru Super no Shuchū Shōhin" ["An Increase in the Number of Products Sold Predominantly by Supermarkets"], *Nihon Keizai Shinbun*, November 17, 1969, p. 5.

"Sangyo Tokushu" ["Industry Report"], *Nihon Keizai Shinbun*, March 24, 1970, pp. 21–26.

Suzuki, Tsuneo. "1966 Nendo Keiei no Ugoki—Wagakuni Shuyo 317 Sha no Anketo Bunseki Kara" ["Major Managerial Developments in 317 Major Japanese Corporations in Fiscal Year 1966"] in Fujiyoshi Sakamoto, *Keiei Nenpo, 1967* [*Management Annual, 1967*] (Tokyo: The Diamond Publishing Co., 1967), p. 14.

"Teikei Gappei de Kyodaika" ["Growing to Giant Scale Through Cooperative Relationships and Mergers"], *Nihon Keizai Shinbun*, May 3, 1969, p. 3.

"Wakamono no Hijuwa masu" ["A Growing Importance of the Youth"], *Nihon Keizai Shinbun*, August 19, 1969, p. 22.

"Zenko Ku Chain Keisei e Hashiru" ["Toward National Chains"], *Nihon Keizai Shinbun*, January 21, 1970, p. 8.

### Government Publications

*Annual Report on the Family Income and Expenditure Survey, 1968* (Tokyo: The Office of the Prime Minister, 1969), 452 pp.

*Bushibetsu Ryutsu Jittai Chosa Hokokusho* [*Report on Actual Status of Distribution of Certain Commodities*] (Tokyo: The Ministry of International Trade and Industry, 1969), 353 pp.

*Chūshō Kigyō Hakusho, Showa 42 nen ban* [*White Paper on Small- to Medium-Size Enterprises, 1967*] (Tokyo: The Small-Medium-Size Enterprise Agency, 1968), 329 pp.

*Chūshō Kigyō Hakusho, Showa 43 nen ban* [*White Paper on Small- to Medium-Size Enterprises, 1968*] (Tokyo: The Small-Medium-Size Enterprise Agency, 1969), 340 pp.

*Chūshō Kigyō Shisaku no Aramashi, Showa 44 nen do* [*A Summary of Governmental Programs for Small- to Medium-Size Enterprises, 1969*] (Tokyo: The Small-Medium-Size Enterprise Agency, 1970), 271 pp.

*Economic Statistics Annual, 1968* (Tokyo: The Bank of Japan, 1969), 292 pp.

*Economic Statistics Annual, 1969* (Tokyo: The Bank of Japan, 1970), 294 pp.

*Honpo Keizai Tokei, 1968* [*Economic Statistics of Japan, 1968*] (Tokyo: The Bank of Japan, 1969), 304 pp.

*Hundred-Year Statistics of the Japanese Economy* (Tokyo: The Bank of Japan, 1966), 362 pp.

*Kakei Chosa Nenpo, Showa 43 nen* [*Annual Report on the Family Income Statistics, 1968*] (Tokyo: Office of the Prime Minister, 1969), 469 pp.

*Kanko Hakusho, Showa 43 nen ban* [*White Paper on Sight-Seeing, 1968*] (Tokyo: Office of the Prime Minister, 1968), 276 pp.

*Kappu Hanbai Jittai Chosa Hokokusho: Dai Ikkan and Dai 4 Kan* [*A Survey on the Status of Installment Credit, Vols. 1 and 4*] (Tokyo: Ministry of International Trade and Industry, 1967), 326 pp.

*Keizai Hakusho, Showa 44 nen ban* [*White Paper on Economics, 1969*] (Tokyo: The Economic Planning Agency, 1970), 288 pp.

*Keizai Yoran, 1969* [*Summary of Economic Statistics, 1969*] (Tokyo: The Economic Planning Agency, 1969) 330 pp.

*Keizai Yoran, 1970* [*Summary of Economic Statistics, 1970*] (Tokyo: The Economic Planning Agency, 1970), 332 pp.

*Kensetsu Hakusho, Showa 44 nen ban* [*White Paper on Construction, 1969*] (Tokyo: The Ministry of Construction, 1969), 275 pp.

*Kokumin Seikatsu Hakusho, Showa 41 nen ban* [*White Paper on National Life, 1966*] (Tokyo: The Economic Planning Agency, 1966), 282 pp.

*Kokumin Seikatsu Hakusho, Showa 42 nen ban* [*White Paper on National Life, 1967*] (Tokyo: The Economic Planning Agency, 1967), 275 pp.

*Kokumin Seikatsu Hakusho, Showa 44 nen ban* [*White Paper on National Life, 1969*] (Tokyo: The Economic Planning Agency, 1969), 437 pp.

*Kokumin Seikatsu ni Kansuru Seron Chōsa, Showa 42 nen* [*A Public Opinion Survey on National Life, 1967*] (Tokyo: The Office of the Prime Minister, 1968), 210 pp.

*Kokumin Seikatsu ni Kansuru Seron Chōsa, Showa 43 nen* [*A Public*

*Opinion Survey on National Life, 1968*] (Tokyo: The Office of the Prime Minister, 1969), 285 pp.

*Kokumin Seikatsu Tokei Nenpo, Showa 43 nen ban* [*Annual Statistics on National Life, 1969*] (Tokyo: Kokumin Seikatsu Kenkyūjo, 1969) 271 pp.

*Kosei Torihiki Iinkai Nenji Hokokusho, Showa 44 nen ban* [*The Fair Trade Commission, Annual Report, 1969*] (Tokyo: The Fair Trade Commission, 1969), 310 pp.

*Monbu Tokei Yoran, Showa 42 nen ban* [*A Summary of Educational Statistics, 1967*] (Tokyo: The Ministry of Education, 1968), 172 pp.

*Regular Chain Chōsa Hokokusho* [*A Report on Regular Chains*] (Tokyo: The Ministry of International Trade and Industry, 1968), 17 pp.

*Rodo Hakusho, Showa 43 nen ban* [*White Paper on Labor, 1968*] (Tokyo: The Ministry of Labor, 1968), 248 pp.

*Rodo Hakusho, Showa 44 nen ban* [*White Paper on Labor, 1969*] Tokyo: The Ministry of Labor, 1969), 116 pp.

*Ryutsu Chitsujo ni Kansuru Jittai Chōsa* [*A Study on Actual Conditions of the Distribution Process*] (Tokyo: Ryutsu Mondai Kenkyukai, 1967), 172 pp.

*Ryutsu Kindaika no Tenbo to Kadai* [*A Perspective and the Challenge of Modernization of the Distribution Sector*] (Tokyo: The Ministry of International Trade and Industry, 1968), 95 pp.

*Ryutsu Kindaika Yushi Nitsuite* [*Outline on Loans for Modernization of the Distribution Sector*] (Tokyo: The Ministry of International Trade and Industry, 1970), 32 pp.

*70 Nendai no Chusho Kigyo Ryutsu* [*Problems of Small- to Medium-Size Enterprises and Distribution in the 1970s*] (Tokyo: Keizai Shingikai, 1970), 399 pp.

"Shinki Kigyo ni Kansuru Chosa" ["A Study of New Entrants"], in *Shogyo Ryutsu Kozo Chosa* [*An Investigation of the Distribution Structure*] (Tokyo: Ryutsu Mondai Kenkyu Kyokai, 1968), pp. 4–32.

*Shōgyō Kindaika Chihiki Keikaku Sakutei Nitsuite* [*Outline for Regional Planning for Modernization of the Commercial Sector*] (Tokyo: Small–Medium-Size Enterprise Agency, 1970), 14 pp.

*Shōgyō Richi Kankei Shiryoshi, Showa 44 nen* [*Data on Location of Commercial Establishments, 1969*] (Tokyo: The Ministry of International Trade and Industry, 1969), 99 pp.

*Shōgyō Tokei Sokuho, Showa 43 nen ban* [*Preliminary Report on Commercial Statistics, 1968*] (Tokyo: The Ministry of International Trade and Industry 1969), 55 pp.

*Shohi to Chochiku no Doko, Showa 43 nen ban* [*A Survey of Consumption and Savings, 1968*] (Tokyo: The Economic Planning Agency, 1968), 140 pp.

*Shohisha Doko, Showa 44 nen* [*Consumer Trends, 1969*] (Tokyo: Shohisha Doko Kenkyukai, 1969), 191 pp.

*Shohisha Shinyo no Riyoni Kansuru Seron Chosa* [*A Survey of Public Opinion on the Use of Consumer Financing*] (Tokyo: Ministry of International Trade and Industry, 1966), 120 pp.

*Shohizai no Ryutsu Kiko* [*Distribution Patterns of Consumer Goods*] (Tokyo: Ministry of International Trade and Industry, 1964), 282 pp.

"Shokibo Kouriten ni Kansuru Chosa" ["A Study of Small-Scale Retail Establishments"], in *Shogyō Ryutsu Kozō Chōsa* [*An Investigation of the Distribution Structure*] (Tokyo: Ryutsu Mondai Kenkyu Kyokai, 1968), pp. 60–99.

*Showa 39 nen, Zenkoku Shohi Jittai Chosa Hokoku* [*1964 National Survey of Family Income and Expenditure*] (Tokyo: The Office of the Prime Minister, 1966), 483 pp.

*Showa 45 nendo Ryutsu Kindaika Shisaku no Juten* [*Outline for the Program of Modernization of the Distribution Sector for Fiscal Year 1970*] (Tokyo: Ministry of International Trade and Industry, 1970), 29 pp.

*Sogo Nokyo Tokei, Showa 41 nendo* [*Statistics on Agricultural Cooperatives, 1966*] (Tokyo: The Ministry of Agriculture, 1968), 179 pp.

*Unyu Hakusho, Showa 44 nen ban* [*White Paper on Transportation, 1969*] (Tokyo: The Ministry of Transportation, 1969), 559 pp.

*Wagakuni no Shōgyō, 1967* [*Commerce in Japan, 1967*] (Tokyo: The Ministry of International Trade and Industry, 1968), 327 pp.

*Wagakuni no Shōgyō, 1969* [*Commerce in Japan, 1969*] (Tokyo: The Ministry of International Trade and Industry, 1970), 351 pp.

# Index